The Art of
FAUX

The Art of
FAUX

THE COMPLETE
SOURCEBOOK OF DECORATIVE
PAINTED FINISHES

Pierre Finkelstein

WATSON-GUPTILL PUBLICATIONS/NEW YORK

Art Notes

On the front cover: The central panel is painted with Rouge Royal (see pages 94–96), the corners are Portor (pages 103–105), and the stiles and rails are Sarancolin (a brèche marble similar to Violet Brèche but with a different palette and surface design; see pages 109–111). The moldings and bronze medallions were painted using trompe l'oeil techniques (see pages 310–316).

On the back cover: The central panel is painted with feather chestnut (similar to Cuban feather mahogany; see pages 191–193), the stiles and rails are straight-grain mahogany (pages 188–190), the geometric inlays in the stiles and rails are walnut painted with a water-based glaze (see page 181 for an example), and the narrow inlays that border them are ivory (pages 260–262).

On pages 2–3: (Left) Marble panel featuring Violet Brèche, Portor, and Rouge Royal, with faux moldings and trompe l'oeil bas-relief. (Right) Oak panel (pages 182–185) with walnut inlay (pages 179–181) and carved ornaments and moldings.

On page 6: Author photo by Norman McGrath.

Senior Editor: Candace Raney
Developmental Editor: Joy Aquilino
Art Director/Designer: Areta Buk
Production Manager: Ellen Greene

First published in the United States in 1997
by Watson-Guptill Publications,
a division of VNU Business Media, Inc.,
770 Broadway, New York, N.Y. 10003
www.watsonguptill.com

Library of Congress Cataloging-in-Publication Data
Finkelstein, Pierre.
    The art of faux: the complete sourcebook of decorative painted finishes / Pierre Finkelstein.
        p.   cm.
    Includes index.
    ISBN 0-8230-0858-4
    1. House painting. 2. Interior decoration. 3. Finishes and finishing. I. Title.
    TT323.F56 1997
    698'.14—dc21
                                            97-840
                                            CIP

Manufactured in Malaysia

First printing, 1997

9 / 05 04 03

Pierre Finkelstein, the owner of Grand Illusion Decorative Painting, Inc., creates faux finishes for internationally acclaimed interior designers and architects that can be seen in some of the most beautiful homes in the United States and Europe. A 1986 gold-medal graduate of the Van Der Kellen Painting Institute in Brussels, he was awarded the distinguished title of "Best Craftsman of France" for decorative painting by the French government in 1990, and has also won an award from the Painting and Decorating Contractors of America. Finkelstein is director and instructor at the Pierre Finkelstein Institute of Decorative Painting, and serves as the technical advisor for a decorative painting brush manufacturer and importer. He is also the co-author of and faux finisher for the best-selling *Recipes for Surfaces* (Simon & Schuster, 1990). He lives in New York City with his wife and two children.

To share your suggestions, recipes, and experiences, or if you have any comments or questions, write to the author at the following address:

Pierre Finkelstein
Pierre Finkelstein Institute of Decorative Painting, Inc.
175 Fifth Avenue – Suite 2162
New York, N.Y. 10010
http://www.pfinkelstein.com/

Photo Credits

Except as noted below, all the photographs in this book were taken by Patrick Gries. All faux finishes were conceived and executed by Pierre Finkelstein.

Pages 18–19 and 226–227: Photos by Pierre Finkelstein. Courtesy of homeowners Phoebe Cowles and Robert Girard.

Pages 72–73: Photo courtesy of Gloria P. Cowen. Interior design by George Dandridge Associates, Inc.

Pages 136–137 and 294–295: Photos courtesy of Candace and Frederick W. Beinecke.

Pages 148–149: Interior design by Jean Charles Moriniere of Trade France.

Pages 200–201: Photo by Pierre Finkelstein. Interior design by Genevieve Favre.

Pages 116–117, 242–243, 256–257, and 280–281: Photos by Pierre Finkelstein.

In memory of my dear friend
CHRISTIAN HERBAUT

Acknowledgments

First and foremost, I would like to thank my teacher—our "old master," as my fellow students and I affectionately called him—Clement Van Der Kellen, who not only taught me the ABC's of my craft, but also gave me the passion for it.

Thanks are also due to the many decorative painters I met while traveling and at various jobs and conventions who were nice enough to share their professional secrets with me, particularly Don Gray, Philip Waite, and Marc Gardereau. I would also like to recognize all the anonymous decorative painters, both past and present, whose magnificent work in the Louvre, the Palace of Versailles, and other public and private spaces has been a ceaseless source of inspiration for me. The challenge of deciphering the techniques that were used to create some of those finishes has taught me much about our craft.

I would also like to thank all the architects, interior designers, and clients with whom I have worked, who have allowed me to realize some of my finest and most interesting work. I would especially like to thank my dear friend Thierry Despont, for the exceptional opportunities he has offered me, and for

his continued use of fine decorative painting in the remarkable residences he designs and builds. I particularly appreciate the graciousness of those clients who permitted me to use photographs of the interiors in which I created my work.

I would like to express gratitude to two decorative painters with whom I have worked over the years, Pieter de Liagre Bohl and Alan Carroll. Special recognition goes to my assistant Ryan Pollastro, for his dedication and perseverance.

I would like to extend a fond thank you to Nick Bienes and Rhea Gallaher, for their support and advice during the early stages of this book, as well as for their long-standing and unwavering friendship.

A special thanks goes to Patrick Gries, an accomplished and talented photographer who took the vast majority of the photographs in this book. He imaginatively solved all our photographic problems, and managed to shoot wonderful images under the worst of conditions. His boundless energy, patience, composure, and generosity made this book possible.

Thank you to the staff at Watson-Guptill Publications: To senior acquisitions editor Candace Raney for her confidence in me; and to art director and designer Areta Buk and production manager Ellen Greene, whose superb work helped bring this book to fruition. A very special and heartfelt thank you to Joy Aquilino, my remarkable editor, whose incredible kindness, patience, and expertise made this book a reality.

For their work on the French edition, I would also like to thank Thaddée Thomas, a writer and editor who assisted me with my research and helped translate my ideas and techniques, and editor Nathalie Duval at Diderot Multimedia.

I am enormously grateful to my wonderful wife Clarisse and my children Eleonore and Roman, for being so patient and understanding on all those days and weekends when I came home late because I was working on the book; and to my parents, Patrick and Annie, and my sister, Anne, for their support. I love you very much.

Contents

Contents

Preface

Over the last few years, the number of books on decorative painting has increased considerably. Typically, these books cover such fundamental techniques as sponging and ragging, as well as more ambitious finishes like "fantasy" woodgraining and marbleizing. While many of these books have been well received, a somewhat superficial treatment of the subject has left many professional decorative painters, interior designers, and enthusiastic amateurs craving a more substantial source of knowledge. My desire to write *The Art of Faux* was primarily motivated by the realization that none of the books that is currently available provide an in-depth, complete text supported by an accessible format and clear, step-by-step photographs, all of which would allow the reader a complete understanding of some carefully chosen aspects of decorative painting.

The basic model I had in mind for the book was a cookbook, with step-by-step "recipes" arranged within several categories of finish based on their degree of difficulty. In addition to covering the techniques necessary to create the basic graphic elements of each category—preparatory "exercises" for practicing hand and brush movements—I include finishes that reflect the prevailing tastes of today's best interior decorators and architects, as well as those of their clients. As a result, the recipes are more complex and diverse than those found in most other decorative painting books. Throughout the book, I adapt traditional techniques to accommodate the latest technological advances in materials and tools, and try to take into account such practical considerations as time constraints, budgetary limitations, and environmental guidelines. For all of these reasons, I use acrylics and other water-based media wherever possible, while attempting to maintain the beauty and superior quality of the recipes that were passed on by our decorative painting forebears. Since oil-based paints are still available in many locations, and in some cases are recommended for beginning professionals and home decorators, I provide guidance on recycling

and creating environmentally sound recipes, and frequently offer alternate instructions on the potential benefits and drawbacks of using these media.

My primary objective in writing *The Art of Faux* is to document the traditions and creative demands of the art and craft of decorative painting and, by doing so, to consider it within the context of the overarching tradition of fine-arts painting. It is unfortunate that contemporary fine-arts painting has made such an effort to "free" itself from the rigorous techniques once taught by the academies in order to emphasize subject matter to the exclusion of everything else. Decorative painting is one of the only areas of fine-arts painting in which knowledge is carefully maintained, willingly shared, and graciously passed on to subsequent generations. With this in mind, I have tried to summarize the many years of experience and research I have devoted to my craft in as complete a manner as possible, given the physical restraints of the book. Because there are virtually thousands of recipes, I realize that this book cannot be an exhaustive encyclopedia of decorative painting, but instead must serve as a sourcebook and instruction manual.

After working more than ten years throughout the United States and Europe, I have determined that decorative painting is practiced by four principal categories of individual:

- *Professional housepainters or basepainters,* who face an ever-increasing demand for decorative painting services from their clientele, which consists mainly of middle-class homeowners and the owners of small to medium-sized businesses. Until just a few years ago, faux finishes were requested exclusively by clients who worked with interior designers, typically affluent homeowners and large corporations. In order to satisfy their clients' demands and diversify their sources of income, many housepainters have been forced to learn some basic decorative painting techniques, though even the most professional and skillful often lack artistic and technical training. This book offers this particular category of reader the essentials of decorative painting, as well as some important "tricks of the trade," so they can feel completely at ease when creating most faux finishes.

- *Fine artists,* who turn to "commercial painting"—creating faux finishes as well as murals—because they find it difficult to derive adequate income from their own artwork. While most fine artists have a good sense of color and composition, they generally lack technical knowledge and skill. This book gives them the information they need to become accomplished decorative painters.
- *Professional decorative painters*—the category I fall into—are always on the lookout for new formulas and secrets, and this book offers some new procedures as well as ideas that might turn them on to new ways of painting. Although some professionals might not follow my recipes to the letter, or disagree with my approach to design, they are sure to pick up on some techniques and adapt them to fit their own recipes and working styles.
- *Skilled, resourceful amateurs* (usually homeowners) who may have some basic knowledge of decorative painting techniques, or aspire to be professional decorative painters. All these enthusiastic beginners need to quench their thirst for creativity—to beautifully decorate their own or their friends' homes—is more complex and challenging faux finishes.

The Art of Faux also serves as a visual reference for interior designers and architects, both as a source for faux finishes and for decorative ideas. Even when designers and architects have a working knowledge of a variety of woods, marbles, and surface textures in addition to a well-developed sense of color, balance, style, and period, they often don't have enough experience to accurately judge the quality of a faux finish. This book not only gives them basic guidelines for evaluating finishes but also a way to ensure that both the work in progress and the completed finish are of the highest quality. If the choice of finishes is limited to a painter's portfolio samples, the following pages can provide a wealth of possibilities.

HOW TO USE THIS BOOK

The Art of Faux was conceived, written, and designed to avoid some of the shortcomings that can be found in many other decorative painting manuals: an overwhelming amount of text, inconsistent organization, unclear photographs, and samples painted at an unrealistically small scale. While the book is organized into chapters, its information can be classified into two distinct types: a general historical and technical overview, which can be found in the Introduction and in Chapter 1, "The Elements of Faux"; and the step-by-step recipes, which are in chapters 2 through 11. As is mentioned above, the organization is based on that of a cookbook, in which the introductory chapters would define terminology and describe utensils, ingredients, seasonings, and various cooking methods, followed by chapters containing recipes.

As with a cookbook, your level of experience and individual needs will affect how you read and use this book. For example, those interior designers and architects who are simply looking for samples and ideas would not have to read the Introduction or Chapter 1, and could instead proceed directly to a specific chapter or recipe. However, I would encourage them to browse through the sections on decorative painting media (pages 20–28), color (pages 33–35), and surface preparation (pages 53–58) to gain a working knowledge of the materials and processes involved in decorative painting, as well as the historical background in the Introduction and the section on planning a faux finish in Chapter 1 (pages 70–71).

In contrast, anyone planning to execute a finish—regardless of their level of experience—must read and have a thorough understanding of all of the information in both the Introduction and Chapter 1 before reading the general information on each category of finish or selecting a recipe. Because recipes are organized within each chapter based on their degree of difficulty—from easiest to most challenging—it is recommended that less experienced painters begin by attempting to paint the initial recipes in a chapter.

Introduction
This section briefly summarizes the history of decorative painting, the two most influential movements within the craft, and the professional requirements and legacy of decorative painters.

Chapter 1: "The Elements of Faux"
This chapter is a comprehensive summary of all the "faux basics": paints, glazes, and related media, including how to mix a glaze and how to select the right medium for each job; basic color terminology and tips on mixing color; decorative painting brushes and other essential tools; guidelines on surface preparation for the most common surfaces; varnishing; and cleanup and recycling. In addition, I have included some "tricks of the trade" designed to improve working habits and reduce working time, as well as some advice on how to plan a faux finish.

Chapters 2 through 11: The Finishes
The information in each chapter is organized according to a consistent arrangement.

General Information on the Specific Type of Finish. This section must be read before *any* recipe in that chapter can be painted. In most cases, the following subjects are covered:

- *The various types of materials.* To enable the reader to better understand the various materials or textures within a category of finish, detailed descriptions of their physical characteristics are provided so they can be simulated more effectively.
- *Suitable applications.* The reasons for recreating the material in a faux finish, and the settings, decorative styles, and surfaces to which it is most appropriately suited.
- *Choosing the right technique.* In this section, the finish is discussed within the context of the two principal approaches to

decorative painting—Italian and French—and the most suitable applications for each.
- *Layout.* This a brief discussion of how the painted surface should be organized, relationships of color and value among individual units, and the accurate scale for a finish.
- *Basic procedure.* This section outlines the essential sequence of events for a finish: the type of surface preparation needed; the recommended media—either oil- or water-based—including varnish; general guidelines for rendering a finish; and common mistakes to avoid.

Exercises. This feature, an indispensable learning tool, is unique to *The Art of Faux*. Combining clear, concise descriptions with step-by-step photographs, the exercises demonstrate the brush and hand movements that are used to create the discrete visual elements of a finish. The samples for the exercises are painted in sepia on a white ground so that color will not detract from the resulting brushstrokes and how they are arranged to create an accurate and realistic surface design. The exercises distill the essential techniques for all the recipes in a chapter, so it is necessary to practice and refer to them in order to better understand the step-by-step instructions and photographs.

It is important to make a clear distinction between the surface design of a finish and the movements of the hand and brush that are required to produce it. (For this reason, I have included one or two reference drawings when the finish calls for it; these appear at the back of the book.) Before you can begin painting a faux finish, its related exercises (listed in the technical notes) must be practiced and mastered, so that you can focus exclusively on the design of the surface and not have to worry about how to hold a brush.

Step-by-Step Recipes. The recipes are generally structured as follows:

- *Technical notes.* These list all the necessary ingredients for each recipe: a difficulty rating of 1 to 5; the system or systems used (oil, water, or both); the basecoat color, medium, and surface finish; glazes and their formulas; a complete palette listing; a list of brushes and tools, which can be varied and expanded based on medium, working preferences, and availability; related exercises; and reference drawings (where applicable).

- *Instructions.* Each set of instructions begins with a detailed description of the specific finish, including its common decorative uses. Noted within the instructions are the various colors mixtures that are used for each step. Exact percentages for each color in a mixture were deliberately omitted to keep from locking the reader into a specific palette. Faux finishes—even those whose coloration can be somewhat limited, such as wood and marble—can be painted in literally hundreds of colors, so their color should be adjusted to fit the setting in which they are painted and the other elements of the decor (furniture, draperies, decorative objects, lighting, and so forth). Therefore, the palette listings in the technical notes and the color mixtures noted in the recipe instructions, which reflect the colors I used to create the finish in the demonstration photographs, should be treated as general recommendations. In a color mixture "equation," a + indicates that colors should be mixed together to create a single color; for example, **yellow ochre + red ochre + white** would create a salmon-colored mixture. On the other hand, an arrangement such as **yellow ochre, red ochre, white** would mean that the colors are chosen from or mixed on the palette each time in different proportions, or added to another color to vary its tonality.

- *Photographs and captions.* Each set of instructions is accompanied by several generously sized photographs, in which the steps in the development of the finish are clearly visible. Every effort was made to keep the brush hand from intruding into the frame and from casting a shadow onto the panel—two more regrettable shortcomings of many decorative painting books. Where it is necessary to clarify a point by showing a detail of the surface, closeup photographs are provided.

The captions summarize the procedures illustrated by their corresponding photographs. The photographs of the completed finishes, which are as large as the book's format permits, usually feature a faux molding, and in some cases another finish or two that complements it. Some of my fellow craftsmen might argue that the surface designs of some finishes are too complex and active—particularly the woods and marbles—but this was done purposely, to show as many effects and design variations as possible within a single panel.

- *Using other media and alternate techniques.* Frequently, guidelines for using a medium different from the one specified by the recipe and/or alternate methods of painting the finish are given.

Reference Drawings

Corresponding to the recipes for marble, wood, and two organic materials are over thirty black-and-white reference drawings. In addition to the enlarged photographs of these completed finishes, the drawings are to be used as examples of surface design. They will prove particularly helpful when painting an entire room in a single finish, allowing you to paint large areas without having to refer to an actual example of the material.

Introduction

A BRIEF HISTORY OF DECORATIVE PAINTING

Humans have always decorated the walls of their shelters. In prehistoric times, the first artists used just a few earth pigments bound with animal fat to paint the walls of their caves with scenes of hunting and daily life, either for ritual purposes or simply to enhance their surroundings. In ancient Egypt, artists painted the walls of tombs and sarcophagi with a still-limited palette of earth pigments using waxes and gums as binders; the ancient Greek palette also included primary colors, which they used to decorate their temples. The ancient Romans invented mural painting, mixing their earth and plant-based pigments with water-based binders to paint frescoes featuring faux moldings, marbleizing, and other forms of ornamentation.

During the Middle Ages, decorative painting consisted primarily of religious iconography and scenes from courtly life adorning walls in churches and castles. The palette was still limited by today's standards but continued to expand; the most common binders in use at that time were resins, gums, casein, and animal-based sizes or glues. By the late Middle Ages, the use of fresco was on the rise, and an oil-based paint similar to the artists' oils that are still used today had been invented, a development that is attributed to 15th-century Flemish artists Jan and Hubert van Eyck.

With the advent of the Renaissance, the binder in oil paints was further refined, related products such as driers were developed, and the palette was expanded with the development of the first chemically derived pigments. In Italy, the fresco technique reached lofty heights with the work of such luminaries as Titian, Raphael, Leonardo, and Michelangelo, as well as the Italian decorative painting masters who created some of the best examples of trompe l'oeil architectural details and ornaments.

Lacquer objects were first imported into Europe from China and Japan during the 16th century, and European methods of lacquering and varnishing were invented in the early 17th century. While the Flemish painters of the 17th century were mastering the genre of still life, the European aristocracy luxuriated in sumptuous styles of decorative painting. Masterful gilding, marbleizing, trompe l'oeil moldings, and grisaille ornaments could be seen in such magnificent residences as the Palace of Versaille. Oil paint formulations were updated once more, and the primacy of oil painting, which was maintained by artists like Poussin, was continued into the 18th century by the likes of Chardin and Boucher. At this time, transparent watercolor and gouache first flourished as fine-arts media.

During the 19th century, decorative painting reached glorious heights. The Empire style, which was popular not only in France but throughout most of Europe, made extensive use of marbleizing, wood graining, trompe l'oeil moldings and architectural ornaments, stenciling, metal patinas, and all manner of simulated textures and patinas. The burgeoning middle and upper classes began decorating their homes lavishly, rivaling the elegance that was once reserved for nobility. This created such a demand for decorative painting that schools were founded and professional standards and practices were established by such prominent decorative artists as Thomas Kershaw in England. This demand also fostered the emergence and subsequent growth of art materials manufacturing: Paints, varnishes, brushes, and other tools that were once made by artists themselves were now mass produced, with paints and varnishes sold in tubes and cans. Advancements in paint chemistry produced new pigments such as ultramarine blue and vermilion. In fine-arts painting, the work and techniques of Academy-trained artists such as Ingres, Delacroix, and David were dominant prior to the rise in the late 19th century of the Impressionists and Neo-Impressionists, including Monet, Renoir, Seurat, Pissarro, and Van Gogh.

The interest in and growth of decorative painting continued into the early 20th century; most notably, the art deco style of the 1920s and 30s employed stenciling, gilding, and wood graining extensively. After World War II, the craft declined to its lowest point, a result of the rejection of academic standards of aesthetics and traditional painting techniques in favor of innovative styles and techniques practiced by such influential artists as Picasso and Matisse.

The introduction of synthetic resin binders (alkyds and acrylics) in the 1930s and improvements in wallpaper manufacturing eventually led to the widespread and ease of use of premixed housepaints and wallpapers. In the 1980s, decorative painting experienced a rebirth and embraced a range of styles, including a return to classical decor. In the United States, the large outdoor mural was developed, then scaled down and adapted for homes, restaurants, and corporate lobbies.

Today, some form of decorative painting—most commonly stenciling, glazing, marbling, and mural painting—can be found in virtually every home. The prevalence of faux finishing is due in part to the widespread accessibility of the right materials, reference books and other sources, and seminars.

INFLUENTIAL MOVEMENTS IN DECORATIVE PAINTING

Historically, two major "schools" or styles of decorative painting can be discerned. One is referred to as the Italian school; the other, the French school (which is also sometimes called the English or Belgian school). Both of these styles can be used to render all types of faux finishes.

The Italian Style

The first use of painting for purely decorative purposes can be attributed to the Italians; examples of their earliest work still survive among the ruins of Pompeii and Herculaneum. The distinguishing features of the Italian style is its very loose, painterly technique, highly decorative and theatrical renderings, and translucent use of color. In the case of marble, for instance, the goal is to achieve the impression or effect of a marble, rather than to precisely render its specific physical characteristics. While evoking a certain type of marble, an Italian-style rendering would be executed with the highest degree of spontaneity, so that the resulting finish might almost seem a product of the imagination. Despite its loose and spontaneous technique, the Italian style should not be considered amateurish, or even more accessible to amateur painters. On the contrary, it requires a great deal of expertise; because this style of finish does not exploit a realistic surface design, it must rely solely on a skillful use of color and composition to create the illusion.

Italian-style finishes are generally rendered in water-based paints, painted on light or white grounds, and executed in very few steps, often without overglazing. On close observation, brush and sponge marks and dripped paint are visible in a completed finish, but from a distance the work is convincing. The lightness of color and effect makes them well suited for large surfaces and spaces, and permits the use of brighter and more colorful palettes.

The Italian style also has an element of fun. It is said that the most accomplished Italian-style decorative painters concealed drawings of horses' heads, birds, and other animals within the veining of their marble finishes so they could have fun at the expense of their unknowing viewers. At the Brighton Pavilion in England, for example, one of the rooms is painted with the imaginary "dragon wood," in whose grain the drawing of a dragon's head can barely be distinguished.

The Italian approach is still widely used by European decorative painters, primarily for its spectacular decorative effect, which is particularly effective in large rooms and with theatrical decor.

The French Style

In contrast to the Italian approach, the French style is very precise, with an emphasis on reproducing the physical characteristics of a material almost exactly. The technique is more complex, often involving at least three steps and one or two overglazings, as well as several coats of varnish to give the completed finish depth. Typically, the basecoat is tinted to reflect the general coloration of the final finish, and water and oil media are combined, either as an initial oil-based glaze followed by a water-based glaze, or vice versa. Overall, these finishes are very detailed and tightly rendered. The use of the term trompe l'oeil to refer to faux wood and marble is derived from this approach, because its finishes are so accurately rendered that the eye is "fooled" into thinking they are real.

The French style is perfect for matching existing finishes that can no longer be found or easily installed. For example, the baseboards in many of the rooms in the Palace of Versailles were marbleized to match the real marble of the mantels. At the height of decorative painting's popularity during the 19th century, the preference for ornate decor held that rare species of wood should be painted over existing millwork and that plaster columns should be marbleized—and the work was done so well that untrained eyes would be unable to discern that it was painted. Because of this, the French style was often employed to maintain budgets and working schedules; in fact, during the 18th century it was often easier and less costly to apply a faux finish to existing architectural details than to replace them with real materials that might take years to produce because they were milled by hand. Continuing the trend, many 19th-century restaurants, hotels, museums, and other public interiors were decorated with faux finishes—a highly productive and rewarding period for the craft as well as for many craftsmen.

Choosing the Right Technique
Is the French style preferable to the Italian, or vice versa? Actually, both approaches are valuable and valid, but each must be used appropriately.

Though more complex and time-consuming, the French technique is well suited to producing high-quality finishes that must match existing materials. Within a dramatic decor, the Italian technique is ideal because it is less imposing. The French style is more difficult than the Italian in that it requires a great deal of knowledge about the physical details of materials, such as grain patterns of various woods and the arrangement of veins and fragments within various marbles, as well as a rigorous execution. As mentioned earlier, a beginning decorative painter should avoid the common misconception that the Italian technique is easier to master, because although it doesn't rely on a precise rendering of surface design or physical details, it requires a well-developed sense of color and composition, which is probably the hardest thing for a decorative painter to learn.

The finishes in *The Art of Faux* are done in the French style, which were modified or simplified slightly to accommodate the use of artists' acrylics. Today, both the French and Italian approaches are used equally by decorative painters, but the Italian technique's speed of execution makes it a favorite of newly established decorative painting studios. For this reason, interior decorators must be able to distinguish between a poorly executed French-style finish and one done using the Italian approach.

DECORATIVE PAINTING: CRAFT AND CRAFTSMAN

Like cabinetmakers and blacksmiths, decorative painters are first and foremost craftsmen rather than artists; the profession's carefully preserved theories, formulas, recipes, rules, and tips confirm its status as a craft, and so its students must be taught and make a disciplined commitment to its standards and methods in order to become skilled decorative painters. While decorative painting is a craft practiced by trained technicians, these technicians must also have an aesthetic sensibility. In fact, knowing only the ABC's of the craft will not enable a beginning painter to spell a word much less write an entire a sentence, because only experience and personal taste can provide the artistic values and sensitivity necessary for creating high-quality work. For example, a well-trained cabinetmaker may be able to make a durable and well-constructed chest of drawers, but he must use his aesthetic judgment in order to select a pleasing combination of woods, molding profiles, and carvings to enhance its basic design.

To ensure success, decorative painters must follow a basic set of rules. They must possess an in-depth knowledge of the materials and tools they use to prevent their work from deteriorating due to incompatibility between systems or poor surface preparation. (See Chapter 1, "The Elements of Faux.") They must also behave in a professional manner; that is, to show up for work on time, to dress appropriately, to keep all brushes and tools in good working condition, and to maintain a professional attitude toward other tradesmen as well as toward clients and interior decorators. I would personally prefer to work with a less experienced and less talented painter who behaves like a professional and is willing to learn than with a so-called "true artist" who acts like a spoiled diva, showing up at work only when the mood is right, and who considers decorative painting only as a way to make money that is secondary to their "true," personal art.

Good decorative painters must also be able to work quickly and efficiently, qualities that can only be acquired with practice. They must also have a thorough understanding of the physical characteristics of each category of finish, and a good working knowledge of a variety of recipes as well as of specific historical and decorative styles, geometry, and perspective. Such a well-rounded craftsman could execute a Rouge Royal marble one day, and panel of feather mahogany the next, and recreate the finishes used in an 18th-century French salon later that same week, all without hesitation or a lack of confidence.

In the past, decorative painters began their careers at age 13 as apprentices in a reputable studio. Except for a small weekend allowance and a few tips, they received no salary. In 1870, an English painter described Thomas Kershaw's apprenticeship: "The working time in those days was 60 hours a week, being 10 hours a day, Saturday included; and in addition, Kershaw always worked 2, 3, or 4 hours extra every day, without receiving any additional pay for overtime." After seven to ten years of instruction in surface preparation, pigments, and mixing paints and glazes, apprentices would begin their training in wood graining, marbling, and creating patinas, as well as lettering and ornament painting, all under the supervision of a senior craftsman; any "free" time was spent studying and drawing the surface designs of wood and marble. As Kershaw himself recounted, "On every opportunity, I visited the timber and veneer merchants, and the marble factory yards, getting the proprietor's permission to allow their men to turn out specimens of woods and slabs for my inspection, and paying them for their trouble. And it was well spent money, as every specimen taught me a lesson which could not be acquired in any other way."

After this long training period, a competent decorative painter would be able to render the grain patterns and veining configurations of over 100 finishes; to imitate organic materials and metal patinas; to glaze, distress, stencil, and gild a variety of surfaces; to paint trompe l'oeil moldings and other architectural details; to handletter signs; and to paint small landscapes. Only once these prerequisites were met could someone earn the title of decorative painter. In light of this rigorous training, I always find it amusing to hear someone who "specializes" only in glazing, or sponging, or painting marble and malachite, call himself a decorative painter.

Today's decorative painter is the heir of a legacy that was once passed on from master to apprentice. Unfortunately, the recipes and professional secrets of the decorative painting masters of the late 19th and early 20th centuries were lost after World War II, when decorative painting was considered obsolete. Since very few books have been written on the subject and good schools with comprehensive curricula are rare, it is difficult to develop interest in and talent for the craft; given the demands of the modern world, it is nearly impossible to learn a trade and earn a living at the same time. This problem can be solved by consulting books and other documents, and perhaps by developing a rolling-admissions approach to decorative painting education, in which seminars are scheduled at regularly spaced intervals so that students can work between sessions while dedicating themselves to learning and practicing their craft.

The Elements of Faux

This chapter provides the decorative painter with indispensable information on the art of faux. However, it is not intended as an encyclopedia of terms and technical data, but rather as a solid foundation for general painting knowledge. As a result, the technical information has been simplified so that it is accessible even to a beginner.

The two most important elements of decorative painting—paint and glaze—are given a thorough review, including their use, compatibility, and coloration. Each part of the decorative painting process is covered, from surface preparation to cleanup and recycling, and a few "tricks of the trade" and tips for planning a faux finish are offered as well. The equipment required to carry out the recipes in this book is covered in detail, from an exhaustive listing of brushes to the key items every decorative painter should keep in his or her fanny pack. Although in some cases I have noted the brands that I use regularly, they are by no means the only brands you should use. Naturally, experimentation, working preferences, and local availability will determine which products will become your own personal favorites.

A decorative painting job site. The tools shown are those of a professional base painter, whose work has already been completed. The dados are set up for painting trompe l'oeil ornaments (see Chapter 11), and the areas that have already been painted are protected with brown masking paper and plastic.

Paint

Paint is one of the essential ingredients of decorative painting. It is used to impart color and texture to both interior and exterior surfaces, as well as to provide protection from the effects of day-to-day use or exposure to the elements.

While there are many different types of paint on the market, each is always composed of three elements—*pigment, binder,* and *solvent*—which combine to create an opaque paint. (Note that the binder and solvent, which make up most of a paint's liquid, are sometimes referred to jointly as the *vehicle.*)

Pigment. The pigment, which comprises the solid part of a paint, is used to create its most obvious attribute: its color. Pigments are colored powders obtained from a variety of sources, both organic (derived from animal or plant sources) and inorganic (processed from mineral sources). (See "The Faux Palette," pages 34–35.)

Binder. The binder is the component of the paint in which the particles of pigment are suspended and that dries and/or oxidizes (changes from liquid to solid) to form the basis of the cured paint film. This element affects quality, durability, and surface finish to such an extent that the names of paints often reflect the type of binder they contain. For example, linseed oil is the standard binder used in artists' oil paint, alkyd resin is the primary binder component in alkyd paint, and acrylic polymer resin is the binder in artists' acrylic paints.

Solvent. As a paint ingredient, a solvent regulates a paint's consistency by diluting the binder. A solvent evaporates after the paint has been applied, leaving behind a curing film of binder and pigment. Paints containing pine resin– or petroleum-based solvents—usually either gum turpentine or mineral spirits—are referred to as "oil-based," while those that contain water as a solvent are called "water-based."

A solvent is called a *thinner* when it is added to paint in order to thin down its consistency or to reduce its working time, such as when mixing a glaze (see page 29).

Note that certain materials such as acetone, lacquer thinner, and denatured alcohol are referred to as solvents when they are used to remove dried paint films (see page 65). Lacquer thinner and denatured alcohol are also used as thinners, respectively, for lacquer and shellac.

PROPERTIES OF PAINT

The proportion and type of pigment, binder, and solvent in a paint's formula affect its primary characteristics, which include degree of opacity, finish, and durability, as well as its consistency and drying time. All of these factors determine whether a paint will meet the needs of your project.

- *Drying time* is the amount of time it takes for a solvent to evaporate and the binder to dry, leaving behind a dry paint film. Paint is said to have *dried* when it is dry to the touch; it is considered *cured* only after the binder has hardened completely.
- *Reversibility* refers to a paint's capacity to be reactivated, or reliquified, with the application of its thinner. For example, dried gouache, transparent watercolor, and casein paint—all water-based paints—can be reversed by applying water. A paint is said to be *irreversible* when its paint film cannot be reactivated. This occurs when a paint's binder *oxidizes,* which means that its molecular structure changes permanently from a liquid into a solid. Water-based paints that contain synthetic binders and all oil-based paints are irreversible. When dried, irreversible paints can be removed from a surface with certain chemicals.
- *Opacity* is the extent to which a paint can cover another color without show-through, which is sometimes referred to as "ghost."
- *Durability* refers to how long a paint will endure wear and abrasion before cracking, while *strength* is its resistance to scratches and other damage.
- *Stability* is the resistance of the paint to the degradation of heat and ultraviolet light.
- *Finish* or *sheen* describes a paint's degree of luster after it has dried. Most basecoat

paints are available in a range of finishes, from no luster to high luster: flat or matte, eggshell, satin, semigloss, gloss, and high gloss. A painted surface always retains the sheen of its last coat; even if the first two coats are high gloss, the surface will be flat if the final coat has a matte finish.

- *Thickness* is the measure of a paint's dried film. A thick coat of paint is at greater risk for degradation than a thinner one, which is less susceptible to change over time. It is better to use two or three thin coats of paint than one thick one.

Both oil- and water-based paints have advantages and disadvantages, so the criteria for selecting a paint should be dictated by the specific needs of your project: the condition of the surface, the technical requirements of the recipe, the timetable for creating the finish, and your level of experience. In addition to reading this chapter (see "Choosing the Right Medium," page 31, and "Surface Preparation," page 53), you can consult with an expert at a local paint retailer or contact a paint manufacturer if you have specific questions about a product. You might seek the advice of a professional painter—there's no substitute for experience when working with paint.

Quality is an important consideration when choosing a paint. Some paint companies use better manufacturing methods and higher-quality ingredients than others. The cost of paint makes up a fairly low percentage of the budget of decorative painting projects, but buying a "bargain" brand is more often than not an unreliable way to save money. Many inexpensive paints contain ingredients of questionable quality that may result in a weak paint film, or worse, poor coverage, requiring additional coats of paint, not to mention the time needed to apply them. If you're on a limited budget, it's best to look for sales on reputable brands of excellent quality. The following proverb applies to all elements of a painted finish, from the basecoat to the final varnish: A painted finish is only as strong as its weakest coat.

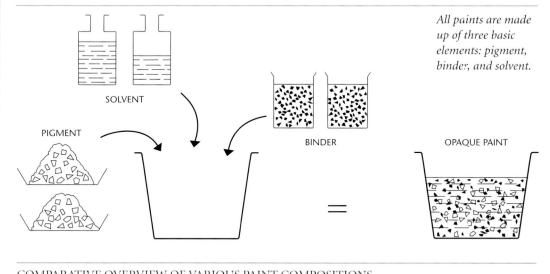

SOLVENT

PIGMENT

BINDER

OPAQUE PAINT

All paints are made up of three basic elements: pigment, binder, and solvent.

COMPARATIVE OVERVIEW OF VARIOUS PAINT COMPOSITIONS

Paint Type	Composition (Pigment + Binder + Solvent)	Consistency	Container
Latex	pigment + polymer resin + water	Concentrated liquid	Can
Alkyd	pigment + alkyd resin + mineral spirits	Concentrated liquid	Can
Artists' Oils	pigment + linseed oil + gum turpentine	Paste	Tube
Gouaches	pigment + gum arabic + water	Paste	Tube
Acrylics	pigment + polymer resin + water	Paste	Tube

Glaze

The vast majority of decorative painting work is done with glazes of various types. In its most basic form, a glaze is a translucent liquid to which color has been added. By incorporating additional vehicle (binder and solvent) into a paint, it can be modified to create a glaze. The added binder and solvent make the paint translucent so that when it is applied over a basecoat it will add depth and radiance, changing its color and texture without obscuring it. The single most important faux painting technique is *glazing*, in which two translucent colors are layered, rather than mixed, to create a third.

NOTE: Do not confuse glazing with varnishing. Glazes have color and can be used to create texture, while varnishes are completely transparent and are used to protect rather than to embellish finishes.

PROPERTIES OF GLAZE

As with paint, the proportion of pigment, binder, and solvent in a glaze's formula affect its physical characteristics.

- *Drying time*, as a glaze must remain open long enough to allow its surface to be manipulated, often several times over, and then dry and cure fully.
- *Reversibility* or *irreversibility* depends on the binder in a glaze. As is the case for each type of paint, reversible glazes can be reactivated from a dry, solid film with the application of thinner; once dry, irreversible glazes can only be removed from a surface with certain chemicals.
- *Transparency* is the degree to which the glaze will permit light to pass through it and reflect off the underlying surface.
- *Strength* is usually very low because the paint film is so thin. The higher the proportion of solvent, the weaker the film, while a higher proportion of binder will strengthen a film. Since glazes are applied in thin coats and are therefore susceptible to scratches, a protective varnish is sometimes required, depending on the application.
- *Finish* or *sheen* can range from matte to high gloss, as determined by the glaze's ingredients and their proportions. Because glazes are usually mixed by hand, there are no predetermined degrees of luster. If you apply varnish over the glaze, the finish will have the sheen of the varnish.

Your choice of glaze type and formula will be determined by qualifying factors of the both the project and the faux finish (see page 21). See "Media Compatibility," page 31, for a detailed review of what is most suitable for each type of surface.

Glazes made by commercial manufacturers are sold in art supply, paint, and home decorating stores, or you can prepare glazes yourself from a variety of painting ingredients and adapt them to your project requirements (see "Mixing a Glaze," page 29). As with other materials, prices and quality can vary greatly. Buy the best glazes or glazing ingredients you can afford; in the long run, the better quality justifies the higher price.

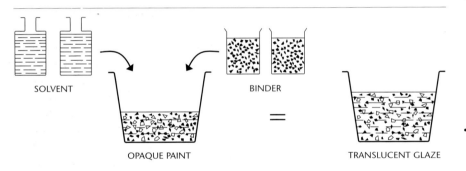

A glaze is made by diluting paint with extra solvent and binder.

Because they are translucent, light passes through a glaze, reflects off the basecoat below, and passes through again. Glazes reflect light and enrich the look of the basecoat, adding depth, shading, and texture.

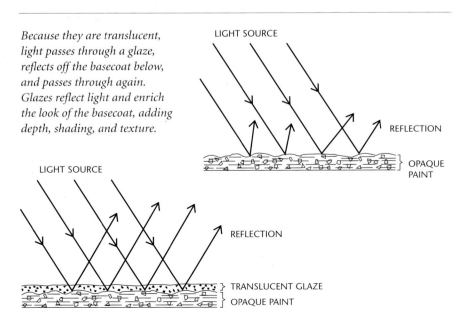

Decorative Painting Media

OIL-BASED MEDIA

In this section, a range of oil-based products is reviewed. The original formula for oil paint has been adapted over the last five centuries to serve a variety of uses, from traditional, slow-drying artist's oils, to strong, quick-drying, flexible alkyds. Refer to "Media Compatibility," page 31, to determine whether an oil-based paint or glaze is appropriate for your surface and project.

Paints and Other Products Used to Color Oil-Based Glazes

Although raw pigments are an economical alternative to many other glaze colorants and can be used to color oil-based as well as water-based glazes, it's easier to mix commercially prepared colors on a palette before incorporating them into a glaze (see page 29). Listed below are three commonly used products for coloring oil-based glazes.

Artists' Oils. Artists' oils were first developed in the early 15th century by Flemish painters Jan and Hubert van Eyck. These paints were revolutionary because the translucency of the linseed oil binder made it possible to use some of the colors as glazes, producing more lustrous and highly reflective surfaces than could be achieved with fresco, casein, or tempera, which were the principal painting media at that time. Artists' oils are still widely used to impart color to most of the oil glazes used to create faux finishes (see page 29).

One of oil paint's double-edged attributes is its slow drying and curing times—one day for the former and as much as several weeks for the latter. While this leaves the paint "open," or workable, for at least a few hours, allowing time to smooth out the surface and to make adjustments and correct mistakes, it also lengthens the painting process significantly. With the addition of a drier (see "Related Products," below), an oil paint film will be dry to the touch in 12 to 24 hours, but may need up to a week to cure completely, depending on its thickness, the nature of the pigment, the amount of drier that has been added, and the humidity.

(CAUTION: Because the oxidation of oil paint produces heat, rags that have been soaked with oil paint can spontaneously combust in very confined spaces. See page 66 for more information.)

Oil paint can be thinned with gum turpentine or mineral spirits, and its semigloss finish can be further enhanced by adding linseed oil and gum turpentine—the more oil, the higher the sheen (and the slower the drying time). While it is possible to paint over an oil paint or glaze after just 24 hours (usually when a drier has been added), if the initial coat is not completely dry to the touch, all subsequent coats may crack or wrinkle, since the first coat continues to expand as it dries. Artists' oils adhere well to properly prepared surfaces (see "Surface Preparation," pages 53–55), and once cured the paint film is very strong. A dried layer of oil paint is irreversible, but it can be removed with lacquer thinner or acetone. Unfortunately, linseed oil can sometimes yellow and become brittle, affecting the color of the surface and causing it to crack.

Produced in tubes of various sizes as well as in pint-, quart-, and gallon-size cans, artists' oils are manufactured by many companies, but considerations of quality should precede those of cost when making a selection. As with most paint brands, price tends to reflect the quality of the product's ingredients. Sennelier, Gamblin, and Talens all make excellent artist-quality oil paints. Experiment with a few name brands, get to know the working properties of each, then choose the one you like most.

Universal Colorants or Tints. These colorants, which are an inexpensive alternative to artists' oils and raw pigments, can be used with oil-based paint and to color some water-based products (see page 28). Usually produced in a limited palette of about 12 to 16 colors, they are used primarily to tint housepaints but can also be used to color ready-mixed commercial glazes. Mixol, a German product imported by Sepp Leafing (see the list of suppliers), offers an incredible 26-color selection with high tinting strength that can be mixed with virtually any medium.

NOTE: The proportion of universal colorants should never exceed 20 percent of the total volume of a paint or glaze. Because they have no siccative properties, an excess of universal colorants can prevent a glaze from drying fully.

Japan Colors. Japan colors (also known as japan paints) were originally developed by sign painters who wanted a quick-drying, irreversible paint well suited to hard surfaces. These paints, which are made by grinding pigments into a resinous varnish containing little or no oil, are thinned with either gum turpentine or mineral spirits. They dry to an opaque, matte finish in about 20 minutes and cure completely in 6 hours. In decorative painting, japan colors are used as coloring agents for oil-based glazes, to paint architectural ornaments, and for stenciling.

Japan colors can be puchased in art supply and paint stores and are generally sold in small cans. They are made by very few manufacturers, and their palette is limited to about 20 colors.

Oil-Based Paint for Basecoating
Even though traditional oil basepaints are still available in most areas, alkyds offer decorative painters exceptional value, a virtually unlimited palette, and a superior smoothness.

Alkyds. Developed in the 1930s, alkyd paints were first formulated and marketed as interior and exterior housepaints, a role they've played successfully since their introduction. In decorative painting, alkyd paints are used exclusively for basecoating. The synthetic binder in alkyd paints offers decorative painters some clear advantages over traditional oil paints.

One of the most compelling features of alkyd paints is their rapid drying and curing rates. They're dry to the touch—and, under normal conditions, ready for a second coat—in 6 to 12 hours, and cure in as little as 24, all without the addition of a drier. An alkyd paint film is also more durable, flexible, stable, and far less likely to yellow than a regular oil paint film. Alkyds are available in a range of finishes—flat, eggshell, satin, semigloss, and gloss—and the strength of the paint film increases as its sheen increases; the flat finish is most susceptible to dirt and scratches. While a dried alkyd paint film is irreversible, it can be removed with acetone or lacquer thinner.

Sold in several sizes, from quart to 5-gallon cans, alkyds are made by almost every major housepaint manufacturer and can be found at most paint and hardware stores. For the consumer, this abundance provides a dazzling array of colors as well. Most alkyd paints are opaque (depending on the pigment), and though most are also thickened with whiting, this doesn't necessarily enhance their opacity. If you can't find the color you desire, most stores will gladly create it for you by tinting it to your specifications. Benjamin Moore and Pratt & Lambert, both widely distributed brands, make several lines of alkyd paint in a wide range of finishes; Benjamin Moore's Satin Impervo and Dullamel eggshell finish are good, all-purpose, decorative painting oil basepaints. Alkyds take the guesswork out of making your own basepaint with linseed oil and pigment—something most professional painting contractors did until the mid-1960s.

Related Products
The following is a list of accessory products that are used to adjust the physical or working properties of oil-based paints and to mix oil-based glazes (see page 29).

Linseed Oil and Other Drying Oils. Used as a binder in the manufacture of artists' oil and alkyd paints, linseed oil, which is irreversible, is also an essential ingredient for heightening the transparency of oil-based paints and for making oil-based glazes. For these purposes, refined linseed oil is the preferred form; commercial-grade raw or boiled linseed oils are less-than-satisfactory substitutes.

Linseed oil is pressed or extracted from the seeds of the flax plant, then treated to improve thickness, color, or drying action. Sold in glass bottles and metal cans, linseed oil is produced by many manufacturers, and the level of quality varies from brand to brand. The importance of working with a high-quality linseed oil cannot be overstressed, particularly for glaze making; as when purchasing paints, you should buy the best you can afford. A linseed oil should be clear and light (the darker the oil, the more quickly a glaze will yellow). The linseed oil products that are carried by paint stores are industrial-grade and are generally not considered by decorative painters to be as desirable as those sold in art supply stores. Winsor & Newton's refined linseed oil, sold in 1-liter bottles, is a good example of the latter. Once you find a brand you like, stick with it so you can become familiar with the way it handles, dries, and ages. NOTE: Dampness and a lack of sunlight will accelerate the tendency of linseed oil to yellow, but exposing a yellowed oil paint film to sunlight can diminish this effect.

Several other drying oils can be used to make glazes, though their paint films are not as strong. Safflower oil and poppy oil are both pale oils that work well with light-colored paints and are less likely to yellow with age. Walnut oil, which is also very light, is excellent for use with white paints. Oil paints should never be mixed with olive oil or peanut oil, because they are not drying oils.

Thinners. A wide selection of thinners can be used to adjust the consistency of oil paint, but only those used in this book are covered here. *Gum turpentine* (properly referred to as "gum spirits of turpentine") and *kerosene* are generally used to make oil-based glazes and to thin down artists' oils, while *mineral spirits* (also known as paint thinner or white spirit) is used for cleaning oil brushes and thinning alkyd paint. All are considered moderately toxic (and highly toxic when ingested), are either flammable or combustible at around 90°F (32°C), and should be used and stored according to label directions.

But if these thinners can all be used to accomplish the same goals, why choose one over another to do different jobs? In each case, their physical properties determine their function. Gum turpentine (distilled pine sap) and kerosene (a fuel oil) are both "greasy" spirits, which means that they evaporate more slowly than mineral spirits (a "dry" spirit). Greasy spirits have a longer open time and heighten the sheen of the paint, making them well suited for mixing and working with glazes. Generally speaking, the drier a solvent's formula, the flatter the finish of the paint or glaze.

Driers or Siccatives. Available in both liquid and powdered forms, driers are metallic salts that are added to oil glazes to reduce drying and curing times. Of course, oil paints will dry on their own, but adding a drier can accelerate the oxidation process significantly. Manganese drier (Manganese linoleate), cobalt drier, japan drier, and Courtrai drier (*siccatif de Courtrai*) are all widely used in decorative painting. They are usually sold in small bottles or cans and can be purchased at most art supply and paint stores.

NOTE: Because driers are progressive—that is, their drying action continues even after the paint has dried to the touch, which can lead to cracking—they must be used very sparingly, and should never exceed 10 percent of the total volume of a paint or glaze. Driers can also darken colors, both in their liquid state and after they have dried,

A selection of oil-based media and related products.

because they contain ingredients that tend to darken with age.

Oil-Based Glazing Liquids. Commercially prepared oil glazes—available in 1-quart to 1-gallon cans—are easy to use and tint well with universal tints or colorants, or artists' oils. They work well on walls but are not as suitable for fine finishes such as faux wood, marble, or organic textures as a linseed-oil glaze because they are thick and gummy; they are also not appropriate for exterior surfaces. Their thick consistency usually requires that they be thinned down before using them. Pratt & Lambert is the brand I sometimes use. Test a few others before deciding on one.

Oil-based glazing liquids dry to the touch in 2 to 6 hours and cure in about 24 hours, depending on sheen, thickness of application, and weather conditions. A second coat can usually be applied after 12 hours. Driers are not generally necessary unless you want to speed up the drying time. "Open" time varies from 15 to 35 minutes, depending on the mixture. Once oxidized, oil-based glazes are irreversible, but can be removed with acetone or lacquer thinner.

Oil Paint Mediums. From the Renaissance until the early 20th century, artists made their own paints by handgrinding pigments and developing recipes for vehicles. Because the vehicle played a fundamental role in the aesthetic character of the paint—and, therefore, in the artist's work—most recipes were well-kept secrets. As a result, recipes were lost when the artists who developed them died.

Modern conservators and art materials scientists have tried to recreate some of these mediums, which are believed to have been instrumental in creating the radiance and depth of many works by the Old Masters. Although they are used primarily by fine artists, in some cases they are useful to decorative painters as well. Sold at many art supply stores, usually in small glass containers, such oil paint mediums as wax medium, the Maroger Medium, and amber varnish are used to add sheen, create transparencies, and strengthen oil paint films.

Several alkyd-based painting mediums can also be used with oil paint. These are available in two forms: a thick gel and a heavy-bodied liquid similar to that of drying oils.

Waxes. Although waxes are not actually oil-based, they are listed here because they can be thinned with turpentine and used as a varnish; as such, wax is particularly suited to faux leather and some types of wood (see page 61). Colored wax crayons are also rubbed over dried surfaces to create "distressed" textures.

WATER-BASED MEDIA

Prior to the invention of oil paints in the early 15th century, artists used several versions of water-based paint: fresco, casein, tempera, and various gum arabic–binder paints (including watercolor and gouache). As oil paint reached the height of its ascendency, water-based paints were relegated to making quick studies and sketches, and their quick-drying properties, ease of handling, and portability suited them well to these tasks, with the exception of fresco, which was still used exclusively on walls.

In the late-19th and early 20th century, the development of synthetic binders updated, and in some ways improved upon, the traditional water-based paints. In addition, many of the newer paints require less-toxic and potentially less-hazardous solvents for thinning and cleanup than their oil-based counterparts.

Paints Used to Color Water-Based Glazes
Note that in addition to the two paints discussed below, universal colorants (see page 23) and raw pigments (page 29) can be used to color water-based glazes.

Artists' Acrylics. The vehicle in an acrylic paint consists of tiny beads of a synthetic acrylic resin (the binder) dispersed in water (the solvent). As the water evaporates the resin binder oxidizes, creating a hard, flexible, usually opaque, satiny finish. Depending on its thickness, an acrylic paint film will dry in about 15 minutes and cure in as little as 30 minutes, permitting rapid recoating and reglazing. Once dry, acrylic paints are irreversible but can be removed with denatured alcohol, lacquer thinner, or acetone. Acrylics are usually very stable, adhere well to both interior and exterior surfaces, and almost never yellow with age.

Versatile and easy to use, acrylics are a favorite among decorative painters. Made by several manufacturers and available in a wide range of colors, acrylics are sold in tubes, jars, and large plastic containers. To create faux finishes, artists' acrylics are used straight for basepainting small areas and ornaments as well as for stenciling, and are mixed with water and acrylic medium to make glazes. Available in many consistencies—including paste, gel, and liquid—and a range of sheens, acrylic medium is basically raw acrylic binder without pigment.

Another auxiliary material for acrylic paints is retarder, which is mixed with paint or glaze to extend its working time. NOTE: Acrylic retarder should be used sparingly, never exceeding 10 percent of the total volume of a paint or glaze. Excessive use of retarder will weaken the paint film and possibly prevent it from curing fully.

Two companies, Golden and Lascaux, both make high-quality acrylic products, offering an exceptionally wide range of consistencies, finishes, and degrees of opacity. There are several other good brands of acrylic paint available, so experiment with a few to find what is best for you. Acrylic paints and their related materials can be purchased in art supply stores.

Vinyl Paints. Except for a small molecular difference in their binders, vinyl paints are very similar to acrylics in appearance and handling. Used primarily by sign painters and scenic artists, vinyls are used by decorative

painters for light basecoating, painting ornaments, and stenciling. Their opaque colors dry to a matte or low-sheen finish.

In contrast to acrylic paints, vinyls are made by only a few manufacturers, and are more frequently sold in jars rather than tubes. Vinyl paints are sold in art supply stores as well as in some paint stores.

Gouaches. Also known as opaque watercolors, gouaches are bound with gum arabic, a product of the acacia tree. They are rendered opaque by adding precipitated chalk to the vehicle and by using opaque pigments. Many manufacturers produce gouaches, which are available in art supply stores in a variety of qualities and price ranges and are generally sold in small tubes. Depending on pigment quality, gouaches may be opaque or semi-opaque; a good gouache will provide smooth coverage and will not yellow. The finish is always matte.

Gouache dries in about 5 minutes and cures in 10 minutes, depending on the thickness of the application. Since it is reversible, a final coat or glaze of gouache must be sealed with a non-water-based varnish or glaze. Gouaches are an excellent medium for wood graining (see Chapter 5).

NOTE: Because gouache is a popular medium among illustrators—whose work is meant for reproduction rather than long-term duration—many gouaches fade very quickly. In general, you should avoid

A selection of water-based media (acrylics are shown here) and related products.

paints labeled "designers' gouache," which indicates that they are primarily intended for applications that do not require permanence. Winsor & Newton and Lascaux both offer artist-quality gouaches containing high-quality pigments.

Water-Based Paint for Basecoating
Because they are less toxic than their oil-based counterparts, latex paints are the only type of basepaint sold in some regions of the United States.

Latex Paints. Containing yet another type of polymer binder, latex paints are essentially an industrial version of acrylic paints, and share many of their working properties. Latex paints are used exclusively for basecoating.

Sold and used primarily as housepaints, latex paints are available in numerous premixed colors and in several sheens: flat, eggshell, satin, semigloss, and gloss. Depending on its thickness, a coat of latex dries in about 30 minutes and cures in 2 hours. The paint film is strong, stable, adheres well, and is resistant to yellowing. As with acrylics, a dried latex paint film is irreversible, but can be removed with denatured alcohol, lacquer thinner, or acetone.

Latex paints are sold in quart, gallon, and 5-gallon cans and can be purchased at most paint and hardware stores. They tend to be affordably priced, though they also vary widely in quality, depending on the manufacturer. Most are either opaque or semi-opaque, depending on the quality of the pigment. (They often contain a high percentage of whiting [see next column, this page], which imparts body but provides little coverage.) Benjamin Moore's Latex House Paint is a reliable brand. While latex paints are typically formulated for indoor use, some manufacturers also produce exterior grades.

Related Products
The following water-based materials have specialized applications in creating or accenting faux finishes.

Artists' Watercolors. Similar to gouache in handling and reversibility but made with transparent pigments, watercolor provides transparent paint effects and dries extremely quickly. Because high-quality watercolors are extremely expensive and because they produce such a transparent finish, they have limited use in decorative painting. They can be utilized to glaze real gold gilding to give it an antique look; the extreme transparency of the medium provides an effect of aging and barely tarnishes the shine of the gold.

Casein. The binder of casein paint is a protein derived from skim milk. Widely used in the 17th and 18th centuries, casein is nowadays marketed as an inexpensive craft paint in a limited color range. Because it shares many of the characteristics of gouache, casein can be used in decorative painting applications in ways similar to gouache.

Universal Colorants or Tints. In addition to artists' acrylics, these can be used to color such water-based products as latex paint and commercial water-based glazes (see below).

NOTE: The amount of universal colorants should never exceed 20 percent of the total volume of a paint or glaze. Because they have no siccative properties, an excess of universal colorants can prevent a glaze from drying fully.

Water-Based Glazing Liquids. Commercially prepared water-based glazing liquid has a much slower drying time than most water-based preparations (about 12 hours), allowing it to be handled more like an oil-based glaze. Once dry, water-based glazing liquid is irreversible, but can be removed with denatured alcohol, acetone, or lacquer thinner. Because its consistency is very thick and quite gummy, it is suitable only for use as a glazing finish for walls, and is not appropriate for marbling or wood graining. This product is currently being developed as a substitute for oil-based glaze. Available in quart- and gallon-size cans, it can be purchased in paint stores.

Whiting. Composed of ground chalk (calcium carbonate), whiting is used to add body to paint. Though it does not have coloring power, it may whiten a paint slightly. Whiting is also used to "degrease" an oil-basecoated surface so that it will accept a reversible water-based glaze (see page 32). Whiting can be found in paint stores and retailers specializing in gold leaf supplies. Buy the refined grade used by gilders.

Mixing a Glaze

Vehicles for glazes are available in several ready-made forms, but most of the recipes in this book call for glazes made from scratch. Your choice of glaze media and its formula will depend on the requirements of each particular recipe. To illustrate how the proportions of a glaze are determined, the following is a sample glaze formula:

> Modified ready-mixed glaze = 1 glazing liquid + $3/4$ kerosene + $1/4$ linseed oil + colorant

The number preceding the first item in the formula indicates the amount per volume; in the example, 1 part of glazing liquid is mixed with amounts of kerosene and linseed oil equaling, respectively, $3/4$ and $1/4$ of the volume of that part. Any unit of measure can be used, as long as it is applied to all the ingredients. A percent sign indicates that the amount of the ingredient should be a percentage of the mixture's total volume.

The colorant you use to tint your glaze will depend on its compatibility with the medium you're working with. Raw pigments can be incorporated into any medium, but require more handling than paints and other commercially prepared colorants. Even nontoxic pigments require that a dust mask and gloves be worn; toxic pigments in their raw form should be avoided altogether (see "The Faux Palette," page 34). Mix the pigment with linseed oil (for oil-based glazes) or water or beer (for water-based glazes), then let it sit overnight so that the pigment dissolves completely before adding the remaining glaze ingredients.

NOTE: When adding a colorant to a glaze, begin with a small amount and mix thoroughly. Always test the mixture on the surface to be glazed, then add more colorant or more medium as needed to achieve the correct degree of translucency.

Always mix more glaze than you think you need, for several reasons. Some may accidentally spill; there may be more surface to cover than originally planned; it is helpful to have some left over for touch ups; and most important, it is extremely tricky to mix more glaze in a middle of a project and attain just the right consistency, color, and transparency to match what you have already used. For small projects and surfaces, glazes can be mixed on a palette or in a small cup. Larger projects and surfaces require a bucket for mixing. I always use a small $1/2$-gallon bucket and fill it with only about 1 inch of liquid, which means a lot less mess and waste if I accidentally drop it. More importantly, the thinner evaporates because the glaze is exposed to the air, and after about 2 hours it becomes thicker, darker, harder to work with, and contaminated with dust. Although you may not even be aware of them, these changes in the glaze will also affect your faux finish, so it's better to refill the bucket with fresh batches of glaze as you need them.

OIL-BASED GLAZES

Although ready-mixed commercial oil-based glazes are widely available, being able to make a glaze from scratch allows the decorative painter to control its drying time and consistency. In each case, the amount of linseed oil can be varied to satisfy the needs of the specific application.

Artists' Oil Glaze

To prepare a glazing medium that can be tinted with artists' oil paints, combine 1 part linseed oil and 2 to 4 parts turpentine (the amount of turpentine will make the glaze "slim" or "greasy"—the more turpentine, the slimmer the glaze). Add an amount of drier equal to no more than 10 percent of the total volume. Add colorant as noted above. Whiting can be used to add more body.

> 2 to 4 turpentine + 1 linseed oil + 10% drier + colorant

Glazing Liquid

To make a glaze with glazing liquid, combine 1 part ready-mixed glazing liquid with $1/2$ part kerosene. Add colorant, following the directions given above.

> 1 ready-mixed glazing liquid + $1/2$ kerosene + colorant

By varying the amount of solvent and adding linseed oil, you can greatly alter the open time of a ready-mixed glaze. For a longer open time, use 1 part ready-mixed glazing liquid, $3/4$ part kerosene, and $1/4$ part linseed oil.

WATER-BASED GLAZES

As with oil-based glazes, it is preferable to mix a water-based glaze from scratch than to use a commercial glaze product. As a rule, ready-mixed water-based glazes cure extremely slowly, offering virtually no advantage over their oil-based counterparts, and are so thick and gummy in consistency that they are difficult to manipulate even after only 15 minutes. In general, the only value of these products is that they are not likely to yellow with time.

Using water-based glazes on large surfaces can be somewhat tricky, especially on hot days, but there are several ways to reduce their fast-drying properties. You can water down your surface with a sponge or a bottle sprayer or run a humidifier while you work. If you're working with acrylics, you can add retarder gel to the glaze (but be sure the amount of gel does not exceed 10 percent of the total volume); a few drops of glycerin (glycerol), available at most pharmacies, can be added to a gouache or beer glaze to produce the same result. Don't turn on a fan because the increased air circulation will speed up the drying time. You can also work in smaller sections, leaving a 2-inch-wide "grease mark," or a heavy application of glaze. The grease mark will dry more slowly than the rest of the surface, allowing you to complete work on one section before moving on to the next, thus preventing overlap marks where the sections join.

Acrylic Glaze
To make an acrylic glaze from scratch, combine 1 part acrylic medium with 1 or 2 parts water. Add a compatible colorant. If the glaze is too runny, you can add whiting to give it more body, add gel medium, or remix it using less water.

> 1 acrylic medium + 2 water + colorant
> (+ whiting, if needed)

Gouache Glaze
This reversible water-based medium makes an excellent transparent glaze that's particularly well suited to wood graining. To make a gouache glaze, just combine gouache and water; add gum arabic if it seems a little too weak. Whiting can be added to give the glaze more body.

> 1 tube of gouache + $1/2$ pint (or less) of water (+ gum arabic or whiting, if needed)

Beer Glaze
Beer can provide a medium for a reversible water-based glaze that has one important advantage over gouache: It is less expensive. On the other hand, beer glaze doesn't keep well; it will turn after 3 or 4 days. As with gouache glaze, you can use gum arabic and/or whiting to add body.

> 1 beer + pigment (+ whiting, if needed)

1. *Mixing a glaze:* Begin by measuring out the proportions of the glaze ingredients using a consistent unit of measurement. (Here, an oil-based glaze is used as an example.)

2. *The elements of the glaze:* $3^1/2$ turpentine + 1 linseed oil + 5% drier.

3. Mix the glaze ingredients, adding them one at a time to a clean container. Label the mixture with its formula.

1

2

3

Choosing the Right Medium

The choice of medium depends on several factors: the nature and scope of the project, the type of faux finish chosen, weather conditions, dust, time constraints, and your own skill level. Oil-based and water-based systems each have advantages and disadvantages, and knowing the facts about each type will help you to chose the kind most appropriate to the job.

MEDIA COMPATIBILITY

Decorative painting often requires numerous steps of glazing and reglazing, sometimes in different systems. Although oil- and water-based media can often be combined on the same project, if done incorrectly it can result in nonadhesion or in degradation of the paint. It is therefore important to understand the details of compatibility and to be certain that the surfaces are *completely* dry before proceeding to the next step. In the case of oil-based media, this means the basecoat must be fully cured, not simply dry to the touch. Glazing over a flat basecoat is not recommended because the surface is too porous; it will "drink" the glaze. Glazing over a gloss finish can be tricky because it repels the glaze and causes beading. Oil-based paint in an eggshell finish is the most versatile basecoat.

General Compatibility Rules
- Oil glaze may be applied over an oil basecoat, with little or no preparation.
- Oil glaze may be applied over a water basecoat, with little or no preparation.
- Water-based glaze must not be applied over an oil basecoat unless the surface is specially prepared (see "'Degreasing' an Oil Basecoat for a Reversible Water-Based Glaze," page 32.)

OIL-BASED MEDIA

Advantages	Disadvantages
Long drying time, allowing more time for achieving effects and permitting stoppage of work mid-project	Long drying time means long waits between steps, and wet surfaces can attract dust that will ruin the finished product
Strong, durable coverage, even for exterior surfaces	Susceptible to yellowing
Available in a wide variety of colors, sheens, and textures	Requires the use of flammable products that emit dangerous fumes
Similarity of color between wet and dry states makes color mixing easier	Cleanup can be time-consuming

WATER-BASED MEDIA

Advantages	Disadvantages
Fast drying, requiring shorter waits between steps, encouraging spontaneous paint effects, and preventing dust from settling on surface	Open time is short, allowing less time for complicated effects; brushmarks may show; working on large surfaces can be tricky
Permanent types are durable and color-stable	Reversible types are fragile and must be sealed with non-water-based finishes
Available in a wide variety of colors, packaging, fluidity, and textures	When dry, water-based paint looks darker than when wet, so all color mixtures must be tested first
Virtually no yellowing effect; can be used in dark areas and over white basecoats	An acrylic varnish may cause an oil-based glaze to turn yellow
Glazes are very transparent and fresh looking even after many years	In very cold weather, polymer paint may produce a weak film
Most related products are environmentally safe	Incompatible with certain types of surfaces
Cleanup with water is relatively fast and easy	Irreversible types require the use of synthetic brushes because the polymers damage natural hairs; brushes must be rinsed often to prevent drying out

Over an Oil Basecoat, Eggshell or Satin Finish
- Any type of oil-based glaze can be used; no sanding required.
- Before applying acrylic glazes, lightly sand the surface to give it some "tooth."
- Before applying reversible water-based glaze (such as gouache or beer glaze), the surface must be "degreased" (see below) to prevent beading.

Over an Oil Basecoat, Semigloss or Gloss Finish
- Any type of oil-based glaze can be used, but lightly sand the surface first.
- Before applying acrylic glazes, lightly sand the surface to give it some "tooth."
- Reversible water-based glazes will not work well, even with thorough sanding.

Over an Oil-Glazed Surface
- Any type of oil-based glaze can be used; no sanding required.
- Before applying acrylic glazes, gently dust the surface with whiting; no sanding required.
- Before applying reversible water-based glaze, gently dust the surface with whiting; no sanding required.

Over a Water Basecoat, Any Finish
- Any type of oil-based glaze can be used; no sanding required.
- Any type of acrylic glaze can be used; no sanding required.
- Any type of reversible water-based glaze can be used; no sanding required (except for gloss-finish latex, which should be sanded lightly to give it some tooth).

"DEGREASING" AN OIL BASECOAT FOR A REVERSIBLE WATER-BASED GLAZE

When a reversible water-based glaze is applied over an oil basecoat, it can result in "beading," whereby the basecoat repels the glaze, causing it to form small beadlike puddles on the surface. The more watery the glaze, the more it has a tendency to bead; heavier glazes will bead less.

Begin by sanding the surface well. Using a scrub pad or 220-grit sandpaper, apply a fair amount of pressure, except on the edges, where sanding must be lighter to avoid burning them. Dust off the surface thoroughly.

Dip a damp sponge (either an industrial sponge or an old sea sponge) into some whiting, or prepare a mixture of whiting and water (combine 2 parts water with a $1/2$ part of whiting) and apply it to the surface with a used spalter or round-bristled brush. Rub the entire surface energetically, let dry, then wipe off the dried film with a clean, damp sponge. You can also put whiting directly into the water-based glaze, but don't use too much or it will dull the glaze.

Some alternatives to the water-and-whiting mixture are commercial surface deglosser (which has a strong odor and is only effective for about 30 minutes, depending on the size of the surface), white vinegar, or a mixture of Panama wood chips and warm water (add a heaping teaspoonful of chips to 32 ounces of water). Experiment with a few of these; your choice will be based on the size, intricacy, and accessibility of your project's surface.

1. If a cured oil-basecoated surface is not "degreased" before a reversible water-based glaze is applied, the basecoat will repel the glaze, causing it to bead.

2. Apply a mixture of whiting and water to the surface, then rub energetically. Let dry.

3. Wipe off the surface with a clean, damp sponge.

1

2

3

Color Basics

Color theory is a complex topic, with many books devoted to the subject. A thorough treatment is beyond the scope of this book, but it is important to understand certain basic principles of color that apply to decorative painting. With practice, you can learn how to determine what colors will work best for a wide variety of applications.

Light is an essential component in color perception. White light contains all the colors of the spectrum (red, orange, yellow, green, blue, violet). Color results when light hits a surface and a particular shade is reflected back; when a surface appears yellow, for example, that means it is reflecting the yellow portion of the light and is absorbing all the other colors. Black absorbs all colors and reflects none back.

THE COLOR WHEEL

The easiest way to understand colors and how they work (or don't work) together is through the color wheel. The three *primary colors* are red, blue, and yellow; they cannot be made by mixing any other colors. Theoretically any color can be achieved by combining various mixtures of the three primaries, but certain bright colors are better purchased as such. The three *secondary colors* are made by combining two primary colors: red + yellow = orange; blue + yellow = green; and red + blue = violet. The six *tertiary colors* are obtained by mixing a secondary and a primary: yellow + orange = yellow-orange; red + orange = red-orange; blue + violet = blue-violet, and so on. Warm colors are those in the red-orange-yellow portion of the spectrum; cool colors run through the green-blue-violet portion.

PROPERTIES OF COLOR

Notions of what makes a color beautiful or ugly are very subjective. Yet it is possible to learn how to get colors to harmonize and to judge what colors will work well together. Color harmony can be thought of like harmony in music. Just as certain sounds combine to produce pleasing music, certain colors go very well together and show one another off to best advantage. Certain musical instruments sound wonderful individually but do not work with others because they are not in harmony or because one instrument is so loud that it drowns out the others. The same is true for colors; certain colors may be individually pretty but they may be unbearable in some combinations.

The adage "less is more" often holds true in decor: combining numerous colors or finishes in one room or one project does not necessarily mean better decor. In music, silence can be used to enhance the arrangement; in decor, fewer colors or finishes can enhance the beauty of a finished piece. Extending the auditory analogy one step further, just as the setting affects sound (the slightest sound may be heard in a library, but the same sound may not be heard in a crowded cafeteria), setting must also be taken into account when planning use of colors. A vivid environment can handle bolder colors and finishes, while a very plain setting can make even the slightest color change seem drastic. Keep in mind that colors can set moods; warmer colors produce a more intense ambiance, while cooler colors often evoke tranquility.

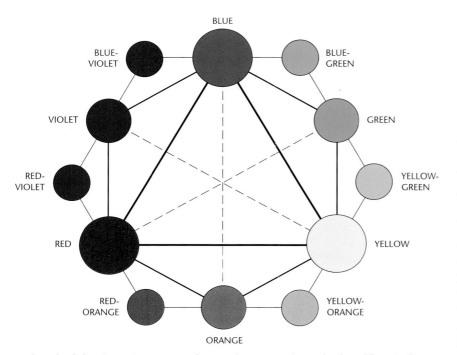

A color wheel showing primary, secondary, and tertiary colors. The dotted lines indicate complementary colors, which lie opposite one another on the wheel (see page 35).

The Faux Palette

Every paint contains pigment, and its color is essentially a pigment or a mixture of pigments. Pigments may be of mineral, vegetable (obtained from plants), or animal origin, but they all share certain characteristics:

- *Tinting strength* is a pigment's capacity to impose its color on a mixture.
- *Opacity* is a pigment's ability to cover another color.
- *Stability* is a pigment's power to resist deterioration from exposure to higher temperatures and to weather.
- *Lightfastness* is a pigment's ability to resist fading caused by exposure to light. Lightfastness is generally indicated on the paint's label.
- *Toxicity* is a measure of the pigment's potential health hazards, often indicated on the paint's label.

Although the majority of decorative painters, both amateur and professional, use commercially prepared paints or tints rather than raw pigments to impart color to glazes, it is important to be aware of the basic characteristics of the pigments they contain and how they may affect a glaze. Armed with that knowledge, you can make informed color choices because you'll know what to expect from each pigment. It should be noted, however, that a pigment's characteristics can vary from paint to paint, depending on the quality and amount of pigment in a paint, as well as the medium.

The following is a partial list of colors—grouped by color family—that are often used in decorative painting.

Whites
- *Titanium white.* Very opaque, excellent lightfastness, slow drying rate, nontoxic.
- *Zinc white.* Semi-transparent to semi-opaque (depending on source), excellent lightfastness, very slow drying rate.

Yellows
- *Chrome yellow.* Opaque, unstable (may react with other pigments), poor lightfastness (may turn black or green), toxic (derived from lead).
- *Chrome orange.* See chrome yellow.
- *Cadmium yellow.* Very opaque to semi-opaque (depending on source), very stable, excellent lightfastness, nontoxic.

Reds
- *Cadmium red.* Very opaque to semi-opaque (depending on source), very stable, excellent lightfastness, nontoxic, very slow drying rate.
- *Vermilion.* Very opaque, low stability, poor lightfastness, toxic.
- *English red.* Similar to red ochre: High tinting strength, very opaque, stable, excellent lightfastness (also known as light red).
- *Alizarin crimson.* Transparent, excellent stability, fair lightfastness, very slow drying rate (similar to crimson lake and carmine lake).

Blues
- *Ultramarine blue.* Opaque to semi-transparent (depending on source), low stability outdoors, excellent lightfastness, slow drying rate.
- *Cerulean blue.* Very opaque, very stable, generally excellent lightfastness, toxic.
- *Prussian blue.* Very high tinting strength, opaque, low stability, excellent lightfastness, fast drying rate.

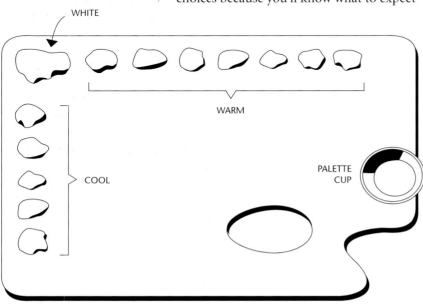

Use a consistent arrangement to organize the colors on your palette: Place white in the upper left-hand corner, then align warm colors in a row to its right, and cool colors in a column below it. Keep a palette cup filled with glaze on the right.

Colors should be carefully mixed on a palette before they are incorporated into a glaze.

Ochres and Earth Pigments

- *Yellow ochre.* Semi-opaque to opaque (depending on source), very stable, excellent lightfastness, slow drying rate.
- *Red ochre.* Very high tinting strength, very opaque, very stable, average drying rate, may cause brittle oil paint films (similar to Venetian red).
- *Raw sienna.* Low tinting strength, transparent to semi-opaque (depending on source), very stable, excellent lightfastness.
- *Burnt sienna.* Calcined (roasted) raw sienna; see raw sienna.
- *Raw umber.* Semi-opaque (variable color), stable, excellent lightfastness, fast drying rate.
- *Burnt umber.* Calcined raw umber; see raw umber.

Browns

- *Cassel earth.* Semi-transparent, stable, very slow drying rate.
- *Vandyke brown.* Opaque, very stable.

Greens

- *Chrome green oxide.* Opaque, weak tinting strength, stable, excellent lightfastness, nontoxic.
- *Chrome oxide deep.* See chrome oxide green (but has good tinting strength).
- *Veronese green.* Transparent, weak tinting strength, unstable, good lightfastness, toxic, average drying rate (somewhat similar to viridian and emerald green).
- *English green.* Opaque, stable.

Blacks

- *Lamp black.* Opaque, very stable, excellent lightfastness, very slow drying rate.
- *Ivory black.* Semi-transparent, stable, excellent lightfastness, very slow drying rate.

TIPS ON COLOR MIXING

Because light is crucial to the way colors work, you must always consider what type of light your decorative painting will be seen in. Is the room used primarily by day or by evening? Does it receive a lot of sunlight, or is it lit mostly by electric light? Preparation of samples should of course be done under the same lighting conditions that will illuminate the finished work.

One of the most important precepts of color mixing, harmony, and contrasting is the concept of complementary colors. Complementary colors are those opposite each other on the color wheel: red and green are complementary, blue and orange are complementary, and yellow and violet are complementary (see page 33). The greatest color contrasts are between two complementaries, so when you want to set off a color, place its complementary next to it. If you want to emphasize a red marble, for example, frame it with a green marble.

To lower a color's intensity, add a few drops of its complementary. An orange glaze mixture that appears too intense, for example, can be toned down by adding a bit of blue. This principle also applies when selecting a glaze for a particular basecoat. If a yellow basecoat seems too strong, applying a purplish glaze over it will greatly reduce its intensity.

Combining more than five colors to make a paint or a glaze will most likely "kill" at least one of the colors because those in the mixture begin to cancel each other out. Thus, more colors in a mix does not mean more intensity. If you add too much of a certain color when mixing, you can add its complementary to help counteract it.

Mixing together two complementary colors often produces a gray tone. The best grays can often be obtained not by mixing black and white but by mixing two complementaries and some white.

One way to harmonize many different colors or finishes is to use the same glaze over all the different tones. Since glaze is transparent, each area will retain its basic color, but the glaze will help to unite them.

When trying to achieve a gradation of the same color, use a palette knife to compare the different shades. Dip the blade all the way into the first color, three-quarters of the way into the second color, halfway into the third color, and a quarter of the way into the last color. This will show you all four colors in direct relation to one another.

Brushes

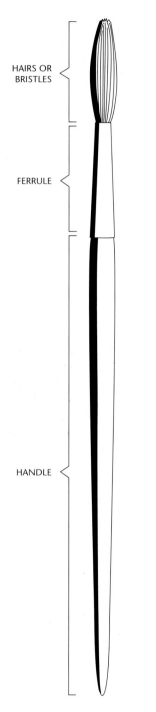

HAIRS OR BRISTLES

FERRULE

HANDLE

The basic elements of a brush.

Choosing the right brush is crucial to the success of a decorative painting project. Though brushes all share the same three elements—hairs or bristles, ferrule (the metal portion that attaches the hairs to the handle), and handle—they are available in an almost bewildering array of different shapes, types of hair, ferrule styles, and price ranges, and each is designed for a specific use. Trying to work with the wrong kind of brush, or using one that is in poor shape, will prohibit proper completion of your work. If you're a professional you should cultivate the habit of bringing your entire brush kit on a project. The condition of your tools reflects your attitude at work, so it is very important to take good care of them. Moreover, brushes are expensive, so proper maintenance will prolong the life of your investment, which is especially important because "broken-in" brushes are preferable to brand new ones, since they don't shed hair and are more responsive to your hand.

Because decorative painting brushes are expensive and are not always offered by every art supply or paint store, I have included in the list of suppliers a few mail-order companies that sell competitively priced brushes and carry some hard-to-find brushes. I use brushes that I import from France through my own company, which offers a complete selection of traditionally handcrafted decorative painting brushes.

BRUSH HAIRS

Brushes are distinguished primarily by the type of hair from which they are made. There are two basic categories of hair, natural and synthetic, but each of those categories boasts a variety of different types. The type of brush hair will often indicate what usage is appropriate for the particular brush (see below). Because brushes are the most expensive tools of the decorative painter, it is important to be able to recognize the type of hair in order to avoid ruining a brush by using it with the wrong system. Some brushes are intended only for oil-based products, others only for products that are water-based.

It is also extremely important to clean them properly with the right products (see page 62).

White Bristle. This is the most frequently used of the natural-hair brushes. All very large brushes and a number of small brushes are made from bristle, which comes from the pig. It is an inexpensive brush, with good "spring," though it tends to be a little stiff. It is recommended primarily for oil systems but it is used also with water. Brushes made from black bristle are of a lesser quality than white.

The poorest-quality white bristles are used to make disposable brushes, which are made to be thrown away after a single use. They usually feature uneven bristles, cheap metal ferrules, and unvarnished handles. Similar in appearance to spalters (see page 40), disposable brushes are an inexpensive alternative to spatter and stippling brushes, and good for use with hard-to-clean materials.

Ox Hair. Ox hair, which comes from the ears of oxen, produces a soft brush with medium spring. It is often used instead of the more expensive sable. It is recommended for oils.

Badger. A very soft, fluffy brush with no spring, the badger brush is expensive. It is used as a softening brush, mainly with reversible water-based paints, but can also be used with acrylics and oils if it is cleaned immediately.

Squirrel. Made from the tail of the squirrel, this type of brush is quite absorbent, has low spring, and comes to a very fine point when wet. It works well for applications that require a very smooth finish. It is somewhat expensive, particularly the best-quality squirrel-hair brushes, which are Kazan and blue squirrel. It is meant primarily for reversible water-based paints, though it can also be used with oils, and with acrylics if it is cleaned immediately.

Sable. Sable brushes, made from the hair of the sable and other related animals such as the weasel, have excellent spring and keep their shape very well. There are numerous types of sable brushes; the very best is the Kolinsky, but most are generally of good quality and are quite expensive. They can be used either with oils or with reversible water-based paints.

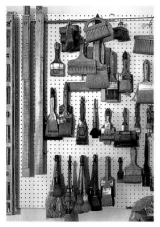

Keeping brushes organized and in good condition will prolong the life of your investment. (For information on cleaning brushes, see page 62.)

Other Natural Hairs. Brush hair is derived from a number of other animals, including the horse, mongoose, goat, skunk, and fitch (polecat, a relative of the weasel). Such brushes are generally intended for specific tasks.

Synthetic Hairs. As the name implies, the hairs in synthetic brushes are made from synthetic filaments instead of animal hairs. Quality varies with the thickness and spring of the hair. Some are thick and strong, and are excellent for basecoating or glazing in acrylic. This type is similar in quality to white bristle and is sometimes a blend of natural and synthetic bristles. The small brushes are thin and soft, resembling sable in quality; these are used for all water-based media and tend to be expensive.

FERRULES

The hair is fastened onto the brush handle by means of the ferrule. The ferrule is usually a small piece of metal, but plastic, horn, quills (feathers shafts), metal wire, and thread are also used. Ferrules may be made of copper, brass, or tin; the best are made of nickel-plated copper. The ferrule's size and shape (either round or flat) affect the size and shape of the brush. The hairs are tied in a bundle of the appropriate shape and set into the ferrule with adhesive. The ferrule is then crimped onto the handle. Better brushes have two or three crimps; the cheapest ones have just one or may have small nails instead.

HANDLES

Brush handles are generally made of wood, and shaped round or flat according to the style of brush. The wood may be varnished, painted, or left raw. Plastic handles are usually used for very cheap brushes.

TYPES OF BRUSHES

There are often a variety of ways to approach the same paint recipe using different brushes. Painting faux marble on a very large area such as a wall, for example, will require bigger and wider brushes than will a small tabletop; in other words, the recipe is essentially the same but the sizes and types of brushes will differ according to the task. Once you become familiar with a recipe you can vary it by using different brushes.

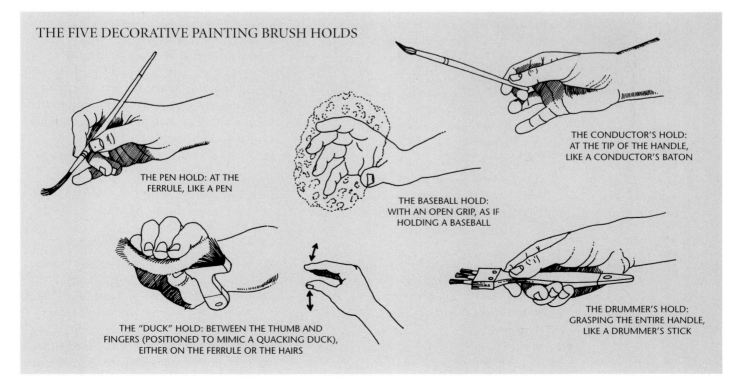

THE FIVE DECORATIVE PAINTING BRUSH HOLDS

THE PEN HOLD: AT THE FERRULE, LIKE A PEN

THE CONDUCTOR'S HOLD: AT THE TIP OF THE HANDLE, LIKE A CONDUCTOR'S BATON

THE BASEBALL HOLD: WITH AN OPEN GRIP, AS IF HOLDING A BASEBALL

THE "DUCK" HOLD: BETWEEN THE THUMB AND FINGERS (POSITIONED TO MIMIC A QUACKING DUCK), EITHER ON THE FERRULE OR THE HAIRS

THE DRUMMER'S HOLD: GRASPING THE ENTIRE HANDLE, LIKE A DRUMMER'S STICK

The following list of brushes presents those most often used in decorative painting. The recipes were done using a 30-×-40-inch board, so the tool specified applies to work on small and medium-sized areas. Depending on your budget and preferences, as well as on the availability of certain brushes, this list may be expanded or condensed. I have selected average brush sizes, but each decorative painter will find a tool that "fits" best. Brush sizes are indicated on the handle, given in inches, millimeters, or the manufacturer's own numbering system.

Key to the Listing
Each entry details four elements about the particular brush.

- The name is followed by the type of hair, ferrule, and handle used; its basic shape; and the method used to indicate its size. (Size numbers often correspond to the measurement in millimeters; #40 may indicate a width of 40 millimeters.)
- The medium for which it is intended. "Oil" means the brush can be used for any oil-based medium. "Water" refers to all water-based systems, both irreversible (acrylics, vinyl, latex) and reversible (watercolors, gouache, casein, beer glazes). "For reversible systems only" means that the brush should *not* be used with irreversible paints. "Dedicated" indicates two sets of the same brush, one for oil and one for water.
- The technique(s) for which it is used
- How it is held. There are five basic holds (see page 37): at the ferrule, like a pen; at the tip of the handle, like a conductor's baton; grasping the entire handle, like a drummer's stick; between your thumb and fingers (positioned to mimic a quacking duck) on the ferrule or on the hair itself; or with an open grip, like a baseball.

DECORATIVE PAINTING BRUSHES

Number	Brush	Description	Medium or System/Use/Hold
1	Round Glazing Brush for Water	Synthetic hair mixed with white bristle; size given in inches or manufacturer's number	• For water only • Used to apply glaze, and sometimes for the basecoat (the pointed types are used to "cut a line," or paint defined areas precisely) • Held at the ferrule, like a pen (see page 37)
2, 3	Flat Painting Brush	White or black bristle or synthetic hair with flat or slanted top, metal ferrule, and flat wooden handle; size given in inches	• Bristle types for oil; synthetic for water • Generally used to apply the basecoat, sometimes for varnishing • Held at the ferrule, like a pen (see page 37)
4–7	Round Glazing Brush for Oil	White bristle with square or pointed top, copper ferrule, and round wooden handle; size given in inches or manufacturer's number; also known as a domed sash brush	• Mostly for oil, but can be used for water when dedicated • Used to apply glaze, and sometimes for the basecoat (the pointed types are used to "cut a line," or paint defined areas precisely) • Held at the ferrule, like a pen (see page 37)
8	Varnishing Brush	White bristle or synthetic hair with oval handle, metal ferrule, and flat wooden handle, size given in inches or manufacturer's number	• Bristle types for oil; synthetic for water • Used for varnishing small surfaces or cabinetry; on large areas use a roller first, then smooth out with a #200 spalter • Held at the ferrule, like a pen (see page 37)
9, 10	Staining Brush	White or black bristle or synthetic hair with flat top, metal ferrule, and round wooden handle; size given in inches or manufacturer's number	• Bristle types for oil; synthetic for water • Primarily used for staining, but decorative painters use them to glaze large areas like walls; also great as a cheap alternative to the expensive stippling brush • Held like a drummer's stick, or in an open hand, like a baseball (see page 37)

1. Round glazing brush for water; 2, 3. Flat painting brushes for water (2) and oil (3); 4–7. Round glazing brushes for oil; 8. Varnishing brush; 9, 10. Staining brushes for water (9) and oil (10).

DECORATIVE PAINTING BRUSHES

Number	Brush	Description	Medium or System/Use/Hold
11, 12	Spalter	Short white bristle (sometimes synthetic) in one medium-thick row with flat top, metal ferrule, and very short wooden handle; size given in millimeters; commonly used sizes: 100, 60, 40; also known as mottlers; disposable brushes (page 36) are a cheap alternative	• Mostly for oil, but can be used for water when dedicated, especially synthetic type (see page 44) • Wide variety of uses, including stretching glazes, smoothing paint or varnish, and creating moiré, ripple, and striated effects • Held between thumb and fingers on the ferrule or on the hair itself; near the end of the handle, like a conductor's baton; or like a drummer's stick (see page 37)
13, 14	Badger Brush	Badger hair arrayed in three rows with horn or plastic ferrule or hairs sometimes set directly in the wood (one row with metal ferrule on smaller sizes) and round wooden handle; size given in millimeters; commonly used sizes: 100, 60, 40	• For reversible systems only; oil or acrylic okay if dedicated as such but can damage the hair; may be replaced by a wide veinette • Used to smooth out water glazes, or for moiré and ripple effects • Held at the tip of the handle, like a conductor's baton, or between thumb and fingers on the hair itself (see page 37)
15, 16	Codtail	Long white bristle in one medium-thick row with metal ferrule and long, flat handle, size given in millimeters; commonly used sizes: 100, 60, 40; also called flat, long-haired softeners	• For oil only • Used to smooth out paint and glaze (the codtail is the oil version of the badger brush; can be substituted with a long flat-bristled oil basecoating brush) • Held at the tip of the handle, like a conductor's baton (see page 37)
17, 18	Flogger	Long black horse hair with flat top, metal ferrule, and long, flat wooden handle; size given in millimeters; commonly used sizes: 100, 60, 40	• For reversible systems only • Used to simulate wood pores • Held like a drummer's stick (see page 37)
19	Veinette	Long white bristle in a thin row with flat or fan top, metal ferrule, and flat handle; size given in millimeters; commonly used sizes: 100, 60, 40	• For oil or water, as dedicated • Used to create wood graining; can also dedicate one to acrylic as an alternative to badger • Held like a drummer's stick, or at the tip of the handle, like a conductor's baton (see page 37)
20, 21	Teeth Spalter	Short white bristle in one medium-thick row as in regular spalter but with spaces at intervals, with metal ferrule and short, flat wooden handle; size given in millimeters; commonly used sizes: 100, 60, 40	• Mostly for oil; old ones can be used for water • Used to create veins or to establish a design in wood graining, also to give the look of old patina • Held like a drummer's stick, or at the tip of the handle, like a conductor's baton (see page 37)
22	Pencil Grainer	White bristle (ox hair and synthetic also available) arrayed in three to six "pencils," with pointed top, metal ferrule (sometimes hinged), and flat wooden handle; size usually the number of "pencils" (a #3, for example, has three pencils)	• White bristle and ox hair for oil; synthetic for water • Used to create intricate underveining of certain marbles, or figured effects of certain woods • Held like a drummer's stick, or at the tip of the handle, like a conductor's baton (see page 37); affect can be approximated by holding two or three pointed brushes together in the palm of the hand

11, 12. Spalters; 13, 14. Badger brushes; 15, 16. Codtail brushes; 17, 18. Floggers; 19. Veinette; 20, 21. Teeth spalters; 22. Pencil grainer.

DECORATIVE PAINTING BRUSHES

Number	Brush	Description	Medium or System/Use/Hold
23–26	Striping Brush	Small flat hairs (sometimes fitch) with slanted or slightly rounded top, metal ferrule, and long, thin wooden handle; size given in manufacturer's number; also known as a striping fitch	• For oil only • Slanted edge used for striping, rounded edge for fine striping and veining • Held at the tip of the handle, like a conductor's baton, or at the ferrule, like a pen (see page 37)
27	Small Flat Brush	Small, flat bristle with square or slightly rounded top, metal ferrule, and long, thin wooden handle; size given in manufacturer's number	• For oil only • Used for veining and touchups • Held at the ferrule, like a pen, or at the tip of the handle, like a conductor's baton (see page 37)
28, 29	Halftone Brush	Short goat or mongoose hair (also synthetic variety) with square or rounded top, metal ferrule, and long, thin wooden handle; size given in manufacturer's number	• Goat or mongoose for oil; synthetic for water • Used to create shading in faux molding • Held at the tip of the handle, like a conductor's baton (see page 37)
30, 31	Synthetic Flat Brush	Short synthetic hair with flat top, metal ferrule, and long, thin wooden handle; size given in manufacturer's number	• For water only • Used for striping and shading • Held at the tip of the handle, like a conductor's baton (see page 37)
32–35	Lettering Brush	Ox hair, squirrel, or sable (also synthetic variety) with long, square tip, metal ferrule, and long, thin wooden handle; size given in manufacturer's number	• Squirrel and sable for oil only; ox hair for oil or water when dedicated; synthetic for water only • Used for lettering, ornament painting, lining, and veining, and for basecoating very small areas • Held at the ferrule, like a pen, or at the tip of the handle, like a conductor's baton (see page 37)
36–39	Long Pointed Brushes	Assortment of ox hair, goat, sable, and synthetic brushes with pointed tips, metal ferrules, and long, thin wooden handles; size given in manufacturer's number	• Goat and sable for oil only; ox hair for oil or water when dedicated; synthetic for water only • Used for ornament painting, lining, veining, and touchups • Held at the ferrule, like a pen, or at the tip of the handle, like a conductor's baton (see page 37)
40, 41	Short Pointed Synthetic Brush	Synthetic hair with short, pointed tip, metal ferrule, and medium-length wooden handle; size given in manufacturer's number	• For water only • Used for ornament painting, veining, and touchups • Held at the ferrule, like a pen, or at the tip of the handle, like a conductor's baton (see page 37)
42, 44, 45	Marbling Brush	Long bristles with slightly rounded tip, wire- or string-tied ferrule, and long, thin wooden handle; size given in manufacturer's number	• For oil only • Used only for marbling • Held at the tip of the handle, like a conductor's baton (see page 37)
46–48	Small White Bristle Brushes	Assortment of white bristle brushes in both long and short bristle styles, with flat, round, pointed, and square tops, metal ferrules, and long, thin wooden handles; size given in manufacturer's number	• For oil only • Used for many techniques, including ornament painting, marbling, striping, lining, veining, and touchups • Held at the ferrule, like a pen, or at the tip of the handle, like a conductor's baton (see page 37)
43	Cat's Tongue	Squirrel hair with flat, pointed, or square top, metal ferrule, and wooden handle; size given in manufacturer's number	• For oil only; can be dedicated to reversible media • For establishing undergraining and designs for certain woods • Held at the ferrule, like a pen, or at the tip of the handle, like a conductor's baton (see page 37)
49	Fan Brush	Bristle, mongoose, or synthetic hair arrayed in a thin, fan-shaped row, with metal ferrule and long, thin wooden handle; size given in manufacturer's number	• Bristle and mongoose for oil; synthetic for water • Used for smoothing out or veining in small areas • Held at the tip of the handle, like a conductor's baton (see page 37)

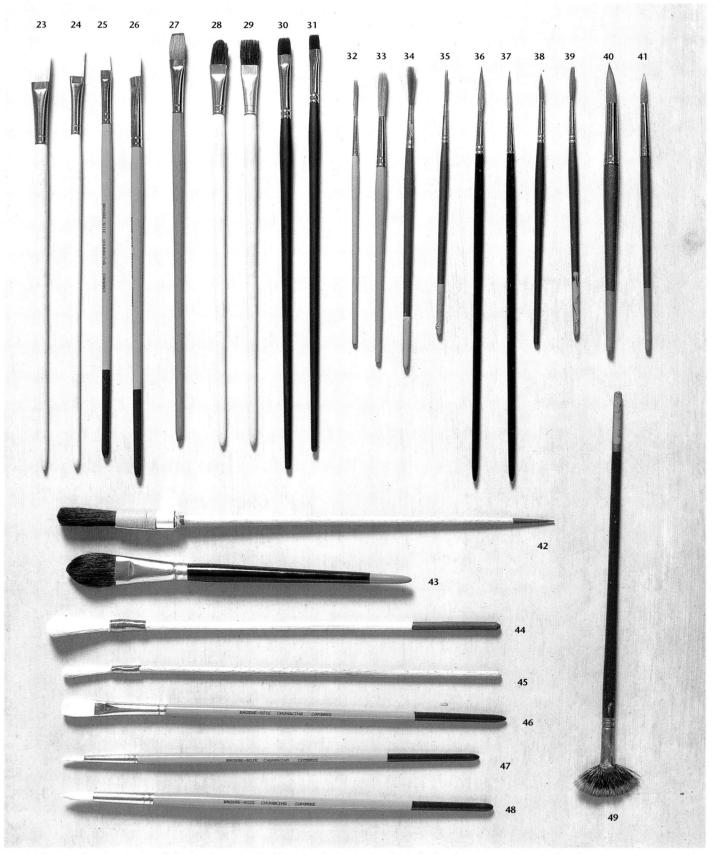

23–26. Striping brushes; 27. Small flat brush; 28, 29. Halftone brush; 30, 31. Synthetic flat brushes; 32–35. Lettering brushes; 36–39. Long pointed brushes; 40, 41. Short pointed synthetic brushes; 42, 44, 45. Marbling brushes; 43. Cat's tongue; 46–48. Small white bristle brushes; 49. Fan brush.

DECORATIVE PAINTING BRUSHES

Number	Brush	Description	Medium or System/Use/Hold
50	Skunk Brush	Very short skunk or ox hair arrayed in thick or thin row, with metal ferrule and medium-length flat wooden handle; size given in millimeters; commonly used sizes: 60, 40	• For reversible systems only • Used for creating fine moiré or ripple effects in faux mahogany and walnut; a used #40 spalter is good alternative • Held like a drummer's stick (see page 37)
51	Bird's-Eye Brush	Round bristles arrayed in a hollow shape, with string-tied ferrule and long, thin wooden handle; size given in manufacturer's number	• For reversible systems only; can be used for oil too, if dedicated • Used for imitating bird's-eye maple and burl • Held at the ferrule, like a pen (see page 37)
52, 53	Rondin Brush	Fat, round skunk-hair brush with slightly rounded top, metal ferrule, and short, round wooden handle; also called a porcelain brush because it is used primarily for striping china and earthenware	• For oil or water, as dedicated • Used for lining or striping on faux three-dimensional molding • Held like a pen but pinched on the heel and the ferrule (see page 208)
54	Chiqueteur	Fat squirrel-hair brush (sometimes Kazan or blue squirrel; sometimes mixed with goat hair to make it less expensive) with square tip, quill ferrule, and short, fat, round wooden handle; size given in manufacturer's number	• For oil only; rinse often if used with water systems, or substitute with a worn and fray-edged sea sponge • Used to create the small fragment patterns in faux marble • Held at the ferrule, like a pen (see page 37)
55	Brecheur	Round squirrel-hair brush (sometimes Kazan or blue squirrel) with pointed tip, quill ferrule, and long, round wooden handle; also called a washer or veiner; size given in manufacturer's number	• For oil or water, as dedicated • For fine reglazing, creating effects of brèche (fragments) in marbling, and achieving figural effects in wood graining • Held at the ferrule, like a pen, or at the tip of the handle, like a conductor's baton (see page 37)
56–58	Two-Header	Two long, round brecheur-type brushes mounted on a forklike handle, with either square or pointed tip, quill ferrule, and long, thin wooden handle; size given in manufacturer's number; also available as three-header (see brush number 58)	• For oil only, or water when dedicated • Pointed type used for marbling and creating brèche effects (fragments), but can be approximated by holding pointed brushes held in the palm of the hand; square type is used for side and figure veining in wood graining, but can be replaced by the veinette • Held just below the ferrule, like a pen, or at the tip of the handle, like a conductor's baton (see page 37)
59	Stippling or Patina Brush	White bristles grouped in long bunches and arrayed in six rows; the wooden handle also serves as the ferrule; size given in manufacturer's number	• For oil or water, as dedicated • Used to create stippled effects or textures in glazes; wide staining brush may be used instead • Held with an open grip, like a baseball (see page 37)
60	Square Stippling Brush	White bristles grouped in long bunches and arrayed in twelve or more rows in a rectangular shape; the rectangular wooden base serves as the ferrule, with a wooden handle attached to the back; size given in manufacturer's number	• For oil only • Used to create stippled effects evenly over a large area • Held by the handle, like a briefcase
61, 62	Stencil Brush	Fat, round, short white or black bristles with square tip, metal ferule, and short, round wooden handle; size given in manufacturer's number	• For oil or water, as dedicated • Used for stenciling • Held at the ferrule, like a pen (see page 37)
63	Synthetic Spalter	Long synthetic hair arrayed in a thin row, with metal ferrule and short, flat wooden handle; size given in millimeters; commonly used sizes: 100, 60, 40	• For water only • Used for glazing and for certain types of fragmenting or brèching • Held at the tip of the handle, like a conductor's baton (see page 37)

50. Skunk brush; 51. Bird's-eye brush; 52–53. Rondin brush; 54. Chiqueteur; 55. Brecheur; 56, 57. Two headers: Pointed (56) and square (57); 58. Three-header; 59. Stippling or patina brush; 60. Square stippling brush; 61, 62. Stenciling brushes; 63. Synthetic spalter.

TYING A BRUSH

Tying a brush yourself is a great way to make a new round brush a little stiffer so it will be easier to apply a glaze. Always remember to undo the tie when you clean the brush so that it gets thoroughly cleaned.

1. Hold the brush at the ferrule in one hand. Use the other hand to loop a piece of string at the edge of the ferrule nearest the hairs. Make sure to leave about 3 inches of string at the top.

2. Hold the loop in place with your thumb.

3. Begin winding the string around the hairs, starting at the base immediately above the ferrule.

4. Continue winding the string until the hairs have been narrowed to the desired width. Insert the end of the string through the loop.

5. Pull the short end of the string at the top of the ferrule so that the point where the string was inserted through the loop lies beneath the wound string.

6. Tie a knot to secure the string.

7. Cut both ends close to the knot.

8. The tied glazing brush.

Other Decorative Painting Tools

Decorative painting often calls for a wide variety of tools in addition to brushes. The following list provides many suggestions, but you may discover many more. As you experiment with various methods, you will no doubt begin to customize your tool kit to fit your own preferences and skill level. One of the great pleasures of the work is to invent new uses for materials that might not at first seem applicable to painting techniques. The spliced end of a piece of rubber hose, for instance, can make a great implement for painting faux cork. A piece of cardboard or a rectangle cut from the plastic lid of a food container can be turned into a striating tool by notching the edges. By using your imagination and looking at old things in new ways, you can invent new ways to do old techniques, or create brand new ones.

PREPARATION ITEMS

Sandpaper. Sandpaper is available in two forms. *Dry sandpaper* is used on a rough surface, or one that is not yet basecoated. *Wet sandpaper* can be used either dry or with water. For the wet method, moisten the surface with a sponge and then sand, dipping the sandpaper in a bucket of water to rinse it every so often. Wet sanding produces a finer and more gentle sanding than dry sandpaper, and is especially good as a finishing sanding between coats of varnish.

Both types are used by folding the sandpaper before sanding, and both are sold in different grades, from coarse (50 to 150; grade 50 is not available in wet form) to medium (220 to 300) to fine (400 to 600) to extra fine (1000 to 1500; the finest grades are not available in dry form).

A *sanding block* is a wooden or rubber block covered with sandpaper that is usually equipped with a handle. You can make a sanding block by taping sandpaper to a small piece of wood.

For information on how to sand a surface, see "Sanding," page 56.

Dusting Brush. Also known as a hand duster, this 9-inch-long brush should be used *exclusively* for removing sanding dust and other debris from a surface. Although a dusting brush looks similar to a stippling brush (see page 45), it will contaminate a surface with dust if it is used to manipulate a glaze. A 3-inch disposable or old square painting brush can be substituted for a dusting brush; once they've been used for dusting, they should *never* be used for painting or glazing.

Tack Cloth. A tack cloth is a gauzy rag treated with a waxy, sticky substance. It is used to remove dust and other debris from a surface, usually before varnishing. NOTE: A tack cloth should always be stroked *gently* over a painted or glazed surface.

Scrub Pad. This item, which is a soft sponge on one side and a scouring or scrubbing pad on the other, is used to sand intricate surfaces, to dull down shiny surfaces without "burning" the edges, or to clean dried mistakes. It is also used in "degreasing" an oil-basecoated surface to prepare it to accept a reversible water-based glaze (see page 32).

Industrial Sponge. Much less expensive than a sea sponge (see page 50), this type is good for scrubbing a surface, especially a large one. It is used to wipe off a degreased or wet-sanded surface.

Set of Compound Knives. For filling holes, spackling, or, when painting wood, for marking a cut (making a distinct line) between two boards, I use a set of plasterer's knives and a set of small flexible blades of the type used in auto body shops, also known as Japanese blades.

Tape. Tape can be very useful to protect areas that have already been painted or to cover areas that will not be painted. Projects may call for several different types of tape, in varying widths (from $1/16$-inch pinstriping tape to 3 inches wide) and degrees of stickiness (from low tack to high tack). Before using a tape, always test it for tack and bleed resistance (not all tape is bleedproof). If tape is left on a surface for too long it may leave a glue residue or may pull off some paint when the tape is removed. Remember that tape is not foolproof; the work must still be done with care even if you use tape to help you. Note that a hair dryer can be used to soften tape if removal is problematic (see the entry on page 52). Several types of tape are used in decorative painting:

- *Masking tape.* This beige tape is available in 1- to 3-inch widths and is very inexpensive. It bleeds, and its very high tack will leave a residue after two days, so use it only to tape floor paper, never on painted surfaces.
- *Packing tape.* Packing tape is transparent or brown, available in 2- to 3-inch widths, and is somewhat expensive. It is quite strong, with very high tack. It is good only for packing and for taping plastic cloth together.
- *Blue tape or green tape.* This type comes in 1- to 2-inch widths and is medium-priced to expensive. It has medium tack, low bleeding, and leaves little or no residue. It is useful for general taping on walls and cabinetry, but be careful when removing it.
- *White tape.* White tape is paperlike, available in 1- to 2-inch widths, and is medium-priced to expensive. It has very low tack, low bleeding, and no residue. It is good for taping over wallpaper or freshly painted surfaces.
- *Tape with plastic or paper drape.* This type is sold either already set up or with a dispenser on which you can put any sizes of any tape with either paper or self-stick plastic film of different widths. It is great for taping off surfaces to protect them.
- *Pinstriping tape.* Pinstriping tape, sold in auto supply stores, is available in $1/16$- to $3/4$-inch widths and is expensive. It has good tack, no bleeding, and no residue. It is good for creating grout or joint lines in a faux stone layout.

Scaffolds and Ladders. Made of metal, wood, or fiberglass, scaffolds and ladders are sold in different sizes and shapes. Use the kind you are most comfortable with, but try to use the least cumbersome or smallest one that will safely reach an area. A small collapsible scaffold is also great and will enable you to work on most wall sizes.

CUTTING AND MEASURING TOOLS

Measuring Tape. This should be long and strong, so that heights can be measured easily.

Rulers. You will need a range of different-sized rulers, from 18 to 48 inches.

Striping Edge. Made of light wood, a striping edge is beveled on both edges. There are very few sources for this tool, but a carpenter can make one for you. The tool must be cleaned often while in use, and it must not be used for any other task, so that the edges stay smooth and free of nicks. A cheap alternative is to use a yardstick from the hardware store. (Chapter 11, "Trompe l'Oeil: Faux Moldings and Grisaille.")

Chalk. A stick of white chalk is used to do a rough tracing, or to lay out a preliminary design; it is easy to erase.

Snap Line. This tool is used to ensure a very straight line between two points. The device consists of a string reeled inside a housing full of tinted chalk. Working with an assistant, you unreel the string, stretch it between two points, hold it taut, and then snap it against the surface. This leaves a chalk deposit that should be easily removable. However, the blue or red chalk that often comes in the snap line is so highly tinted that it may be hard to erase, so I empty it and replace it with a mixture of $3/4$ part talcum powder and $1/3$ part powdered charcoal or raw umber pigment.

Levels. To create paneling or to lay out blocks for faux stone work, you need a small level and a 48-inch level.

Compass. It is useful to have both a small regular compass and a beam compass for large circles or arcs.

X-Acto or Craft Knife. An X-Acto knife is used to cut stencils.

Five-in-One or Five-Way Tool. This is a truly versatile tool. One part is for cleaning roller sleeves, one for opening cans, one for punching holes or scraping, and the front is good for scraping or cutting tape to make 45-degree angles. A slightly dulled five-in-one can also be used as a burnisher.

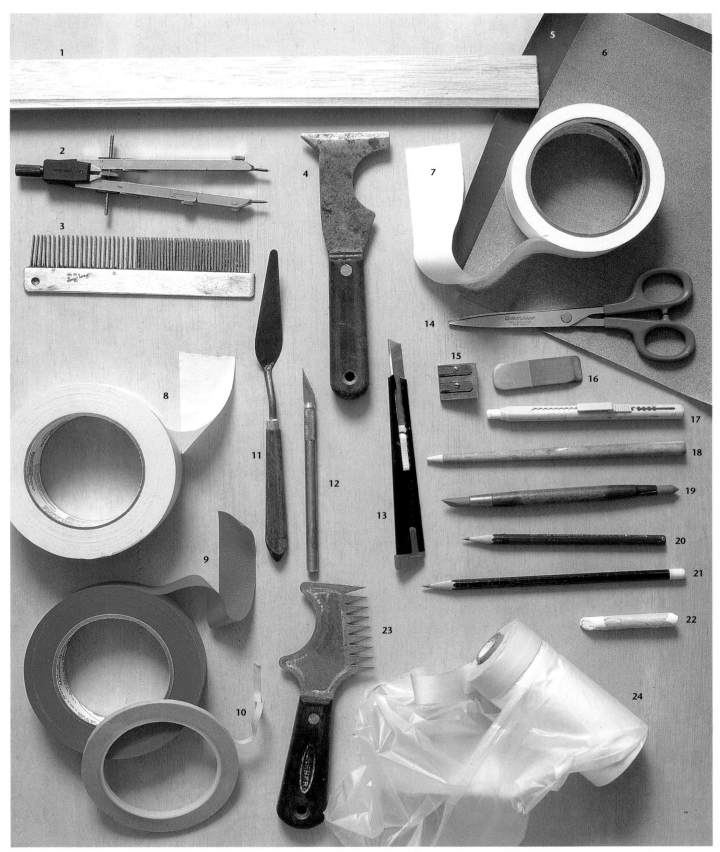

1. Striping edge; 2. Compass; 3. Metal pet comb; 4. Five-in-one tool; 5, 6. Wet and dry sandpapers; 7. White tape; 8. Masking tape; 9. Blue tape; 10. Pinstriping tape; 11. Palette knife; 12, 13. X-Acto and craft or hobby knives; 14. Scissors; 15. Pencil sharpener; 16–22. Erasers, pencils, and chalks; 23. Five-in-one with a comb for cleaning brushes; 24. Tape with plastic drape.

PAINT AND TOOL ORGANIZATION ITEMS

Palette. The most important tool after the brush, the palette is used for most projects, except those large enough to require a bucket. Palettes are sold in various shapes and sizes; some types are disposable. Be sure to get one with a hole for your thumb, and be aware that there are palettes for right- and left-handed people. There are three basic types of palettes, for different mediums:

- *For oil paints.* Wood palette, preferably grade-A lacquered plywood. If it is not lacquered, it must be rubbed with four or five coats of boiled linseed oil before use. Oil palettes must be cleaned after every use or colors will not mix properly. Every month or so I strip my palettes and paint them with satin-finish white oil paint.
- *For acrylic paints.* Disposable, water-grade palette, or transparent Plexiglas.
- *For gouaches and other reversible water systems.* Wood palette dedicated to water-based paints, or a disposable palette

Palette Knife. Palette knives are sold in different shapes and sizes. I use a small one for removing hairs from a dried surface or pulling up tape, and a large one that looks like a regular knife for mixing colors on my palette.

Palette Cup. This small tin cup has a clip underneath to attach it to the edge of the palette. It is also available as a double cup, but that style tends to be too shallow. (Palette cups may be hard to find—see the list of suppliers).

Buckets. Five-gallon buckets are useful for mixing quantites of glaze (the large size helps prevent splatters when mixing). Half-gallon buckets are good for holding mixed glaze. Use metal buckets for oils and plastic buckets for water-based systems. Remember to clean them well; if you don't, the residue can spoil the next mixture.

Containers. Containers should have a lid to preserve mixtures. Various kinds will serve: film canisters, baby-food jars, tin cans, food containers from the delicatessen, and wide-mouth glass jars.

Funnels. Plastic and metal funnels are very useful for filling up bottles when you need to store mixed glazes.

Brush-Cleaning Tool. Similar to a pet comb, this tool is used to detangle brush hairs.

Tool Kit. Sold in different shapes and sizes, in wood or aluminum, storage kits resemble either compartmentalized briefcases or tool boxes that open up on the side. You can also make your own, customized with small drawers. To protect your tools, it must be rigid and strong (canvas bags will not work), and must be able to travel well and be fairly lightweight.

Fanny Pack. Keeping the following frequently used items in a belt pouch while you work will make them easily accessible at all times:

- Small pair of sharp scissors
- Pencils (HB, 2H, 5H, 9H—one of each) and one pen
- Small notepad
- Mat knife with disposable blades
- Eraser with a soft and a hard side, or an erasing strip in a dispenser that allows you to erase as though holding a pencil
- Pencil sharpener
- Five-in-one

PAINT MANIPULATION ITEMS

Rags. Use cotton rags, free of lint and seams. They should be large enough to be cut up if necessary, and they should be white so you can see exactly what you are wiping off surfaces or brushes.

Cheesecloth. Cheesecloth is a gauzy material used to create texture in certain glazing techniques. It must be washed with water before using it to get rid of the lint. It can also be used to filter dirty mixes (fold it two or three times; one layer is not enough to act as a sieve).

Sea Sponge. Natural sponges come in wide variety of shapes and sizes. Though they are somewhat expensive, they can be used for a number of applications. Large flat ones are good for glazing, and an old one can be used for marbling and wood graining by first tearing away bits from

1–6. Graining combs; 7. Japanese blade; 8. Upholstery burlap; 9. Ribbon of billiard cloth; 10. Palette; 11. Scrub pad; 12. Industrial sponge; 13. Elephant ear sponge; 14. Sea sponge; 15. Cheesecloth; 16. Palette cup; 17. Snap line.

the edges to "fringe" them and to make the shape irregular.

Billiard Cloth. Available from a billiard parlor or a shop that repairs billiard tables, billiard cloth is best when old and worn and will not shed lint. Cut the felt in $1/2$-inch-wide ribbons. It is used as a wiping tool, mostly to create the silver grain characteristic of oak.

Upholstery Burlap. Burlap is used for the preliminary design in some wood graining recipes. It must first be treated so it does not shed lint, either by soaking it in a solution of 4 parts water and 1 part acrylic medium and then letting dry, or by running it quickly above a candle to burn off the lint, then dipping it in water and letting it dry. CAUTION: Be extremely careful with this procedure. Do not allow the fabric to touch the flame directly.

Elephant Ear Sponge. This flat natural sponge is used for cleaning off or wiping off a distinct line from a glazed or painted surface.

Metal Graining Combs. Graining combs are sold in four widths and three tooth sizes. When a recipe calls for a small, medium, or large comb, that refers to the tooth size, not the width. The size of the painting surface will determine the width of comb needed.

Gilding Tips. These brushes are used to apply gold leaf to a sized surface. They consist of a thin row of long hairs (generally badger, sable, or squirrel) mounted on a cardboard handle.

A check roller.

Metal or Plastic Pet Comb. This type of comb is used with the veinette brush, and also to comb out white-bristle brushes.

Corkboard. A notched piece of corkboard $1/8$ inch thick can be used to create the side and figure graining of oak.

Check Roller. A check roller consists of an array of small, notched metal disks on an axle held in a bracket and attached to a short wooden handle. To imitate the pores of certain types of wood, the device is rolled over the surface; the effect is then softened with a spalter.

Tracing Paper. Use a good-quality tracing paper that can accept paint as well as pencil and other dry media.

Frisket. This self-adhesive, low-tack transparent film is used to mask off selected areas of a surface when painting an intricate image. It can be cut very easily and will leave no residue on the surface.

Hair Dryer. When making samples in acrylics, using a blow dryer to speed up drying will allow you to reglaze within 5 minutes. It also helps show how a color will look when dry; though this will dry only the very surface in oil systems, it is sufficient to evaluate a color. The dryer is also handy to use on tape that has been left on a surface for long time; the heat softens the glue and makes the tape easier to remove.

Spray Bottle. On hot days, a spray bottle is useful for wetting down a surface with water before using water-based glazes.

Gilding tips.

Surface Preparation

Many people might be tempted to neglect preparation of the surface to be painted, but it is a crucial step that must not be overlooked. In fact, it could be considered the first step of any painted finish; at least 20 percent of the time it takes to create a finish should be devoted to preparing the surface. The layers of glaze over the basecoat are extremely thin, so they will not hide nicks, roughness, brush marks, hairs, bumps, cracks, or any other imperfections. The faux finish on any painted surface is always done over a basecoat, which allows decorative painting to be done on almost any surface. Taking the time to do the right preparation will ensure a solid surface on which to paint. Remember, the painting is only as strong as its weakest coat.

Professional decorative painters often have base painters prepare the surfaces for them. Nevertheless, all decorative painters should understand surface preparation, whether to actually do it themselves or to simply be able to specify the type and quality of the preparation expected. This knowledge will also enable you to check on the progress of the preparation if it is performed by someone else. If you are having a surface prepared by a base painter, have him or her give you a detailed list of the work to be done, as well as a list of the materials to be used. Fortunately, reputable painters are qualified craftspeople who understand the needs of the decorative painter. But even if you have someone else prepare the surface for you, try to spend some time familiarizing yourself with the different aspects of base painting.

There are two basic types of surfaces to consider when beginning preparation. *Raw surfaces* have no paint finish on them. They may be porous or not, soft or hard, smooth or rough; these characteristics will direct the preparation. *Painted surfaces* already have paint or finish on them, whether old or new. Within this group are two subcategories: (1) painted surfaces in good condition, in which, though the paint may be dirty or old, it is solid, with no flaking and few damages; or (2) painted surfaces in bad condition,

in which the paint may not only be dirty but is also cracking, chipping, or otherwise loosened.

The preparation table in this chapter presents general information on surface preparation. You may need to adapt this information to individual situations, taking into account such variables as drying time, weather conditions, size of the project, and budget. Note that the table does not refer to any particular sheen of paint; that will vary according to the recipe used. Also note that the material presented here applies to relatively flat surfaces; preparation for small, intricate surfaces may vary slightly (see note on millwork, page 54).

The table specifies the use of oil-based products, since they tend to give the better finish in most cases, but water-based products have their own advantages and should not be overlooked. (See "Media Compatibility," page 31.) CAUTION: Be sure to read manufacturers' labels to see if the products you are using are compatible with one another.

Throughout the table, the term "skim coating" is used to refer to the application of a fine coating of spackling compound over an uneven or damaged surface. Working in sections (from top to bottom and from left to right), apply the spackle to the surface, then use a large compound or spackling knife to smooth it out.

The tools used for preparation will vary from roller to fine brush to sprayer, depending on the size and type of surface in question. Use common sense, or ask the advice of a professional painter to find out the best way to go about a particular preparation. (Do not, for example, use a heavy nap roller to prepare a tabletop.)

Several entries call for industrial detergent, which is a very strong powdered cleanser available at paint or hardware stores. You can vary its strength depending on the amount of water added; follow the manufacturer's recommendations. CAUTION: This substance is extremely caustic; exercise care when using it.

SURFACE PREPARATION GUIDELINES

Surface	Cleaning/Scraping	Priming	Basecoating
Raw drywall	• Scrape rough spots lightly • Dust off surface thoroughly	• Top preparation: skim coating, then sand • Oil primer; sand when dry • Patch and spot-prime lightly where needed • Sand lightly when dry	• First coat: oil, thinned down 5%; sand lightly when dry • Second coat: oil, thinned down 15%; sand lightly when dry
Raw plaster	• Scrape rough spots lightly • Sand • Dust off surface thoroughly	• Top preparation: skim coating, then sand • Oil primer or linseed oil; sand when dry • Patch and spot prime lightly where needed • Sand lightly when dry	• First coat: oil, thinned down 5%; sand lightly when dry • Second coat: oil, thinned down 15%; sand lightly when dry
Raw wood: plywood, MDF (medium-density fiberboard), all solid woods, cabinets, furniture, doors, millwork	• Scrape rough spots lightly • Sand • Dust off surface thoroughly • On resinous wood (pine), shellac knots; if wood type is unknown but may be tropical, shellac all	• Oil primer; sand when dry • Top preparation: oil skim coating; sand then prime, when dry • Patch and spot prime lightly where needed	• First coat: oil, thinned down 5%; sand lightly when dry • Second coat: oil, thinned down 15%; sand lightly when dry
Raw fabric and canvas	• If canvas is rough wash it, then stretch or iron • If fabric is fragile, don't wash, just press if needed	• Water-based primer or gesso • Sand well and dust off	• First coat: oil or water, thinned down 5%; sand lightly when dry • Second coat: oil or water, thinned down 15%; sand lightly when dry • Use textile paint if needed for small areas
Raw paper, cardboard, craft paper, vellum	• Dust off surface	• Oil primer only (or oil primer, then shellac primer, if desired); sand when dry	• First coat: oil, thinned down 5%; sand lightly when dry • Second coat: oil, thinned down 15%; sand lightly when dry
Raw plastic, laminates, PVC	• Wash with strong chemical (acetone, lacquer thinner, or surface deglosser) • Sand thoroughly to give tooth	• Oil primer or very strong plastic-grade primer • Sand lightly; dust off	• First coat: oil, thinned down 5%; sand lightly when dry • Second coat: oil, thinned down 15%, sand lightly when dry
Metals subject to rust (iron) or oxidization (copper, bronze)	• Wash with strong chemical (acetone, lacquer thinner, or surface deglosser) • Sand thoroughly to give tooth	• Antirust primer for iron; clear lacquer for copper or bronze; sand lightly when dry • Oil primer	• First coat: oil, thinned down 5%; sand lightly when dry • Second coat: oil, thinned down 15%; sand lightly when dry
Nonrusting metals: aluminum, aluminum alloys, stainless steel	• Wash with strong chemical (acetone, lacquer thinner, or surface deglosser) • Sand thoroughly to give tooth	• Oil primer; sand and dust off when dry	• First coat: oil, thinned down 5%; sand lightly when dry • Second coat: oil, thinned down 15%; sand lightly when dry

SURFACE PREPARATION GUIDELINES

Surface	Cleaning/Scraping	Priming	Basecoating
Raw marble or polished stone	• Wash with strong chemical (acetone, lacquer thinner, or surface deglosser) • Sand thoroughly to give tooth	• Oil primer; sand and dust off when dry	• First coat: oil, thinned down 5%; sand lightly when dry • Second coat: oil, thinned down 15%; sand lightly when dry
Ceramics: tiles, old tub, appliances with baked ceramic finish	• Wash with strong chemical (acetone, lacquer thinner, surface deglosser, or industrial detergent) • Sand thoroughly to give tooth	• Oil primer or special ceramic primer; sand and dust off when dry	• First coat: oil enamel, thinned down 5%; sand lightly when dry • Second coat: oil, thinned down 15%; sand lightly when dry • If working directly on unprimed tiles, use acrylic enamel paint
Raw concrete	• Scrub with a plastic scrub brush; sand • Wash with Muriatic acid, then with water	• Concrete-grade primer; sand and dust off when dry	• First coat: oil, thinned down 5%; sand lightly when dry • Second coat: oil, thinned down 15%; sand lightly when dry
Glass: windows, lettering on glass, painting on the undersurface of glass	• Wash with industrial detergent, then Bon Ami powder; wipe off with clean rag	• Oil or glass-grade primer if painting over the glass; none if painting on a glass undersurface	• Two coats oil-based paint, or use sign painter's One Shot enamel for painting directly on the surface
Painted surface in good condition: wood, plaster, drywall	• Identify last basecoat and substrate • Wash lightly with industrial detergent; rinse well; let dry • Sand thoroughly and dust off	• Oil primer if compatible; sand and dust off when dry • Fill cracks and patch nicks with compound or filler; sand and dust off • Spot prime; sand and dust off	• First coat: oil or water, thinned down 5%; sand lightly when dry • Second coat: oil or water, thinned down 15%; sand lightly when dry
Painted surface in poor condition: wood, plaster	• Identify last basecoat and substrate • Scrape off dry paint • Deepen cracks with a scraper • Wash lightly with industrial detergent; rinse well; let dry • Sand thoroughly and dust off	• Oil primer if compatible; sand and dust off when dry • Fill cracks and patch nicks with compound or filler; sand and dust off • Spot prime; sand and dust off	• First coat: oil or water, thinned down 5%; sand lightly when dry • Second coat: oil or water, thinned down 15%; sand lightly when dry
Varnished surfaces	• Identify varnish and substrate; be sure it is not waxed • Wash with industrial detergent; rinse well; let dry	• Revarnish, or oil primer; sand and dust off when dry	• First coat: oil, thinned down 5%; sand lightly when dry • Second coat: oil, thinned down 15%; sand lightly when dry
Waxed surfaces	• Remove wax with naphtha or mineral spirits, using clean rags and hard brushes (CAUTION: Do not leave any trace of wax); sand lightly when dry	• Oil primer; sand and dust off when dry	• First coat: oil, thinned down 5%; sand lightly when dry • Second coat: oil, thinned down 15%; sand lightly when dry

SANDING

Sanding is an important part of the preparation and finish. Basecoats are sanded to make them smooth; surfaces are sanded to give to give them some tooth (see "'Degreasing' an Oil Basecoat for a Reversible Water-Based Glaze," page 32); varnish coats are sanded to get rid of the "grain" in the varnish. A variety of materials are used for sanding, including wet and dry sandpapers, scrub pads, and pumice on a wet rag. But no matter what the material, sanding always follows the same basic process: As you sand with your right hand, feel the surface with your left hand to be sure you have not missed a spot. (Or, if you are left-handed, sand with your left hand and feel the surface with your right.) You can sand in circular motions or follow the direction of the surface. The amount of pressure applied should vary according the surface: use lighter pressure on smooth surfaces, and firmer pressure on rough surfaces.

To get the most out of a piece of sandpaper, fold it as shown in the photos below. This will give you a total of six "sides" to work with; as each one is used, refold the sandpaper to reveal a new side.

1. *Folding sandpaper:* Fold the sandpaper in half so that the back is folded over on itself.

2. Fold one-third of the folded sandpaper onto its center third.

3. Repeat with the unfolded third of the sandpaper. The sandpaper is now ready to use.

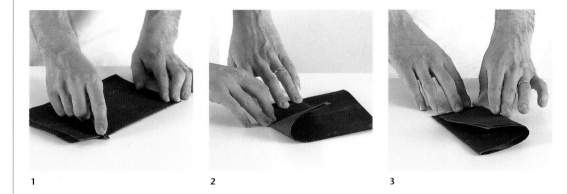

1   2   3

MAKING A "CUT" WITH SANDPAPER

There are several ways to make a miter or a straight cut to imitate wood paneling or the construction cut of marble. You can use tape when working in oil, but you must wait until the next day to tape off the areas you painted the first day. When working with oil-based media, you can use a strip of 100-grade sandpaper turned face down to mask a clear line of demarcation. No marks will be left on the fresh surface. Simply place the sandpaper face down on the surface, hold it in place, and apply the glaze (see photo). You can also use a metal blade or the flat part of a metal graining comb, but if your hand slips you will damage your work.

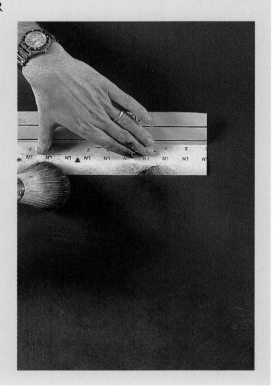

TAPING

Although some decorative painters might disagree, I am in favor of taping, as long as you use the right tape, do not rely on it to do all the work for you, and know how to do without it at times. Different jobs call for tapes of various types, widths, tacks, and prices. Know and test your tapes so you can make the right choices and can use them properly. Remember to remove tape carefully to avoid damaging the painted surface; if necessary, you can use a hair dryer to soften tape. (See page 47 for information about types of tape and their specific uses.)

1. Use a pencil to mark the dimensions of the area to be taped.

2. Draw the taping lines with a pencil and a straight edge.

3. Affix the tape to surface, aligning it with the taping lines.

4. Use a five-in-one to cut the tape at the corners at a 45-degree angle.

5. The taped surface, with a correctly cut edge.

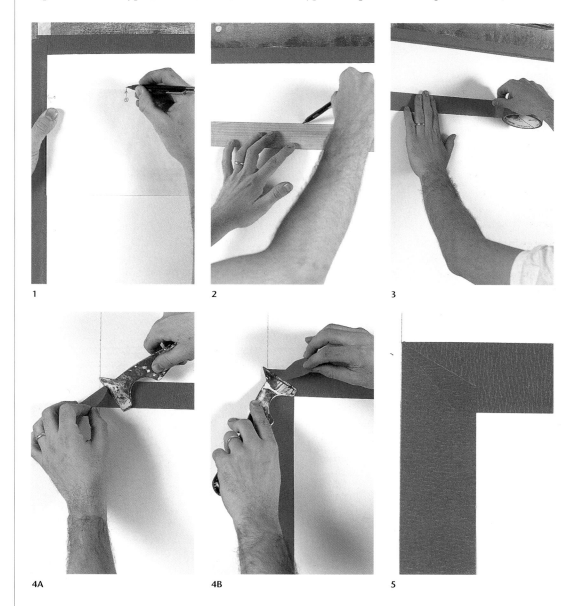

1

2

3

4A

4B

5

Removing Lint from a Roller

To remove the lint and loose hairs or fibers from a roller, wind 1 1/2-inch masking tape around the sleeve, then remove it fast. Repeat as necessary.

Removing a Hair from a Wet Surface

Using the tip of a white bristle brush, scoop the hair off the surface with a short, jerky movement.

CHOOSING THE RIGHT BASECOAT

Making the correct decision about a basecoat can be quite difficult, because you must anticipate what the end result will look like over it. Making a sample is the best way to know whether the basecoat is right. But when you have to match an existing finish, you must guess what color basecoat will give the right result after it has been glazed. In this case, choose the lightest value you can see, then make it one tone lighter. Don't make it too light, however, because that will entail more work to attain the correct match. Always confirm the match by making a sample.

APPLYING A BASECOAT

Smooth paint application depends greatly on making the environment as dust free as possible. Next to lack of organization and of proper tools, dust is your worst enemy. To minimize dust, clean the room before you begin, and vacuum as the work progresses. If construction or renovation work is being done in another part of the house, seal off the room you're painting.

On Large Flat Areas

- *Ceilings.* Use a medium-nap roller.
- *Walls.* If the surface is smooth, use a fine- to medium-nap roller. Then, if a rolled look is called for, follow this immediately by a dry rolling with a mohair-nap roller to minimize the small puckers of the "orange peel" effect. If a brushed look is preferred, follow immediately by brushing down with a dry #200 spalter. If the surface is not smooth, it should be cleaned, patched, primed, and sanded as needed.

On Medium and Small Flat Areas

- Use a fine roller, followed immediately by brushing down with a dry #200 spalter, or move the paintbrush in a crisscross pattern, with the final pass in the direction of the "grain."

On Millwork

- Use a brush, in crisscrossed pattern whenever possible, with the final pass in the direction of the "grain," or sprayed on with an HVLP (high-volume, low-pressure) spray gun (see "Applying a Finish Coat," page 60).

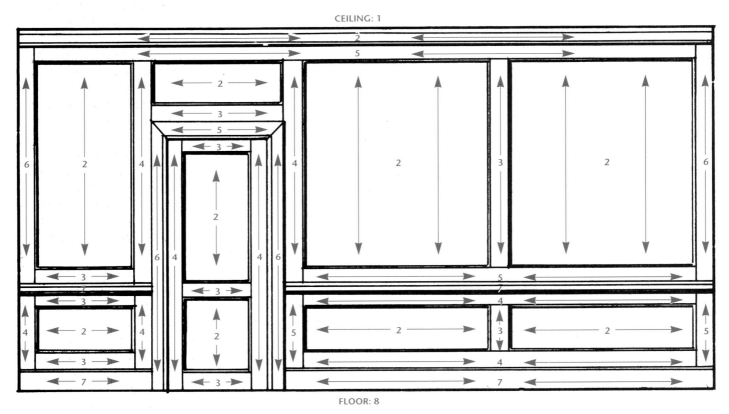

When applying base paint, orient the brushstrokes as indicated by the arrows. The areas that comprise a wall should be painted in the order indicated on the diagram. Always paint the ceiling first and the floor last.

The Finish Coat

A finish coat seals and protects your completed faux finish. The product you choose for this task—either varnish, polyurethane, shellac, or wax—must satisfy the rules of compatibility (see page 31) and the requirements of the project, as well as complement and enhance the type of finish you've created. For example, a textured surface such as faux sandstone or limestone blocks usually doesn't require a finish coat, but if one were desired only a flat finish would look right. Sometimes, the way that a finish coat might age is a significant factor. An oil-based varnish, which has a tendency to yellow with time, would be a poor choice for a white or light-colored marble.

The instructions for the finish coat given in each recipe should be regarded as recommendations, not hard-and-fast rules. Several conditions must be evaluated before committing to a specific product or application technique: the last or most recent medium, surface size and intricacy, time constraints, dust, temperature, and exposure to light.

VARNISH

Varnish is a transparent liquid made of a resin and a solvent. Once the solvent evaporates, the resin oxidizes, leaving a hard, dry, transparent, and generally irreversible film. Since glazes are very thin and therefore fragile, varnish is used to seal them, thus protecting them from the rigors of wear over time. Also, working in different systems and with various tools can produce dissimilar textures and shines, so varnish is used to give an even shine to the glazed surface.

Varnish is available in different sheens. Always remember that the final shine on a project results from the final coat of varnish. Choosing the right sheen will help to reinforce the proper look of the finish. A stone finish, for example, should have a very flat varnish to look like real stones, while a faux marble finish might have a gloss varnish to simulate real polished marble. Applying many coats of gloss or satin varnish (sanding between coats) builds a transparent thickness that lends tremendous depth to your finish.

Keep in mind that a good varnishing is not a guarantee of durability, nor can it hide problems inherent in the applications over which it is applied. As with other materials, varnish is part of the metaphoric chain—the project is only as strong as its weakest link. So no matter how good the varnish is, if the paint preparation is not impeccable the finish may deteriorate from the inside rather than the outside. Talk to your supplier or to other decorative painters to find out which type of varnish is best suited for you.

Oil-Based Varnishes

Oil-based varnishes have a base of oil or alkyd resin and can be cut with mineral spirits or turpentine (not to exceed 25 percent of the total volume). Sold in paint and hardware stores in 1-quart to 1-gallon metal cans, oil varnishes are available flat, eggshell, satin, semigloss, gloss, and high-gloss sheens. They are made by many manufacturers in many different qualities, but don't buy cheap materials if you expect good performance, especially since the varnish coat will be seen on top of all other finishes.

For a variety of reasons, oil-based varnishes are used often in decorative painting. They can be used as protection over all finishes (however, an oil finish must be fully cured before varnish is applied, otherwise crackling might result), they spread well, and they should be applied in a crisscross pattern (see Chapter 6). Open time varies from 15 to 30 minutes, depending on sheen and thickness of application. They dry in 1 to 6 hours and cure in about 12 hours. Once oxidized, oil varnishes are irreversible. Most are quite strong, though the glossier finishes are generally stronger than the flatter finishes because they are less susceptible to scratches. I frequently use Pratt & Lambert Clear 38, which has a dull satin gloss.

Oil-based varnishes have the same basic advantages and disadvantages of other oil-based media (see page 31). One of their biggest disadvantages is their tendency to yellow. Like oil-based paint, different oil-based varnishes yellow at different rates and to different degrees, due mostly to lack of sunlight. To check the yellowing effect of different varnishes, apply a sample of each to a piece of cardboard that's been painted white, date it, and hide it in a closet for at least two months, then check to see which ones yellow the most. To some degree, yellowing is reversible. If a varnished floor has been covered with a rug, for example, and the rug is later moved, you will see a yellow "stain" where the rug blocked the rays of the sun from reaching the floor. If you let the sun hit the yellowed patch for a few weeks, the varnish will often bleach back close to its original color.

Water-Based Varnishes
Acrylic and vinyl varnishes are made with polymer resin suspended in water and are usually very fluid. They can be cut with water (not to exceed 15 percent of the total volume, or according to the manufacturer's recommendations). They are sold in 1-quart to 1-gallon plastic containers, in eggshell, satin, gloss, and high-gloss sheens. As with oil-based varnishes, exercise common sense when weighing quality against price. I use Varathane Diamond Hard Finish, mostly in satin and gloss sheens; there are many other water-based varnishes of comparable quality available.

Water-based varnishes—sometimes called water-based polyurethanes—can be used as protection over all irreversible water-based finishes. Although most of these products do not yellow with time, they may cause an oil-based glaze to turn yellow. (To check the potential yellowing effect, follow the same technique given above for checking oil-based varnishes.) Open time varies from 2 to 5 minutes, depending on shine and thickness of application. They dry in 15 to 30 minutes and cure in 2 to 4 hours. Once cured completely, they are irreversible. They are generally very strong, though the glossier finishes tend to be stronger than the flatter ones. In general, water-based varnishes exhibit the same advantages and disadvantages as water-based paints (see page 31).

Some water-based varnishes contain UV protection, which means they help protect paint from the deteriorating effects of ultraviolet light. This is particularly important if a finished project will be exposed to direct sunlight, which will fade certain pigments.

POLYURETHANE

Available in both oil- and water-based forms, polyurethane is generally stronger than varnish and is often used as a protective coat on floors. Polyurethane often comes with a separate catalyst, a sort of hardener that is mixed into the polyurethane to start the drying and hardening process. In decorative painting, polyurethane is used on areas that will be subject to a lot of abuse: floors, countertops, tables, and restaurant doors or walls. If an extremely strong coat is need, sometimes car-grade polyurethane is used; however, this type must be sprayed on and is highly toxic, requiring elaborate ventilation and someone trained in its use, so its application is best left to professionals.

SHELLAC

Shellac is actually made from lac, a resinous substance secreted by an insect and gathered off the branches of certain trees in India and Indochina. In its basic form shellac comes in amber flakes that are then dissolved in alcohol, but you can buy shellac at paint or hardware stores already mixed and ready to use.

There are three types of shellac: clear shellac, which is slightly yellow; blond shellac, which is amber or light orange; and white-tinted shellac (also called shellac primer), which contains white pigment and is opaque, for use as a primer. Shellac is fairly unique among finish coats in that it is reversible; it can be reactivated with alcohol. It dries extremely fast—in 30 seconds to 1 minute—and cures in 5 to 10 minutes, so it is used when quick isolation of a reversible water-based paint is needed. You could, for example, use shellac over gouache in order to be able to reglaze over it with water or oil (see page 197). Shellac is compatible over cured water-based paint, and over oil-based paint that is absolutely, completely cured, otherwise wrinkling or cracks may result. It is not a strong protective finish coat.

APPLYING A FINISH COAT

In decorative painting, the finish coat essentially completes the work. Varnishing is not particularly difficult, but it is fairly labor-intensive and requires some practice. Because it is the last coat, and the coat that will be touched, if it is not smooth it will ruin the faux effect (real marble or finished wood does not have drips or a sandpaperlike feel to it). There are two different ways to apply varnish: brushing or spraying.

Using a Brush

On cabinetry and millwork, varnishing is done with a good varnishing brush: oval-shaped bristle brushes for oil varnish; flat, used synthetic brushes for water. When using oil varnish, you must really work your varnish in a crisscross pattern, with the final one running in the direction of the grain. Since water-based varnish dries more quickly, it does not allow as much working time, but try for a crisscross pattern here too (see page 205). NOTE: Do not dip the brush into the can roughly; just dip the tip of the bristles in gently and lightly tap the brush on the inner wall of the can.

A technique that works well on walls or other large, flat surfaces (particularly for the harder-to-apply water-based varnishes) is to roll the varnish onto the surface with a mohair roller, then brush it with a large, wide brush, such as a #200 spalter just as you finish applying it with the roller.

Using a Sprayer

Spraying a varnish onto a surface produces the best finish because the varnish goes on in fine droplets and has no brushmarks, resulting in a very smooth and even coat. This process, however, requires more setup and preparation than brushing, and by itself can be a job for a professional. If you're a professional painter, you'll be familiar with the equipment setup, know how to deal with the potential hazards of the process, and probably be willing to invest in a good-quality sprayer. If you want to paint faux finishes in your home, or if you're a novice decorative painter, you'll most likely apply your finish coat with a brush or roller, and read the next paragraph solely for your own edification.

Everything that is not to be varnished must be masked off, and all exposed floors must be protected. Proper lighting is important, and proper ventilation and protective gear (respirator, goggles, and protective suit) are absolutely crucial. Above all, you must be trained by a professional in the proper way to spray. My favorite sprayer is an HVLP (high volume, low pressure) because it produces very little overspray (about 20 percent), making it easier to do a good job, particularly with water-based media. (Conventional sprayers, which have high pressure, produce about 40 percent overspray.) Spraying is a more demanding job than brushing but is twice as fast—even with the long setup—and the finish is excellent.

APPLYING A WAX FINISH

Even though wax is not technically a varnish, it is used as such. It is very clear; the clearest beeswax is like crystal. It does not yellow, which makes it the preferred finish for white faux marbles and light patinas. It is not very strong—it is easily scratched with a fingernail—but it repairs easily by adding a little more wax and buffing it. Carnauba wax, which is a product of a Brazilian palm tree, is clear or amber, and polishes quickly and well. Wax is very natural-looking (it does not have the "dryness" of some water varnishes) and is especially suited to faux wood, leather, parchment, and white marble.

Wax is sold in cans as a paste that is applied with a rag and then buffed with a clean rag. It is also sold in blocks or beads that can be cut into small flakes and dissolved at room temperature with turpentine, or heated in a double boiler; the wax is then brushed or sprayed onto a surface. Once it dries, the wax can be left as is or buffed. (CAUTION: Be extremely careful if heating the wax, as the turpentine is highly flammable.)

This finish is reversible; it can be reactivated with any thinner (mineral or turpentine), so it can be refreshed and reapplied. It may require some maintenance, which simply entails applying a new coat of wax once in a while.

NOTE: Once a wax coat is applied, only more wax can be applied on top of it; it is incompatible as a base for any other media. If you are working on a surface that has been waxed—even if there are only traces of wax—you need to wash the surface with a dry thinner such as naphtha. However, wax is compatible when used *over* any other system: It can be applied over oil, water, or alcohol systems as long as they are completely dried.

Cleanup and Recycling

Some painters may be tempted to view cleanup as an afterthought, but it is an essential part of any project. If you work dirty, your work is likely to be dirty; even if it is not it may still be perceived as such. Clean up and organize the job when you stop working every night so when you start the next day everything is ready. People tend to lower their standards when working in a messy environment, so organization is important in preventing this. Just before painting, always dust off the work surface one more time. Always have a clean rag to wipe your hands; don't get into the habit of wiping your hands on your clothing. And always be sure to dispose of used cleaning solutions properly (see "Recycling," page 66).

CLEANING BRUSHES

Because brush cleaning takes time, some paint shops find it more cost effective to dispose of all but the most expensive brushes when a job is done, rather than going to the expense of paying employees to clean them. Of course, most people do not have this luxury; I, for one, hate to throw brushes away, especially those that are hard to obtain. Moreover, I like working with brushes that have been already broken in, because a new brush often sheds hair and is not "worn" to my hand.

The instructions in this section explain how to wash your brushes thoroughly and yet relatively quickly. To wash a brush well, three things must be taken into consideration:

- The type of hair from which the brush is made
- The type of paint used with the brush
- Whether the brush is small (all brushes with thin handles) or large (anything bigger than a small brush)

NOTE: If you don't have time to clean your glazing brushes right after a job, you can keep them in a bucket of water overnight. To do this, tape the brush handles to the side of the bucket (above the water line) so the hairs don't touch the bottom of the bucket. The next day, wring them out by spinning them between your hands until there is no water left in the brush. This works for both oil- and water-based systems.

CAUTION: Exercise care when cleaning brushes, especially when using mineral spirits. Do not work near the freshly finished surface, because splattering will have a disastrous effect on it. As when working with other materials, cleanup must be done with adequate ventilation.

Cleaning Brushes Used with Oil-Based Materials

NOTE: If you forget to wash a brush and it becomes caked with dry glaze, you can salvage the brush by giving it a bath of lacquer thinner or acetone or even brush cleaner, but just for a few minutes. Then wash it with soap and water as explained below. You can also use a metal or pet comb to help untangle the hairs.

Large White Bristle Brushes (*glazing brushes, spalters, teeth spalters, codtails, veinettes, stipplers, stencil brushes, stainers, disposable brushes*). Clean the brushes with a little thinner in a bucket, followed by a second and then a third cleaning if necessary. (It is better to do three cleanings in three small containers of thinner than one cleaning in a big bucket of thinner.) Work the brush in a rag between your fingers, concentrating especially on the heel, until the brush barely leaves a trace on the rag. Then spin out or wring out the brush until there is little or no thinner left in it; otherwise, the soap will not foam if there is any thinner left in the brush. Finally, wash the brush with soap (either a "black" soap such as Murphy's Oil Soap Paste or a dishwashing liquid) and warm water (cold water does not work well and hot water can be harmful to handmade brushes that contain organic glues, which will soften in hot water). Repeat the soap-and-water washing several times because the first washing generally just dissolves the thinner and the subsequent ones will wash off the oil. Be sure to work the soap into the heel of the brush with your fingers. If the brush is really soiled, let the lathered soap sit on the brush for a few minutes while you work on less dirty brushes. Rinse the brush *very* thoroughly (soap left on a brush will foam when used with a water-based glaze). Finally, hang the brushes dry by threading a string through the holes in their handles and then tying each end of the string to an opposing rung on an A-frame ladder, or rest them flat on a tray away from each other so they can dry completely overnight and so the bristles don't become bent. Don't stand clean, wet brushes bristles-up in a container.

Small White Bristle Brushes *(small flats, stipplers, pencil spalters, fan brushes).* Clean the brushes with a little thinner in a bucket, followed by a second and then a third cleaning if necessary. (It is better to do three cleanings in three small containers of thinner than one cleaning in a big bucket of thinner.) Work the brush in a rag between your fingers, concentrating especially on the heel, until the brush leaves no trace on the rag.

Once clean, small brushes must be reshaped. To reshape an oil brush, work a glob of lard or Vaseline into the hairs, covering them from heel to tip. (Lard—which is sold in butcher shops, Spanish grocery stores, and sometimes supermarkets—works very well because it not only conditions the hairs and protects them from dust, but when it hardens it keeps the shape you gave the brush. Vaseline works just as well but does not harden.) Using your thumb and index finger, shape the brush back into its original form, then let it rest in its case or a canvas roll. When you want to use the brush again, rinse it in thinner and wipe it twice with a clean rag to ensure that all grease has been removed (if it is not, it will ruin your glaze).

Large Sable, Squirrel, Skunk, Goat, Ox, and Badger Hair Brushes *(chiqueteurs).* Follow the directions given above for large white bristle brushes, but since this type is the most expensive brush in your kit, take even more care. Be sure to do three thorough rinses and a good washing, checking that the foam squeezed from the brush is completely white before you rinse it. NOTE: For a badger brush dedicated to oil, rinse the tip with thinner and then wash with mild soap and water. Never wet the ferrule because the brush will start losing its hair.

If you don't have time to clean your brushes at the end of a working session, keep them in water overnight. Also, when working with acrylics (an irreversible water system), your brushes will harden if you don't rinse them often or let them rest horizontally in a tray filled with water.

Small Sable, Squirrel, Skunk, Goat, Ox, and Badger Hair Brushes *(lettering brushes, pointed brushes, halftones, two-headers, rondins)*. Follow the directions given above for small white bristle brushes. Take special care with sable and squirrel brushes, and use a good amount of grease when reshaping.

Synthetic Hairs and Other "Water" Brushes Dedicated to Oil. If you use a synthetic or other "water" brush with an oil-based medium, clean it as follows: Follow the directions given above for large white bristle brushes, taking extra care as specified in the section on other large natural-hair brushes. Remember that thinner deteriorates synthetic hair, so work quickly.

Cleaning Brushes Used with Water-Based Materials
NOTE: Brushes used with irreversible water systems such as acrylics dry quickly and will harden if you don't rinse them often during use them or let them rest horizontally in a tray filled with water. If a brush becomes caked with paint, rinse it with alcohol and work the hairs between your fingers and a rag to remove most of the hardened paint. Then proceed with the appropriate washing, as determined by the brush type. You can use a metal or plastic pet comb to help untangle the hairs.

White Bristle Brushes *(round glazing brushes, spalters, stipplers, veinettes)*. Even though most bristles are used for oils, you

may have some bristles dedicated to water. First rinse the brush in warm water (cold water does not work well and hot water can be harmful to handmade brushes that contain organic glues, which will soften in hot water), then in warm water with a bit of black soap or dishwashing liquid. Be sure to use a very small amount of soap or you will have a hard time rinsing out the brush. Work the soap into the heel of the brush with your fingers. Repeat the soap-and-water washing several times, using only a little soap each time. If the brush is really soiled, let the lathered soap sit on the brush for a few minutes while you work on less dirty brushes. Rinse the brush *very* thoroughly (soap left on a brush will make a foamy mess on your next finish). Finally, let the brushes hang down or rest them flat on a tray away from each other.

Synthetic Hair Brushes *(pointed and flat brushes, synthetic spalters, round synthetic brushes, glazing brushes)*. Follow the directions given above for water-based white bristle brushes. When you work the small brushes between your fingers, be very careful not to apply too much pressure or you may impart a curve to the hairs.

Sable, Squirrel, Skunk, Goat, Ox, and Badger Hair Brushes *(lettering brushes, floggers, badger brushes, small brushes)*. Follow the directions given above for water-based white bristle brushes. Because natural-hair brushes are generally used

1. When cleaning a brush with soap and water, squeeze the hairs or bristles to work the soap into a lather.

2. Make sure to work the soap into the heel with your fingers.

3. Repeat the process until the brush rinses clean.

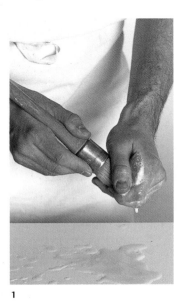
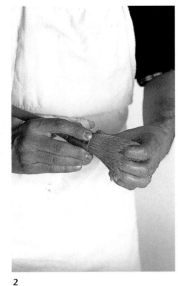
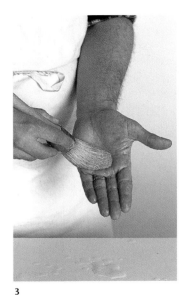

1

2

3

KEY TO
SOLVENTS
All of the following
products should be
used with caution and
tested before use.
- For acrylics:
  alcohol, lacquer
  thinner, acetone
- For reversible
  water-based
  paints: water
- For oil paints:
  lacquer thinner,
  acetone
- Commercial spot
  remover

only with reversible systems (gouache or beer glazes), which reactivate easily with water and rarely produce a seriously soiled brush, these brushes require only a quick wash, with very little soap. When washing badger-hair brushes, use only warm water and no soap (soap hardens badger hair, destroying its softness), and never wet the ferrule because that will loosen the glue. However, if you use the badger with irreversible water-based paint (acrylic), you must use a little mild soap.

Reshaping Small Brushes
Once clean, small brushes must be reshaped. To reshape a water-based brush, dip it into a mixture of 80 percent water and 20 percent gum arabic, then shape it between your thumb and index finger and let dry. The next day the brush will seem like new. To remove the film, work the hair with your fingers or wet the brush in the proper solvent.

CLEANING TOOLS

Equipment Used with Oil-Based Products
Since oil paint is irreversible, you must clean your tools at the end of each working session. If you wait, you won't be able to clean them completely.

Metal Tools. To clean all metal tools (including buckets, combs, palette cups, knives, and blades), first wipe the tool with a dry rag, then wipe again with a rag moistened with thinner. Wipe off again with a clean rag. If a tool is caked with paint, you can use a chemical such as stripper, acetone, or pipe cleaner.

Wood Tools. To clean all wood tools (including palettes and striping edges), follow instructions for cleaning metal tools, but after each use, condition the wood by rubbing it with leftover glaze to add a layer of protection. If you wish to continue working the next day with the same paints that are already on the palette, you can save oil-based paints by storing the palette overnight in the refrigerator, but do this only if it is used exclusively for your decorative painting work and doesn't contain any food.

Equipment Used with Water-Based Products

Metal Tools. Wash the tool with soap and water and wipe dry to prevent rust.

Wood Tools. Scrub the tool with a scrub pad or rag and wipe dry, then oil it with linseed oil. As with oil paints, you can save water-based paints by putting the palette in the refrigerator for the night. Before doing so, mist the palette with water, then lay a damp rag over it. This should only be done if the refrigerator doesn't contain any food.

REMOVING SURFACE SPOTS
As when cleaning brushes, in order to clean spots efficiently you must first identify the surface and the type of dry or wet paint to determine the appropriate type of cleaning. Always proceed with caution. First, make a test with the least damaging solvent on the least conspicuous area. If it does not work, repeat the test with another solvent. When you find the correct solvent, work on one small area at a time, and be careful not to smudge it out and make an even bigger mess. Often, stain removal works best when you gently dab or blot the stain, rather than rub it. Remember, this process is meant to improve the surface, not deteriorate it.

Wet Spots
If a spot is still wet, you will most likely know what type of paint it is. On a hard or nonporous surface (wood, plastic, glass), carefully wipe off the spot with a clean rag and clean solvent (water or thinner, as appropriate). On a porous or soft surface (fabric, leather), rather than wiping, dab the spot with the correct solvent. Once this has dried, you may be able to use a commercial spot remover, but be sure to make a test first, in an inconspicuous area if possible.

Dry Spots
On a hard or nonporous surface, if you know what type of paint made the spot, use the appropriate solvent on a used scrub pad or a rag, then wipe it off with a clean rag. For a known stain on a porous or soft surface, follow directions above for cleaning wet spots on porous surfaces.

If you don't know what made the spot, test out various solvents, beginning with the least corrosive. Proceed carefully, and use common sense. For a dried acrylic spot on a dried oil basecoat, for example, clean the spot with alcohol, since that will remove only the acrylic and not the basecoat; using lacquer thinner in this case would remove not only the acrylic but the oil basecoat as well.

RECYCLING

Although recycling is not always cost effective (especially when cleaning inexpensive materials that may be cheaper than the cost of the labor to clean them), it is very important for environmental reasons. In addition, it is a good habit that forces a painter to be organized, and to learn proper cleaning techniques.

Recycling Thinner. Thinner is one of the easiest things to recycle. At the end of the day when you have finished rinsing your oil brushes in thinner, rather than disposing of the dirtied thinner, let it sit in a container with the lid closed. The next day, when the pigment (which is heavier than the thinner) has settled at the bottom of the bucket, gently poor the recycled thinner into a clean container, being careful not to stir up the pigment at the bottom. This thinner can now be reused for subsequent cleaning jobs and can be recycled in this manner as many times as you like. If the thinner is very dirty, it will need to sit in a closed container for about a week to become usable again. The "goo" that is left at the bottom can be scooped out and disposed of properly. I transfer the goo to an empty paint container, which I use to collect several months' worth of "goo," then eventually have a private sanitation company cart it away. Contact the local waste management authorities for guidelines on disposal and recycling such materials in your area.

Recycling Old Paint. There is really no way to recycle old paint, but you can pour leftover mixtures into containers according to paint type (oils with oils, and so on), and use the resulting gray paints to repaint storage crates or the floor of your work space. Leftover glazes cannot be recycled and should be disposed of properly (see "Recycling Thinner," above).

Recycling Rags. Good-quality white cotton rags can be expensive, so you should not use them to wipe up a paint spill, but rather save them to manipulate a glaze, wipe off brushes while glazing, and to clean mistakes from projects. At the end of the day, spread out the soiled rags to dry. (CAUTION: To avoid spontaneous combustion, soak rags soiled with oil-based paints overnight in a bucket of water, then spread them out to dry.)

The next day, sort them into two piles, one for the very dirty rags and one for the semidirty. You can use the very dirty rags to wipe out buckets and clean up spills; use the semidirty rags to wipe off tools. Once the rags are too dirty and stiff to work with, dispose of them properly.

Recycling Old Brushes. Even when a brush is too well worn to be suitable for its original purpose, you may still discover a second life for it. Old round brushes are great for stirring glaze or mixing paint; old small brushes are good for achieving certain wood-grain effects, especially for wiping off or refining the jagged contours of the figure grain; old rounds or spalters are good for scrubbing surfaces; old flats are good for dusting off floors near the baseboard; and old two-headers can be used with acrylics without the worry of damaging them.

Recycling Cardboard Boxes. Keep the boxes in which your supplies were packaged. Cut off the upper part and use the bottom as a tray in which to carry and rest your tools and supplies.

Recycling Containers. Many types of containers can be recycled as painting supplies. Baby-food jars and other small jars with lids are great to hold small quantities of paint or glaze for touchups; film canisters can be strapped on your chest while you're striping (see Chapter 11); and aluminum cans, deli containers with lids, empty paint cans, and wide-mouthed glass jars are excellent for storing glazes.

Tricks of the Trade

The following tips are based on my professional decorative painting experience, as well as that of other painters. Feel free to supplement this relatively short list of suggestions with your own. If you would like to share some of your suggestions, write to me at the address on page 4. These tips can be as useful to the beginning decorative painter as they are to a professional, as they offer simple ways for improving painting skills.

GETTING ORGANIZED

Shop Setup. Good organization is the key to a successful work area. Your shop or work space must be as clean and dust-free as possible, with good natural light and good ventilation. Sweep the area clean every morning before you start working. To keep dust to a minimum, sprinkle some water on the floor before you sweep. Sort your supplies by type and keep them on shelves. Label the shelves so you can easily find supplies and can readily return them to the proper place when finished. Store flammable products in a cool area with a fire extinguisher nearby. Your work space should have a table or an easel on which you can make samples and drawings, and another table on which to let samples dry (or an enclosed space, if possible). If you venture into the decorative painting business professionally, you should also have an office space in which to take care of office activities and to store books, research materials, and photographs.

Job Setup. The job site is different from the shop because it is not a permanent situation and you may be sharing a space with other tradespeople. You will often have to move from room to room and will not have the luxury of space to spread out equipment. It is especially important to be very neat, because job sites are often messy and the working conditions will affect your finishes. Once again, organization is the key. You must be able to pack your supplies into only a few boxes. I use large plastic containers (they resemble big coolers with hard tops) that can be locked with padlocks, and I label them according to what supplies they contain.

When starting a job on a site, I introduce myself and my crew to the contractor and to the other tradespeople. I always make sure to ask where I can start and whether any other work is scheduled in that room. When I'm ready to start working, I cover the floor with plastic cloth and lay a dropcloth in the center of the room, where I set up my collapsible "paper hanger" table. I sort my supplies so that one container holds tapes and small paint containers, another one holds only brushes, and another holds sandpaper, rags, and palettes. I place all my paints on the table, and I put all my mediums, varnishes, and thinners under the table. I always use this same setup for every job so that no matter where we work, my crew and I can find and put away anything without having to ask.

Make Checklists. When preparing for a job, make a checklist of all the materials you'll need, including all paints, tools, and other supplies that may be necessary. You don't want to get to a job site and discover that you've forgotten something. Be sure to include your complete brush kit.

Take Notes. Get into the habit right away of taking thorough notes. Not only is it important to have the written information to refer to later, but the process of writing something down helps you to retain the information longer and may even clarify a point as you write it. Develop a filing system or keep a notebook in which to record all your recipes. Write down recipe details when you make a sample, so that when you do the actual job (sometimes months later) you will have no trouble matching your sample; this will also enable you to do touchups on jobs that were done a few years earlier. Keep lists of everything you must do, buy, or ask for at each job site.

Label Everything. Label all your mixed paint and glazes according to a system that works best for you, and record that system in your recipe log to avoid any confusion. When I label containers, I use a permanent marker, either directly on the container or on a piece of masking tape wrapped all the way around the container. I label the container on both sides so I can read the label no matter which way the container is turned. I also label the lid. (Don't just label the lid; once you remove it, the container will have no identification.) Include the location, room, glaze formula, where or at what stage it was used, and the date.

Practice. Practice is the cornerstone of your entire operation; it is the only way to develop skill, speed, and confidence. Exploit any slow time to practice familiar techniques or invent new ones. The day before starting a job, rehearse by spending some time studying your reference materials on that particular faux finish and its techniques, and by doing a sample. That way you will already be immersed in the subject and confident in your approach when you start the work.

Make Samples. Whenever you prepare a sample, write down every detail of the recipe and the technique. Also, keep a small area of the different steps untouched so you will have something to match in case you need to remake the same recipe later, after you no longer have the colors you mixed for the sample. I protect every step of the sample with a piece of low-tack tape (see page 115 for an example of this technique). I paint my samples on draw-down board, a special grade of treated cardboard used by paint manufacturers to test their products.

Make Maquettes. Making maquettes is an important part of the sample process only when you are presenting an elaborate decor idea that needs to be embodied more fully in order to be better understood. (A maquette is not required for small or simple projects.)

Several examples of maquettes, which are full-scale samples used to illustrate a complex decorative painting concept.

A maquette is usually a full-scale sample that shows precisely what the painted finish looks like. I usually do my maquettes on chart paper or watercolor paper with acrylics so I can glaze and add as I would on large scale.

THE RIGHT ATTITUDE

Positive and Confident Attitude. A positive and confident attitude toward the work at hand is the main ingredient to success. Enjoy what you are accomplishing—namely, turning a blank surface into fabulous decor. When you leave a job, you leave behind a reminder of yourself in the form of your work, so be proud of what you do and aim for high standards. (See also pages 15 and 70.)

Attitude with Client and Designer. When dealing with clients, you must not only exhibit a positive attitude, you must also appear professional in all aspects of your work. Always be on time for a job and wear a clean painting outfit; this will project a good image right from the start. Give the client as few options and as detailed an explanation as possible, presenting them both clearly to avoid confusion. Clients often have trouble viewing a small sample and trying to envision what the finished room will look like. When dealing with subjective topics such as color and decor, you must establish a relationship of trust with the client so that he or she will look to your expertise for help in making decisions and will be confident in having made the right choices. (Always keep this adage in mind: "Clients may not know what they want, but they'll always know what they *don't* want.") If you think that the selected color or decor will not work, be courteous but frank; politely explain why you feel that way and suggest an alternative plan. Never disagree openly with the decorator in front of the client; confrontations are not only unnecessary, but when a client witnesses a disagreement within the design team, it can undermine the client's trust.

PAINTING PRECAUTIONS

Safety Advice. Safety is of paramount importance. Never take any risks that might injure you or someone else. When working with flammable products such as paint thinners or oil-based paints, work in a well-ventilated area. If this is not possible, be sure to bring along a fan, and face it away from you and your surface and toward an open door so that it will pull the toxic vapors out of the room. This will also prevent dust from blowing onto your freshly painted surface. CAUTION: Spontaneous combustion is a very real threat and precautions must be taken against it. When oil dries it creates heat—heat that may be hot enough to cause an oil-soaked rag to self-ignite, particularly if it was placed in bundle, bag, or other confined space. To prevent this, spread out all rags at night or dip them in water. Use common sense and try to anticipate a problem before it arises.

Never smoke while working with paint—even water-based paints. Not only does it create a fire hazard, but it forces you to work with one hand instead of two, since one hand is kept busy holding a cigarette. Also, avoid eating on the job site.

Body Movements. Working on a job requires climbing up and down ladders, moving about from room to room, and carrying equipment around; in other words, you will be in fairly constant motion while painting. At the end of the day you will be exhausted, so you must learn to spare your movements and conserve your energy. To do that, you must develop a system for carrying your tools that anticipates your needs. If you are right-handed, your work should progress from left to right, with the ladder to the left of the area on which you are working. (If you are left-handed, reverse these directions.) This will provide access to a greater area of work and require less ladder moving, and your movements will not be restricted by the ladder placement. To avoid unnecessary torso rotations, put your bucket of glaze on your right side if you're right-handed, and hold your palette and all your brushes in your left hand. Keep your tools as nearby as possible. (See page 50 for tips on keeping certain items in a belt pouch.) A good trick to make movement easier when painting a baseboard is to sit on a skateboard or a mover's dolly.

Before You Begin: Planning Your Faux Finish

Before starting any of the recipes, spend some time looking over this section to acquaint yourself with the artistic ingredients of good faux painting.

HONING YOUR POWERS OF OBSERVATION

All good faux finishes are based on a thorough observation of nature and of other painted finishes. Begin building your own library of reference materials—including books, magazine clippings, photographs, and drawings—that will help you to document examples of wood, marbles, and other finishes. Ask lumberyards and home improvement stores for samples of wood veneers, and a marble quarry or distributor for some marble chips.

Decorative painting, however, goes beyond simply imitating nature and attempts to improve upon it by concentrating on only what is best in nature: the most interesting marble veins or wood grains, the colors that will best harmonize with the setting in which the work will be seen. Faux painting aims to highlight the best of each type of wood or marble as well as its most quintessential characteristics so that the viewer will more easily be fooled into thinking it is the real thing. On some projects you may find it more realistic to add more veins, knots, or other details than are actually visible on the real thing. Because a good faux finish has more visual impact than the average grade of wood or marble, you may even hear someone comment that it looks better than the real wood or marble on which it is modeled. By selecting the best in nature for your painted finishes; by playing with color, highlight, and shadow; by bringing into play a sense of composition and harmony, you can create very striking work indeed.

In order to understand how to paint faux marble or wood, you must understand how a cabinetmaker and a marble craftsperson work. The marble craftsperson selects slabs of marble from a supplier by wetting each slab to approximate the effect that the color and design will have when polished, eliminating the slabs in which the pattern is too busy and the color clashes, and looking for marble with "quiet" parts to balance the busy areas. A cabinetmaker goes to the lumberyard and selects board that exhibits beautiful and consistent figure design, rejecting wood with too many knots (this would indicate lesser-grade wood) or imperfections. When painting faux marble or wood, keep these considerations in mind to achieve a more realistic look, but at the same time, as mentioned above, learn to embellish nature and copy what is best and most decorative.

Get into the habit of experimenting with techniques and colors, and make a lot of samples. The colors given in the recipes are just suggestions, not absolute rules. The same applies to the steps themselves: You can improve them, add more steps, or eliminate some, just as you might customize a cooking recipe. If you like your food hot, for example, you might add more spices; if you can't have salt, don't use any. As a decorative painter you have the freedom to do what is best suited to each project, something that is not always an option when using real wood or marble, or even wallpaper.

SPONTANEITY AND CONFIDENCE

As the French decorative painter Eugene Blot (active 1930–50) declared, "The best is the enemy of the good." By this he meant that you must learn when to stop. Spontaneity and confidence are important components in successful painting; by going too far and adding too many effects, you risk destroying what may already be a successful painted finish.

Spontaneity is actually a true mark of confidence in yourself and of knowledge of the finish you are painting. Spontaneity is necessary because hesitation is a source of errors, bad design, and slow work. A spontaneous painting with few changes or touchups—even though it may contain some inaccuracies—will always be more attractive than an overworked painting with an unsure touch. If, for instance, you try to paint a straight line freehand with a brush by moving slowly, biting your tongue, and sweating it out because you're worried that it won't be straight, you will almost certainly end up with a crooked line of varying thickness. However, if you are relaxed and you move your brush quickly in one go, your line will be fairly straight and relatively even.

BALANCING YOUR DECOR

There are many ways to achieve harmony in a decor, but the end result should be pleasing to the eye and should be balanced:

- Balance the strength of a color by using another strong color next to it, or by glazing over it with its complementary to mute it. (See "Tips on Color Mixing," page 35.) Experiment with color to get a feel for how colors interact. Also remember that too many glazes will make your work heavy; after the fourth reglazing the next one will most likely "kill" your first one.
- When deciding which elements of the decor should be darker or lighter, take into account size variations of different elements (such as rails, panels, or walls). In general, the smaller elements of a finish should be darker than the larger or primary one, to give it added emphasis.
- Learn which techniques complement each other; a marbleized baseboard, for example, might go well with a stenciled wall.
- Don't isolate individual touches; a gold stripe alone on the crown, for instance, should be balanced with other stripes on other parts of the millwork.
- Learn to appreciate the visual equivalent of silence. Don't overdecorate; use the quiet parts to make the more elaborate part stand out.

One of the most important precepts of decorative painting is that it is easier to add than to remove. If you are not convinced whether a certain element—such as stripes—belongs on a project, start with a little. You can always add more little by little until you are satisfied, but taking off an element once it is added (especially if it is already dry) will require a lot more work.

For effective composition, the bottom of a panel should generally appear weightier than the top, either through the use of a darker color or by making the faux effect a little more involved or broader in width. This provides a sense of support at the bottom, much like the base of a column. The same idea applies to a marbleized wall (the more intricate and colorful veining should appear at the bottom and the more tranquil parts at the top to give a sense of rest) and to wood graining (where the weight of the figural design should be at the bottom). So that the stiles and rails don't compete with or overwhelm the panels they frame, panels usually feature the best grain figure or veining patterns, while straight-grain wood and subdued marble punctuated with small, rounded fragments or less visually active veins are frequently reserved for stiles and rails.

Another very important concept is that it is much easier to darken than to lighten. If you are uncertain about what intensity to use on a certain element of decor, start with a light value. You can always add another glaze to change or darken the color, but the reverse is almost impossible. Bear in mind that using white glaze will tend to dull a surface and obscure details. This also applies to mixing a glaze: Add just a few drops of color at a time, because if you add too much too quickly you might accidentally make it too dark and have to throw some of it away in order to reduce its volume, add more transparent glaze, or even throw the entire glaze away and start over again.

There are many ways to change the look of a room's dimensions, so experiment with different techniques. You can manipulate the direction of the design to give an effect of height or width to a room. For an impression of height, use a lot of verticals (such as a stripe motif), paint the ceiling in a light color, and paint the crown as part of the wall. If you want to lower the height, use a dark color on the ceiling and paint the crown to match it. To give the impression of width, emphasize the horizontal lines of the room. Rooms painted in dark colors generally appear smaller and more intimate; those painted in light colors will have the opposite appearance.

Marble

Marbles are metamorphic rocks composed of fine-grained, dense, crystallized calcium carbonate (usually limestone) that can be honed to a high polish. White in its purest state, marble is often colored with a variety of minerals and other organic materials. The presence of these substances and the process of metamorphosis—the intense heat and pressure that cause layers of rock to fragment and shift—produce the patterns and color combinations specific to each type of marble.

This elegant circular foyer features White Veined Carrara panels framed with Gray Brèche moldings and baseboards and accented by Rouge Royale insets.

Painting Marble

Decorative painters must examine relationships of color and design so that their painted interpretations capture the vigor and diversity within a marble's surface. Despite the fact that there are thousands of different marbles, a knowledge of and familiarity with just twenty examples will enable you to paint most of the others. Of these twenty, the eight that are demonstrated in this chapter are representative of the most popular decorative marbles. In general, the most highly prized marbles come from France, Italy, Belgium, North Africa, and California.

A SYSTEM OF CLASSIFICATION

In order to recognize various types of marble more easily, decorative painters have devised a general system of classification. Once you have familiarized yourself with the four basic types of marble—veined, brèche, cloudy, and onyx or agate—you will be able to paint almost any marble because you will be able to compare it to at least one of the recipes in this book. It's important to note that these categories are based on a marble's visual elements rather than its geological characteristics.

- *Veined marbles* are monochromatic stones that are striped or streaked with veins in one or more colors. During metamorphosis, the background stone cracked and shifted without spreading apart completely. The resulting gaps or cracks, which are generally consistent in size and scale, were subsequently filled with various mineral and organic sediments, both white and colored. Among the most commonly used veined marbles are White Carrara (pages 88–90), Sea Green (pages 97–99), Yellow Sienna (see page 93), and Yellow Flower (pages 91–93).
- *Brèche marbles* (from the French word *brèche,* which means "break") are composed of broken fragments of one or more rocks that, as a result of geological upheaval, were first scattered and shifted, then finally reunited, though in disarray. The shapes and sizes of the fragments can vary widely, but the severe fracturing that occurred also makes them all extremely angular. In contrast to veined marbles, the sizes of the gaps between the fragments of brèche marbles are very diverse. After the larger fragments settled, the gaps between them were filled with mineral or organic sediments of various colors. Once formed, the marble usually underwent another slight shift, in which fissures within the fragments themselves were filled with white calcareous matter (a characteristic of many veined marbles as well). A few examples of brèche marble are White Brèche (pages 106–108), Imperador (pages 100–102), Violet Brèche (pages 109–111), Portor (pages 103–105), and Grand Antique (see page 99). (Note that although Portor and Grand Antique are technically veined marbles, because of their angular fragmentation they are classified decoratively as brèche.)
- *"Cloudy" marbles,* actually a subcategory of veined marbles, are composed of multicolored stones dappled with cloud-shaped fragments, or *twists,* and veined with a profusion of thin white veins. Saint Anne, Rouge Languedoc (page 108), and Rouge Royal (pages 94–96) are a few examples.
- *Onyx or agate marbles* are another type of veined marble, but the process of their formation distinguishes them visually from the others. This type of stone is formed similarly to stalagmites and stalactites, in which minerals and sediments are deposited around a central point in more or less parallel layers, some of which are translucent. Algerian onyx (pages 129–131) and Brazilian onyx are both examples of this type of marble. The exercise for onyx veining (page 119) and the recipe for Algerian onyx are in the chapter on semiprecious stone because onyx and agate marbles are often referred to as such. In contrast to other types of marble, onyx marbles are only quarried in small amounts, and thus are more expensive. Because of this, they are often used similarly to other semiprecious stones, mainly in small panels or as inlays for furniture, walls, and floors.

The four basic types of marble: veined, brèche, cloudy, and onyx or agate.

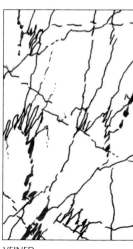

VEINED

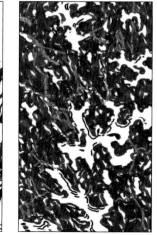

BRÈCHE

CLOUDY

ONYX OR AGATE

The development of a veined marble: The original stone (drawing 1) shifted and cracked in response to heat and pressure (drawing 2). The gaps were then filled with mineral sediments, producing veins of various colors (drawing 3). After a second shift, small fissures were filled with a white calcareous matter (drawing 4).

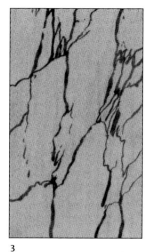

1

2

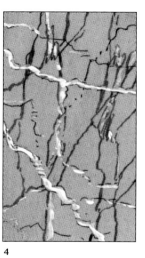

3

4

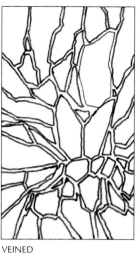

VEINED

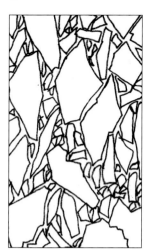

BRÈCHE

These drawings illustrate the basic differences in structure between veined and brèche marbles. A veined marble resembles a mirror that has been set on the floor and smashed with a hammer, so that the pieces more or less fit together. In contrast, a brèche marble looks similar to several mirrors that have been dropped on the floor and swept together, so that the pieces look jagged and disjointed.

A NOTE ON THE TERMINOLOGY: MARBLING VS. MARBLEIZING

Although the terms "marbling" and "marbleizing" are often used interchangeably, they each have a distinct meaning. *Marbling* means to paint a marble realistically, while *marbleizing* means to paint a fantasy marble or a marble effect.

Another word that is often misused when describing painted finishes is "faux." For example, a painted marble can be accurately described as either a "faux marble" or an "imitation marble." In contrast, the expression "faux marble imitation" is not only redundant, but it implies that the finish is merely a badly painted approximation.

A marble block is sliced into slabs using either the pass cut (near right) or the counterpass cut (far right).

CUTTING METHODS

The way in which marble is cut plays a large part in the appearance of its surface. There are two principal ways to cut a block of marble:

- With *the pass cut* (also known as the "with-the-bed cut" or "vein cut"), the marble slab is sliced parallel to the main direction of the veining, creating elongated shapes. Of the two types, this cut is the most commonly used.
- With *the counterpass cut* (also called the "across-the-bed cut" or "fleuri cut"), the slab is sliced perpendicular to the main direction of the veining, similar to the way a salami is sliced. This cut yields tighter, smaller, and more angular fragments and veining patterns than the pass cut. It is used primarily on brèche marbles, mainly to create a contrasting surface design.

SUITABLE APPLICATIONS

Marble is imitated with paint for several reasons, most of which have to do with cost and convenience. Marble is very heavy and damages easily, which makes it expensive to ship and store and difficult to work with, and requires heavy equipment at every step, from excavation to polishing to installation. In light of these drawbacks, it is almost always easier to paint marble than it is to install the real thing, especially in existing structures. It is interesting to note that the interior of the Marie Antoinette Opera House in the Palace of Versailles was marbled because the project had overrun its budget and its schedule.

Frequently, the marble of an existing installation can only be duplicated by painting it. Older marbles can often no longer be matched because the particular type of marble is currently quarried in another location, or merely because the new marble will be cut from a different slab or block. In 18th-century Europe, it was common practice to paint baseboards to match the real marble in the room, which was usually found on the mantelpiece. Painting marble also makes it possible to supplement nature's supply; for instance, when a particular color or surface design is either unavailable or simply doesn't exist. This is especially true in the case of Italian-style "fantasy" marble (see pages 112–115), where coloration and surface design are created solely for decorative value.

Marble is a timeless decorative finish that can be used successfully in either modern or traditional decors, though it is more often identified with classic interiors, as it conveys a richness and solidity that was much prized during the eras they evoke. In general, marble is appropriate for such architectural elements as walls (including chair rails, dadoes, and baseboards), pedestals, columns, pilasters, and door casings, but it is visually too imposing for crown moldings. In spite of marble's decorative versatility, surfaces that would not customarily be fashioned in marble—doors, cabinetry, windows, objects with moving parts, or utilitarian items such as telephones—should not be marbled.

CHOOSING THE RIGHT TECHNIQUE

Before reading this section, review "Influential Movements in Decorative Painting," page 15. More than in any other category of faux finish, the expressiveness of the Italian style of decorative painting is most fully realized in faux marble. The transparency and diversity in color of Italian-style marbleizing

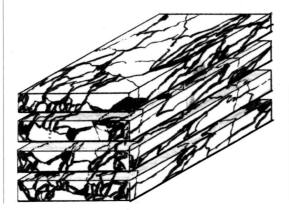

make it preferable to the precise, highly rendered, and somewhat labored French technique. The Italian technique is more fluid and highly decorative, since the focus is on conveying the aesthetic value of the marble rather than on painstakingly reproducing its every detail. However, the unpracticed painter (whether an unprepared amateur or an inept professional) should not assume that he or she can use the creative latitude of the Italian style to conceal a lack of skill or to avoid the accuracy of the French technique. In fact, in order to capitalize on it fully, the Italian approach requires more of a sense of color and composition than the French. Regardless of technique, veins and fragments should always be dynamic and angular, never weak or soft.

With the exception of the Italian-style fantasy marbles, the marbles in this chapter are rendered in an accurate French style, but using a water-based medium (acrylics) whose spontaneity and fluidity are traditionally associated with the Italian approach.

LAYOUT

To present faux marble most effectively, the methods for laying out and installing real marble must be considered, regardless of the technique used to paint it. Since marble is usually not cut into slabs large enough to cover the wall of an entire room, walls are divided into panels that can be framed by stiles and rails. The basic arrangement can be approached in a variety of ways, depending on the style of the room. However, certain rules must be adhered to:

- In a marble layout, stiles (vertical elements) and rails (horizontal elements) are "cut," or arranged, so that the rails frame the stiles by overlapping them.

Panels of marble should be arranged to create symmetry and contrast. In this example, the center panel is a veined book-matched marble and framed by darker brèche stiles and rails, while the adjoining panels are mirror images of one another.

- Immediately adjoining panels, as well as the stiles and rails that frame them, should always contrast with one another, either dark versus light, colored versus predominantly white, or active versus tranquil.
- The orientation of the surface design of adjacent slabs should also create contrast. This is sometimes done by painting panels in a *book-match* layout. This woodworking term refers to wood veneers that have been cut from the same tree or marble slabs that have been cut from the same block, so that their surface designs are essentially identical. The veneers or slabs are then arranged like facing pages in an open book (hence the term "book-match") as mirror images of one another. This spectacular effect is done by making a rough tracing of a completed panel, then transferring the flopped tracing to the opposite panel and painting it using the same palette and technique that was used for the first.

BASIC PROCEDURE

Because real marble is so smooth, the intended surface must be prepared well. Begin by skimcoating, then priming, following each procedure with a sanding. Apply two or three coats of basepaint (preferably alkyd, in either an eggshell or a satin finish), sanding between each coat, then sand the final coat with a scrub pad. Make sure the basecoat does not have any brush marks or the small puckers of the "orange peel" effect caused by poor rolling.

Artists' oils have traditionally been used to paint marbles because the final results are generally more subtle than can be achieved with water-based paints. Of course, their longer working time also means a waiting period of at least 24 hours between glaze applications, and there is always the possibility of a yellowing effect.

All of the marble recipes in this book specify that acrylic paints be used. Although their fast drying times demand greater accuracy, acrylics can be reglazed in practically no time, which for me outweighs the fact that they aren't as smooth or as subtle as oils. I also prefer acrylics because they can be worked either transparently or opaquely. Where appropriate, alternate glaze mixtures (and, where necessary, painting instructions) are provided for oil-based paints, which may be most desirable for large surfaces. Acrylics' working time can be extended by adding gel retarder.

In most cases, it is recommended that the basic acrylic glaze indicated for each recipe (generally a 1-to-1 ratio of matte medium and water—a fairly heavy mixture) be made more fluid with the addition of another part of water after the background texture has been established.

Basic acrylic glaze = 1 matte medium + 1 or 2 water

Basic oil glaze = 2 to 4 turpentine + 1 linseed oil + 2% cobalt drier

Regardless of medium, you should paint samples in order to analyze relationships between color and technique. As you carry out the tasks within a step, you must anticipate the steps that will follow, so that each step will contribute to the development of the surface's color and design.

Varnishing is an essential element of a painted marble finish. When using brush-on varnish, care should be taken to avoid leaving brush marks. For this reason, a spray-on varnish is most preferable, but there are some drawbacks to this method of application (see page 61). On white marbles, use a nonyellowing varnish or apply a coat of wax.

Marble Exercises

Before you lay a paint-filled brush on your prepared surface, turn to the first page of the marble recipe you plan to paint and review its technical notes to see which of the following exercises you'll need to practice. (In fact, it's best to familiarize yourself with *all* of the exercises before you start.) You should spend as much time as possible learning how to create the individual elements of a finish (repeating an exercise at least five times), so that when you combine them you can do so with confidence. If you're completely new to painting, the strategy of isolating the movements of the hand and brush or tool and the configuration of the shapes they produce will also provide you with an opportunity to become accustomed to handling paint, holding a brush, and getting a sense of how the hairs of a brush respond to pressure. Exercises are also useful for warming up the hand and loosening up the wrist.

The exercises were painted on a double-ply posterboard sealed with a white oil-based primer, then painted with one coat of eggshell-finish basepaint, creating a slick surface that allowed brush hairs to flow smoothly. (In addition to posterboard, draw-down card can also be used.) The exercises themselves were executed in gouache so that the surface could be easily wiped clean and reused.

When painting marble finishes, the single most important principle is *variation*—in the sizes of the veins and fragments, in color and value, and in the orientation of the marble's elements—all within the context of the particular marble. So that your strokes will vary in value and intensity as you practice the exercises, use your brush or application tool until it runs out of paint before reloading it. To emphasize the marble's natural structure, all its elements should vary in size corresponding to three visual levels: Those of the first level are the largest, the second level are medium-sized, and the third level are the smallest.

In some of the exercises that follow, the term "small brush" is used to refer to any of the narrow-handled, pointed or flat brushes (either long- or short-haired) discussed on pages 42–43. (Either oil- or water-based versions can be used, depending on the medium you're working in.) In fact, using more than one of these brushes would contribute to the visual variety that is so crucial to a well-painted marble. Experiment with different brushes to find a few you feel most comfortable using.

SPONGING ON

Dip a sea sponge in water, then wring it out so that it's slightly damp. Load the sponge by touching it to some of the colors on the palette, then distribute the paint evenly by working it on the palette in a circular motion. Hold the loaded sponge between your fingers using the baseball grip (see page 37) and tap or dab it on the surface repeatedly, rotating your hand and working from the wrist rather than the elbow (photo 1). Work from left to right and from top to bottom, overlapping the prints slightly and varying their pattern by adjusting the position of sponge after each hit so that none of the individual sponge prints is clearly discernible (photo 2). A heavily loaded sponge produces wide, open impressions, while a lightly loaded sponge creates small prints. Repeat until the sponge is out of paint before reloading.

1

2

SPONGING OFF

Apply a water-based glaze with a glazing brush. (If desired, add random strokes in a darker value.) Smooth out the surface with a badger brush using a figure-eight motion (photo 1). Using the motion described in "Sponging On" (see page 79), tap the surface repeatedly with a sea sponge that's been moistened with water but is not loaded with color (photo 2). Rinse the sponge often to avoid reapplying the paint you've already removed. Smooth out the completed surface with a badger brush (photo 3).

1

2

3

VEINING WITH A SMALL BRUSH

Using the conductor hold (see page 37), hold the brush at a 45-degree angle to the surface. Working from top to bottom, paint long, energetically trembled lines so that they look almost like lightning bolts, *not* softly curving worms (photo 1). This first set of veins, which are also the heaviest, establish the orientation of the connecting secondary and tertiary veins. Without reloading the brush, paint the secondary veins, which run at various angles to the first set. Use the brush to knit (see opposite) in a few areas (photo 2), then add some fine, broken veins that run across the surface as well as a group of elongated dabs of paint whose course follows the general direction of the primary veins (photo 3).

1

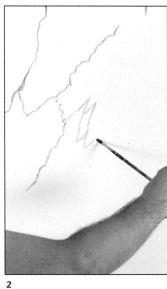

2

3

KNITTING

The knitting technique is used both alone and in conjunction with other veining techniques (see "Veining with a Small Brush," opposite). Using the conductor hold (see page 37), hold the brush at a 45-degree angle to the surface. Paint a series of very loose N shapes, trembling your hand as you work (photo 1). Overlap the first set with a second set of interlocking Ns to create diamond-shaped fragments of various sizes (photo 2). Without reloading the brush, use the first set of fragments as a guide to expand the design by adding fragments of various sizes above and below (photo 3). Work until the brush is out of paint before reloading.

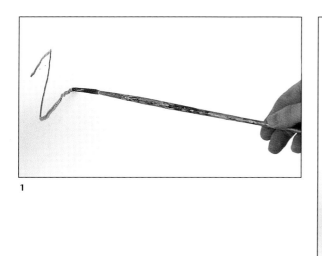

1

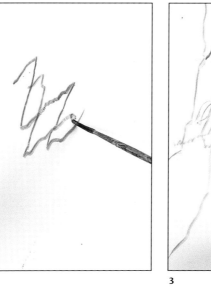

2

3

KNITTING WITH TWO SMALL BRUSHES

Using the drummer hold (see page 37), grasp two small brushes so that the ends of their handles rest in the palm of your hand. (You can also hold the brushes like chopsticks.) Rotating your wrist back and forth as if you were turning a knob on a radio while simultaneously trembling your hand, paint very fragmented yet compact knitted forms in a configuration similar to a lightning strike, first working down the surface, then back up (photos 1 & 2). Use one of the two brushes to add lighter individual veins that interconnect the major shapes and create fragments of various sizes (photo 3). Work until the brushes are out of paint before reloading.

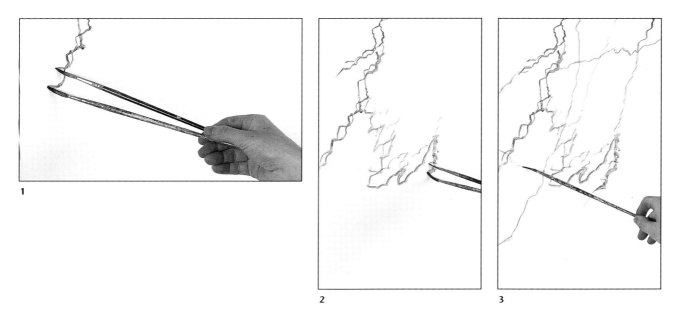

1

2

3

FISSURES

Common to most marbles, fissures are white veins that are formed during a marble's final or most recent shift. Grasp a small brush in the conductor hold (see page 37) and hold it at a 45-degree angle to the surface. Working either from top to bottom or across the surface in a steplike movement (either from left to right or from right to left), vary the width of the vein, giving it a slight trembled effect as you paint (photo 1). Note, however, that it should be jagged like a bolt of lightning, not softly curved like a worm. Establish the configuration of the fissures with first-level veins, then embellish it with second- and third-level veins (photos 2 & 3).

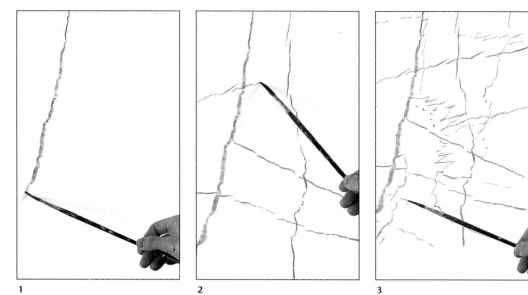

1   2   3

COMMON VEINING ERRORS

Shown below are the three veining mistakes most often made by beginners. It is essential that these unnatural configurations be avoided, as they will surely ruin a marble finish.

All veins are parallel and aligned at a 45-degree angle, resulting in an unrealistic and contrived surface (photo 1).

Soft, wormlike shapes, with cross-veins painted at a 90-degree angle. Weak veining looks unattractive, and such X shapes do not occur in real marbles (photo 2).

A "spider web" of veins radiating from a central point. This configuration is almost nonexistent in nature (photo 3).

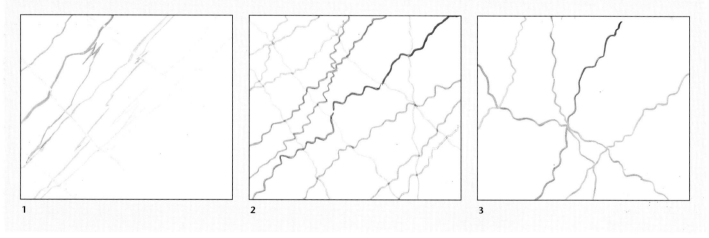

1   2   3

ESTABLISHING AN UNDERLYING NETWORK OF VEINS AND FRAGMENTS WITH A PENCIL GRAINER

Using the conductor hold (see page 37), hold the pencil grainer at a 45-degree angle to the surface. Knit with a trembled hand and in no particular direction, simulating the action of a Slinky going down a flight of stairs, turning the brush from side to side by rotating your wrist while moving it up and down the surface (photo 1). Repeat to crisscross the previous strokes, varying their intensity, until the surface is full (photos 2 & 3). Using the network as a foundation, add some first-level veining with a small brush (photo 4). Work until the paint has been exhausted from the brush before reloading.

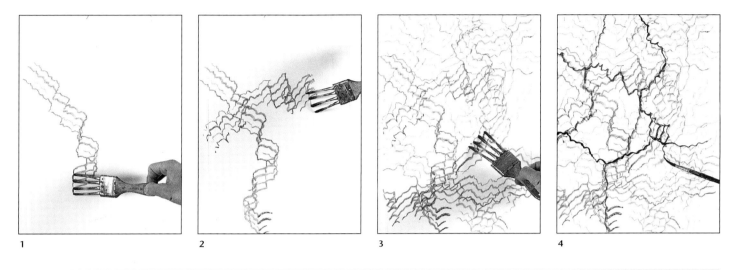

1   2   3   4

FRAGMENTING OR BRECHING

Using a small round brush held in the conductor's grip (see page 37) at a 45-degree angle to the surface, imitate the swing of a pendulum, flattening the hairs of the brush at the downswing and lifting it up to its tip at the upswings (photo 1). Vary the pattern and width of the swings to produce a chain of angular fragments in different shapes and sizes, then link the fragments within the chain with some fine trembled veins (photo 2). Start a second chain of fragments (photo 3), then connect it to the first one with some fine veins. Cross the chains with short, fine veins (photo 4).

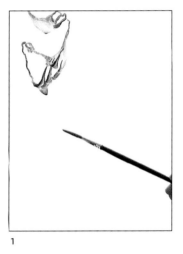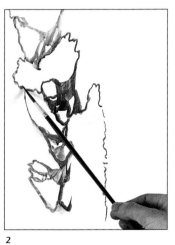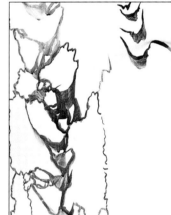

1   2   3   4

FRAGMENTING WITH A POINTED TWO-HEADER

Holding the brush like a pen (see page 37) near the fork, turn it from side to side to simulate the action of a Slinky going down a flight of stairs, while moving it up, down, and across the surface (photo 1). Using your wrist, vary the pressure on the brush to vary the width of the fragments, so that large ones are surrounded by small and medium-sized ones (photo 2). (The fragments are the negative spaces between and within the painted forms.) Work on different areas of the surface, then tie the painted forms together with a few veins (photo 3). Compared to "Fragmenting or Brèching" (see page 83), the orientation of the fragments is less obvious, but there still is one. Work until the paint has been exhausted from the brush before reloading.

1

2

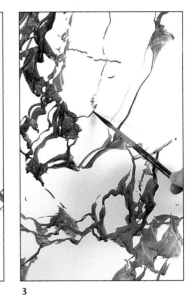

3

FRAGMENTING WITH SEVERAL DIFFERENT BRUSHES

Establish the orientation and sizes of the main fragments by working the pointed two-header like a pendulum (photo 1). Tie them together by veining with various small brushes. Use a liner brush to add connecting veins (photo 2). Develop the surface with other small round brushes (photo 3). Complement the connected forms with small dabs of paint (photo 4).

1

2

3

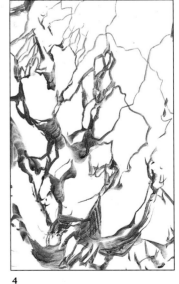

4

KNITTING WITH A POINTED TWO-HEADER

As for "Fragmenting with a Pointed Two-Header" (see opposite), hold the brush like a pen (see page 37) near the fork and simulate the action of a Slinky going down a flight of stairs, turning it from side to side by rotating your wrist while moving it up, down, and across the surface, but in this case using only the *tips* of the hairs (photo 1). Exerting a minimum of pressure on the brush, give the chaining a consistent direction. Use a small brush to add veining by following the framework established by the knitting (photo 2). Create fragments (the spaces between the painted forms) in a range of sizes. Work until the brush is out of paint before reloading.

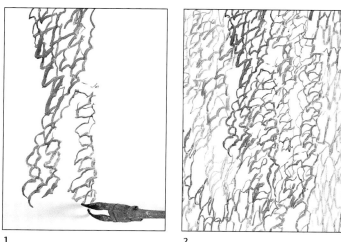

1

2

TWISTS

Load one side of a spalter or a glazing brush with a light-colored glaze, then load the other side with a dark glaze. Holding the brush in a drummer's hold (see page 37), use a trembled hand to paint winding, twisted shapes (photo 1). Repeat, varying size, shape, length, orientation, and intensity of color (photo 2). In the example at right, the same movement was repeated so that it could be copied easily.

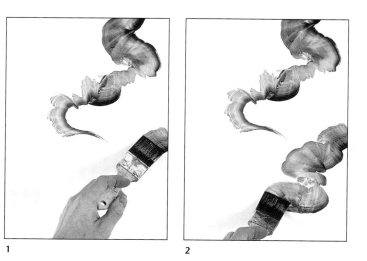

1

2

COMMON FRAGMENTING ERRORS

Shown below are the three most common mistakes made when painting brèche and cloudy marbles.

Fragments that are rounded, too similar in size and shape, too uniformly spaced, and oriented in one single direction (in drawing 1, all the fragments are aligned at a 45-degree angle).

Fragments that are so widely spaced they appear to be floating, so that the surface looks like a slice of salami (drawing 2).

The surface seems to have no direction at all, with fragments that are too similar in size and spaced too consistently (drawing 3).

Fragments should be oriented in a general direction, show variation in form and spacing, and look very angular (drawing 4).

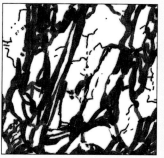

1

2

3

4

CLOUD-SHAPED FRAGMENTS

Hold a pointed two-header like a pen (see page 37) near the fork at a 45-degree angle to the surface. The tips of the brush hairs should barely leave the surface as the brush is turned from side to side by rotating the wrist (photo 1). Create small rounded fragments, positioning adjacent masses so that they are surrounded by curved, twisted, unpainted areas of various sizes (photo 2). Work until the paint has been exhausted from the brush before reloading. Smooth out with a badger brush (photo 3).

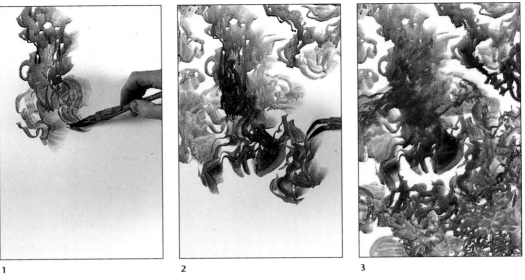

1   2   3

SPATTERING

Load an old or stiff small round glazing brush with very fluid glaze. Grasping it in a drummer hold (see page 37), hold it bristles-end up at a 45-degree angle away from the surface. Use a palette knife to the gently stroke the tips of the hairs *away* from the surface. (Always draw the knife *toward* you—otherwise, you'll spatter yourself.) Spatter the surface methodically, moving from top to bottom and from left to right, to avoid leaving bare spots (see photo). Work until the brush is out of paint before reloading.

When spattering, keep the following rules in mind:
- The farther the brush is held from the surface, the larger and more widely distributed the spatters will be.
- The closer the brush is held to the surface, the smaller and closer together the spatters will be.
- A more fluid glaze will produce more and larger speckles, while a thicker glaze result in fewer and smaller speckles.
- The greater the force that is used to stroke the tip of the brush, the more and larger the speckles, whereas a gentle caress will yield fewer and smaller speckles.

DABBING WITH A CHIQUETEUR BRUSH

Hold the chiqueteur brush like a pen (see page 37) just above the quill ferrule. Dip into some untinted glaze, then load it by touching it to some of the colors on the palette. Using very little pressure, evenly distribute the glaze through the hairs by working them on the palette in a circular motion (photo 1). (The more glaze, the fatter the dabbing marks; the less glaze, the finer the marks.) Dab the surface in curving bands, rotating the brush between your thumb and index finger to vary the patterns of the marks (photo 2). The bands should run parallel to one another and overlap each other slightly, so it is hard to distinguish how many times the surface has been dabbed (photos 3 & 4). Wait until the paint has been exhausted from the brush before reloading. This exercise can also be done with a worn sea sponge (see "Sponging On," page 79), but it won't produce the same pattern of small fragment-shaped marks.

1

2

3

4

FLAMING

Hold and load the chiqueteur brush as described in "Dabbing with a Chiqueteur Brush," above. Hold the brush perpendicular to the surface, then drag it across (photo 1), changing pressure as you work to vary the widths of the strokes (photo 2). This technique is often done with a sea sponge, usually after a final overglaze has been applied to the surface with a sponge.

1

2

White Veined Carrara

Carrara is a veined marble striped with soft, blue-gray veins that fade gently into its white background. Its name is derived from its primary quarry site, Carrara, Italy, though it can also be found in France. The number and shape of the veins vary, depending on where the slab was excavated. This marble can be used on most surfaces and works especially well on walls, where its light value can be heightened with dark marbles.

In addition to the veined version, Carrara marble is available in a spotted white used exclusively for stiles and rails, as well as in an almost pure white traditionally used for statuary, which is never painted as a faux finish because it is too plain.

1. Lightly sand and dust off the cured basecoated surface. Load the glazing brush with a transparent mixture of glaze #1 (see Technical Notes) + **white**, then glaze the surface heavily. While the surface is still wet, apply mixtures of glaze #1 + **white** + **ultramarine blue** + **raw umber** and/or **white** + **yellow ochre** + **black** with the glazing brush to establish an undertone that provides the surface with a distinct direction.

2. While the surface is still wet (if necessary, mist it with water to keep it wet), break up the undertone by sponging on glaze #1 + **ultramarine blue** + **raw umber** over the entire surface to provide blended undertones for the veining (see the exercise on page 79). When the glaze has been exhausted from the sponge, use it to sponge off the surface (see page 80). Soften well with a badger brush, working first from top to bottom, then from left to right, to create a smooth, faded underwork. Wipe off the bristles frequently in a clean rag to prevent the paint from drying in the hairs. Let dry.

3. Mix **white** + **ultramarine blue** + **black** to create a cold blue-gray, then use it to tint a small amount of glaze #1. Following the general direction of the undertones, use a small round brush to establish the major veins as shown in the exercise on page 80. Add knitted forms at random using two small brushes, alternating among large, medium, and small masses and making

the veining progressively finer. Vary the intensity and color of the veining by working with different colors from the palette and by using the brushes until they run out of paint (see page 81). Soften with a badger brush as you work. Let dry.

4. Use a small brush (either pointed or flat) and a darker value of the cold blue-gray glaze to accentuate certain veins. Using the same glaze, add some fine veins that run counter to the general direction of the veining and move across the surface in descending steps. Soften with a badger brush as you work. Let dry.

5. Overglazing: Tint glaze #2 (see Technical Notes) with some **white**. Load the glaze mixture on the sea sponge, then sponge it on the surface. Finally, "flame" the surface as shown in the exercise on page 87, holding the sponge on its side and dragging it across the darkest and heaviest veins. Soften with a badger brush as you work. Let dry.

6. Use a small round brush to paint almond-shaped dots of pure **white** at the intersection of selected veins and within the smallest knitted forms to represent areas of intense crystallization.

7. Use a small round brush to add some final white fissures across the surface and alongside a few of the darker gray veins (see the exercise on page 82). Let dry.

8. Lightly sand and dust off the surface. Varnish with two coats of satin-finish acrylic polyurethane.

USING OTHER MEDIA

To achieve a smoother finish, this recipe can also be painted in oils. Mix the glaze with poppy oil (3 turpentine + 1 poppy oil + drier), which has less of a tendency to yellow than linseed oil. Use the same palette and techniques, but replace the synthetic brushes with natural bristle brushes and the sea sponge with a chiqueteur brush. Let the surface dry completely before overglazing and adding the fissures. Let dry a few days before finishing with wax instead of oil varnish to help minimize the yellowing effect.

1. Coat the surface heavily with white glaze, then provide direction for the veining with toned white glazes.

2. Break up the undertone by sponging on a glaze over the entire surface. Soften with a badger brush. Let dry.

3. Paint the first set of veins. Soften well with a badger brush.

4. Add progressively finer veins with one brush (A) and knitted forms with two brushes (B), alternating among large, medium, and small masses (C). Soften with a badger (D). Let dry.

5. Emphasize certain veins, then add some fine veins that run counter to the general direction of the veining. Soften. Let dry.

6. Overglaze and flame the surface.

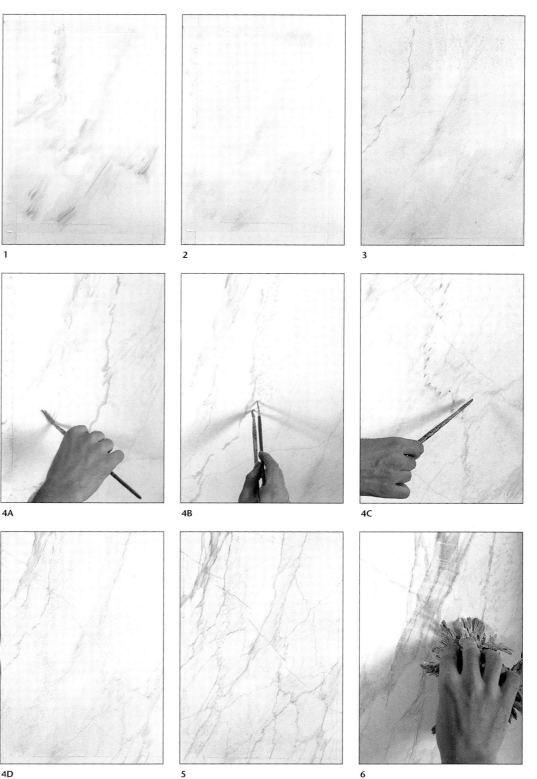

1

2

3

4A

4B

4C

4D

5

6

7. Soften the flamed surface with a badger brush. Let dry.

8. Paint almond-shaped dots (A) and add some final fissures (B).

9. The completed finish. The stiles and rails are painted with a brèche marble similar to White Brèche (shown on pages 106–108) except that the tone is grayer and the example here was essentially worked wet-on-wet because the painting area was so small.

7

8A

8B

9

Yellow Flower

TECHNICAL NOTES

Difficulty Rating

1.5

System

Water (acrylics)

Basecoat

White OR straw yellow
(white + chrome yellow)
alkyd, eggshell finish

Acrylic Glazes

Glaze #1: 1 matte medium +
1 water

Glaze #2: 1 matte medium +
2 water

Palette

Artists' Acrylics

White

Chrome yellow

Chrome orange

Raw sienna

Yellow ochre

Red ochre

Cadmium red

Raw umber

Black

Brushes and Tools

Glazing brush

Chiqueteur brush or sea
sponge

Badger brush

Pointed two-header

Assorted small round
brushes

Synthetic spalter

Exercises

Dabbing with a Chiqueteur
Brush (page 87)

Knitting with a Pointed
Two-Header (page 85)

Twists (page 85)

Veining with a Small Brush
(page 80)

Flaming (page 87)

Fissures (page 82)

Reference Drawings

See Drawings 3 and 4

Yellow Flower is a yellow veined marble that is streaked with orange and striped with many small, angular red, ochre, or black veins as well as white ones. It is quarried in France, and belongs to the same family of marbles as Saint Sylvester. Though it works well on walls and most other architectural elements, Yellow Flower is not recommended for use on detailed milled pieces, as its veining is very difficult to paint on intricate surfaces.

1. Lightly sand and dust off the cured basecoated surface. Use the glazing brush to glaze the entire surface with glaze #1 (see Technical Notes) + **chrome yellow + white + raw sienna**, alternating it with a glaze of **chrome orange + raw umber.** While the surface is still wet, load a chiqueteur or sea sponge with glaze #1 + **yellow ochre, chrome yellow, raw sienna, or chrome orange** and dab it on the surface in a slightly slanted vertical configuration as shown in the exercise on page 87, varying the values as you work. Soften with a badger brush, wiping the bristles frequently to prevent paint buildup. Let dry.

2. Mix glaze #2 (see Technical Notes) with **raw sienna + red ochre + white.** (White can be substituted for other colors from the palette, but avoid black and raw umber.) Load the two-header with the glaze and knit a transparent network of thin yellow veins as shown in the exercise on page 85, softening with a badger brush as you work. Let dry.

3. Load the synthetic spalter with **cadmium red + yellow ochre** on one side and a transparent tone (glaze #2 + the same colors) on the other. Paint a few long "twists" similar to those shown in the exercise on page 85, but less contorted. The twists should run parallel to and alongside some of the major lines of the knitted underwork. Use the chiqueteur brush or a sea sponge to create soft breaks within the twists. Soften with a badger brush as you work. Let dry.

4. Using a slightly darker glaze than the one used for the underwork (glaze #2 + **yellow ochre + red ochre + raw umber**), add a stratum of trembled but dynamic veining with various small round brushes (see page 80). Work until the paint has been exhausted from the brushes, and use a badger brush to soften the veins.

    Darken the glaze with **black,** then use it to emphasize the major veins and the darker edge of each twist. Soften with a badger as you work. Darken the glaze with **red ochre,** then repeat. Add some dots in **black** or **raw umber** at the intersection of certain veins. Let dry.

5. Overglazing: Mix a transparent off-white glaze (glaze #2 + **white + chrome yellow + yellow ochre**). Load the chiqueteur brush or a sea sponge, then apply the glaze over the entire surface as shown in the exercise on page 87, softening with a badger brush as you work. Flame the twists by dragging the brush or sponge across them and away from their darker edges (see page 87).

6. Using several different pointed brushes and glaze #2 + **white** + a touch of **chrome yellow,** paint the fissures as shown on page 82 so that some of them run between two parallel dark veins. Place almond shapes at the intersection of certain veins. Soften as you work. Use a transparent gray glaze (#2) to break up some of the larger fissures. Soften as you work. Let dry.

7. Lightly sand and dust off the surface. Varnish with two coats of satin-finish or semigloss acrylic polyurethane.

USING OTHER MEDIA

This marble can also be painted using an oil-based glaze (3 turpentine + 1 oil + drier) following essentially the same steps but working wet-in-wet from steps 1 through 4. Instead of paint and brush, use a Conté crayon to add some of the dark veins. This will result in a softer-looking marble, but you have to wait for the veining to dry before overglazing.

1. Loosely glaze the entire surface with two yellow-orange glazes (A), then dab on various colors from the palette with a chiqueteur brush (B). Soften with a badger brush. Let dry.

2. Use the two-header to knit a transparent network of veins. Soften with a badger. Let dry.

3. Use a double-loaded synthetic spalter to paint a few long twists. Soften the twists with a chiqueteur brush, then with a badger. Let dry.

4. Add veining with assorted small brushes.

5. Emphasize major veins and the darker edge of each twist. Let dry.

6. Apply the overglaze with a chiqueteur brush or sea sponge.

7. Flame the twists by dragging the brush across them and away from their darker edges. Let dry.

8. Place almond-shaped dots of white at the intersections of the certain veins, then add the final fissures. Let dry.

9. The completed finish. The Yellow Flower panel is framed with Yellow Sienna, a veined marble that contains some brèche forms. Working over a sponged background of dirty yellow with green and red ochre streaks, it was veined with darker values of yellow ochre, red ochre, raw umber, and chrome green oxide, then overglazed with off-white.

1A

1B

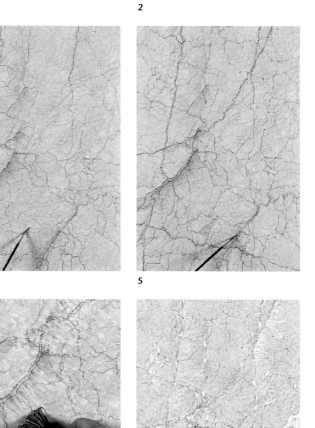

2

3

4

5

6

7

8

9

Rouge Royal

Quarried in Belgium and northern France, Rouge Royal is a cloudy veined marble whose predominant color, which is derived from various metal oxides of red or brownish hue, is blotched with gray calcium deposits and covered with a network of thin brown and black veins. Its white fissures are a variety of shapes and sizes, and appear to occur throughout the entire surface. Similar in appearance to Cerfontaine, Rance, and Saint Remy, Rouge Royal is suitable for wainscoting, baseboards, columns, and mantels. It goes well with White Veined Carrara (page 90), Sea Green (page 99), and Portor (page 105).

This recipe presents a Rouge Royal that is somewhat intermediate in complexity. Depending on the desired effect, the surface design of this marble can be made more complex by adding more veins and overglazings, or simplified by omitting some of the overglazing steps.

1. Lightly sand and dust off the cured basecoated surface. Mix a gray from the palette using glaze + **white** + **ultramarine blue** + **burnt umber** OR **raw umber**. Varying the gray with **black,** sponge on the surface as shown in the exercise on page 79, but with a more open print to create a loose, rippling pattern. Let dry.

2. Load the synthetic spalter with glaze + **white,** then lightly load one end of the bristles with **black** and the other with **raw umber**. Paint gently curving twists ranging from 3 to 7 inches (7.6 to 17.8 cm) long, varying the values of their gray tones (see the exercise on page 85) as well as their orientation. Soften as you work with a badger brush. Let dry.

3. Load the two-header with a mixture of glaze + **burnt sienna** + **red ochre** + **cadmium red** + **raw sienna,** then modify the color with a little **burnt umber, chrome orange,** and **yellow ochre** from the palette. Surround the twists with cloud-shaped fragments as shown in the exercise on page 86, reloading only when the glaze has been exhausted from the brush. Soften with a badger brush as you work. Vary the palette colors when reloading to create depth. Let dry.

4. Emphasize selected masses by knitting with the two-header loaded with a darker maroon. Use a small pointed brush loaded with glaze + **raw umber** + **burnt umber** to add a network of small veins. Use the same brush to reinforce one side of each twist with a mixture of **black** + **raw umber**. As you work, smooth out and soften all elements with a badger brush. Let dry.

5. To create depth, break up the twists by running a two-header loaded with a transparent mixture of glaze + **burnt umber** + **black** across their width, softening them with a badger brush as you work. Then sponge on a brownish red glaze only over the red areas. Let dry.

6. Overglazing: Sponge on an off-white glaze (**white** + **yellow ochre** + **burnt sienna**) over the entire surface as shown in the exercise on page 79. Use a small pointed brush and the off-white glaze to add major fissures and to create a network of fine, interlacing veins, adding a few heavier ones for contrast (see page 82). Though the veining follows no particular direction, it should be very vigorously painted. Vary the intensity of the veins by waiting to reload the brush until it runs out of paint. Soften as you work.

   Place almond- and half-moon-shaped spots here and there on the white fragments. Underline some of the large fissures with a thin line of **burnt umber.** Let dry.

7. Lightly sand and dust off the surface. Varnish with two coats of satin-finish or semigloss acrylic polyurethane.

USING OTHER MEDIA

This marble can also be painted using an oil-based glaze (3 turpentine + 1 oil + drier), and replacing the sea sponge with a chiqueteur brush. Steps 1 through 5 are done wet-in-wet, then let dry before overglazing the surface in oil as well. This approach is preferable for intricate or large surfaces because it allows more time to create the effect, but requires a long wait before overglazing.

1. Sponge on gray and black glazes to create a loose, rippling pattern. Let dry.

2. Triple-load a synthetic spalter (A), then use it to paint gently curving twists that follow the contours of the sponged-on underwork (B). Soften with a badger brush (C). Let dry.

3. Use a pointed two-header to create cloud-shaped fragments over the entire surface (A). Emphasize certain areas with a darker red (B). Soften with a badger. Let dry.

4. Add a network of small veins, then reinforce one edge of each twist with a dark tone. Soften all with a badger. Let dry.

5. Break up the twist by running a two-header loaded with transparent brown glaze across their width. Soften with a badger.

6. Sponge on a brownish red glaze over the red areas only. Let dry.

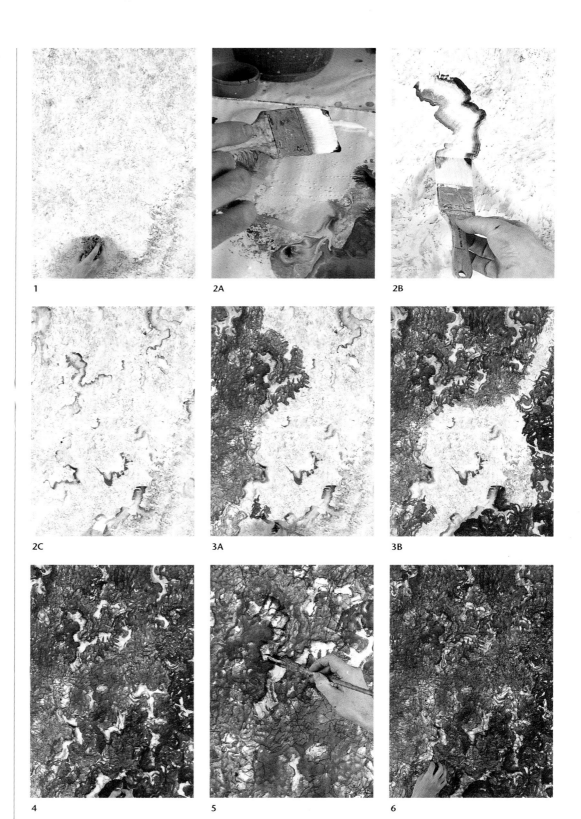

1

2A

2B

2C

3A

3B

4

5

6

7. Sponge on an off-white glaze over the entire surface.

8. Use a small brush to add fissures and a network of fine, interlacing veins. Let dry.

9. The completed finish. The baseboard beneath the Rouge Royal panel was painted in a dark brown Henriette marble, which was created by sponging a dark maroon on and off the surface several times, leaving some lighter areas in which beige veins were then painted.

7

8

9

Sea Green

Sea Green is a veined marble whose black cement and green veins are a result of decomposed plant matter. Its dense veining forms a network of torn fragments of different shades of green, creating an impression of a profusion of tiny brèches.

There are actually several marbles in the same family that exhibit a variety of greens and veining configurations. Quarried in France (both in the Alps and in Corsica), Italy, and Egypt, Sea Green has been used since antiquity, and is particularly common on wainscotting and casings. It looks beautiful with mahogany woodwork and also works well with dark marbles such as Portor (page 105) and Grand Antique (which was used to frame the completed finish on page 99), as well as a variety of red marbles.

1. Lightly sand and dust off the cured basecoated surface. Use the glazing brush to glaze the surface heavily with a mixture of glaze #1 + **chrome oxide deep + ultramarine blue + yellow ochre** + a touch of **white.** Change the proportions of the colors to vary the tonality within the panel. While the surface is still wet, add irregular blotches of pure **black** with the glazing brush.

2. While still wet, load a chiqueteur brush or a small sea sponge with untinted glaze #1, then dab it over the entire surface to break the undertones, smooth out the background, and create a nice underwork of small fragments (see page 87). Smooth out again with a badger brush. Let dry.

3. Load the pencil grainer with a transparent mixture of glaze #2 + **chrome green oxide + yellow ochre+ raw sienna+** a touch of **white,** then modify the color with a little **ultramarine blue** or **burnt sienna.** Tremble your hand as you paint the underwork, crisscrossing the veining and creating masses in a range of sizes (see page 83). Wait until the glaze is exhausted from the brush before reloading. Soften with a badger brush as you work. Let dry.

4. Repeat step 3, using a lighter version of the mixture by adding more **white.** Emphasize the veining in certain areas and redefine the sizes of some of the dark background

masses. Soften with a badger brush as you work. Let dry.

5. As shown in the exercise on page 84, begin fragmenting with the two-header loaded with the mixture used in step 4 lightened again with **white.** After each level of veining has been completed, continue to lighten the mixture by gradually adding more white. Soften with a badger brush as you work. Let dry.

6. Link the fragments by veining with a round brush loaded with the glaze mixture used in step 5, lightened yet again with **white** and modified by adding **yellow ochre** or **alizarin crimson.** Refer to the exercise on page 80 but work on a smaller, less open scale, increasing the definition of the masses while continuing to gradually lighten the color by adding more **white.** Soften with a badger as you work. Let dry.

7. Overglazing: Using a variety of small round brushes, paint the fissures with an off-white glaze (glaze #1 + **white+ yellow ochre + chrome green oxide**) as shown in the exercise on page 82. Follow the general direction of the underwork and earlier veining, then add a few thin veins across some of the larger masses. Let dry.

8. Load a chiqueteur brush or a sea sponge with a dark transparent mixture of glaze #1 + **black + chrome oxide deep,** then dab it over the entire surface as shown in the exercise on page 87. Add a touch of **alizarin crimson** here and there to vary the tonality. Blend and soften the fissures and light veins by flaming them with the brush or sponge as shown on page 87. Soften with a badger as you work. As shown in the exercise on page 86, spatter the surface with black to break up some of the green areas. Let dry.

9. Lightly sand and dust off the surface. Varnish with two coats of semigloss acrylic polyurethane.

USING OTHER MEDIA

This finish can also be painted with an oil-based glaze (3 turpentine + 1 oil + drier), which gives it a softer look and allows more time to work on large or intricate areas, but

1. Glaze the surface heavily with a gray-green glaze, then add blotches of pure black.

2. Smooth out the background and break up the undertones by dabbing the surface with a chiqueteur brush loaded with untinted glaze. Soften with a badger brush as you work. Let dry.

3. Use the pencil grainer to create a network of trembled veins. Soften with a badger. Let dry.

4. Use the pencil grainer and a lighter glaze to emphasize selected veins and redefine the sizes of some background masses. Soften with a badger. Let dry.

5. Add fragments with the pointed two-header. Soften with a badger. Let dry.

6. Link the fragments with a small pointed brush. Soften with a badger. Let dry.

7. Add fissures and a few thin veins that run across some of the larger masses. Let dry.

8. Use a chiqueteur brush or a sea sponge to dab the surface with a dark transparent glaze (A). Flame the fissures and lightest veins to blend and soften them (B), then spatter the surface. Let dry.

9. The completed Sea Green panel is framed here with stiles and rails painted with Grand Antique; the corners are painted with Portor (see page 105). For the Grand Antique, a black background was modified with some gray undertones, then painted with very broken and angular white fragments as shown in "Fragmenting with a Pointed Two-Header" (see page 84). After the fragments dried, they were overglazed with black.

requires a much longer wait between steps. The instructions for working with a water-based glaze are essentially the same, except that visually heavy areas can be opened up by dabbing on some pure turpentine with a chiqueteur brush. Allow the veins and fragments to dry before adding the fissures and white veining, and before applying the final glaze.

ALTERNATE TECHNIQUE

On small surfaces, this marble can be done in either acrylics or oils using a wipe-off technique. Glaze a white basecoat with a deep greenish black, then use a chamois wrapped over your thumbnail (see Chapter 5) to wipe off the white veins. Smooth out with a badger or codtail brush, let dry, then overglaze with a transparent green.

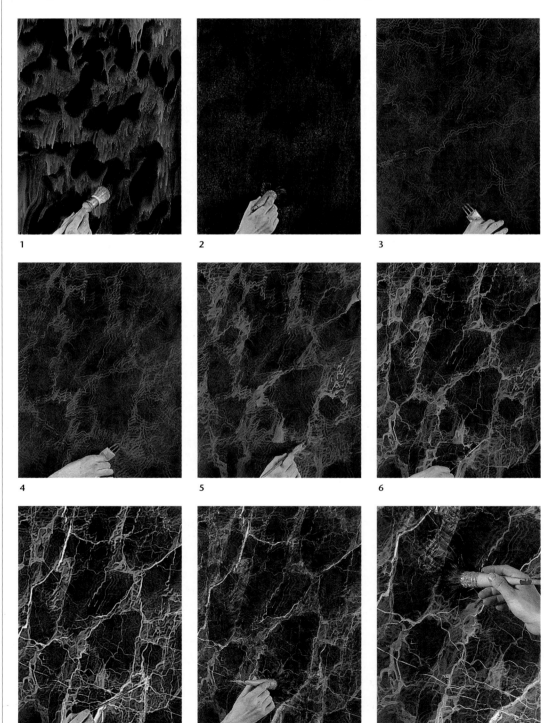

1

2

3

4

5

6

7

8A

8B

9

Imperador

Imperador is a brèche marble whose tobacco brown background contains an intricate network of golden and beige veins and tiny black speckles. The type of Imperador shown in this demonstration is quarried in Belgium, but similar varieties can be found in the United States and Italy. Imperador is a little too busy for walls, so it is often used on stiles and rails to frame other marbles, in tub and shower enclosures, and for baseboards. Though it makes an attractive molding, the intricacy of its veining makes it very difficult to paint on small, detailed surfaces.

1. Lightly sand and dust off the cured basecoated surface. Load the glazing brush heavily with glaze #1 (see Technical Notes) and some of the colors from the palette (**black, raw umber, burnt umber,** and **chrome orange**). Glaze the surface heavily, creating variety and contrast within the coloration.

2. While the surface is still wet, sponge it off with the used sea sponge as shown in the exercise on page 80. Rotate the sponge so that it picks up more color, dragging it across the surface as shown in "Elm, Amboina, and Thuja Burl" (see Chapter 5). Smooth out with a badger brush. Let dry.

3. Repeat steps 1 and 2, this time working with glaze #1 and a slightly darker palette. Soften with a badger brush as you work. Let dry.

4. Paint wide, open brèches using the synthetic spalter and a transparent mixture of glaze #2 (see Technical Notes) + **white + raw umber + burnt umber + yellow ochre,** modifying it with some of the other colors of the palette. Create large as well as small masses. Soften with a badger brush as you work. Let dry.

5. Begin the veining with a long, pointed synthetic round brush and a mixture of glaze #2 + **white + raw umber + chrome yellow + chrome orange,** varying the tonality with the colors of the palette.

    Using the same glaze mixture, paint knitted forms using two brushes, changing the tones of the glaze often while keeping it transparent. Create first-, second-, and third-level veining. Soften with a badger brush as you work. Let dry.

6. Use the pencil grainer to paint a network of thin light veins with glaze #2 + **white + raw umber + chrome yellow + chrome orange** varied with the palette (see the exercise on page 83). (If you prefer, this step can also be done after the second glazing and sponging off and before the brèches are painted [between steps 3 and 4].) Let dry.

7. Use an assortment of small round brushes to paint many thin veins that run across the brèche masses as shown in the exercise on page 80. Avoid making Xs and spider webs. Work with the same beige tonalities as in step 6, but lighter. Soften with a badger brush as you work. Let dry.

8. Overglazing: Sponge a transparent mixture of glaze #2 + **burnt umber + black + chrome orange** over the entire surface as shown in the exercise on page 79, but use a more open print. Over the lighter veins, hold the sea sponge on its side and drag it across the surface (see "Flaming," page 87). Soften with a badger brush as you work. Spatter the surface (see page 86) here and there with **black** or **burnt umber.** Let dry.

9. Use a small pointed brush loaded with an off-white glaze (glaze #2 + **white + yellow ochre**) to add the fissures as shown in the exercise on page 82, varying their tones and widths. Use the two-header to overglaze some of the stronger veins with a very transparent mixture of glaze #2 + **burnt umber + raw umber.** Let dry.

10. Lightly sand and dust off the surface. Varnish with two coats of semigloss or gloss acrylic polyurethane.

USING OTHER MEDIA

This recipe for Imperador can also be done in oil (3 turpentine + 1 oil + drier), which will give you more time to work on each step but requires a much longer wait between glazings. If necessary, open up the background and create more variety by spattering the surface with mineral spirits.

1. Glaze the surface heavily, producing variety and contrast.

2. Sponge off the surface, rotating and dragging the sponge to create light areas. Smooth out with a badger brush. Let dry.

3. Repeat the preceding steps using a darker palette.

4. Paint light, transparent fragments with the synthetic spalter. Soften with a badger. Let dry.

5. Begin the veining, then paint knitted forms with two brushes. Soften with a badger. Let dry.

6. Use the pencil grainer to paint a network of thin light veins. Let dry.

7. Add thin veins across fragments with long pointed brushes. Soften with a badger. Let dry.

8. Sponge on a transparent glaze over the entire surface. Flame the lightest veins, then spatter here and there. Let dry.

9. Add the final fissures, then overglaze the strongest ones with the two-header.

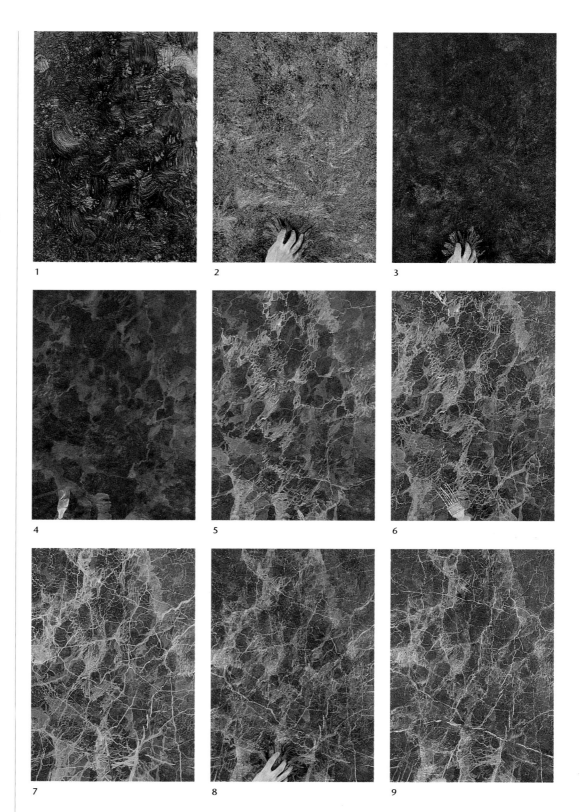

1 2 3

4 5 6

7 8 9

Imperador

10. The completed finish. The African Brèche on the stiles and rails is painted similarly to the White Brèche shown on pages 106–108, except that it has more yellow, ochre, and brownish red tones.

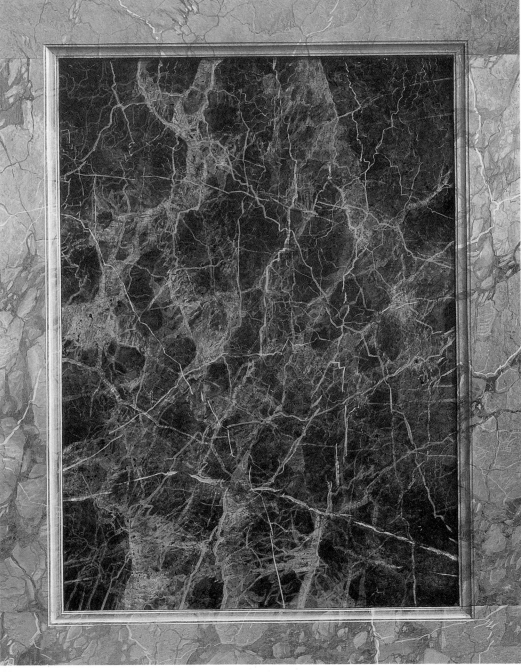

10

Portor

Although it is actually a veined marble, Portor (also referred to as Black and Gold) is decoratively classified as a brèche marble due to the visual predominance of rounded brèche shapes. Its black calcareous cement features parallel golden chains of iron oxides, which are actually veins. Though it is primarily quarried in Italy, it is also found in France, Corsica, and Algeria.

As one of the most decorative marbles, Portor can be used on a wide variety of surfaces, including baseboards, mantels, tabletops, pilasters, columns, casings, and medium-sized panels, but it is not appropriate for large walls. It is set off very nicely by yellow marbles such as Yellow Flower (pages 91–93) and Yellow Sienna (see page 93), as well as red marbles such as Rouge Royal (pages 94–96). Portor is always painted so that its veining runs either vertically or horizontally, but never on an angle or a slant.

1. Lightly sand and dust off the cured basecoated surface. Load the heel of a long-haired pointed round or lettering brush with a beige tone (glaze + **white** + **raw sienna** + **chrome yellow**), then touch one of the other colors on the palette with just the tip of the brush. Working on a few "links" but on one chain at a time, begin the brèching process as shown in the exercise on page 83, but paint rounder, less angular forms. "Swing" the brush down the surface like a pendulum without slanting the chain. When you paint with the tip of the brush, the color will be, for example, red ochre, but as you press down on the hair to paint with the heel, the color will change to beige, creating a "candle flame" effect. To avoid smudging your work, wait until it is almost dry before softening it lightly with a badger brush.

2. Repeat step 1 to paint the remaining chains of brèche. Load the tip of the brush with a different color for each chain, alternating the colors of the chains within a panel or section between slightly grayed and more intense; for example, from **yellow ochre**, to **red ochre**, to another subtle or neutral tone, and so on. Creating chains of first-, second-, and third-level importance will give the finish variation and movement. Let dry.

3. Tie the chains together by painting a network of thin, trembled veins with a long pointed brush, loaded as described in step 1 with the predominant colors of each individual chain. Let dry.

4. Run the two-header loaded with a transparent mixture of glaze + **black** + **burnt umber** across certain brèches to break them up and add depth and mirrorlike ripples reminiscent of sunlight on water. Soften with a badger brush as you work. Let dry.

5. To add more depth, use a small flat brush loaded with a transparent dark gray glaze (**black** + **raw umber** + a touch of **white**) to fill in some areas of the black background, then drybrush them with a small stencil brush. Work only within the black areas; do not overlap the brèches or veins. Soften with a badger brush as you work. Let dry.

6. Overglazing: Add some tiny fissures in an off-white glaze (**white** + **yellow ochre**) with a small pointed brush as shown on page 82. Paint a few large fissures alongside and over the chains, then add more finer ones that run across the surface in steps. Tone down and break up these veins using a two-header loaded with transparent brown or black. Soften with a badger as you work. Let dry.

7. Lightly sand and dust off the surface. Varnish with two or three coats of semigloss or gloss acrylic polyurethane. (This marble gains a lot in depth by being well varnished with either of these lusters.)

USING OTHER MEDIA

This recipe can also be done in an oil-based glaze (3 turpentine + 1 oil + drier) following the same instructions. However, the only advantage to working in oil when painting Portor is that you will have more time to smooth out the brèches on very detailed moldings or fluted surfaces.

1. Using a tip-loaded brush, create vertical chains of rounded fragments (A–D). The "candle-flame" effect is created as pressure is shifted from the tip of the brush to the heel. Wait until the chain is almost dry before softening it lightly with a badger brush. Let dry.

2. Tie the chains together with a network of thin, trembled veins. Let dry.

3. Blend certain fragments with the pointed two-header and a dark glaze, adding mirrorlike ripples to the surface. Soften with a badger. Let dry.

4. Use a small flat brush to fill in some of the black background with a transparent gray glaze, then drybrush them with a stencil brush. Soften with a badger. Let dry.

5. Add fissures and fine veins in white, then soften them with a two-header loaded with a dark transparent glaze. Soften with a badger. Let dry.

6. The completed finish. The baseboard was painted with the same marble using the same technique but a grayer palette.

1A

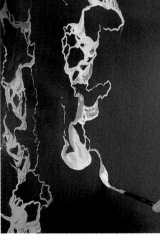

1B

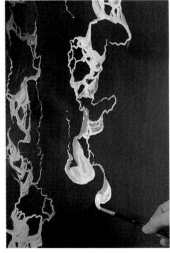

1C

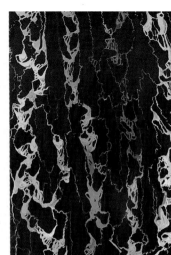

1D

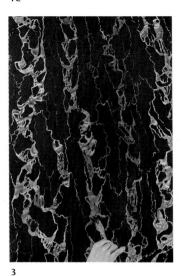

2

3

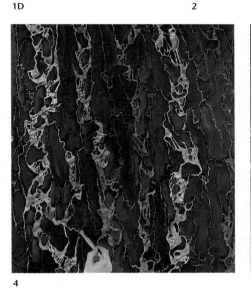

4

5

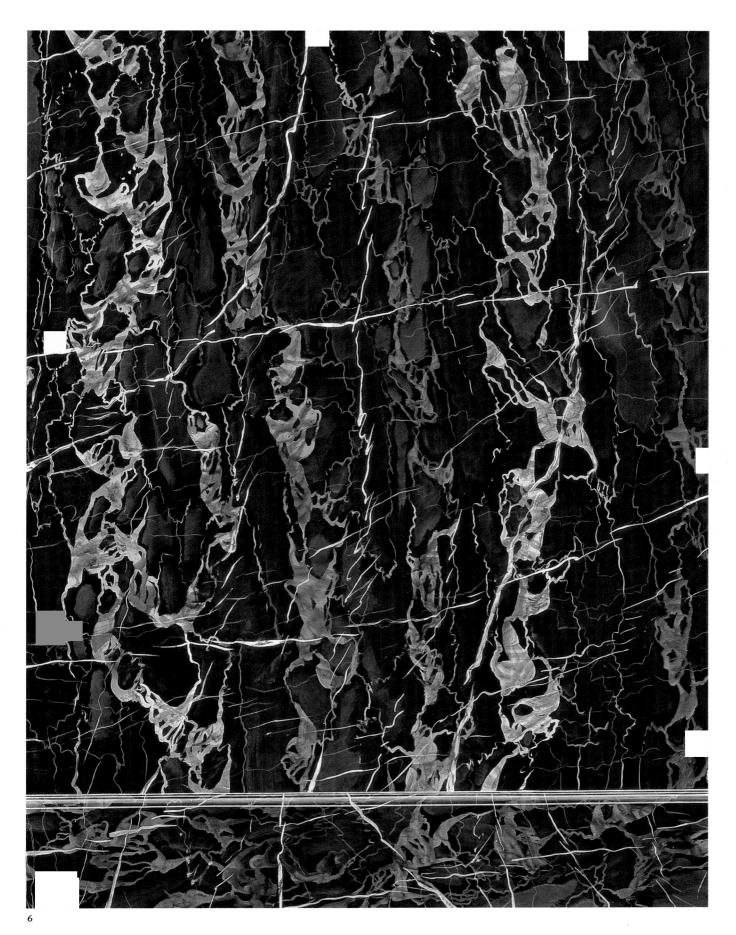

6

White Brèche

Quarried in Italy and France, White Brèche is a fragmented white marble agglomerated in a gray calcareous cement. Its fragments, which are angular and elongated, vary greatly in size and are randomly placed, with major shifts in orientation. Though White Brèche is suitable for most surfaces, especially panels (as long as the wall is not too large), its fragments are difficult to paint on small, intricate surfaces. It harmonizes well with most marbles.

1. Lightly sand and dust off the cured basecoated surface. Using the glazing brush, glaze the surface heavily with glaze #1 (see Technical Notes) + **white.** While wet, add some streaks of gray (glaze #1 + **white + ultramarine blue + black**) varied with other colors from the palette with the pointed glazing brush to establish the orientation of the surface.

2. While still wet, break up the pattern slightly by dabbing the surface with the chiqueteur brush (see page 87) loaded with glaze #1 + **white + ultramarine blue + black.** Soften the entire surface with a badger brush, first from top to bottom and then from left to right. Let dry.

3. With the two-header and glaze #2 (see Technical Notes) tinted with a mixture of **white + ultramarine blue + black** varied with colors from the palette, paint the fragments as shown in the exercise on page 84, softening with a badger brush as you work. These brèche chains, which should be very angular, establish the position and orientation of the main fragments. Wait to reload until the paint has been exhausted from the brush. Let dry.

4. Using several of the small pointed brushes and the same gray mixture used in step 3, tie the brèches together by veining as shown in the exercise on page 80, varying their color and intensity. Working vigorously, add knitting here and there (see the exercise on page 81), varying the size of the fragments from large to medium to small. Soften with a badger brush as you work. Let dry.

5. Use a small pointed brush and an even more transparent gray glaze to add fine veins within the largest fragments. Accentuate some of the dark areas while minimizing the weak ones. Soften as you work. Let dry.

6. Using the two-header or synthetic spalter and a very transparent gray glaze (glaze #2 + **ultramarine blue + raw umber + black**), create depth by adding some transparent tones within certain fragments (but along one side only), holding the brush at an angle to the surface. Soften with a badger brush, moving the transparent tone against the dark side of each fragment. Finally, add very transparent brèche forms within some of the large fragments to break them up. Let dry.

7. Overglazing: Sponge on a transparent mixture of glaze #2 + **white** over the entire surface as shown in the exercise on page 79, but use a more open pattern. Drag the sponge sideways across some of the darker fragments as shown in the exercise on page 87. Soften as you work. Let dry.

   Use a pointed brush and the white glaze to accentuate areas opposite those that were darkened within certain fragments in step 6. Place some almond-shaped dots inside the small fragments, then add a few fissures (see the exercise on page 82). Soften as you work. Let dry.

8. Lightly sand and dust off the surface. Varnish with two coats of satin-finish acrylic polyurethane.

USING OTHER MEDIA

In general, acrylics are preferable to oil paints for predominantly white marbles because they do not yellow over time; however, oils will give this marble a softer look. Substitute poppy oil for linseed oil when mixing the glaze (2 turpentine + 1 poppy oil + drier), as it has less of a tendency to yellow.

1. Glaze the surface heavily with white. Add streaks of gray with a pointed glazing brush.

2. Dab the surface with a chiqueteur brush loaded with a light gray tone. Soften with a badger brush. Let dry.

3. With the pointed two-header and a gray glaze, begin painting the main fragments. Let dry.

4. Tie the fragments together with veining. Add knitting here and there. Soften with a badger. Let dry.

5. Add fine veins within the largest fragments. Soften. Let dry.

6. Create depth by adding some dark transparent tones and brèche forms within some of the fragments. Let dry.

7. Sponge on a transparent white glaze, then flame some of the darker fragments. Let dry, then add fissures.

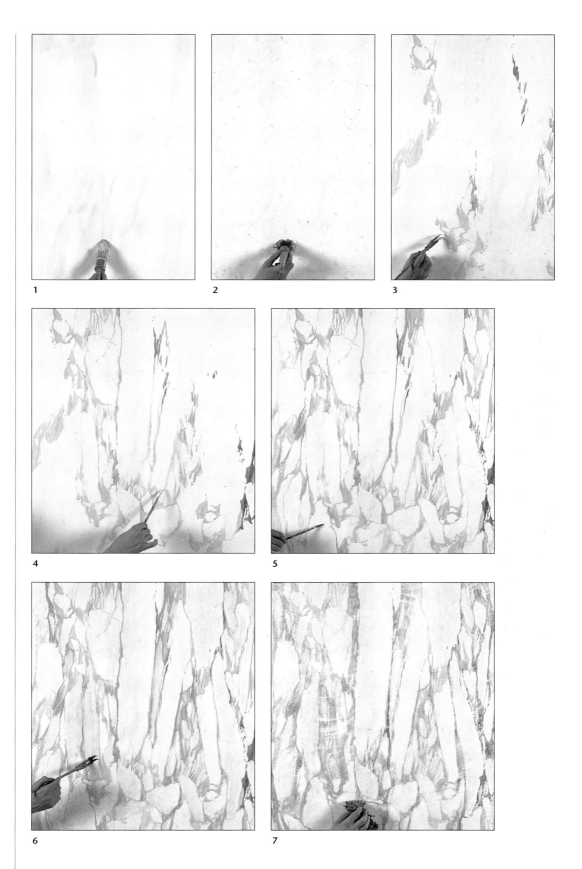

8. The completed finish. The baseboard, which is painted in Rouge Languedoc, provides a striking contrast for the subtle coloration of the White Brèche panel. Rouge Languedoc is from the same marble family as Rouge Royal (see pages 94–96), but its white fragments are more defined. In this example, the white cloud-shaped fragments (see the exercise on page 86) were delineated in red with a small pointed brush over a sponged gray surface. After the white twists were emphasized with transparent glazes in off-white, brown, and gray, veining was added in dark brown and white.

8

Violet Brèche

Violet Brèche is composed of remnants of white and other marbles agglomerated in a grayish green or dark iron oxide cement. In contrast to White Brèche (see pages 106–108), its angular, elongated fragments generally run parallel to one another and are oriented only vertically or horizontally. Quarried in Italy and the French Alps, this beautiful marble is a little too busy for large areas, but looks spectacular on pilasters, columns, wainscoting, and panels. The pass cut is more widely used than the counterpass cut, which is used mostly for stiles and rails. Violet Brèche works well with dark marbles such as Sea Green (see pages 97–99) and Portor (pages 103–105).

Before you begin, practice creating brèche forms by working on the recipe for White Brèche, which is somewhat easier to paint because its palette is far more limited.

1. Lightly sand and dust off the cured basecoated surface. Load the glazing brush brush heavily with an off-white mixture of glaze #1 (see Technical Notes) + white + yellow ochre + raw sienna, then modify it with other colors from the palette (purple, ochre, and gray-beige tones). Glaze the surface, using the various tones to establish the orientation of the main fragments.
2. While the surface is still wet, sponge it off as shown on page 80, but use a more open pattern to break up the undertones. Lightly smooth out the surface with the badger brush. Let dry.
3. With the two-header and an assortment of pointed brushes, use glaze #2 (see Technical Notes) and tones mixed from the palette to paint the fragments (see the exercises on pages 83 and 84). Use a purple-gray (alizarin crimson + ultramarine blue + black + white) and a green-gray (white + yellow oxide + raw sienna + raw umber + chrome green oxide) varied with other

colors of the palette. Paint angular and elongated brèche similar to those in White Brèche, but with a more consistent orientation and more rounded edges. Soften as you work with a badger brush. Let dry.

4. Working progressively darker, use a small pointed brush and glaze #2 + various colors from the palette to emphasize and redefine certain areas and to link fragments together. Soften as you work with a badger brush. Let dry.
5. Create depth by adding some transparent tones (glaze #2 + purple, blue, and yellow ochre within certain fragments (but on one side only) by holding the two-header at an angle to the surface. Soften as you work with a badger brush. Let dry.
6. Overglazing: Sponge on a transparent off-white mixture of glaze #2 + white + yellow ochre over the entire surface as shown in the exercise on page 79, but use a more open pattern. Drag the sponge sideways across the surface to "flame" some of the darker fragments as shown in the exercise on page 87. Let dry.
7. Use a small round brush and the off-white glaze from step 6 to add the fissures (see the exercise on page 82) and accentuate areas opposite those that were darkened within certain fragments in step 5. Soften as you work with a badger brush. Let dry.
8. Lightly sand and dust off the surface. Varnish with two coats of satin-finish acrylic polyurethane.

USING OTHER MEDIA

For a smoother finish, this marble can be painted in oils (glaze: 3 turpentine + 1 linseed oil + drier). Aside from the fact that the wait between overglazings will be significantly longer, the steps in the recipe are virtually the same.

1. Glaze the surface heavily with off-white, then modify it with other colors from the palette.

2. Sponge off the surface, then smooth it out with the badger brush. Let dry.

3. Use the two-header and some small brushes to paint the fragments. Soften with a badger. Let dry.

4. Emphasize and redefine certain areas with a small brush, working progressively darker. Soften with a badger. Let dry.

5. Create depth by adding some transparent tones within certain fragments (but on one side only) by holding the two-header at an angle to the surface. Soften with a badger. Let dry.

6. Sponge on a transparent off-white glaze, then flame some of the darker fragments. Let dry.

7. Add fissures, then accentuate areas opposite those that were darkened within selected fragments. Soften with a badger. Let dry.

8. The completed finish. The stiles and rails are painted with Violet Brèche in the counterpass cut, which makes brèche smaller and compact rather than elongated. The painting technique is the same; only the surface design is different.

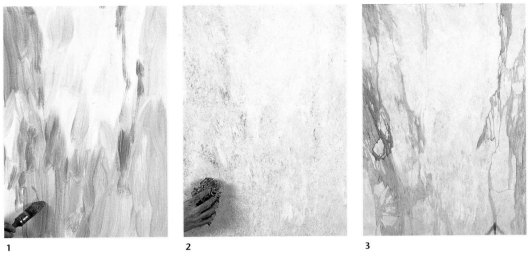

1

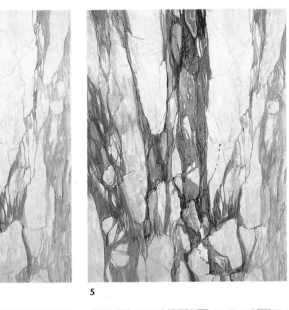

2

3

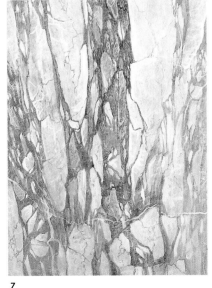

4

5

6

7

Italian-Style "Fantasy" Marble

TECHNICAL NOTES

Difficulty Rating

1 to 2

System

Water

Reversible (gouache, watercolor, or beer) OR *irreversible (acrylics)*

Basecoat

White OR any other light color alkyd, eggshell finish

Glaze

For reversible water-based media: Water only

For acrylics: 1 matte medium + 3 water

Palette

Since these marbles are imaginary, any of the colors listed on pages 34–35 can be used. Use paints or colorants that are compatible with your chosen glaze media.

Brushes and Tools

Glazing brush

Badger brush

Sea sponge

Synthetic spalter

Assorted small pointed synthetic brushes

Billiard cloth ribbon

Exercises

Sponging On (page 79)

Sponging Off (page 80)

Veining with a Small Brush (page 80)

Fragmenting or Brèching (page 83)

Spattering (page 86)

Flaming (page 87)

The marbles in this recipe are neither veined nor brèche, though they could be either. Though these "fantasy" or decorative marbles are usually inspired by actual marbles (or are an amalgam of the characteristics of several), their elements are simplified so that they are both more decorative and easier to paint. What matters most when painting these "Italian-style" marbles is a sense of color, composition, and the final effect. Since they are imaginary virtually any palette can be used; the more extensive the palette, the more compelling the result. Nevertheless, it is important to bear in mind the caveats of using too many colors (see page 35). There are thousands of different combinations you can invent using the basic principles of marble formation. By experimenting with color, composition, and form, you can come up with your own techniques, but this creative freedom should never be used as an excuse to paint marble poorly. The development of each marble can be seen at the top of the completed panels. After each layer of glaze dried, a band of white artists' tape was used to cover a segment of the finish. The tape was then removed after the final glaze had dried.

Fantasy marbles can be painted on any area or surface. (Because water-based media are fast-drying, don't attempt to work on too large a surface at one time; it's easier to divide an area into panels.) Since they are more transparent and lighter than most real marbles, they are well suited for large walls and can appear with a variety of other such marbles. They should never be combined with realistically rendered marble or wood, and should be limited to dramatic decors in order to avoid an unflattering clash of style or technique.

GRAY-PINK MARBLE

1. Lightly sand and dust off the cured basecoated surface, then degrease it as shown on page 32. Glaze the surface with a glazing brush and a medium **gray** gouache glaze, then add a few strokes in a darker gray to create some contrast. While wet, sponge off the surface as shown in the exercise on page 79 to break up the pattern. Smooth out with a badger brush. Let dry.

2. Paint some fragments using the synthetic spalter loaded with **salmon pink,** then smooth out with a badger. With a small pointed brush, add some veins in a darker value. Use a wet ribbon of billiard cloth to wipe off areas along some of the veins and inside certain small fragments. Let dry.

3. Varnish with an oil-based varnish. (Do *not* use an acrylic varnish, which will reactivate the gouache glaze.)

OCHRE MARBLE

1. Glaze the surface with the glazing brush loaded with an **ochre** tone. Add touches of another color to form the fragments, then smooth out with a badger brush. While wet, sponge off the surface to break it up and soften it further. Let dry.

2. Use an assortment of pointed brushes or a synthetic spalter to paint fragments and veins in darker tones. Soften as you work with a badger brush. Let dry. Add some **white** veins with a small brush. Let dry.

3. Varnish; use an oil-based product if a reversible glaze was used.

GREEN AND BROWN MARBLE

This marble is very similar to the ochre example (above) except that a different palette is used.

1. Glaze the surface with the glazing brush loaded with a **brown** tone. Add streaks of **chrome green oxide.** Sponge off the surface, dragging the sponge to leave some flamed areas. Smooth out with a badger brush. Let dry.

2. Use a ribbon of billiard cloth to wipe off some veins. Smooth the surface with a badger, then add some dark **green** veins with assorted small pointed brushes. Let dry.

3. Varnish; use an oil-based product if a reversible glaze was used.

1. Gray-pink marble: Glaze the surface, adding darker, contrasting strokes. Sponge off to break up the pattern. Smooth out with a badger brush.

2. Add fragments with the synthetic spalter. Smooth out with a badger.

3. Paint some veins with a small pointed brush. Wipe off other veins with a wet ribbon of billiard cloth.

4. The completed finish.

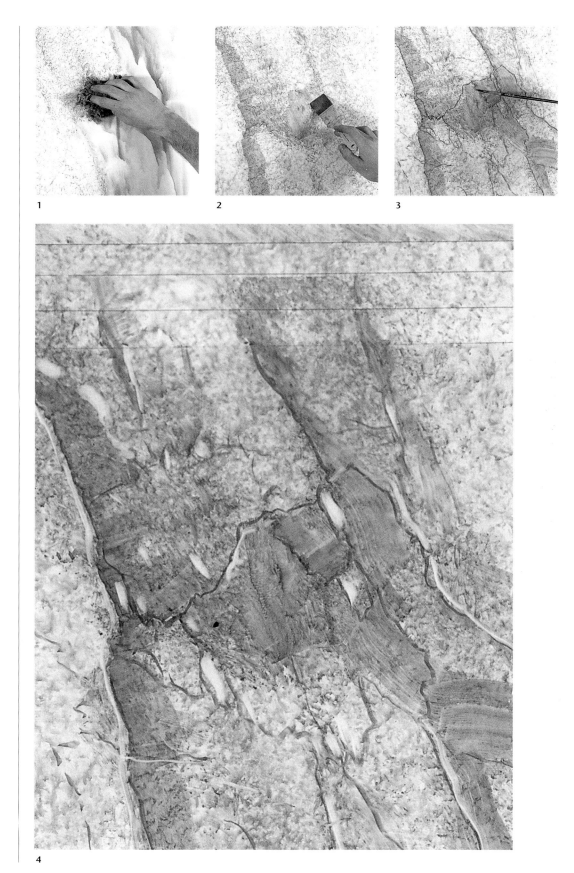

1

2

3

4

Italian-Style "Fantasy" Marble

1. Ochre marble: Glaze the surface, then add touches of color to create fragments. Smooth out with a badger. Sponge off the surface.

2. Add fragments and veins in darker tones.

3. Add white veins with a small brush.

4. The completed finish.

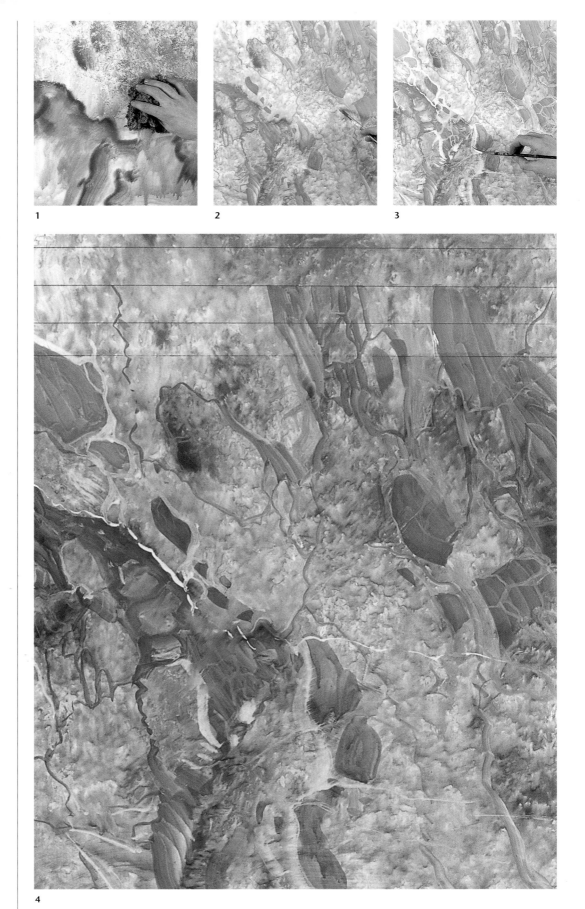

1

2

3

4

1. Green and brown marble: Glaze the surface, then add streaks. Sponge off the surface.

2. Drag the sponge to leave some flamed areas. Smooth out with a badger.

3. Wipe off some veins with a ribbon of billiard cloth. Add some dark green veins with small brushes.

4. The completed finish.

1

2

3

4

Semiprecious Stone

Semiprecious stones are essentially marbles, generally classified as agate, a subcategory of veined marble (see page 74). Composed of fine-grained, dense, crystallized calcium carbonate, semiprecious stones can be honed to a high polish. They are rarer in nature than other marbles and found in smaller concentrations, making them most suitable for jewelry and marquetry—hence the designation "semiprecious stones."

In addition to an Italian-style onyx dado, this dining room is adorned with trompe l'oeil grisaille ornaments that were painted on canvas and installed under glass. Displayed above the mantelpiece is a real ornamental medallion.

Painting Semiprecious Stone

The two practical reasons for imitating semiprecious stones are their high cost, given their relative scarcity, and their unavailability in large quantity. A third, less obvious, reason is that many craftspeople are not trained to work with semiprecious stone in furniture marquetry or as insets of panels on walls. And, of course, their colorful aspect makes semiprecious stones very decorative and appealing.

TYPES OF SEMIPRECIOUS STONE

Of the many varieties of semiprecious stone, the four that are covered in this chapter were selected for the diversity of their color, surface design, and technique.

- *Lapis lazuli* is colored a very intense blue, speckled with white and sometimes little golden flecks.
- *Diaspro di Bohemia* is actually a brèche marble (see page 74). When cut, it shows very decorative stripes, generally of maroon and green.
- *Red jasper* is found in colors ranging from yellow, brown, red, green, blue, and black, and shapes including cloudy, brèche, and onyx.
- *Algerian onyx* is a translucent marble much like alabaster, a pure white calcite.

The fifth recipe demonstrates a technique for faux *pietre dure* (an Italian phrase meaning "hard stones"), or stone marquetry.

SUITABLE APPLICATIONS

By their very nature, semiprecious stones should be simulated only in confined areas, where real forms would be used: to embellish small statues, pedestals, columns, bases or stands, and other fine decorative objects. Imagine how unnatural it would look to panel an entire room in lapis lazuli, unless you were to break it up into small sections (no larger than 8 inches). The only exception to this rule would be onyx, which is found in larger slabs, sometimes measuring several feet, but that, too, would also be used as marquetry or inlays alternated with marble in larger panels.

Italian artisans created entire rooms of semiprecious marquetry in the 17th and 18th centuries. Florentine craftsmen in particular were renowned for their marvelous artistry in creating such inlays, using trompe l'oeil effects on tabletops and setting semiprecious stones in marquetry.

CHOOSING THE RIGHT TECHNIQUE

Before reading this section, review "Influential Movements in Decorative Painting," page 15.

Since semiprecious stones are almost always confined to small areas, they are usually painted using a fairly precise French technique. On the rare occasion when a semiprecious stone (usually onyx) is painted on larger areas such as grottos or walls, it should be rendered in a looser, more transparent Italian style. Examples of this approach can still be seen in the ruins of the ancient Roman city of Pompeii, where most of the marble imitations are onyx.

LAYOUT

Incorporating semiprecious stone finishes into the layout of panels and other areas can vary greatly both in marquetry and as insets into other marble surfaces. For guidance, consult books, photographs, and auction catalogs to study as many potential layouts and patterns as you can find.

BASIC PROCEDURE

In terms of preparation and varnishing, the procedure for semiprecious stone is the same as for marble (see page 78). A water-based medium allows you to overglaze almost immediately—an important consideration, since it often takes two or three coats of glaze to achieve the depth needed to simulate most semiprecious stone finishes. Because these finishes are usually worked in small areas, you needn't worry about the fast drying time of a water-based medium.

An oil-based overglazing can also be used, either for onyx or when a longer working time is desired.

Semiprecious Stone Exercises

Most of the recipes in this chapter involve techniques that are also used to render marble (see "Marble Exercises," pages 79–87). When you decide which semiprecious stone recipe you're going to work with, first review its technical notes to determine the particular marble exercises you should practice in preparation.

The surface and medium used for the onyx veining exercise is the same as those used for the marble exercises. Although this exercise relates primarily to "Algerian Onyx" (page 129), it can be applied to some of the other semiprecious stone recipes, and is used in some marble and wood recipes as well (see chapters 2 and 5).

ONYX VEINING

Using reversible water-based glaze (gouache, beer, or watercolor), load a synthetic spalter as you would in preparation for painting a twist (see the exercise on page 85). Move the brush in a downward, trembling motion, producing a slightly squiggly shape (photo 1). Repeat so that the squiggles are parallel to one another and immediately adjacent, varying their coloration and shape slightly, until the surface is full. While the glaze is still wet, smooth out the surface with a badger brush using a figure-eight motion. Once the glaze is dry, moisten the tip of a veinette in water, run the bristles through a metal or plastic pet comb (photo 2), then draw the brush over the surface, following the path of each squiggle while changing it slightly here and there (photo 3). With the badger, smooth the

glaze again, but this time always working from left to right, to produce a ridge—a light, inner veining with a hard edge (photo 4).

When the onyx veining technique is used to paint finishes other than marble or stone, it is referred to as *au dépouille* (animal hide) veining. This term likens the reactivation of the reversible glaze with the moistened veinette with the sloughing of layers of skin that occurs when an animal hide is converted into leather. The onyx veining technique can also be done in an irreversible medium (either acrylics or oils), requiring the veins and ridges within the parallel twists to be painted on rather than reactivated and removed. An example of this approach can be seen in the recipe for "Algerian Onyx" (page 129), which is rendered in acrylics.

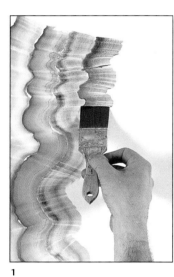

1

2

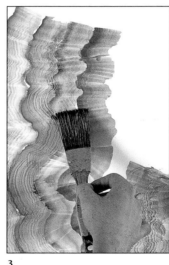

3

4

Lapis Lazuli

Treasured for its beautiful color, lapis lazuli was once ground by artists into a fine powder for the manufacture of ultramarine blue pigment. (Today, that pigment is produced chemically.) Being an expensive and rare semiprecious stone (found mostly in Afghanistan and Chile), its application is limited in area size, but its color is so rich that even when simulated on small pedestals, columns, and panels, its decorative effect is striking.

1. Lightly sand and dust off the cured basecoated surface. Using the glazing brush or synthetic spalter, glaze the surface with **ultramarine blue, Prussian blue,** and a touch of **black,** each in a different zone of the surface and without mixing the colors. Then smooth out each color with the badger brush.

2. While wet, sponge off the surface as shown in the exercise on page 80 to even out the tonality. Proceed to the next step while the surface is wet.

3. Drag a damp but unloaded fringed sea sponge over the surface as shown in the recipe for "Elm, Amboina, and Thuja Burl." Remove paint here and there to create the white streaks characteristic of lapis lazuli. Soften with a badger brush as you work. Let dry.

4. Create some darker areas (in order to accentuate the white ones) by dabbing on some **ultramarine blue** with the synthetic spalter or glazing brush. Soften the newly applied glaze by sponging off these areas, then smooth out with a badger brush. Let dry.

5. Using the sponge-on technique (see page 79), spread a dark blue glaze (**ultramarine blue + Prussian blue + alizarin crimson + a dash of yellow ochre**) across the entire surface, using a fine and open texture. Soften with a badger brush as you work. Let dry.

6. Load a small pointed brush with **white.** Using the techniques shown in the exercise on page 80, add some veins to the white streaks that were made earlier (in step 3), softening with a badger brush as you work. Sponge off the surface here and there. Let dry.

7. With a small flat or pointed brush, add some "golden" speckles using **yellow ochre** (see also "Using Other Media," below). Sponge on some touches of **Prussian blue** in the dark areas and **white** in the light ones. Let dry.

8. Lightly sand and dust off the surface. Varnish with two coats of gloss-finish acrylic polyurethane.

USING OTHER MEDIA

Since the surface areas to which it is applied are usually small (and therefore well suited to the short drying times of water-based media), lapis lazuli is almost never painted in oils. Prior to the development of acrylic paints, decorative painters used a reversible water medium for this finish, either a gouache or beer glaze, which was then sealed with an oil-based overglaze (2 turpentine + 1 oil + drier + **ultramarine blue.**)

Instead of adding golden flecks with a yellow ochre glaze (as in step 7, above), you can apply scraps of real gold leaf (see Chapter 7) or metallic gold paint for added brilliance.

1. Glaze the surface with blue and black, each in a different area. Soften each with a badger brush.

2. Sponge off to even out the tonality, then drag the sponge over certain areas to create white streaks. Soften, then let dry.

3. Reinforce selected areas by dabbing on some ultramarine blue. Sponge off the darkened areas, then smooth out with a badger. Let dry.

4. Sponge on dark blue across the entire surface, using a fine and open texture. Soften. Let dry.

5. Extend the white areas with some veins, then sponge off. Let dry.

6. Add golden speckles, then sponge on touches of blue and white. Let dry.

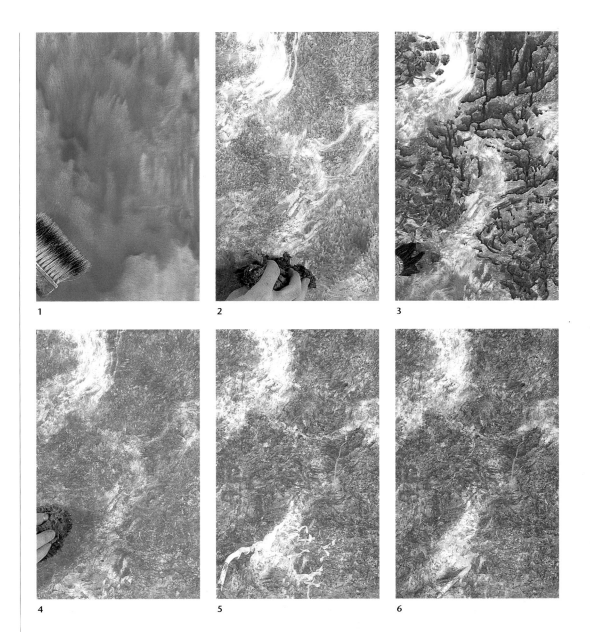

1

2

3

4

5

6

7. The completed finish.

7

Diaspro di Bohemia

Quarried in central Europe, diaspro di Bohemia is actually an unusual form of brèche marble composed of long bands of organic matter and iron oxide. Cut to accentuate its maroon and green stripes and available only in small pieces, it is used to decorate flat or vertical surfaces by fitting together many slices of veneer. Diaspro di Bohemia has been used to striking effect on columns in several Russian palaces.

1. Lightly sand and dust off the cured basecoated surface. With the synthetic spalter, make vertical transparent streaks, using a combination of glaze + **chrome green oxide + alizarin crimson**, OR **yellow ochre + ultramarine blue + red ochre**. Whichever color combination you choose, it should be muted slightly with the complementary color of its dominating hue; for example, if green dominates, use red often. Soften with the badger brush as you work. Let dry. Restripe those parts that need improvement, continuing to soften as you work. Let dry.

2. With the two-header, vein over the first step as shown in the recipe for "Walnut," using a combination of maroon or burgundy tones (**red ochre + alizarin crimson + chrome oxide deep**). Adjust your palette for gradations of tone from warm to cool. The flow should be transparent, creating parallel veins that have a slight undulation. Leave some parts of the background untouched. Soften with a badger brush as you work. Let dry.

3. Repeat step 2, but this time using green tones (**chrome green oxide, yellow ochre, ultramarine blue,** muted with a touch of alizarin crimson or red ochre), that have been varied with some of the other colors on the palette. Continue to paint slightly undulating, parallel veins, leaving some spaces between veinings to allow the background to show through. Soften with the badger brush as you work. Let dry. Select certain parts for emphasis, redefining them with another veining.

4. With a small pointed brush, add some thin transparent veins that descend across the surface as shown in the exercise on page 82, but painting thinner and fewer veins, using a beige tone (**white + chrome green oxide + yellow ochre + red ochre**). Let dry.

5. Give the surface a very transparent overglaze (**chrome green oxide + ultramarine blue + dash of alizarin crimson**) using a synthetic spalter or glazing brush. Smooth out with the badger brush. With a damp spalter, add some moiré effects (see the exercise on page 164) that run almost perpendicular to the streaks. Smooth out with the badger brush, then let dry.

6. Lightly sand and dust off the surface. Varnish with two coats of satin-finish or semigloss acrylic polyurethane.

USING OTHER MEDIA

This recipe can be also be painted in oil using the same palette. After having worked the background in acrylics (as in step 1), apply a transparent glaze (2 turpentine + 1 linseed oil + drier) to the surface, then vein. This procedure will produce a smoother veining, but you will have a longer wait before applying the overglaze.

1. Use a spalter to paint alternating vertical streaks. Soften with a badger brush, then let dry. Repeat to redefine certain areas.

2. Use a square two-header to add vertical streaks, first in maroon (A), then in green (B). Leave some areas of the background exposed. Let dry.

3. Repeat the preceding step to redefine certain areas.

4. Use a small round brush to add a few very thin horizontal fissures. Let dry, overglaze the surface, then manipulate with a moiré effect.

5. The completed finish.

1

2A

2B

3

4

5

Red Jasper

Produced by nature in a wide range of colors and in "cloudy," brèche, and onyx or agate patterns (see page 74), jasper is a generic term for stones made of compact and opaque types of quartz. Red jasper falls into the cloudy category. Some forms are rare and found only in small chunks (including red jasper); others are more plentifully available and found in larger pieces, but are still classified as semiprecious stones, their nonjewelry applications being confined to marquetry and small objects. Given its variety of shapes and colors, jasper is an ideal candidate for faux marquetry, and also lends inspiration to Italian-style marbleizing.

1. Lightly sand and dust off the cured basecoated surface. Use the glazing brush to cover the entire surface with glaze tinted with **white + yellow ochre + burnt sienna,** varying it with other colors from the palette. As shown in the exercise on page 80, sponge off the surface to even out the different zones of color, softening with a badger brush as you work.
2. While the paint is still wet, add a deeper tone (**alizarin crimson + burnt umber + white**) modified with other palette colors by dabbing the surface with the chiqueteur brush as in the exercise on page 87, but more openly, often varying the tonality.
3. As in the exercise on page 80, sponge off while wet, smooth out with a badger brush, and let dry.
4. Load the synthetic spalter with a transparent glaze of **cadmium red + alizarin crimson** + a touch of **chrome orange** to create cloud-shaped fragments (see the exercise on page 86). Soften with a badger brush as you work. Sponge off the outer edges of the light fragments, then smooth out with a badger brush. Let dry.
5. Repeat step 4 using the same or deeper reds to create more depth within the red areas, but without allowing them to become opaque. Let dry.
6. Using a variety of pointed brushes loaded with an off-white glaze (**white + burnt sienna + yellow ochre**), paint a network of thin veins (see page 80) that are distinguished from the light fragments. Apply grayer tones (**white + burnt umber + ultramarine blue + yellow ochre**) to the insides of the light fragments. Soften with a badger brush as you work. Let dry.
7. With pure transparent **white**, redefine and highlight selected edges within the light fragments. Soften with a badger brush as you work. Let dry.
8. Overglaze: Use the synthetic spalter to glaze the entire surface with a transparent red-orange (**cadmium red + chrome orange + alizarin crimson**), alternating with **yellow ochre** or **chrome yellow**. Sponge off the surface as shown in the exercise on page 80, concentrating on the light fragments. Soften with a badger brush as you work. Let dry.
9. Lightly sand and dust off the surface. Varnish with two coats of satin-finish acrylic polyurethane.

USING OTHER MEDIA

This semiprecious stone can also be simulated using oil media, following similar steps. Although a smoother-looking finish will result, you will have long waits between the many overglazings.

In addition to acrylics, reversible water-based media (gouache or beer glaze) may be used, but must be overglazed (see step 8) with an oil glaze (3 turpentine + 1 oil + drier + artists' oil colors).

1. Glaze up the surface with various zones of color, then sponge off to even out the tonality. Soften with a badger brush.

2. Use a chiqueteur brush to dab the surface with a deeper tone, using an open texture. Sponge off, smooth out, and let dry.

3. Use a synthetic spalter to create cloud-shaped fragments. Soften with a badger.

4. Sponge off the outer edges of the light fragments. Smooth out. Let dry.

5. Repeat steps 3 and 4 to create more depth within the red areas. Let dry.

6. Paint a network of thin off-white veins, then apply grayer tones to the interiors of the light fragments. Soften. Let dry.

7. Highlight and redefine the light fragments with white. Soften. Let dry.

8. Overglaze the entire surface, then sponge off, concentrating on the light fragments. Soften. Let dry.

1

2

3

4

5

6

7

8

9. The completed finish.

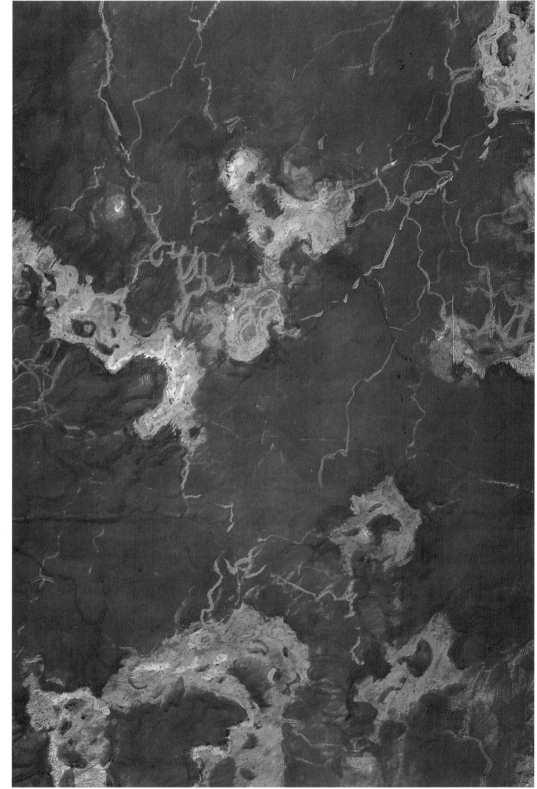

9

Algerian Onyx

A silicate stone from the agate family, Algerian onyx has undulating concentric rings and parallel striations. Since it is composed of crystallized calcium carbonate, a marble formation, it is not actually an onyx, but its shape and design classifies it as such. It has a translucent quality much like alabaster. While nature produces true onyx in small concentrations only, Algerian onyx comes in larger slabs and is used on walls, pedestals, and tabletops. With its many colors and intricate patterns, it is a very decorative stone that varies widely in coloration, ranging from pale beige, to yellows, oranges, reds, greens, and blues.

1. Lightly sand and dust off the cured basecoated surface. Use the glazing brush to cover the surface with glaze #1 (see Technical Notes) + **white + yellow ochre + burnt umber + chrome oxide deep.** While wet, use a spalter or synthetic spalter to create zones of color based on the palette: warm tones of orange and red, and cool tones of blue and green. Use lots of swirling motions, twisting and turning your brush to form the flowing direction and patterns of the onyx.

2. While wet, sponge off the entire surface, following the direction of your underwork. Using the badger, smooth it out. Let dry.

3. Load the fan brush or veinette with a transparent mixture of glaze #2 (see Technical Notes) + **chrome orange + cadmium red + white + a touch of chrome oxide deep** varied with other colors from the palette to impart some warm and some cool tones, and start the veining process as in the exercise on page 119. Use the badger to soften as you work, working the brush across each ring to create a ridge. Let dry.

4. Repeat the previous step using a veinette or a well-worn spalter and a sea sponge and working with only cooler tones (glaze #2 + **white + ultramarine blue + burnt sienna + alizarin crimson**) varied with other colors from the palette. Soften with a badger brush as you work. Let dry.

5. Using an assortment of pointed brushes, start intensifying and refining selected areas, adding some darker edges to reinforce the concentric-rings effect. Choose your palette colors so that the veining harmonizes with its foreground. Soften with a badger brush as you work.

   With a pointed brush dipped in slightly darker tones, create a network of fine veins that runs across the rings (see the exercise on page 82); the smallest veins should hook on the rings. Use a badger brush to soften your work. Let dry.

6. Use a fan brush and an assortment of pointed brushes to add and/or define more rings—but be careful not to create an imbalance and destroy an otherwise good finish by painting too many. Soften as you work. Let dry.

7. Overglazing: Sponge on a glaze as shown in the exercise on page 79, covering the entire surface with transparent off-white (**white + yellow ochre**). To simulate the crystallization that is an important characteristic of onyx, flame certain areas by dragging the sponge across the surface (see the exercise on page 87). Let dry.

8. Use an assortment of pointed brushes dipped in **white + a touch of yellow ochre** to add fissures (see page 82). Emphasize some of the darker veins to create shadow effects. Soften with a badger brush as you work. Let dry.

9. Lightly sand and dust off the surface. Varnish with two coats of satin or semigloss acrylic polyurethane.

USING OTHER MEDIA

This recipe can also be rendered in a reversible water-based medium (either gouache or beer glaze), which must be sealed with shellac before proceeding to step 7.

Following the same steps, this finish can also be painted in oils. The addition of oil-based gloss-finish varnish to the glaze (1 turpentine + 1 linseed oil + 1 oil-based gloss-finish varnish) will make it set faster and impart greater depth to the finish. However, a water-based medium will still permit more overglazings in less time and is far less likely to yellow.

1. Use a spalter to create swirling zones of color.

2. Sponge off the entire surface following the direction of the underwork.

3. Use a fan brush or veinette to add veins that run parallel to the direction of the rings.

4. Repeat using a veinette or a well-worn spalter and a sea sponge, using only cooler tones. Soften as you work. Let dry.

5. Intensify and darken the edges of the rings and create a network of fine veins. Soften as you work. Let dry.

6. Define the veins within selected rings with the fan brush.

7. Soften, working the brush across each ring to create a ridge. Let dry.

8. Sponge on a white glaze over the entire surface, then flame specific areas. Let dry.

9. Add fissures and highlights with a small pointed brush.

10. The completed finish. The stiles and rails are a ribbon onyx that is painted with the same technique, but using more red-orange tones, with straighter, wavelike ripples. The corners are painted with Brazilian onyx, which has a less structured pattern, with deep green and alizarin crimson veins.

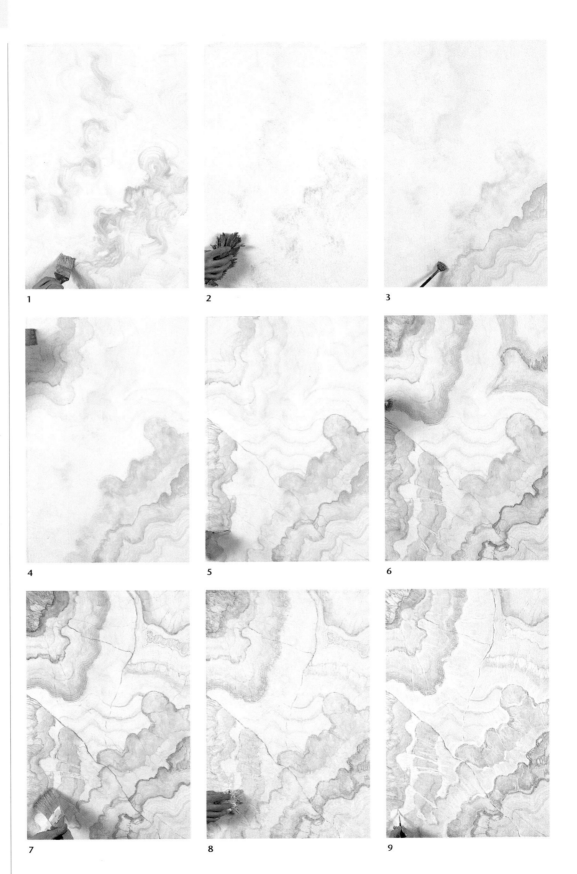

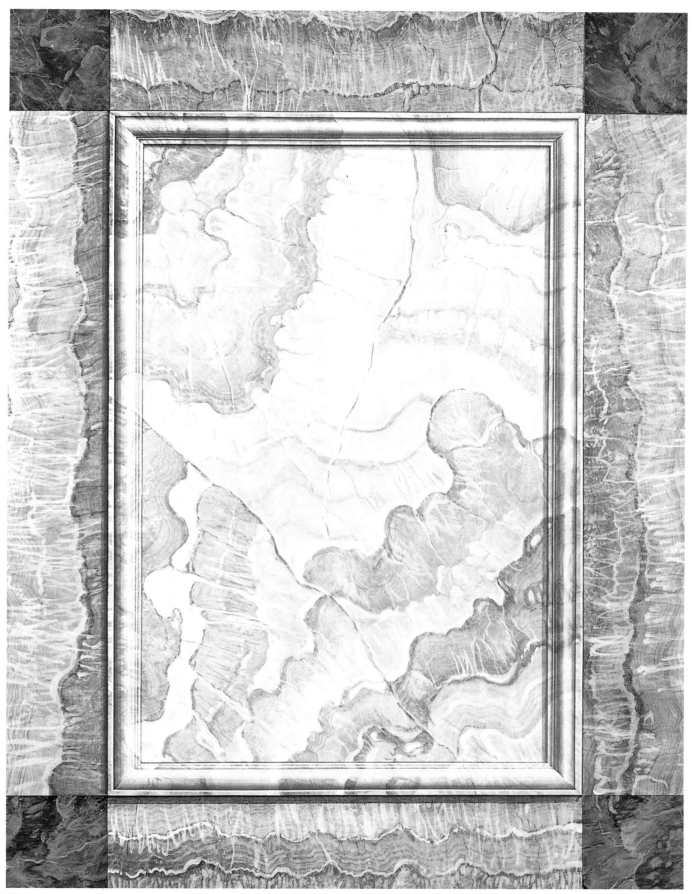

Pietre Dure

TECHNICAL NOTES

Difficulty Rating

4 to 5

System

Water (acrylics)

Basecoat

White alkyd, eggshell finish

Acrylic Glaze

1 matte medium + 2 or 3 water

Palette

Artists' Acrylics

Use as needed to paint each desired finish. Refer to the Palette listing in the Technical Notes for each of the recipes cited in the instructions.

Brushes and Tools

Clear adhesive frisket film

Hobby or craft knife

Hair dryer (optional)

Badger brush

Elephant ear sponge

Assorted small pointed brushes

Black acrylic ink

Refer also to the list of Brushes and Tools in the Technical Notes for each of the recipes cited in the instructions

Exercises

Sponging On (page 79)

Sponging Off (page 80)

Veining with a Small Brush (page 80)

Fissures (page 82)

Onyx Veining (page 119)

Fragmenting or Brèching (page 83)

Spattering (page 86)

Refer also to the list of Exercises in the Technical Notes for each of the recipes cited in the instructions

Marble and semiprecious stone marquetry—decorative work in which elaborate patterns are formed by a mosaic of shaped pieces that is then applied to a surface—is known as *pietre dure*—Italian for "hard stones." It was a specialty of Florentine craftsmen of the 17th and 18th centuries, and major workshops producing this craft remain active in Florence to this day. When rendered with real materials, this exacting technique involves cutting small pieces of marble or semiprecious stone that fit together with the precision of a jigsaw puzzle to form an intricate design. Simulating such patterns also requires great precision to create designs typical of this genre: landscapes, animals, still lifes, geometric and organic shapes, and the most amazing trompe l'oeil renderings—all using the variegation of certain stones to impart remarkable shading effects. Generally produced for tabletops and wall inlays—the form our imitation will take—this time-consuming work is usually executed on a small scale.

For the following recipe, you will use all the techniques of faux marble and semiprecious stone, plus some invented marbles, to get the color effects you desire. For design ideas, images fitting the categories named above, found in all sorts of books and magazines, can provide inspiration. My particular flower motif was copied from a book on *pietre dure*, and the border was inspired by a classical Italian Renaissance pattern.

The image featured in this recipe was developed using a clear frisket film, which is gradually cut away and removed so that each specific element can be painted one by one. A masking technique used with reversible water-based media, which employs isolating coats of shellac to protect elements as they are painted, is shown in the recipe for "Marquetry" (see Chapter 5). Yet another faux *pietre dure* technique paints all the finishes on separate pieces of very thin kraft paper that are precisely cut to fit within a design. These pieces are subsequently assembled and glued on a board or other surface and joined with unifying coats of varnish.

1. Lightly sand and dust off the cured basecoated surface. Transfer your design to the surface, using either the tracing-paper technique or the pounce technique (see Chapter 11). If necessary or desired, use a 5H pencil to retrace the design on the surface. Place frisket adhesive paper over the entire surface; try to avoid creating air bubbles. If the design is too large for one sheet of frisket, overlap the second sheet by 1/2 inch. Burnish the paper slightly to remove any air bubbles.

   Use a pen to mark off with an "X" those pieces of the "puzzle" that you're going to paint first. Using a fine craft or hobby knife, gently cut the frisket film away from the marked areas, being careful not to cut into your painting surface so that the basecoat won't peel off when you remove the frisket.

2. Referring to other recipes on semiprecious stone presented earlier in this chapter, and adding a selection of marble techniques from the previous chapter, begin painting different finishes in different sections of your design. In most cases, do only one or two steps with no overglazing. Select your coloration and zones of tonality as the marquetry artisan would, placing darker sections near lighter ones to create the effects of shadow and transparency. Soften as you work with a badger brush. Let dry.

3. Work an entire element (as shown in the photograph, the yellow iris) before going on to the next, so that you've used all of your palette mixture for that particular motif before the paint dries out. You can speed up the drying process with a hair dryer, enabling you to move along more quickly to another pattern piece next to the one you've just completed. Be careful not to put the dryer too close to the frisket, which might bubble or warp under the heat. Don't bother to mask off a just-completed piece when working on a new piece adjacent to it. Just be sure to use an elephant ear sponge to wipe off

any bleeding or overlap that occurs. Soften with a badger brush as you work. Let dry.

4. On a design such as the one shown, once you've completed a flower, go to the next grouping of the same variety within the same color range. Try to introduce as much texture and variety as possible by painting more veining, more contrast, and more heightened coloration than if you were doing a single panel of one type of marble. Because each motif is small, and there are so many of them, if you start with very muted and similar tones, your finished piece will blend together into a single, monotone panel. To avoid that, remember to create variety and contrast from the beginning. Soften as you work. Let dry.

5. The previous step is repeated until the center motif is finished. The semiprecious stones simulated in the demonstration are lapis lazuli (see page 122), diaspro di Bohemia (page 125), red jasper (page 126), Yellow Sienna (page 93), agates and onyxes (both real and invented), and Violet Brèche (page 111). The border immediately surrounding the central motif is painted with a striped marble (diaspro di Sicilia). Soften as you work. Let dry. Peel off the remaining frisket left on the center motif.

6. Once the center motif was completed, the oval shapes in the frame were painted with an onyx (see the exercise on page 119), softened with a badger brush, then allowed to dry. A petrified wood (similar to diaspro di Bohemia, but with a warmer palette and more fissures) was

created within the vertical shapes. A red brèche (a "fantasy" marble based on the counterpass cut of the Violet Brèche) was painted in the corners. Let dry.

7. The completed center motif was masked off with frisket, and a dark porphyry marble, which was created with a succession of medium to light spatterings (see page 86), was painted in the background. The diamonds on either side were then painted in malachite, which uses a fan brush to paint dark green concentric veins over an intense light blue-green, in a technique somewhat similar to onyx veining (see page 119). The glazes were allowed to dry, then the frisket was peeled off.

8. The band outside the border elements was painted in a Saint Anne marble, which is a brèche marble with a gray-black background and very broken transparent gray fragments painted with a small pointed brush (see the exercise on page 83). Let dry. The band between the center panel and the border elements was painted in an off-white spotted marble. Let dry.

9. Any little defects inside the center motif were touched up and allowed to dry. All the pieces of the motif were then outlined with a hairline rule of black acrylic ink applied with a thin pointed brush or a drafting pen.

10. Lightly sand and dust off the surface. Varnish with two coats of semigloss acrylic polyurethane. If your design is to be used on a tabletop, have it lacquered in a professional shop with a car-grade polyurethane or a good-quality lacquer.

1. Apply adhesive frisket film to the surface. Mark the areas to be painted first with an X. Cut the frisket away from one shape of the motif at a time.

2. Begin painting a different variety of semiprecious stone in each element, completing it before moving on to the next. Continue cutting and removing frisket.

3. Here the surrounding flowers are being painted.

4. The leaves and stems are added and softened.

5. The vase and ornamental forms are developed.

6. The border immediately surrounding the center panel is painted.

7. The corners and ovals of the frame are added.

8. The central motif is masked off and the background painted.

9. The diamond shapes were added and the edges of the elements were cleaned off. The bands surrounding the major elements were painted, and the elements of the central motif were outlined with acrylic ink.

10. The completed finish.

1

2

3

4

5

6

7

8

9

Limestone and Sandstone

Basic to all major building since antiquity, limestone and sandstone remained paramount in construction until the mid-20th century, when concrete replaced both as the material of choice. What these two stones have in common is that both are found almost everywhere the world, and both come in a variety of colors and patterns. In the context of the art of faux, both materials are very suitable for carved sculpture and ornamental architectural embellishment. But how do they differ?

This stairway is graced with a subtle beige interior limestone.

Painting Limestone and Sandstone

Limestone, like marble, is a sedimentary formation composed mostly of calcium carbonate. Much softer than marble, its composition is less dense and compact, and its coarse-grained texture produces a matte finish, even if polished. Being soft, it can be cut by saw and easily carved, making it a prime choice for sculpture. French limestone, a gray, closely grained variety, is the preferred type. Other varieties of limestone come in white, beige, ochre, and red oxide, formed in many patterns, including ribboned, spotted, speckled, and streaked varieties. Some also have fossil encrustations that add to their uniqueness. While quarried in many parts of the world, the limestone most desired for its strength, design, and density comes from France, Italy, England, and North America.

Sandstone, as its name implies, is composed mostly of sand, which is bound with either clay, calcite, silica, or iron oxide, depending on where it's quarried. Granular and porous, it is soft when just cut from the quarry, but hardens considerably when exposed to the elements. Some types can be polished, but only to a matte finish. Like limestone, sandstone comes in a variety of colors and patterns. In contrast to limestone, it is used mainly for exterior construction.

Labor-intensive costs associated with these stones—quarrying, carving or cutting them into blocks, shipping, and installation—make them so expensive to use that since the 19th century the art of faux has replaced real limestone and sandstone in a great many interiors. These imitations are found mainly in entrance halls, lobbies, hallways, and on staircases. The application technique is very easy, it can be executed rapidly, and has great visual impact, turning a simple staircase or lobby into a grand entrance usually associated with such majestic houses as the Palace of Versailles. On exteriors, simulations are occasionally used on new building facades or to match existing, older stonework.

SUITABLE APPLICATIONS

To resemble the real stone and its applications, limestone and sandstone are mostly simulated in blocks (commonly 1 × 2 or 2 × 4 feet × 12 inches thick) for walls and ceilings or in sections devoted to statues or ornaments. Rarely is either seen in slabs (just 2 inches thick). When imitated in blocks for the usual entrance and staircase applications noted above, details such as trompe l'oeil, paneling, molding, and other architectural embellishments are often included. This faux technique is easy to do on high-relief molding and complicated surfaces, because it entails mostly color stippling and some spattering. The only small-scale applications would be bases or pedestals as freestanding elements.

Limestone and sandstone are often painted in landscape or other murals, and are excellent for rendering such architectural details as columns, pedestals, moldings, and carved ornaments.

CHOOSING THE RIGHT TECHNIQUE

Begin by reviewing "Influential Movements in Decorative Painting," page 15, for an overview of faux finishing techniques. Because of the simplicity of limestone/sandstone techniques, there are not as many style distinctions as in faux marble. Mostly, the differences lie in how blocking is laid out. There are two main schools: The French technique uses more rigid, evenly spaced blocking, with very straight dividing lines and minimal textural effects; the Italian technique is looser, using unevenly sized blocks, joint lines painted freehand, and a more patterned stone with lots of color effects—in other words, a more theatrical look. Avoid mixing styles. For example, three-dimensional architectural embellishment on French-style limestone should not be rendered in a loose, Italian-style technique.

PREPARING THE SURFACE

Because limestone and sandstone are granular in texture and always have a matte finish, when these qualities are simulated, they will mask surface imperfections—so you can be less precise with your preparation. Your surface doesn't have to be very smooth; just be sure it's fully covered. The basepaint can be a flat- or eggshell-finish alkyd, or an eggshell-finish latex, depending on the technique. Whenever possible, the basepaint should be rolled on rather than brushed on. When rendering a granular texture, the "orange peel" or pock marks left by a cloth roller will blend in with the finish better than the bristle marks of a brush. Sand the final coat of basepaint well so that the surface will have a good tooth for the heavy-texture paint (see page 140). This enhanced paint mixture is used to create the grainy texture characteristic of certain stone finishes. Once dry, the heavy-textured paint is usually glazed over with an acrylic glaze (1 acrylic matte medium + 2 water). Note that some stones can be simulated without the granular texture; others only with the texture and no overglazing. As always, make samples to experiment with materials that you don't know well, and especially study thickness and drying to avoid shrinkage and crackling.

LAYOUT

The block layout is most often set down before the decorative painting begins. I lay it out on paper first when it is a complicated area, then I trace it down with a 5H pencil, plus I use templates for spacing. Using a snap line (see page 48) loaded with a mixture of ground chalk or talcum and ground charcoal, I snap the horizontal lines, then trace over them with a 5H pencil so I can wipe off the chalk lines. I repeat the procedure with all vertical lines. If I want to establish the joint lines with tape, I use a thin pinstriping tape (see page 140). Otherwise, I apply my paint over the entire surface; then, once dry, I create a grid with a snap line and pencil as described above, then paint the joint lines with a striping brush and striping edge (see "Striping" in Chapter 11).

Another technique consists of applying a heavier, slower-drying textured basepaint (either one that includes more compound and retarding gel or an oil-based compound) over the surface without previously laying out a grid. Stipple the paint; when it's halfway dry, gently snap your lines or use a sharpened piece of chalk to lay out the grid. Using a flat-head screwdriver, score the surface to create the joints.

As for the design and size of your stone-block layout, the basic examples provided here should be supplemented with other documents that you search out in books and magazines to give you a broad perspective on the many effects achieved by stonemasons.

Limestone and Sandstone Exercises

Before starting a limestone or sandstone recipe, review the exercises for faux marble (pages 79–87) and semiprecious stone (page 119). It's most important to practice the appropriate ones before starting a recipe.

There is no set practice order; let the recipe you're working on dictate the sequence. Also review layout information (page 139) as well as the exercises for "Stippling" (in Chapter 6) and "Striping" (in Chapter 11).

TAPING A BLOCK LAYOUT

Using a 5H pencil, lay out your surface with rectangular, horizontally oriented blocks (1 foot high × 2 feet wide is a good average) traced in very thin lines. Place pinstriping tape over all the horizontal pencil lines (photo 1), and then over the vertical lines, using a hobby or craft knife to cut the tape. Don't run your blade over the tape; hold the tape down with the blade, then pull the tape *away* from the wall (photo 2). Burnish the tape with the back of a five-in-one.

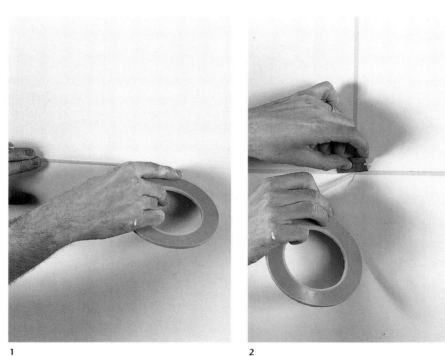

1

2

HEAVY-TEXTURE BASECOAT

In order to obtain the granular texture of certain types of limestone and sandstone, a modified basepaint is stippled onto the surface. The standard heavy-texture basepaint is a mixture of flat latex paint, whiting, and Permalite (see photo), which can then be tinted with artists' acrylics, vinyl paints, or universal tints. A water-based paint is more convenient to use for its rapid drying time, ease of application, and nonyellowing finish. (Because stone is most often laid out in blocks, it's easy to stop at joint lines on a large walls, so a rapid drying time is not really a problem.) The whiting can be replaced by acrylic modeling paste or even joint compound. Available at most paint stores, Permalite is a sandlike material made of plastic resin that can be added to paint to heighten its texture; finely sieved sand or sieved oak sawdust are satisfactory substitutes.

The heavy-texture basecoat is a variation on the "ropey" and heavy-bodied basecoats used to create patinas and aged textures (see Chapter 6).

Interior Limestone of Paris

"French limestone of Paris" is the generic term often applied to all those lobby walls and staircases of Parisian buildings that are gray, buff, or beige with white or gray joint lines. For the most part, those interiors are *not* real; faux limestone has long been the preferred treatment for such settings.

This technique, which is often used in France, is quite simple, economical, and effective: often just a stippling of a grayish paint that is flat, heavy, and smooth, with white stripes added to simulate joint lines. The three-dimensional stippling produces a finish akin to limestone's slightly rough texture, so that painted textures may be kept to a minimum. However, to copy other varieties of limestone, you can enhance the recipe and add more texture. Whichever version you choose, the layout of the stone should be carefully planned first, so you know just how you are going to block out your surface before painting it.

1. Lightly sand and dust off the cured basecoated surface. Lay out and tape the blocks as shown in the exercise on page 140.
2. In a bucket, prepare the heavy paint mixture (see Technical Notes), then add **raw umber + yellow ochre + raw sienna** to make it a light beige. (The heavy paint should be lighter than the basecoat if you want dark grout lines. If white grout lines are preferred, you need to use a white basecoat so that your heavy beige paint becomes the darker color.) With a glazing brush, apply the mixture heavily using a stipple motion, going over everything, including the tape. Limit the area to what you can stipple (see step 3) before the paint sets.
3. While the surface is still wet, stipple it with the stippling brush (see page 206); the finer the stipple, the finer the grain will be. Wipe the brush often so that it doesn't get clogged up.
4. When the surface is half dry (dry to the touch, but soft if you press on it), remove the tape carefully, using a small palette knife to lift the tape ends. This

procedure is done before the surface is totally dry to avoid cracking and peeling the paint as the tape is lifted. When the tape is removed, the surface will have two planes: the joint lines are flat and the stone blocks are raised. Let dry completely before proceeding to the next step.

5. With a sanding block, work over the entire surface vigorously to get rid of any unwanted heavy grain, and also to ensure that it is smooth enough not to be rough to the touch. In the lower part of the sample, I have striped over the joint lines with white so that you can observe the same stone with dark and light joints. In reality, if I knew I wanted white joint lines, I would have started with a white basecoat. This example also demonstrates that you can change joint-line colors without repainting the entire room, but you must do it before overglazing. Let dry.
6. Overglazing: Apply the acrylic glaze (see Technical Notes) tinted with **raw umber,** alternating it with **yellow ochre, raw sienna, burnt sienna** or **burnt umber.** Create zones of color—*not* isolated blotches—over the entire surface, including the joint lines. If you're working on the wall in sections (a grouping of several blocks at a time), you can apply the glaze right up to the edge of a joint line before proceeding to the next.
7. While the surface is still wet, sponge it off as shown in the exercise on page 80, then smooth it out with a badger brush. Should you prefer more varied and contrasting tones in your stone, overglaze selected blocks with the mixture from step 6 after this step dries.
8. Spatter the surface as shown in the exercise on page 86, using the spattering brush with **raw umber + ultramarine blue** varied with other palette colors. Let dry.
9. Load the sea sponge with a transparent off-white glaze (**white + yellow ochre**). Working block by block, sponge the

glaze onto the surface as shown in the exercise on page 79. Let dry.

10. This recipe doesn't usually require varnishing, but for added protection, you may apply one coat of flat-finish varnish, either water- or oil-based, preferably by spraying it on to avoid leaving brush marks.

USING OTHER MEDIA

Until the 1950s, this finish was painted in oils, using zinc white and whiting to mix the heavy paint. In this case, the only advantage an oil-based medium offers over water-based is that it gives you longer working time to score the joint lines, because it takes longer to dry.

1. Apply the heavy paint mixture in a stipple motion over the entire surface, including the taped joint lines.

2. Stipple the wet surface.

3. When the surface is dry to the touch (but still soft), carefully remove the tape. Let dry, then sand vigorously.

4. If you want to change the color of the joint lines, they can be striped over at this point, before overglazing.

5. Apply glazes in various earth colors in zones over the entire surface.

6. Sponge off the wet surface.

7. Spatter, then let dry.

8. Working block by block, sponge on a transparent glaze. Let dry.

9. The completed finish. Dark joints are shown in the top half of the sample and light ones in the bottom.

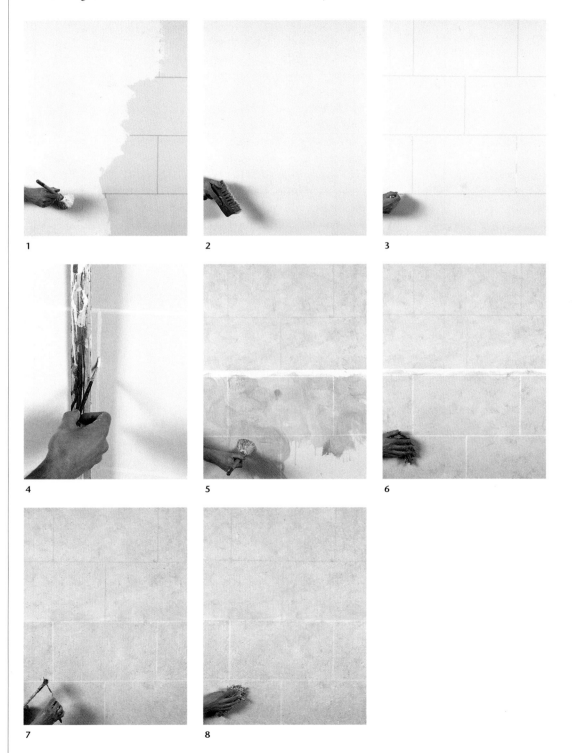

9

Exterior Sandstone and Limestone

TECHNICAL NOTES

Difficulty Rating

1.5

System

Water (acrylics)

Basecoat

White OR beige (white +
raw umber + yellow ochre)
alkyd, eggshell finish

Heavy Paint Mixture

1 white gesso + 1/2 whiting +
1/4 joint compound + a little
Permalite or sieved oak
sawdust

Acrylic Glazes

Glaze #1: 1 matte medium +
1 water

Glaze #2: 1 matte medium +
2 water

Palette

Artists' Acrylics

White

Yellow ochre

Raw sienna

Burnt sienna

Raw umber

Burnt umber

Ultramarine blue

Brushes and Tools

Glazing brush

Wide large-tooth graining
comb

#100 spalter

Sea sponge

Spattering (small glazing)
brush

Assorted pointed brushes

Exercises

Combing (page 167)

Sponging Off (page 80)

Spattering (page 86)

Taping a Block Layout
(page 140)

Sponging On (page 79)

Striping (page 303)

As noted earlier, sandstone is generally used on exteriors, and limestone on interiors, but that is not an absolute rule. Although it's sometimes hard to determine whether the material is actually sandstone or limestone, if the stone is very rough, pock-marked, and with grains of sand imbedded in it, most likely it is sandstone. In this recipe, I made the stone rough and with aged joints of the kind often seen on structures built prior to World War II. By entitling this recipe "Exterior Sandstone and Limestone," I mean to indicate the interchangeability of the two. But mainly, by incorporating rough cuts and effects of aging, I'm demonstrating a technique that resembles stone found on exteriors. In addition, the base of the sample simulates sandstone cut with a handsaw.

EXTERIOR SANDSTONE

1. Lightly sand and dust off the cured basecoated surface. Using a glazing brush in a stipple motion, cover the base with the heavy paint mixture (see Technical Notes) tinted with **white + raw sienna + yellow ochre + raw umber + a touch of burnt umber.**
2. While the surface is still wet, drag a wide large-tooth graining comb across each block in parallel strokes made at a slight angle. Wipe off the comb after each pass to prevent the teeth from clogging. As in the exercise on page 167, leave tiny, parallel, plowlike marks or furrows, all going in one direction—but change direction for each stone. With a spalter or disposable brush, smooth out the surface slightly, working in the direction of the furrows. Let dry.
3. Overglaze: Mix glaze #1 (see Technical Notes) tinted with **raw umber + raw sienna** and dab it over the blocks with the glazing brush. While the surface is still wet, use the glazing brush to add some streaks of **raw umber** and **burnt umber.**
4. Working on the still-wet surface and following the direction of the combed grain, sponge off the block as shown in the exercise on page 80. Let dry. Spatter the

surface as shown in the exercise on page 86, using the spattering brush dipped in **raw umber + burnt umber.** Let dry.
5. Using #150 sandpaper affixed to a sanding block, sand down only the top edges of your sawtooth markings—those furrows that you made in step 2. Sanding will whiten the edges of the furrows, and that contrast will make them stand out more clearly, heightening the dimensional effect.

EXTERIOR LIMESTONE

For a simulation of exterior limestone, a heavy-consistency paint is not used. Instead, the texture is produced solely through painting technique.

1. Begin by laying out your blocks with a thin 5H pencil, using a snap line or level for guidance. Tape off every other stone as in the exercise on page 140. (Note that I have already completed the upper part, leaving the last square for this demonstration.)
2. With a glazing brush, cover the block in a stipple texture, using glaze #1 (see Technical Notes) tinted with **white + raw sienna + raw umber.** On the wet surface, use a spalter or disposable brush loaded with **burnt sienna + raw umber** or **ultramarine blue + white + burnt umber,** painting mostly parallel streaks to lend a definite direction to the block.
3. Working in the same direction, while the surface is still wet, sponge off the block as in the exercise on page 80, leaving perceptible streaks. Following the same direction, smooth out the surface with a badger. Let dry. You may add more transparent sponging to the streaks in selected blocks, which will reinforce the realistic differences among them. Let dry.
4. Make a transparent off-white glaze by tinting glaze #2 (see Technical Notes) with **white + yellow ochre.** Sponge the glaze over the entire surface, proceeding block by block without taping between them, applying the glaze over the joint lines as well, following the respective direction of each stone. Let dry.

5. Load the spattering brush with a medium-gray glaze (glaze #2 + **white** + **raw umber** + **burnt umber** + **raw sienna** + **ultramarine blue**) and spatter the entire surface as shown in the exercise on page 86. Let dry. Using the same gray tone and a pointed synthetic brush, simulate the characteristic tiny elongated gouges that run through the stone here and there. Let dry. Darken the gray glaze with **raw umber** + **burnt umber**; with a pointed brush, use it to shadow the upper parts of the gouges. Let dry. Using the same brush dipped in the off-white glaze (see step 4), paint highlights along the undersides of some of the gouges. (See Chapter 11, "Trompe l'Oeil," for more information on shading and highlighting.) Let dry.

6. Using a pointed brush loaded with the medium-gray glaze, paint joint lines between the blocks. Handle the brush loosely, adjusting the pressure you apply as you paint, so that the width of the lines will vary, creating an open, freehand look. Place shadows and highlights along the joints using a striping edge and the same tones as in the previous step. Let dry.

7. Apply one coat of flat-finish oil- or water-based varnish if desired.

USING OTHER MEDIA

While there is no particular advantage to using an oil glaze, one can be used in this recipe, replacing the sea sponge with a chiqueteur brush.

1. Exterior sandstone: Stipple on the heavy paint mixture, then comb the wet surface with parallel strokes. Change the direction of the furrows slightly for each block. Let dry.

2. Dab a dark transparent glaze on each block, then add some darker streaks.

3. While still wet, sponge off each block following the direction of the combed grain; let dry. Spatter the surface, then let dry.

4. Sand down the tops of the furrows to whiten their edges.

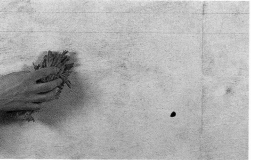

1

2

3

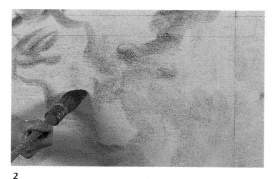

4

1. Exterior limestone:
Stipple on the glaze, then add parallel streaks to the wet surface to create a definite direction.

2. While still wet, sponge off each block, leaving perceptible streaks. Smooth out, then let dry.

3. Sponge on an off-white glaze over the entire surface, following the direction of each stone. Let dry.

4. Paint the gouges that run through the stone. Let dry.

5. Add shadows to the tops of the gouges with a darker glaze. Let dry.

6. Add highlights along the undersides of some of the gouges. Let dry.

7. Loosely paint the joint lines between the blocks.

8. Use a striping edge to add shadows and highlights.

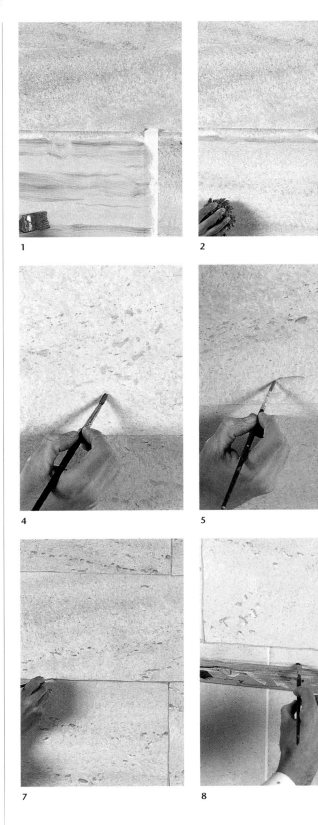

1

2

3

4

5

6

7

8

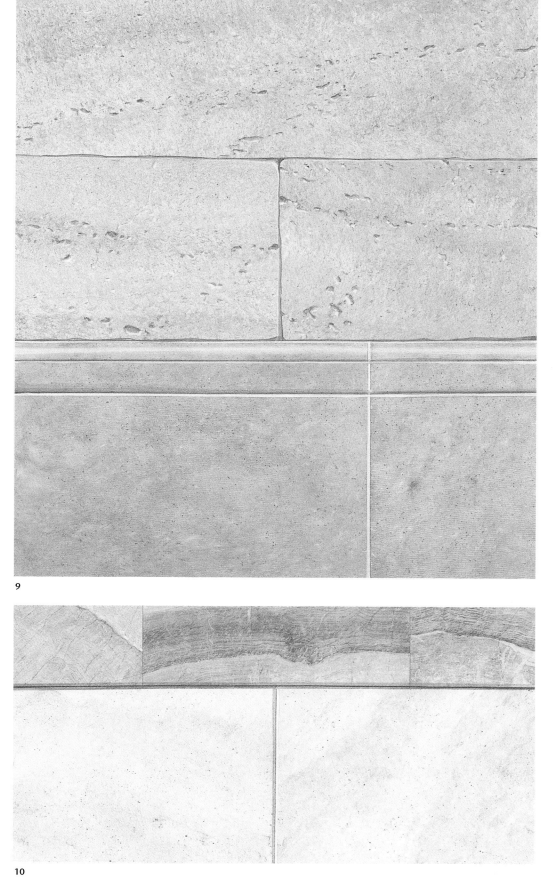

9. The completed finishes: exterior limestone (top) and exterior sandstone (bottom).

10. Variation: Egyptian sandstone (the inlay portion of the sample below left) is a more colorful and more highly textured variation on exterior sandstone. Its colorful stripe, which is reminiscent of ribbon onyx, is applied in streaks with a teeth spalter or disposable brush, sponged off with a worn sea sponge, stippled to refine the grain of the stone, then spattered with a dark transparent glaze. A transparent off-white overglaze is then sponged on one stone at a time following the direction of the streaks. The large blocks are painted with a textured limestone. This combination of finishes would work well in either interior or exterior settings.

9

10

Wood

Trees are comprised primarily of wood, a solid, fibrous material. Though each species of wood exhibits its own distinctive physical characteristics, diversity can always be found not only within a species but within a single tree as well. Because the growth of a tree is continuous, its wood serves as a chronicle of its existence, including its age and history of disease and injury.

The art of simulating wood with paint is referred to as faux wood, graining or wood graining, and faux bois. In order to successfully duplicate a wood's subtle beauty, decorative painters must understand the elements of the tree from which it is taken, the methods by which it is cut and laid out, the configurations of its various grain patterns, and the nuances of its color.

The panels, stiles, rails, and moldings in this library feature a medium caramel color faux walnut with book-match figures.

Relationships Between Cut and Grain

HEARTWOOD

BARK   SAPWOOD

The transversal or ring cut reveals the primary elements of a tree trunk: heartwood, sapwood, and bark.

When the trunk of a tree is cut *transversally*—that is, perpendicular to its length—a series of concentric rings is exposed, each representing the sap that accumulates between the bark and the outermost growth of wood every year, so that the age of a tree can be calculated by counting its rings. Also known as the *ring cut*, this view of a tree displays the three elements of its trunk:

- *The heartwood* consists of the rings closest to the center of the trunk, and is therefore the oldest as well as the hardest and darkest part of the wood. The hardwood is most frequently imitated by decorative painters.
- *The sapwood* is the part of the trunk between the heartwood and the bark (see below). As each new layer of sapwood is formed, the previous one dries and becomes part of the heartwood. As the youngest part of the tree, the sapwood is also the softest and the lightest in color, so it is generally not used for either woodworking or cabinetmaking (making fine furniture), and consequently is not imitated by decorative painters.
- *The bark,* which is the outermost layer of the trunk, acts as a sort of protective sheath, shielding the wood from such external hazards as the weather, insects, and other potential damage. As with sapwood, the bark is never used for woodworking or cabinetmaking, nor is it rendered by decorative painters.

CUTTING METHODS

The way that wood is cut from the trunk determines which of its grain patterns, or *figures,* is revealed (see "Figure or Grain Patterns," below). There are four primary cuts of wood:

- The *horizontal cut* (also called the *crosscut* or *through-and-through cut)* is the most common cutting method, as it produces the best surface designs and yields the least amount of waste. This cut produces the *figure grain* (also called the *heartgrain)* and the *straight grain* (also referred to as

the *side grain.)* Depending on the part of the tree that is being cut, the horizontal cut can produce a number of other figures (see "Figure or Grain Patterns," below).
- With the *quarter-sawn cut,* each quarter of the trunk is sawn into boards at a 45-degree angle. This cut produces a beautiful grain pattern called *silver grain* or *crossfire.* Because the quarter-sawn cut is particularly wasteful (and thus more expensive), yielding only a few usable boards, it is usually reserved for those species of wood in which the silver grain is highly visible, traditionally oak (see page 185).
- Another type of horizontal cut, the *veneer cut* slices the trunk into nearly paper-thin sheets of wood called *veneers,* which are then laminated or glued to cheaper hardwoods. This cutting method is a good way to get the most out of a piece of wood, and is frequently used on expensive woods such as burls and certain other species. The veneer cut makes it possible to arrange grain in the mirror-image pattern of the book-match layout (see page 155).
- *Rotary sawing* clamps the trunk on an axle and rotates it against a blade, peeling away a veneer in one continuous piece, much like a roll of paper toweling. This cut produces a soft, strange figure that is considered unattractive by both cabinetmakers and decorators, and therefore is not imitated by decorative painters. Rotary-sawn veneers are usually used to finish plywood.

FIGURE OR GRAIN PATTERNS

Unlike marble, a wood's natural color can be altered by staining it, making it easy, for example, to mistake a red-stained walnut for a cherry. Therefore, the only reliable way to identify a wood is by observing the configurations of its grain patterns. Depending on how and from what part of a tree the wood is cut, each pattern will vary, even within the same species. As a result, decorative painters must spend a great deal of time studying the grain patterns of each type of wood, so that they can imitate them on large areas without repeating the same figures over and over again, and without having to refer to a real piece of wood.

Except for the silver grain, the horizontal cut produces all of the following grain patterns, which are common to most species of wood:

- The *figure grain* or *heartgrain* is composed of rounded, elongated, more or less concentric diamond shapes. The shapes don't align perfectly because trees don't grow perfectly straight. When a trunk is cut horizontally, the concentric rings of the heartwood are cut at different points, creating the pattern of the figure grain. Each species of wood has a different figure grain, and the figure grain of each tree is as unique as a signature.
- The *straight grain* or *side grain* occurs where the rings of the heartwood extend out toward the sapwood, creating a series of straighter, parallel lines that show a slight movement. The straight grain always appears on either side of the figure grain.
- *Knots*, which are small, dark, round spots of various sizes similar to miniature ring cuts, occur at the start of a branch or a root, or are caused by insect bites. The parallel lines of the straight grain pass on either side of a knot, outlining its contour. Wood artisans, who generally consider knots to be imperfections unless they are extremely small, will often reject a knotty plank of wood. However, there are some instances in which knots are desirable—in those species that are characterized by an abundance of knots, such as bird's-eye maple; in all burl and root cuts (see page 152); and within the figure grains of certain woods—so they are permitted in decorative painting as long as they are done discreetly or are characteristic of a particular species.

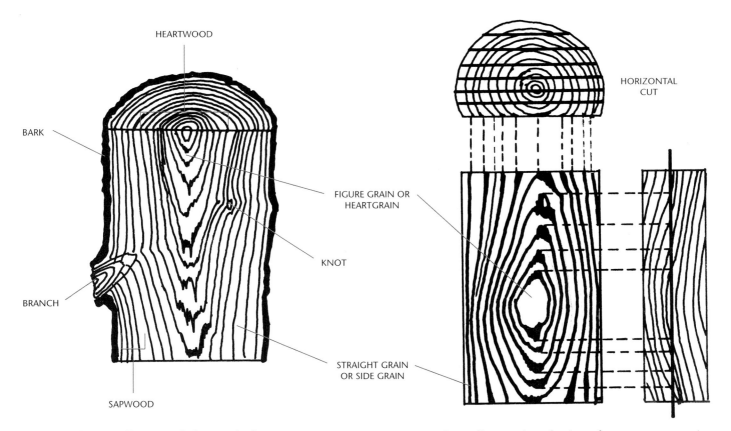

A horizontally cut trunk showing the figure grain or heartgrain and the straight or side grain.

Depending on where the rings of a tree are cut, a variety of figure and side grain patterns are produced.

- The *burl* is a protuberance on the side of the tree, a reaction of the fibrous tissue to a wound or bruise, or from insect bites. Most species of wood have them, but only a few are spectacular enough to be cut. (See "Elm, Amboina, and Thuja Burl," page 178.)
- Visible only in quarter-sawn wood, *silver graining* (also called *crossfire* or *dapple)* consists of overlapping flakelike shapes in a range of sizes arranged in a tight formation that runs counter to the direction of the figure and straight grains. These shapes, which are harder and more lustrous than the surrounding wood, are created by cutting through a network of hardened clots of sap. Though most quarter-sawn woods feature some silver graining, oak exhibits the most distinct example of this pattern (see page 185).
- The *feather, crotch,* or *flame figure* occurs where two major branches split off the main trunk. When this site is cut horizontally, a flamelike shape is produced within the grain. The best examples of the feather figure are usually found in mahogany (see page 193) and chestnut.
- The *root* is the part of the tree that extends below the ground to extract nourishment from the soil. Cutting the root of certain species produces a very intricate figure with a lot of knots, similar in appearance to the burl. Of course, all species have a root figure, but only a few, such as oak, walnut, and ash, are used in cabinetmaking. Note that a *pollard cut,* which is taken from the clustered branches at the top of a trunk to produce a dense, knotty surface design, is often difficult to distinguish from a root cut.

SAP ACCUMULATIONS

In addition to the various grain patterns described above, accumulations of transparent sap are also visible in cut wood. Decorative painters recreate these effects by manipulating a final transparent overglazing with a variety of brushes, mainly spalters and badgers. These effects are the hallmark of fine wood graining.

- *Moiré* are waves or ripples caused by a slowdown of the flow of a tree's sap due to a narrowing or curving of the wood fibers. There are four types of moiré: (1) the basic moiré, or moiré effect; (2) the crisscross moiré; (3) the small moiré or fiddleback; and (4) the butterfly and cat's eyes, which occur only above and below knots or within the heart of the figure grain. Moiré are particularly pronounced in bird's-eye maple (see page 174), walnut (page 181), mahogany (page 190), and pine.
- *Crosspores* can be seen within the sap layer (over the straight graining) of certain hardwoods (oak and walnut) and in exotic woods such as mahogany, lemon, satinwood, and zebrawood. They often occur with small moirés.
- The *spray* or *flame* of the feather figure has a corresponding shape in the sap layer that occurs directly over it. An outstanding example of this effect can be seen in feather mahogany (page 193).

TYPES OF WOOD

Wood can generally be categorized into one of following five groups, which reflect a combination of woodworking and decorative painting terminology.

Hardwoods are used in carpentry and cabinetmaking. Oak (see page 185), walnut (page 181), elm, ash, and chestnut are all examples of hardwoods. This category is subdivided into three categories:

- *White woods* are used to make standard casework and cabinets. Maple, poplar, birch, beech, and horse chestnut are just a few examples of white woods.
- *Fruitwoods* such as pear, cherry, prune, and apple are usually used to make fine furniture.
- *Exotic woods* are used to make fine cabinetry, furniture, and marquetry. Mahogany (page 190), rosewood, palisander, ebony, lemon, teak, satinwood (page 171), bird's-eye maple (page 174), and all varieties of burl (page 178) are considered exotic woods.

Softwoods (also referred to as resinous woods), which include pine, pitchpine, and cedar, are used in certain cabinetry and carpentry work.

The parallel lines of the straight grain pass on either side of a knot, outlining its contour.

KNOTS

QUARTER-SAWN CUT

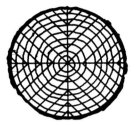

SILVER GRAINING

Quarter-sawing, which cuts each quarter of a trunk into boards at a 45-degree angle, yields silver graining (also called crossfire or dapple), a figure most clearly visible in oak.

The feather or crotch figure occurs where two major branches split off the main trunk.

FLAME OR SPRAY

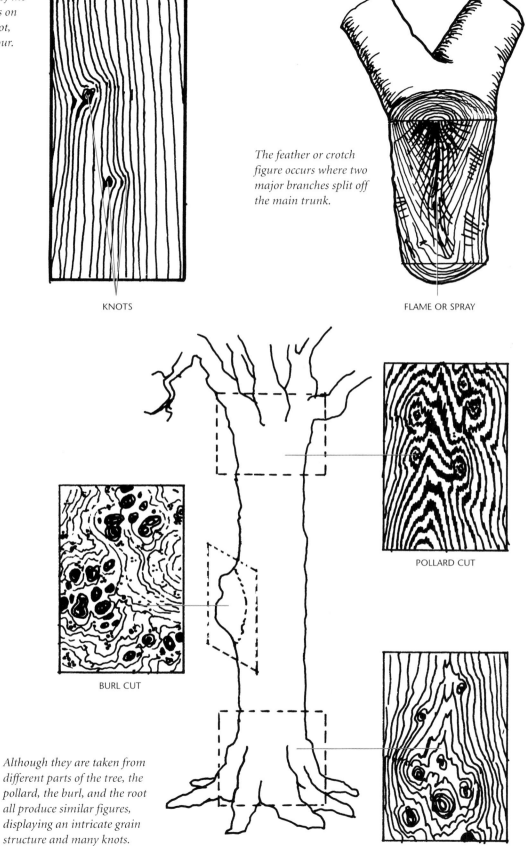

POLLARD CUT

BURL CUT

ROOT CUT

Although they are taken from different parts of the tree, the pollard, the burl, and the root all produce similar figures, displaying an intricate grain structure and many knots.

Suitable Applications

Wood graining is a fairly recent development in decorative painting. There are a few examples from ancient Egypt, mainly sarcophagi painted with rare, precious woods. During the 17th century in Holland, when the Dutch navy had reached the height of its power, oak was reserved almost exclusively for shipbuilding, which boosted its price and created a shortage. Recognizing the desirability of such a scarce commodity, affluent Dutch had the doors to their homes grained with faux oak as a status of their wealth.

But apart from these isolated examples, wood graining was more or less invented in Europe—specifically, France, England, and Belgium—during the 19th century. As with most forms of decorative painting, wood was initially imitated for economic reasons. At the time, trends in interior design required the use of such rare and expensive exotic woods as mahogany, rosewood, palisander, and various types of burl, and it was easier and less expensive to repaint doors and moldings with faux wood than to have them replaced. For legions of less ambitious (and less wealthy) clients in England and France, having a door painted with a comparatively common wood such as oak or walnut was less costly than having one milled. Also, since paint was a better preservative than varnish, wood doors were grained after they were painted so they would still be perceived as wood.

The quality of the wood graining at the time was such that it was almost impossible to distinguish the real from the painted. It was not unusual for an apprentice painter to spend as long as ten years studying and painting oak before he learned any other species. Neither the caliber of training nor the craftsmanship of wood graining is as high today as it was in the 19th century, largely the result of an extended period of neglect that began after World War II (see page 16). Since the 1980s, however, faux wood has become increasingly popular for a number of reasons, including its economic, decorative, and novelty value. Also, many countries have passed laws protecting such exotic woods as Cuban mahogany, satinwood, and rosewood,

providing yet another persuasive argument for imitating rare woods with paint.

Timeless and versatile, wood works well in almost any style of decor and color scheme, from dark, Victorian-style wood paneling, to the art deco elegance of rosewood inlaid with ebony, to the spare, modern beauty of light or bleached walnut or oak. Whereas most marbles are perceived as cold, wood is almost always felt to be warm and inviting. It is recommended that decorative painters study a range of interior styles so that they can make informed decisions about how to use wood graining to its best advantage within a particular setting. In general, dark woods such as oak, walnut, and mahogany presented in a paneled layout suggest a masculine environment, such as a gentlemen's club or a pub, while light woods are better suited to living rooms and dining rooms because they create a more open effect.

Naturally, wood graining can be applied to any milled work or architectural detailing—including panels, moldings, doors, windows, pedestals, and columns—as well as to furniture and small objects such as boxes, though it may be difficult to apply to intricately carved surfaces. As with marble, wood graining should not be applied to anything that wouldn't normally be made out of wood, although it is acceptable to grain such hardware as metal grills or elevator doors so that it blends with an existing installation of wood.

Unlike marble, different species of wood are generally not used in the same installation; only in inlay, marquetry, and furniture do different woods appear together. Even when working with a single species of wood, a cabinetmaker will try to use similar boards of the same cut, and avoid using different cuts of the same wood (for example, never placing silver graining next to figure graining) even though such an arrangement might be highly decorative.

LAYOUT

The dimensions of a board or plank of wood are limited by the size of the tree trunk from which it is cut. For example, a tree that is 4 feet in diameter will yield at its widest point a 2½- to 3-foot-wide board, after the sapwood and bark have been removed. As a result, a large panel must be divided up into several smaller boards, usually of equal width. Sometimes a smaller area, such as a panel within a door, is divided into two unequal-sized boards whose dimensions are generally equivalent to two-thirds and one-third of the width of the space. Although there are no standard lengths, a maximum of 12 feet is recommended. It is important to note that some types of wood are available only in boards of specific dimensions—for example, burl is generally cut into veneers no larger than 1½ feet square—so your painted panels should reflect the specifications that would be used in an actual installation.

The layout should always be drawn or otherwise indicated directly on the surface, so that its design can be developed within specific parameters. In general, the central panels should feature figure graining, while the stiles and rails should be composed almost exclusively of straight graining with only partial (half or one-third) figure grain visible (see pages 160–61). In contrast to marble, the stiles frame the rails. Refer to the drawing below and study books and magazines to obtain more information on the subject, especially when attempting to recreate the proportions, layout, and types of wood used during a particular period.

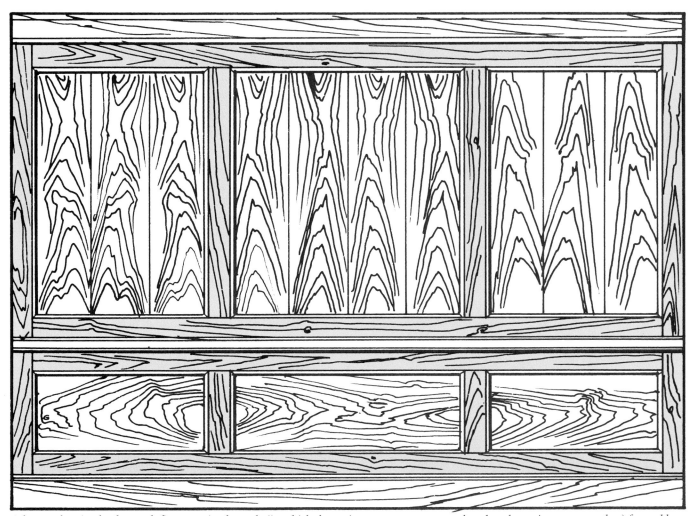

A layout showing book-match figure-grained panels (in which the grain patterns are arranged so that they mirror one another) framed by mainly straight-grained stiles and rails.

CHOOSING THE RIGHT TECHNIQUE

Before reading this section, review "Influential Movements in Decorative Painting," page 15.

For wood graining, I favor the French approach over the Italian. Unlike marble, which usually involves a wide range of colors and forms, wood is relatively limited in color and design, essentially precluding the broader, looser interpretations of the Italian technique. In fact, an entire room wood-grained using a purely decorative Italian-style approach might seem amateurish without a heightened emphasis of certain physical characteristics—the figure grain, knots, and moiré—a variation of the palette, and the addition of ornamentation such as inlay. In general, wood graining painted exclusively with water-based media (either gouache, acrylics, or beer glaze) and in just one or two steps would also be considered an Italian-style approach, because the limited working times of these media require accomplishing a greater impact in fewer steps. The wood recipes in this book combine realistic French-style rendering with a layering of media, by applying oil-based media over reversible water-based media (either gouache or beer glaze), or vice versa.

Distinct from both the French and Italian approaches is *colonial graining*. This so-called "naïve" or "primitive" graining technique, which was developed by settlers during the colonial period of the United States, exaggerates the characteristics of wood to create a decorative effect. These amateur decorative artists, who were active primarily in New England and Pennsylvania, used water-based media and such commonplace tools as carved potatoes, notched leather, feathers, and simple brushes to decorate their homes and furniture. This style of wood graining can be researched in books and historical documents.

BASIC PROCEDURE

The painting surface for faux wood must be as smooth as possible, requiring skimcoating, priming, and two coats of basepaint, with a sanding between each step and coat of paint. Since real wood is fibrous, it's acceptable to have a few brushstrokes remaining in the basecoat, as long as they are barely visible and run in the direction of the grain. The basecoat of choice is alkyd, in either an eggshell or a satin finish. But because many of the graining recipes in this book begin by using a reversible water-based medium (either gouache or beer glaze), you'll need to "degrease" the cured basecoated surface first (see page 32 for instructions). The first glaze is often flogged (see page 157) before the grain is rendered, usually in an oil-based glaze (3 turpentine + 1 linseed oil + drier + artists' oils). The overglazing can also be done in oil; if a water-based glaze is used for the overglazing, the entire surface must first be powdered with whiting, which gives the surface tooth by absorbing the oil. (The surface should be gently dusted with whiting, *not* degreased; degreasing the surface at this point would destroy the dried glazes.) Wood can also be painted exclusively in acrylic inks or oils. As you can see, there are several media combinations for faux wood; the one you choose will depend on the specific circumstances of your project.

Varnishing is a very important step in wood graining. In addition to unifying the surface with a consistent finish, varnish provides a protective coating. With respect to degree of gloss, satin and semigloss are often the most appropriate for wood, as a high-gloss finish tends to look artificial and a flat finish won't adequately enhance the subtlety and richness of the overglazings. Another outstanding finish for faux wood is to wax the surface after first sealing it with a light coat of satin-finish varnish.

Because most woods are medium to dark in value, and lighter versions are usually blond or golden, oil-based varnishes can be used without having to be concerned about their tendency to yellow with time (still, use a good brand). Because a water-based varnish could potentially bead up on an oil-glazed surface, or reactivate a reversible water-based glaze, water-based varnishes are a little trickier to use.

Wood Exercises

These exercises, which isolate the designs of various graining patterns into discrete elements, are one of the keys to successful wood graining. It is essential to practice the exercises that comprise a particular recipe as often as possible before starting, and to refer to them as needed throughout the process.

In most cases, the surface and medium used for the following exercises were also used for the marble exercises (see page 79).

APPLYING A GLAZE FOR FAUX WOOD

In order to make your painted wood even more convincing, it is essential that brush marks be minimized at certain steps in the process. Regardless of medium (a water-based glaze is shown below), a perfectly smooth application of glaze is particularly important for the overglazing.

Sand, dust off, and degrease the cured oil-basecoated surface (see page 32). Apply a reversible water-based glaze with a well-loaded glazing brush, working the brush up and down to cover the surface completely (photo 1). While it is still wet, even out the glaze by working a spalter back and forth across the surface, then make a final downward pass with the spalter to prevent the glaze from running (photo 2).

If the recipe requires it, lightly smooth out the still-wet glaze with a badger brush, holding it perpendicular to the surface and working it in a figure-eight motion while barely touching the surface (photo 3). Proceed immediately to the next step.

1   2   3

FLOGGING

This technique is used to simulate the pores that are created when the cells of hardwoods are cut. With a glazing brush loaded with a water-based glaze (preferably a reversible medium [gouache or beer glaze], but fluid acrylics can also be used), apply glaze to the surface, working the brush up and down, then use a spalter to stretch the glaze in a downward direction only (photo 1). While the glaze is still wet, grasp a flogger (a veinette can be used on small areas) in the drummer hold (see page 37) about 1/2 inch from the ferrule, then hit the surface with the heel of the bristles, working from bottom to top and from left to right in columns, so that each hit always overlaps the previous one (photo 2). Wipe off the brush frequently in a dry, clean rag so it picks up glaze consistently; also, it works best when its hairs are dry and fluffy. When you come to the top of a column, flip the flogger to expose its dry side, and start a new column, overlapping the width of the previous one by one-half or one-third. The glaze should still be wet after the panel has been flogged completely. Repeat the process at least once; the more floggings, the finer the pores (photo 3).

1   2   3

BASIC FIGURE GRAIN

The sloping sides and creased top of the figure grain can be compared to a mountain climb: The mountaineer ascends the mountain on the left, jumps up and down in a kind of "victory dance" when he reaches the top, then descends the mountain on the right (see drawings).

In this book, there are three wood recipes in which the figure grain is a primary visual element: walnut (see page 181), oak (page 185), and mahogany (page 190). In the demonstrations below and opposite, an oil-based glaze (3 turpentine + 1 oil + drier + artists' oils) is used.

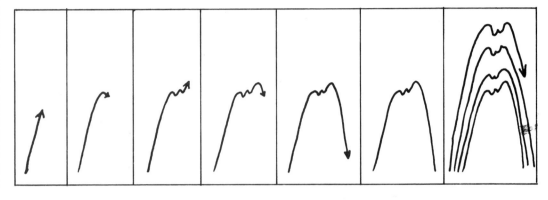

WALNUT FIGURE GRAIN

Apply a light coat of tinted glaze as shown on page 157, then give it an extra stretching with a spalter. Let set for 10 minutes. While the glaze is still wet, lightly load a teeth spalter with various colors from the palette (see page 179), then, grasping it in the drummer's hold (see page 37) use it to sketch out the shape of the figure (see photos 1–3). The sketch is then further developed with a pencil grainer held in the conductor's hold (see page 37). Working quickly to promote spontaneity, begin "climbing the mountain" as shown in the drawing above. Working from the heart of the figure outward, smooth out the figure with #40 spalter, then use a small flat brush to add detail and emphasis at the tops of certain peaks and around selected knots. Smooth out again very gently, always working from the heart of the figure outward.

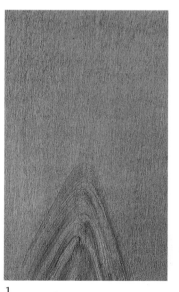

1

2

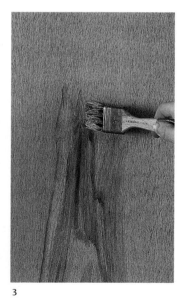

3

OAK FIGURE GRAIN

Apply the oil-based glaze as shown on page 157, then stretch it out with a spalter. Using a folded piece of burlap, begin "climbing the mountain" to create the figure grain as shown in the drawing on the opposite page (photos 1 and 2), then adding the straight grain (photo 3). The figure grain of oak is dense and jagged at the peak and close-grained around the heart, gradually opening as it widens. Once the contour has been completed, refine the figure by adding details with small flat brushes (photo 4). Smooth out the figure with a #40 spalter, this time working from the outside of the heart inward (oak and mahogany are the only woods that are smoothed out in this way). Comb the figure with a narrow, small-toothed comb, again working from the outside inward (photo 5).

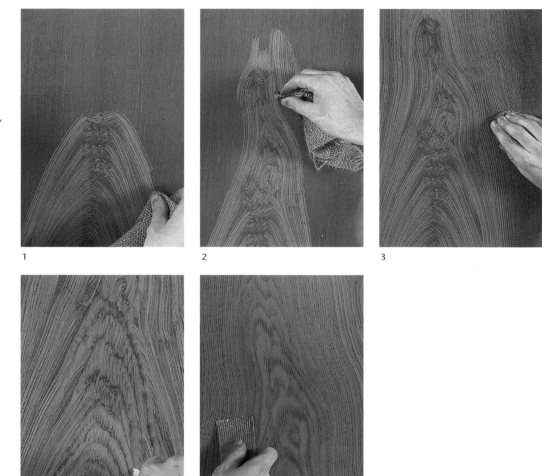

1   2   3

4   5

MAHOGANY FIGURE GRAIN

Apply the oil-based glaze as shown on page 157, then stretch it out with a spalter. Let set for 10 minutes. While the glaze is still wet, lightly load a teeth spalter with various colors from the palette (see page 188); grasping it in the drummer's hold (see page 37) use it to sketch out the shape of the figure (photo 1). Using a folded piece of burlap, begin "climbing the mountain" as shown in the drawing on the opposite page (photo 2). Mahogany's figure grain, which is somewhat softer and less dynamic than oak's, is rounded at the peak with a tiny, less jagged saw-toothed edge (see page 190). Once the contour has been completed, refine the figure by adding details with a ribbon of used billiard cloth. Complete the mahogany figure by smoothing it out with a #40 spalter, this time working from the outside of the heart inward (oak and mahogany are the only woods that are smoothed out in this way).

1   2

GRAINING GUIDELINES

- *Divide the surface to create a natural-looking balance.* A board should be divided visually into areas equaling approximately one-third and two-thirds of its length and width; a board divided directly in half by its grain patterns looks a little rigid. The central peak of the figure should not be aligned slightly off-center, which might also appear unnatural.
- *Develop the grain in the proper sequence.* Begin painting a board by rendering the figure grain in the lower part, where the visual weight should always be concentrated. Next, work on the figure grain in the upper part of the board, then create the juncture between the two "peaks." Finally, add the side graining.
- *Render the grain realistically.* The sides of the figure grain should become progressively straighter the farther away they are from the heart. The straight graining should always show some movement so that it doesn't appear static or unnatural. Such movement can be created by rendering only one-half or one-third of the figure grain, by including a knot, or by rendering a half-figure contour on either side of the board.
- *Grain configuration and relationships.* Avoid aligning any effects symmetrically or directly opposite one another, whether in the graining layer or the sap layer. Opposing points of the figure grain should move in slightly different directions in order to create movement within the board. To avoid painting soft, monotonous patterns, the angles of the graining's curves must be small and varied rather than widely spaced and consistent.

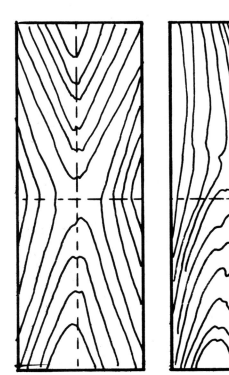

(Left) A symmetrical surface design, where a board is divided visually into halves, either vertically or horizontally, looks a little rigid. (Right) Apply the "one-third/two-thirds" principal—dividing a board into areas equaling approximately one-third and two-thirds of its length and width—to all elements of the surface design.

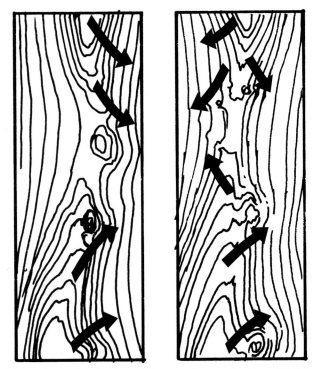

(Left) Avoid aligning the flow of the grain in one direction. (Right) Create movement and visual interest by subtly orienting the flow of the grain in alternating directions.

DO

1. Give straight graining a slight movement.

2. Render a half-figure contour within one-third of a board so that the emphasis is shifted away from the center.

3. Avoid placing knots in the center or at corresponding points within the composition.

4. Render half-figure contours on diagonal corners.

5. Surround a figure that occurs near the center with movement.

6. Render half-figure contours in a one-third/two-thirds configuration on opposite corners.

7. Start at the bottom with a half-figure and end at the top with a complete figure.

DON'T

8. Make grain lines perfectly straight.

9. Align the peak of the figure grain with the center of the board.

10. Place a knot at a halfway point, either vertically or horizontally.

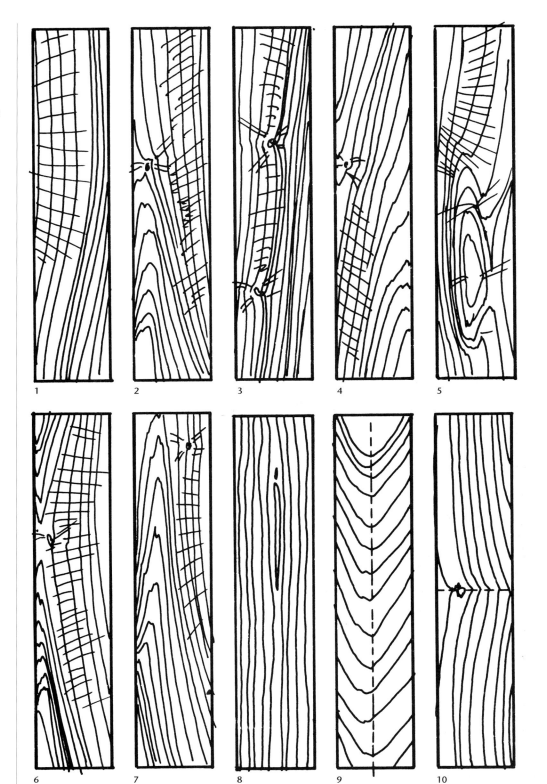

GRAINING WITH A VEINETTE

This technique is used to render the straight grain of many types of wood. Dip the veinette in a small amount of glaze, load it on your palette by touching the tips of its hairs to some of the colors, then work it on the palette in circular motion to even the distribution of paint (photo 1). If the brush seems too heavily loaded, remove some of the glaze by tapping the heel of the bristles gently on the palette. Separate the hairs of the veinette by running them through a metal or plastic pet comb (photo 2). Hold the veinette in the conductor's grip (see page 37) and drag it down the surface; if the wood you're painting requires it, give the strokes a slight trembled effect (photos 3 and 4).

It may be necessary to run the comb through the brush again after two or three passes to vary the configuration of the grain. Also, to avoid creating obvious stop and start marks when you're working on a long surface and can't run the brush from top to bottom in a single pass, slowly lift the veinette off the surface, simulating the way an airplane takes off; after reloading, gently "land" on the surface, slightly overlapping the point where the brush was lifted off.

Note that the cat's tongue brush and the flat two-header are sometimes used to render straight graining in certain types of wood, but their hairs don't require combing beforehand.

1

2

3

4

GRAINING AROUND A KNOT

While this exercise applies directly to pine, which is not covered in this book, it is also very effective for loosening up the hand and for understanding how the contours of grain lines shift as they pass around a knot.

In real wood, a knot can occur at any point in the grain pattern, interrupting the flow of the figure while giving it additional movement. In decorative painting, although the figure is sketched out and developed before the knots are painted, their placement should always be well planned so that they contribute to the overall balance of the design. To paint a knot, make a dot with a small flat brush, then twist it between your fingers.

To grain around a knot, begin by painting the formation of the grain that immediately surrounds it. Hold a long pointed round or flat brush in a pen grip (see page 37). Start with a thin stroke, then rapidly increase pressure on the brush to produce a fat tear shape (photo 1). End the stroke by suddenly lifting the brush from the side of the tear. Reverse the process to create the lower part of the formation (photo 2).

Once you've mastered the tear strokes, start the stroke with a long, thin "tail" that becomes progressively wider and ends in a tear; reverse the process to paint the lower tear and its tail (photo 3). The grain lines that run parallel to these longed-tailed tear strokes are painted similarly, but they are unbroken and less varied in width, becoming progressively straighter until they have "absorbed" the knot (photos 4–6).

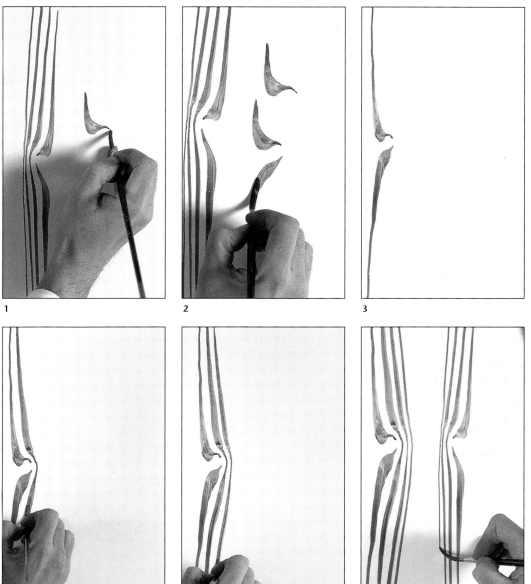

1

2

3

4

5

6

MOIRÉ EFFECT

This movement creates the "ripples" that are found along the grain patterns. These transparent waves of color represent the accumulations of sap that occur wherever the path of the wood's growth has been distorted (see page 152). Moiré are always added to the final overglaze, which can be done either in oil- or water-based media. I prefer to use reversible water-based media because they are slightly more transparent, and their short drying times promote spontaneity and permit varnishing almost immediately.

In the demonstration for this exercise, a reversible water-based glaze was used. Apply the glaze as shown on page 157. Moisten a #100 spalter by dipping it in water and then wringing it out in a sea sponge. Grasp the spalter by the hairs using the "duck" grip (thumb on the bottom, fingers on the top; see page 37), with the fingers flexed slightly so that the hairs are bent into a very wide V

shape. Working from top to bottom, hit the wet surface with the brush repeatedly while dragging it slightly at each stroke (photo 1). Increase the pressure gradually to increase the size of the strokes; when the width of the stroke is more or less equal to the width of the brush, gradually reduce pressure to reduce the size of the strokes. Wipe off the spalter frequently in a damp, used sea sponge so that it leaves clean marks (photo 2). All the ripples should be parallel and occur at regular intervals, but the moiré should have a slight curved movement (photo 3). Smooth out the wet moiré with a badger brush, working it from left to right like a pendulum; on the final pass, smooth the moiré from bottom to top (photo 4).

A badger brush can also be used to produce the moiré effect, with softer results. When working with oil-based media, use a dry spalter and clean off the brush with a rag.

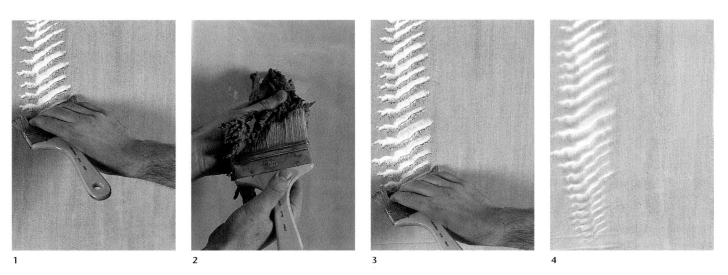

1

2

3

4

CRISSCROSS MOIRÉ

Once you have mastered the moiré effect (above), you will be able to do the crisscross moiré, which uses the same glazing technique, brush, and grip, but whose strokes are "hooked" to each other. The brush should barely leave the surface as it shifts from left to right, imitating the swing of pendulum. The left tip of one ripple should touch the center of the one above it, and the right tip of the one below it should touch the center of the one above it, and so on (photos 1 and 2). The completed stroke is then softened with a badger brush (photo 3). This technique is used in the bird's-eye maple (see page 174) and in some types of burl, and also serves as the basis of satinwood (page 171).

1

2

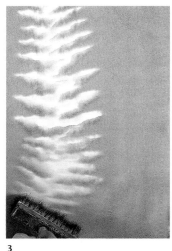

3

SMALL MOIRÉ OR FIDDLEBACK

The small moiré can be seen in straight-grain mahogany (page 190), lemon, tigerwood, and certain types of rosewood. Note that the term "fiddleback" refers to a sap configuration that is characteristic of a particular type of satinwood (see page 171) used to make the backs of violins.

Apply a reversible water-based glaze to the surface as shown on page 157, then smooth it out with a badger brush. Dampen a short skunk brush, then wring it out in a sea sponge. Using the drummer grip (see page 37), drag the brush over the wet glaze, lifting it first on one side, then on the other, so that one corner always remains on the surface (photo 1). Then use a badger brush to smooth it out, working the brush from right to left across the column of teethlike strokes (photo 2).

The small moiré can be done on an oil-based glaze using the same technique, but with a piece of corkboard or cardboard instead of a skunk brush, and smoothed out with a #40 spalter.

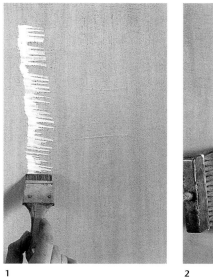

1

2

CROSSPORES

To create crosspores (see page 152), apply the reversible water-based glaze as shown on page 157. Using a badger brush held in a drummer's grip (see page 37), hit the wet glaze with the side of the hairs (see photo). Work the brush either up or down the surface in a column; smooth it out with the badger by stroking it across the column.

When working in an oil-based medium, crosspores are painted with a codtail brush or a spalter instead of a badger.

BUTTERFLY AND CAT'S EYES

These elements, which also represent accumulations of dried sap, occur above and below knots and within the heart of the figure grain. As with the various other moirés and the crosspores, they are also done on the final transparent overglaze. Although in the photos at right a reversible water-based glaze is used, the butterfly and cat's eyes can also be rendered in an oil-based glaze using the same technique, substituting a #80 or #40 spalter for a badger brush to make the butterfly, and using a knuckle instead of a skunk brush to make the cat's eyes.

Apply the glaze as shown on page 157, then smooth it out with a badger brush. Hold the badger brush by the hairs using the "duck" grip (thumb on the bottom, fingers on the top; see page 37), with the fingers flexed slightly so that the hairs are bent into a very wide V shape. Drag the brush over the glaze in a downward motion to form the upper "wings" of the butterfly. Maintaining the same grip, turn your wrist so that the point of the V faces up, then drag the brush upward to form the butterfly's lower "wings." While the glaze is still wet, smooth out the butterfly with the badger from all directions: top, bottom, left, and right (photo 1).

The cat's eyes are added while the butterfly is still wet. Dampen a short-haired skunk brush in water, then wring it out in a sea sponge. Holding the brush in the drummer's grip (see page 37), touch just one of its corners it to the surface on each side of the wings, wiping off the glaze in one quick jerk (photo 2). Smooth out with a badger brush.

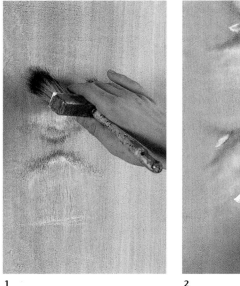

1

2

OUTLINING BAMBOO

The outline of the bamboo stalk (see page 196) is painted using a technique similar to the one described in the exercise for "Graining Around a Knot" (page 163).

Load a long pointed brush (synthetic for water, ox hair for oil) with a dark tone. Holding the brush like a pen (see page 37), begin by painting a long line that follows the contour of the stalk, exerting a consistent amount of pressure on the brush (photo 1). When you come to a ring (which divides the bamboo stalk into sections), lift the brush to release the pressure, which will produce a thinner line (photo 2). As you leave the ring and resume painting the bamboo's outline, immediately increase pressure on the brush to thicken the line (photo 3).

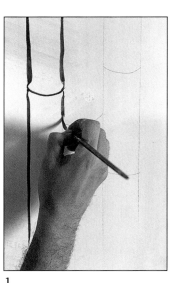

1

2

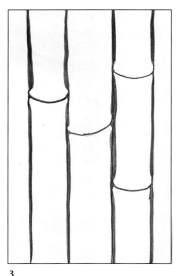

3

COMBING

This technique is one of the steps used to paint faux oak (see page 185). Apply a slightly heavy coat of oil-based glaze to the surface, then smooth it out with a spalter using an up-and-down motion. Add some dark vertical streaks with a teeth spalter (photo 1). Working from top to bottom and from left to right, drag a folded piece of burlap over the surface, overlapping each stroke slightly and using gradually less pressure so that the panel will have a light side and a dark side (photo 2). Wipe off the burlap frequently on a rag. While the glaze is wet, comb the surface from top to bottom with a wide large-tooth comb (photo 3). Vary the size and intensity of the strokes by changing the amount of pressure applied and the angle of the comb. Remove paint that builds up on the comb by wiping it on a rag (photo 4). Then comb the surface with the wide narrow-tooth comb (photo 5), cutting through the first combing while giving the strokes a slightly undulating movement to create the oak's pores (photo 6).

To create an easy silver grain effect (sometimes called a "ghost" silver grain; see "Silver Graining," page 168), comb the burlapped, combed surface with the wide narrow-tooth comb at a more pronounced angle.

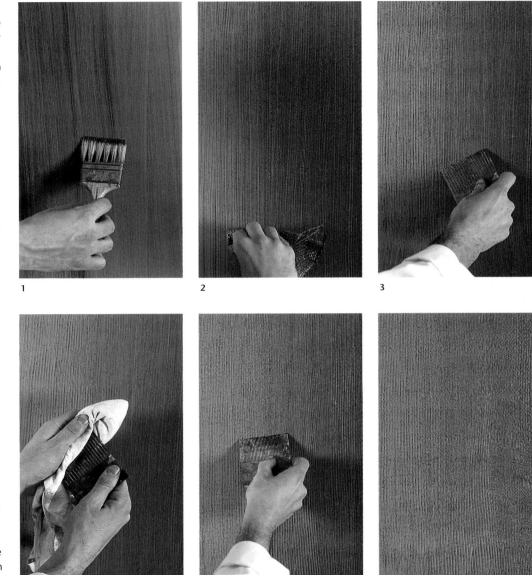

1 2 3

4 5 6

SILVER GRAINING

Silver graining, which appears only in quarter-sawn wood, is most distinct in oak (see "Figure or Grain Patterns," page 150). Although silver graining is always done over a combed background, the demonstration for this exercise was done on a plain dark background in order to give the elements of the grain pattern more clarity.

Wrap a ribbon of used billiard cloth or cotton cloth over your thumbnail. (If your nail isn't long enough, you can wrap a small, flat fingernail-shaped piece of wood.) Using the drawing below, left, as a guide, wipe away the curled "links" of the grain pattern with your cloth-covered thumbnail (photo 1). Before wiping off a link, pull the ribbon toward you slightly to expose a clean piece. The bigger "links" are done using the same technique, but by applying more pressure and by using the side of your thumb as well as the nail. The links should all flow in one general direction and appear to fit into one another like the tiles of a roof (photo 2). Sometimes, the links can radiate from a central point—usually a knot (photo 3)—before conforming to the typical arrangement (photo 4).

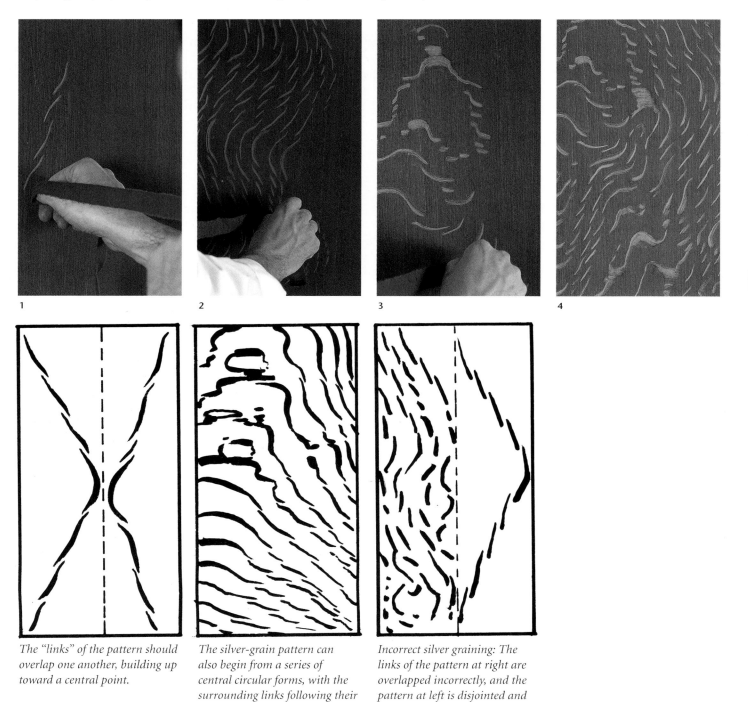

1

2

3

4

The "links" of the pattern should overlap one another, building up toward a central point.

The silver-grain pattern can also begin from a series of central circular forms, with the surrounding links following their contours.

Incorrect silver graining: The links of the pattern at right are overlapped incorrectly, and the pattern at left is disjointed and disorganized.

Satinwood Set in a Diamond Pattern

Satinwood is a generic term for tropical, golden-colored woods from Brazil, Guyana, and India. The satinwood grain pattern consists largely of the moiré effect and crisscross moiré with a light veining, so that the surface suggests the shimmer of silk. Because this pattern is also reminiscent of a tiger's stripes, these woods are sometimes referred to as tigerwood, an effect than can be achieved by increasing the contrast between the color of the basecoat and the color of the glaze.

Satinwood veneers are used on furniture and cabinetry, where they are often combined with other species of wood in marquetry, and are especially decorative when used in a book-match or similar layout. Satinwoods were commonly used to make neoclassical and art deco furniture. The alternating diamond pattern used for the demonstration, which features ivory inlay at the corners, is an example of an art deco layout.

1. Lightly sand and dust off the cured basecoated surface, then degrease it as shown on page 32. Draw the diamond pattern on the surface using a straight edge and a 5H pencil. Using a glazing brush, apply glaze (see Technical Notes) + **raw sienna** + **Cassel earth** + a touch of **yellow ochre** to every other diamond, as shown in the exercise on page 157. Use a damp spalter to manipulate the glaze with crisscross moirés as shown in the exercise on page 164. The groupings of strokes should be close together, but their width and the spacing between them should vary in order to produce light and dark areas. Giving your work a slight movement, orient the moirés for this set of diamonds horizontally. As you work, soften the strokes with a badger brush, working first from left to right, then from bottom to top. Let dry.

2. Load the veinette with glaze + **raw umber** + **Cassel earth** as shown in the exercise on page 162. Following the movement of the moiré, finely grain the surface. Let dry.

3. Tape off the unglazed diamonds, then clean off their edges with a damp elephant ear sponge. (Make sure that the sponge is not so wet that the moisture seeps under the tape.) Glaze up and moiré the surface as described in step 1, but this time orient the strokes vertically instead of horizontally to create visual contrast. Let dry, then grain with a veinette as described in step 2. Let dry.

4. As shown in the exercise on page 285, cut a small diamond-shaped stencil. Place the stencil over each of the intersecting points of the panels, then use a damp rag to remove the dried glaze from within the stencil window. (The reversible water-based glaze makes it possible to use the stencil with a negative, or removal, method.)

5. Glaze, moiré, and grain the baseboard as described in steps 1 and 2. Let dry.

6. Optional: If desired, stencil an ivory color (**white** + **raw sienna** + a touch of **raw umber**) over each of the smaller diamonds. (This step could also have been done without removing the dried glaze first, which was done in step 4.)

7. Varnish with two coats of satin-finish oil-based varnish. (Do *not* use a water-based varnish, which will reactivate the gouache or beer glaze.)

USING OTHER MEDIA

Although this recipe can also be done using either an oil-based or acrylic glaze following the same basic instructions, in this case there are no definite advantages to using these media.

Satinwood Set in a Diamond Pattern

1. Apply glaze to alternating diamonds, then manipulate it with horizontally oriented crisscross moirés. Let dry.

2. Finely grain the surface with the veinette. Let dry.

3. Tape off the unglazed diamonds, then wipe off the excess glaze with a damp elephant ear sponge.

4. Apply glaze, then manipulate it with vertically oriented crisscross moirés. Let dry.

5. Repeat step 2 for the second set of diamonds. Let dry.

6. Use a small diamond stencil and a damp rag to wipe off glaze at intersecting points of the larger diamonds.

7. The completed finish. Here, the stencil was used once more to apply an ivory color to each of the small diamond shapes.

1

2

3

4

5

6

170

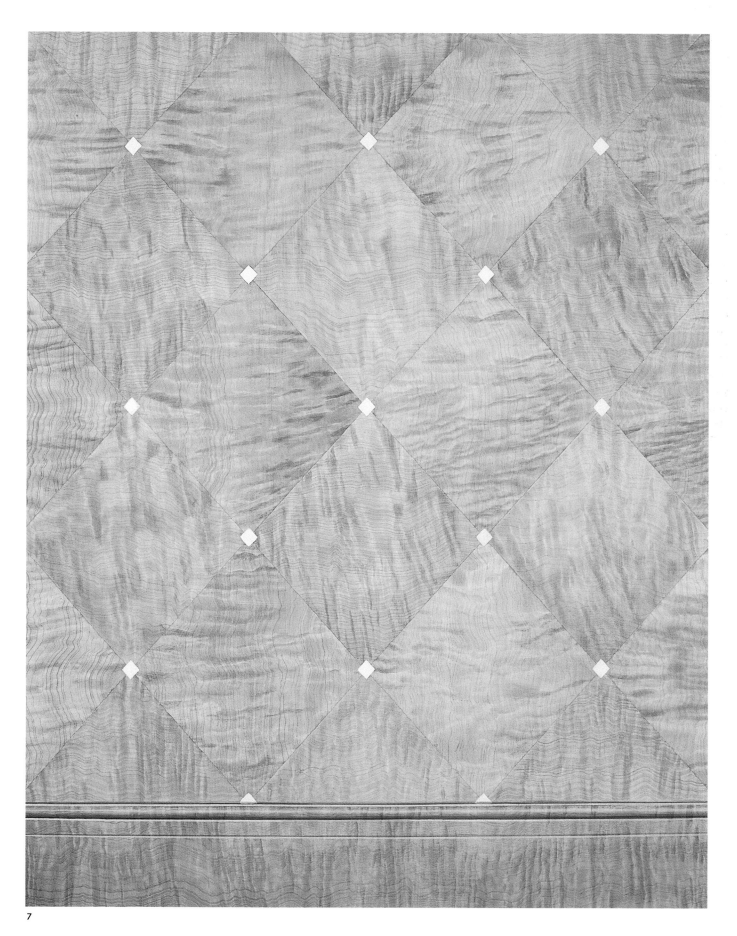

Bird's-Eye Maple

All eighty varieties of maple are found in the Northern Hemisphere; several are native to the Caribbean. Maple is a tight-grained white wood, either pale yellow or gray-beige in color, with lots of tiny knots (the bird's eyes) and sinuous graining that make it very decorative. Bird's-eye maple is used primarily for cabinetry and furniture-making, as well as in marquetry.

1. Lightly sand and dust off the cured basecoated surface, then degrease it as shown on page 32. Using glaze #1 (see Technical Notes) + **Cassel earth** + **raw sienna**, glaze up the surface as shown on page 157, making sure that it's very wet. (It's better for the glaze to be runny than to have it dry in the middle of the process. If you're working on a large panel, begin by glazing up the top half, then work on the top third and leave the middle third very wet, so that when you work on the bottom third you can fade it into the middle.)

   Moisten a #40 spalter by dipping it in water and then blotting it on a dampened sea sponge, then use it to make crisscross moirés as shown in the exercise on page 164. Use the sponge to wipe the spalter often so that the strokes remain distinct. (Hold the damp sponge in your other hand.) Working quickly, give the surface a general direction, alternating between large and small crisscross moirés and sometimes leaving a space in between. Repeat to fill in the spaces with moirés of various sizes. Smooth out with a badger brush using a figure-eight motion.

2. While the glaze is wet, use a bird's-eye brush to create the bird's eyes. Place the brush in a light area and drag it into a darker area, always moving in the same direction. (If you don't have a bird's-eye brush, moisten your fingertips on a wet sponge, then touch them to the surface to create the bird's eyes.) Soften with a badger brush as you work, again always moving in one direction. Let dry.

   If the glaze dries before you have a chance to wipe off all the bird's eyes, you can paint them. Using a small pointed round brush loaded with the same glaze, paint a small half-moon whose ends point downward; immediately beneath it, paint a slightly larger half-moon whose ends point up.

3. Using a pointed brush loaded with glaze #1 + **raw umber** + **raw sienna** and held in the pen grip (see page 37), begin the bird's-eye figure graining by outlining a centrally located burl and its surrounding area, trembling your hand as you work. Bird's-eye graining follows the same general principles as figure graining (see page 160), but it is far more twisted, following the paths set by the little knots, starting out very tight around the heart and following a concentric pattern. Overall, the figure should be relatively straight, while its grain lines are wavy and trembled. As you work, soften the grain lines from the heart outward. Let dry.

4. Using the same glaze mixture as in step 3, grain with the veinette as shown in the exercise on page 162, following the outline of the figure and glazing around knots when you encounter them. Soften the graining with the badger brush, again working from the heart outward. Let dry.

5. Clean off the edges of the panel with a damp elephant ear sponge. Glaze, moiré, knot, and grain the stiles and rails as outlined in steps 1–4, but use glaze #1 + **Cassel earth** + **raw sienna** + **burnt umber**. Mark the cut—a professional painter's term that means "emphasize the contrast"—between the panel and the stiles and rails by making the latter either slightly lighter or slightly darker than the central panel.

6. Overglaze: An oil-based glaze seals the reversible water-based glaze in which the figure of the wood was rendered and heightens its depth. With an oil-dedicated glazing brush and glaze #2 (see Technical Notes) + **Cassel earth** + **raw sienna**, glaze up the entire surface as shown in the exercise on page 157. Here and there, add some transparent touches of cold tones, either **alizarin crimson** or **ultramarine**

blue, at the bottom of some of the crisscross moirés. Smooth out the surface with a #40 spalter, then add some moiré effects in areas that need to be reworked. Repeat for the stiles and rails. Soften all with a codtail brush as you work. Let dry.

7. Varnish with two coats of satin-finish or semigloss oil-based varnish.

USING OTHER MEDIA

Although the bird's-eye underwork (steps 1 and 2) is never done with an oil-based glaze, the bird's-eye figure graining and the veinette graining can be glazed in oil in order to avoid reactivating the underwork, and to offer the possibility of revising the graining if needed.

1. Apply the glaze, then stretch it out with a spalter. Make sure the glaze is very wet.

2. Manipulate the wet glaze with crisscross moirés. Frequently wipe the spalter on a damp sponge so that the strokes remain distinct.

3. Smooth out the surface with a badger brush using a figure-eight motion.

4. Create the bird's eyes by placing the bristles of the bird's-eye brush into a light area and dragging them gently into a darker area. Always move the brush in the same direction. Let dry.

5. Begin the bird's-eye figure graining by outlining a centrally located burl and its surrounding area, trembling your hand as you work. Soften the grain lines from the heart outward as you work. Let dry.

6. Grain the surface with the veinette, following the contour of the figure.

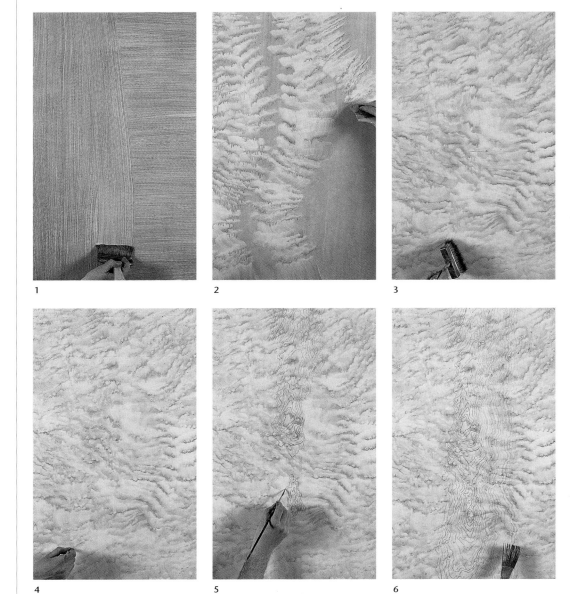

173

7. Glaze around knots while veining. Soften with a badger brush. Let dry.

8. Apply the oil-based overglaze, then manipulate with moiré effects.

9. The completed finish.

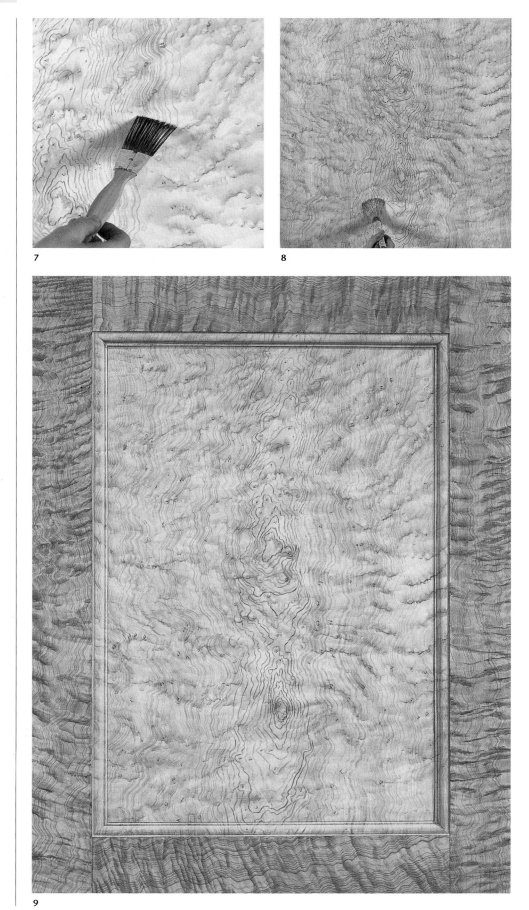

7

8

9

Elm, Amboina, and Thuja Burl

Burls appear in many different types of wood, from the most common to the most exotic. Because the burl figure is always limited in extent (see page 152), it is cut almost exclusively as small veneers and subsequently used for inlay, marquetry, furniture, and small decorative objects. In all these examples, burled wood is often combined with other wood species or with natural materials such as shagreen (a type of sharkskin; see page 277), tortoiseshell (page 270), or ivory (page 260). The recipes for the following species of wood are intended to provide examples that can be used to imitate the most commonly used burled woods.

- *Elm burl.* The fifteen species of elm indigenous to the Northern Hemisphere are nearly extinct. The yellow-white hardwood of the elm is mostly used in roots or burl, which has a warm orange color and features randomly spaced rounded dark knots interspersed with a lot of moiré effects.
- *Amboina burl.* This tree is found only on the island of Ambon or Amboina in Indonesia. Its warm orange wood, which is flecked with thousands of tiny knots, is used exclusively for its burl figure.
- *Thuja burl.* Found throughout the Northern Hemisphere, the thuja (or thuya) is a type of pine tree whose fibrous wood is dappled with many tear-shaped knots. Note that thuja is often incorrectly referred to as tulipwood.

ELM BURL

Note that in the photos on page 177 (steps 1–6), two same-size panels were painted as mirror images to simulate a book-match layout. The top panel was completed before the bottom one was demonstrated.

1. Lightly sand and dust off the entire cured basecoated surface (panels, stiles, and rails), then degrease it as shown on page 32. Glaze the surface as shown in the exercise on page 157 using glaze #1 (see Technical Notes) + **burnt sienna +**

burnt umber, but give the surface some movement with the last pass of the spalter.

2. While the surface is still *very* wet, use another water-dedicated glazing brush or a stencil brush to add some dark knots with glaze #1 + **Cassel earth** or **burnt umber + black.** Vary their size (from the size of a coin to the size of a watch face) as well as their intensity of color. Smooth them out with a badger brush.

3. While the surface is still wet, moisten a well-worn, frayed sea sponge with water, then wring it out. (If necessary, the edges of the sponge can be "fringed" by tearing them.) Following the general direction left by the spalter in step 1, drag the sponge across the surface, working around the knots while leaving streaks in between. Give the sponging a definite flow, always working in the same direction. Occasionally roll the sponge in between your fingers to get a variety of effects. Rinse and wring out the sponge often to keep the glaze from building up on it.

4. While the surface is wet, use a stencil brush and glaze #1 + **Cassel earth** or **burnt umber** to add small spots within the knots. Work over and around the knots with the edge of the sea sponge, then smooth out the surface with the badger brush. Let dry.

5. Add some tiny dots inside the knots and outline certain others with a small pointed brush and glaze #1 + **burnt umber + black** or **burnt umber + Cassel earth.** Let dry. As shown in the exercise on page 162, grain with the veinette, again following the established (but very distorted) direction of the surface and avoiding all the knots. Soften with a badger brush as you work. Let dry.

Once the surface has dried, it is ready for overglazing with an oil-based glaze. In this example, the entire panel was overglazed after the other burled woods were completed. (See "Overglaze and Varnish," page 176.)

1. Elm burl: Apply glaze, then give the surface some movement with the last pass of the spalter. Following the contour of the surface, add some dark knots with a stencil brush. Smooth out with a badger brush.

2. While wet, drag a damp frayed sea sponge across the surface, working around the knots and leaving streaks in between.

3. Add small spots within the knots.

4. Work over and around the knots with the edge of the sea sponge. Smooth out with a badger brush. Let dry.

5. Add some tiny dots inside the knots and outline others. Soften with a badger brush. Let dry.

6. Grain with the veinette, following the established direction of the surface and avoiding the knots. Soften. Let dry.

7. Amboina burl: Apply the glaze, add spots, then stipple the surface.

8. Randomly roll and drag a damp sea sponge over the wet surface, then smooth out with a badger brush. Let dry.

9. Grain with the veinette, this time working randomly (A). Let dry. Repeat on the remaining stiles and rails (B).

10. Thuja burl: Glaze, spot, and stipple as noted in step 7. Drag a damp sea sponge over the surface, creating small, almond-shaped areas; smooth out. Add tear-shaped knots with a small pointed brush. Let dry.

11. Add small dark dots within the knots. Let dry, then grain with the veinette. Let dry.

AMBOINA BURL

1. Glaze the surface with glaze #1 (see Technical Notes) + **burnt sienna** + **Cassel earth** + **burnt umber.** While the surface is wet, use another glazing brush to add some spots of **burnt sienna** + **burnt umber,** then stipple with a codtail or a disposable brush to achieve a stippled texture.
2. To create a knotty and busy texture, roll and drag a damp sea sponge over the wet surface in no particular direction, then smooth it out with a badger brush. If necessary, add more knots using a small pointed brush and glaze #1 + **burnt umber** + **Cassel earth** or **burnt umber** + **black.** Let dry. Grain the surface with the veinette and glaze #1 + **burnt umber** as shown in the exercise on page 162, but this time working randomly. Let dry.

The finish is now ready for overglazing and varnishing. (See "Overglaze and Varnish," below).

THUJA BURL

1. Glaze, spot, and stipple the surface as noted in step 1 for "Amboina Burl," above. (In this case, the spots should be much smaller and more regularly spaced.) Drag a damp, frayed sea sponge across the surface in a distinct and consistent direction, avoiding some areas, which should be smaller and more almond-shaped than those of the elm burl. Smooth out with a badger brush following the established movement of the surface. Let dry.
2. Use a fat pointed brush or rondin loaded with glaze #1 + **Cassel earth** + **burnt umber** to paint some tear-shaped knots whose shape and orientation should follow that of the dark spots in the previous step. Soften with a badger brush as you work. Let dry. Add some small dark dots inside these knots, using a small pointed brush loaded with

black + **burnt umber** or **burnt umber** + **Cassel earth.** Let dry.

Grain the surface with the veinette as shown in the exercise on page 162, but the graining here should be more distorted, following the movement and orientation of the knots. Let dry.

OVERGLAZE AND VARNISH

Although the same overglaze was used on all three woods, the color may be varied by adding any one of the colors listed on the palette for the artists' oils (see Technical Notes).

1. Using a clean and oil-dedicated glazing brush, glaze up the surface with glaze #2 (see Technical Notes) + **burnt sienna** + **Cassel earth,** then smooth it out with a #100 oil-dedicated spalter. Following the curved direction of each surface, manipulate the glaze with moiré effects (see page 164) and small moirés (see page 165). For the latter, hold the skunk brush in a drummer's hold (see page 37), then "zigzag" over the surface with the tips of the hairs, working from left to right in a continuous "Z" motion as you drag the brush down the surface. Smooth out the surface with a codtail or a small #40 spalter, working from left to right and from bottom to top. Let dry.
2. Varnish with two coats of gloss-finish oil-based varnish, sanding in between coats. Since the oil-based overglaze is partially wiped away when the moirés are done, an acrylic varnish should *not* be used, as it might reactivate the gouache or beer glaze underneath.

USING OTHER MEDIA

Because the surfaces on which these burl finishes are painted are small (usually no larger than 12 × 24 inches), oil media offer no distinct advantages over water for the knotting and graining steps.

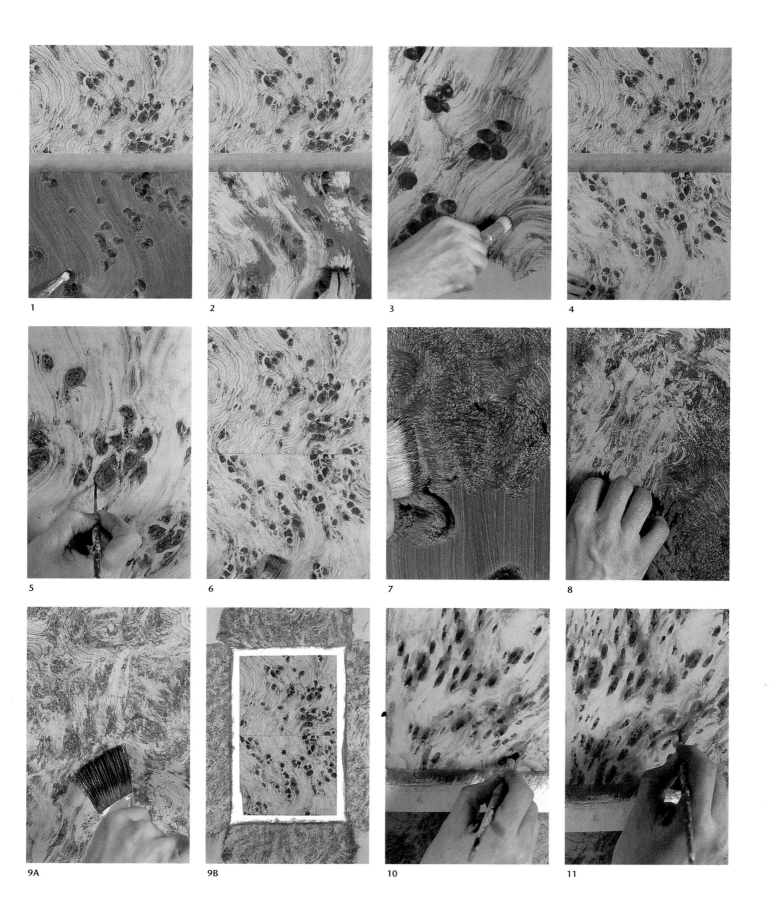

12. Apply the overglaze, then manipulate it with moiré effects.

13. Use a skunk brush to add some zigzag-style small moirés.

14. The completed finishes: elm burl (central panel), Amboina burl (stiles and rails), and thuja burl (corner panels).

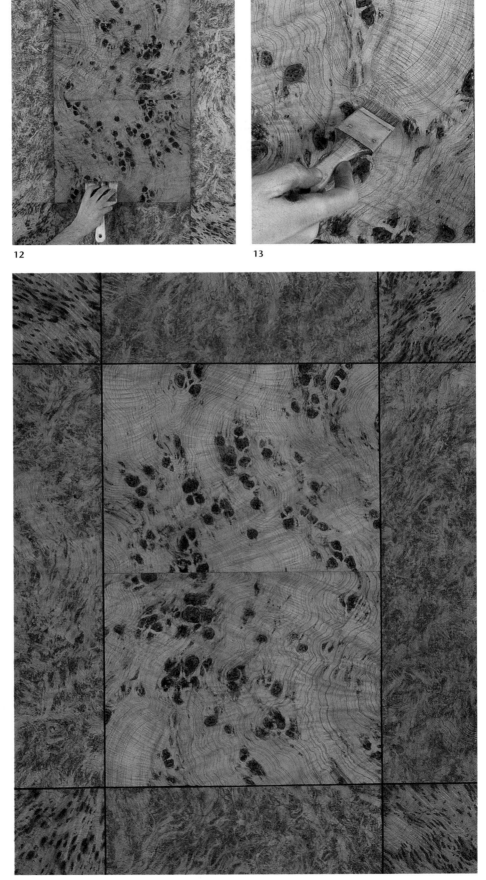

12

13

14

Walnut

Originally from Asia, several varieties of walnut can be found throughout Europe and North America. A hardwood, walnut is yellow-brown with a very deep, tight graining and a smooth, highly varied figure grain, with tiny teeth at the peak. These characteristics make it desirable for sculpting as well as for making cabinets and furniture. The finest grades of walnut are found in Italy, France, Holland, and certain parts of the United States. The nut of this tree is pressed to obtain walnut oil, a painting oil that is very pale in color and less likely to yellow than linseed oil.

1. Lightly sand and dust off the cured basecoated surface, then degrease it as shown on page 32. Draw the boards on the surface using a straight edge and a 5H pencil. Glaze up the surface with glaze #1 (see Technical Notes) + **Cassel earth** or **burnt umber + black.** Flog the wet glaze as shown in the exercise on page 157, using two passes to achieve medium to fine pores. Let dry.

    If desired, the surface can then be sealed with shellac. This step is not absolutely necessary because the oil glaze that is applied in step 2 acts as a sealant, but a layer of shellac will increase the fluidity of the oil glaze and ensures that the flogged texture won't be worn away if the oil glaze is manipulated vigorously.

2. Using a glazing brush, apply a thin layer of glaze #2 (see Technical Notes) + **burnt umber** as shown on page 157, but it should be both stretched and smoothed out with a spalter. Let set for 10 minutes, then proceed to step 3.

3. While the surface is still wet, use the teeth spalter to sketch out the figure grain using all the oil colors, but primarily using glaze #2 + **burnt umber** and **burnt sienna** combined and varied with the others. It's important to have a specific design in mind so you know where you're going. Use the drawings at the end of the book and your own sources as references. Using all the colors of the palette and following the graining guidelines outlined on page 160, design a well composed figure and create a pleasing color effect. Add some dark areas

in the straight graining about an inch or two from the figure. Working from the heart of the figure outward, smooth out with a #40 spalter, then proceed to step 4.

4. While the surface is wet, refine the figure grain using the pencil grainer loaded with glaze #2 and touched with **burnt umber, burnt sienna,** or **black,** as shown in the exercise on page 158. The application of fresh oil glaze will react with the previous application to expose the flogged water-based glaze or the basecoat beneath.

5. Refine the side graining with the square two-header. Load the brush with glaze #2, then touch it to **black,** working it on the palette in a circular motion to even its load and ruffle its hairs. Working from top to bottom, grain as shown in the exercise on page 162.

6. Use a small flat brush to redefine certain peaks of the figure grain and the areas around certain knots as shown in the exercise on page 163. Let set for a few minutes, then smooth out very gently using a #40 spalter or an oil-dedicated badger, always working from the inside of the grain outward. Using the square two-header, complete the last board with straight graining, giving the grain a subtle movement. Let dry for 24 hours, or until the surface is dry to the touch and no longer sticky.

7. Overglazing: Dust the surface with whiting by dipping a folded rag into a can of whiting, then gently tapping it over the surface. (This procedure should *not* be confused with degreasing, which would destroy the surface if done at this point.) This absorbs any of the oil glaze's remaining greasiness, thus preventing the water-based overglaze from beading up. Dust off the excess whiting, then glaze up the surface with glaze #1 (see Technical Notes) as shown in the exercise on page 157. (See also "Using Other Media," page 180.) Working quickly (the manipulations must be completed before the glaze dries), use a badger brush to manipulate the surface with butterflies and cat's eyes (see page 166). Use a #100 spalter to add moiré

1. Glaze and flog the surface. Let dry. Seal with shellac if desired.

2. Apply a thin layer of oil-based glaze. Let set for 10 minutes, then use a teeth spalter to sketch out the figure.

3. Once the lower part of the sketch is complete, develop the upper part.

4. Add some straight graining on either side of the figure.

5. While the glaze is still wet, refine the sketch with the pencil grainer.

6. Develop the side graining with the square two-header.

7. Redefine certain "peaks" of the figure grain with a small flat brush.

8. Let set, then gently smooth out with a spalter, working from the heart of the grain outward. Repeat steps 2–8 to complete the remaining boards. Let dry.

9. Gently dust the surface with whiting to prevent the water-based overglaze from beading. Remove any excess.

10. Apply the water-based overglaze to one board at a time.

11. Manipulate the overglaze with butterflies and cat's eyes and zigzag-style small moirés.

12. Add moiré effects along the sides of the figure grain, following its curves.

13. The completed finish.

effects along the sides of the figure grain, following its curves, then use a skunk brush to add some small moirés. Smooth out with a badger brush, working it in a figure-eight motion. Let dry.

8. Varnish with two coats of oil-based satin-finish or semigloss varnish. (Do *not* use an acrylic varnish, which will reactivate the water-based overglaze.)

USING OTHER MEDIA

Beginners might want to use an oil-based overglaze, which allows for a considerably longer working time and eliminates the need for dusting the surface with whiting after the first oil-based glaze has dried. For a faster, potentially more theatrical faux walnut, see the example on the opposite page.

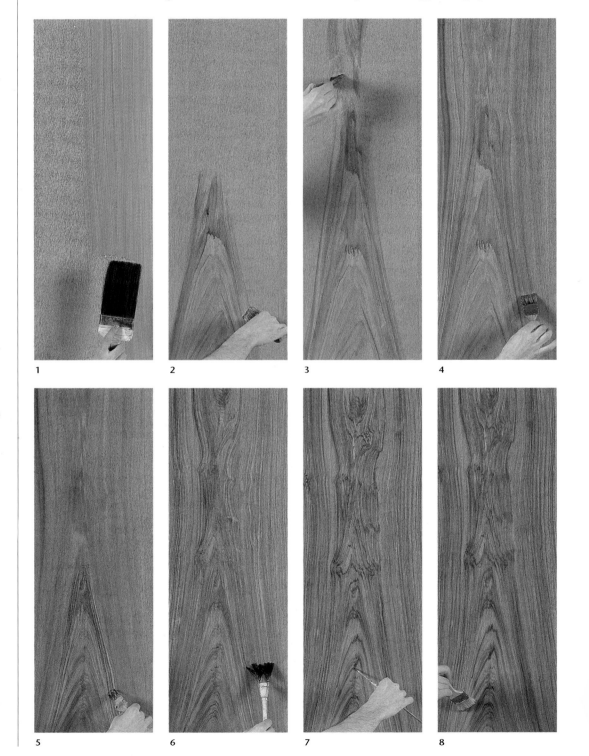

1

2

3

4

5

6

7

8

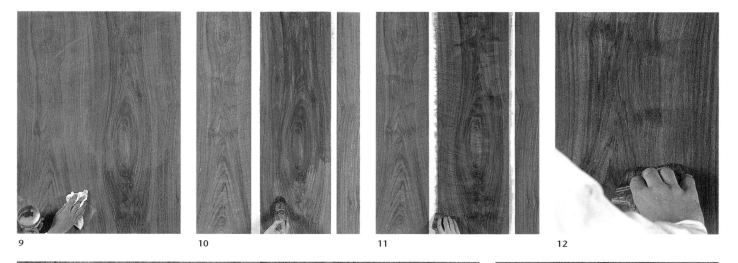

9

10

11

12

13

Variation: Italian-Style Walnut Using a Water-Based Glaze. Instead of three applications of glaze, which were used to create the finish shown at left, two were used here. A reversible water-based glaze was applied, flogged, and then allowed to dry. Using the onyx veining technique (which when used to create wood is referred to as *au dépouille;* see page 119), a damp veinette was used to design the figure grain over the flogged surface. The figure was then smoothed out with a badger brush every two strokes, working from the inside of the figure outward, displacing the reactivated glaze to create the dented, jagged grain lines characteristic of walnut. After the graining was completed and allowed to dry, an oil-based overglaze was applied directly over it (there was no need to dust the water-based glaze with whiting) and manipulated with various moiré effects. The dried surface was then finished with an oil-based varnish.

European Oak

TECHNICAL NOTES

Difficulty Rating

2.5 to 3

Systems

Oil and water

Basecoat

Alkyd, eggshell or satin finish

For a medium-value oak:
Yellow-brown (**yellow ochre + raw umber** + a touch of **white**)

Glazes

Glaze #1: Oil (3 turpentine + 1 oil + drier)

Glaze #2: Gouache + water OR beer + pigment + whiting (optional)

Palettes

Artists' Oils

Raw sienna

Yellow ochre

Raw umber

Burnt umber

Ultramarine blue

Gouaches

Raw sienna

Raw umber

Burnt umber

Cassel earth

Brushes and Tools

Glazing brushes (for both oil and water)

#100 spalter (for oil)

Teeth spalter

Ribbon of billiard cloth

Burlap

Well-worn small flat brushes

#40 spalter

Complete set of steel graining combs

Long pointed brush

Badger brush

Assorted small flat brushes

Exercises

See pages 158–60, 162, 164 (top), 166 (top), 167, and 168

Reference Drawings

See Drawings 23–27

Since the 19th century, decorative painters have sought to capture in paint the exceptional beauty of oak's heartgrain and silver grain (a pattern exhibited only when the wood is quarter-sawn). With over 300 species worldwide, oak can be found in every temperate zone, and was the most prevalent and one of the longest-lived species in European forests, often enduring for many centuries. Oak's extreme hardness, strength, and unusual ability to harden in water without suffering any adverse physical changes made it extremely desirable for shipbuilding. It was also a favorite among cabinetmakers, as fine details can be carved into it easily. In fact, most 18th-century wall paneling, even when it was destined to be painted, was made from oak. Today, oak is still used to make furniture and cabinetry, and though it has lost its elevated status because of its high price and somewhat rustic look, it is still the most frequently used wood for flooring.

Oak can be painted in any one of three versions: young wood (a light yellow-brown), mature wood (a medium yellow-brown), and old wood (brown). The older the wood, the wider the boards and the more impressive the grain patterns. The English, French, German, Hungarian, and American species are best suited for imitation. Heartgrain and silver grain should not appear within the same panel, despite the fact that such an arrangement is highly decorative.

FIGURE AND STRAIGHT GRAIN

1. Lightly sand and dust off the cured basecoated surface. Use a glazing brush to apply a medium layer of glaze #1 (see Technical Notes) tinted with **raw sienna + burnt umber + raw umber.** Stretch it out with the spalter.
2. While the surface is still wet, create contrast by using the teeth spalter and a bit of glaze #1 + **raw umber + ultramarine blue + yellow ochre + burnt sienna** to drybrush some uneven dark streaks. Use the billiard cloth ribbon to create a line of demarcation between the panels.

3. Using the reference drawings as well as images gathered during your own research as visual aids, draw the figure grain with a corner of a piece of folded burlap as shown in the exercise on page 159. While the oak's figure grain pattern can vary greatly, it is always very jagged and tight around the heart. Use a broad edge of the burlap to do the side graining, wiping it frequently on a clean rag.
4. Complete the figure grain by wiping off the jagged contours with a well-worn flat brush, wiping it frequently on a clean rag to prevent paint buildup. Use a #40 spalter to soften the details, working from the outside of the grain inward toward the heart, then use it to smooth the side grain.
5. While the surface is still wet, comb the side grain with a large-tooth comb. Working from the outside of the grain inward, comb the entire figure with a small-tooth comb. Wipe off both combs on a clean rag after each stroke.

SILVER GRAIN

Although the rules of fine woodworking dictate that figure or straight grain and silver grain boards never appear in the same panel, the second board was painted with quarter-sawn oak in order to demonstrate the silver grain. An infinite number of silver-grain configurations are produced by the quarter-sawn cut, so it is important to study actual examples as well as photographs and printed sources.

1. Comb the glazed surface twice: First with the broad side of a piece of folded burlap to create a gradation from light to dark, then with a large-tooth comb. (See the exercise on page 150.)
2. Proceed with the silver graining immediately, using the ribbon of billiard cloth to create the "links" of the silver grain pattern as shown in the exercise on page 168. Use an edge of the ribbon to gently soften the glaze between the central links to create highlights. Shade by outlining them with a long pointed brush lightly loaded with tinted glaze. Let dry.

1. Apply a medium coat of oil-based glaze, stretch it out with the spalter, then add some dark, uneven streaks with the teeth spalter.

2. Use a ribbon of billiard cloth to draw lines of demarcation between panels.

3. Working on the lower part of the board first (A), then the upper part (B), draw the figure grain with a piece of folded burlap, wiping it frequently on a clean rag to prevent paint buildup.

4. Complete the figure grain by using a well-worn flat brush to manipulate the grain pattern with jagged contours. Use a spalter to soften, working from the outside of the grain inward, then use it to smooth the side grain.

5. Comb the side grain with a large-tooth comb, then comb the entire figure with a small-tooth comb, working from the outside of the grain inward. Wipe off the combs after each stroke.

Complete any additional panels, then let dry for a minimum of 24 hours.

OVERGLAZE AND VARNISH

1. Dust the surface with whiting by dipping a folded rag into a can of whiting, then gently tapping it over the surface. (This procedure should *not* be confused with degreasing, which would destroy the surface if done at this point.) This absorbs any of the oil glaze's remaining greasiness, thus preventing the water-based overglaze from beading up. Dust off the excess whiting, then apply glaze #2 (see Technical Notes) tinted with **Cassel earth + raw sienna** to one panel at a time.

2. On the silver-grained panel, create a few moiré effects, then add a slightly undulating strié with the veinette. On the heart- and straight-grained panels, manipulate the glaze with butterflies and cat's eyes and moiré effects. Smooth out with a badger brush. Let dry.

3. Varnish with two coats of satin-finish oil varnish. (Do not use a water-based varnish, as it would reactivate the final glaze.)

USING OTHER MEDIA

In this recipe, the glaze must remain wet for the entire graining process, which makes it appropriate for oil media. While the final glazing can also be done in oil (eliminating the need to dust the surface with whiting beforehand but increasing the drying time considerably), gouache was used here to save time.

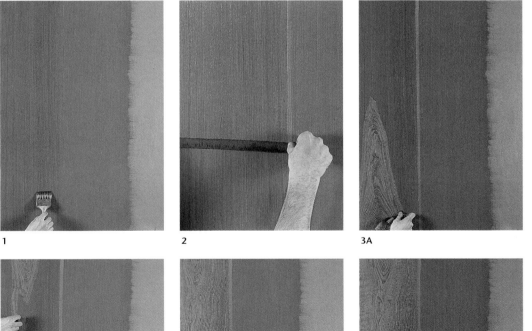

1

2

3A

3B

4

5

6. To begin the silver graining, comb the glazed surface twice: first with a piece of folded burlap, then with a large-tooth comb.

7. Use a ribbon of billiard cloth to create the "links" of the silver grain pattern.

8. Use an edge of the billiard cloth ribbon to gently wipe off glaze between the central links, creating soft highlights. Shade by outlining them with a round brush lightly loaded with glaze. Let dry.

9. Gently dust the oil-glazed surface with whiting to prepare it for the water-based overglaze. (Omit if the final glaze will be done in oil.)

10. Apply the overglaze to one panel at a time.

11. On the silver-grained panel, create a few moiré effects, then add a slightly undulating strié with the veinette.

12. On the figure-grained panels, manipulate the glaze with butterflies and cat's eyes and moiré effects.

13. The completed finish.

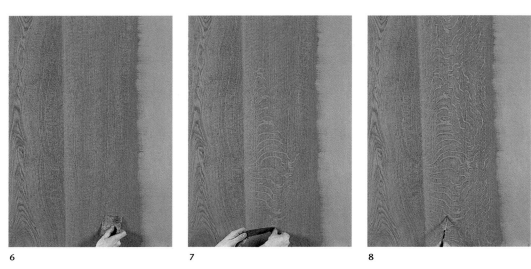

6

7

8

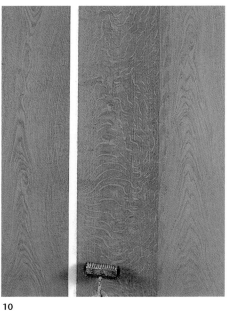

9

10

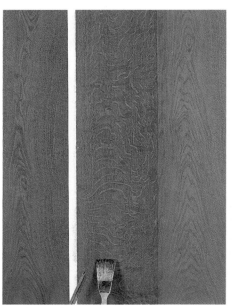

11

12

TECHNICAL NOTES

Difficulty Rating
2.5

Systems
Bleached Oak
Oil
Pickled Oak
Oil OR water (acrylics) and oil

Basecoat
Gray OR warm beige (**white + yellow ochre + burnt sienna + raw umber**) alkyd, eggshell or satin finish

Glazes
Bleached Oak
Glaze #1: Oil (2 turpentine + 1 oil + drier + whiting)
Glaze #2: Oil (3 turpentine + 1 oil + drier)
Pickled Oak
Glaze #1: Acrylic (1 matte medium + 2 water) OR oil (3 turpentine + 1 oil + drier)
Glaze #2: Oil (2 turpentine + 1 oil + drier + whiting)

Palettes
Artists' Oils OR Acrylics
White
Raw sienna
Yellow ochre
Burnt sienna
Raw umber
Burnt umber
Ultramarine blue

Brushes and Tools
Glazing brush
#100 spalter
Teeth spalter
An old or discarded brush whose handle has been sharpened to a point
Steel graining combs
#40 spalter
Assorted small flat brushes
Ribbon of billiard cloth

Exercises
Basic Figure Grain (page 159)
Graining Guidelines (page 160)
Combing (page 167)
Silver Graining (page 168)
Graining Around a Knot (page 163)

Reference Drawings
See Drawings 23–27

BLEACHED AND PICKLED OAK

Real oak can be artificially aged by *bleaching*, in which the wood is washed with a bleaching agent such as oxalic acid, then scrubbed with a wire brush and rinsed with water to raise the grain and deepen the pores. *Pickling* takes this process one step further, by applying a thick wash of titanium white or zinc white oil-based paint to stained and sealed oak, letting it set, then wiping off the excess with a pad, so that the white paint remains only in the pores. The painted versions of these finishes are produced somewhat differently than standard oak, employing the tip of a sharpened brush handle to "etch off" the grain pattern from a thick layer of wet glaze. This technique yields a raised grain that can be felt when the surface is stroked with the fingertips—just like real bleached and pickled oak. Because they are rough rather than polished and smooth, neither finish is overglazed to create ripples of accumulated sap.

Bleached Oak. Over a gray or warm beige eggshell- or satin-finish alkyd basecoat, apply glaze #1 (see Technical Notes) tinted with **white + raw sienna + burnt umber + raw umber** and smooth it out with a spalter. Add darker streaks with a teeth spalter, then smooth it out again. Etch the figure grain (see "Basic Figure Grain," page 159, and "European Oak," page 184) into the surface with the sharpened brush handle, wiping it off in a clean rag after every stroke. (Note that burlap is not used.) Comb the side grain with a large-tooth comb, then very lightly smooth out the entire figure with a #40 spalter, working from the outside inward, before combing it with a small-tooth comb. Use glaze #1 for the silver graining, but comb the surface first with a large-tooth comb, then crisscross it with undulating strokes using a small metal comb. Paint the links of the silver grain (see page 168) using a small flat brush and glaze #2 (see Technical Notes) tinted with **raw umber + burnt umber + raw sienna + a touch of white.** Let dry for a few days before varnishing with two coats of flat-finish oil-based varnish.

Pickled Oak. In contrast to bleached oak, this finish should consist of a light glaze over a comparatively dark background, which was achieved with streaking and spattering. Glaze up the surface with glaze #1 (either an acrylic or oil-based glaze [see Technical Notes]) tinted with **burnt umber + raw sienna + white.** Use other colors from the palette to add dark streaks with a teeth spalter. Smooth out with a spalter, then finely spatter with a darker glaze (**burnt umber + black**) then smooth out again to create pores. Let dry. Apply a thick coat of white-beige oil-based glaze (glaze #2 + **white + yellow ochre + burnt umber**), then smooth it out with a spalter. Etch off the figure grain with the sharpened brush handle, then comb the straight and figure graining as described above. The silver grain can be either wiped off with a ribbon of billiard cloth (see page 168) or painted as described above. Let dry for a few days before varnishing with two coats of flat-finish oil-based varnish.

1

2

3

1. Apply a heavy coat of light-colored oil-based glaze over a slightly darker background. Smooth out, add darker streaks with a teeth spalter, then smooth out again. For the pickled oak, spatter with a dark glaze.

2. Etch the figure grain into the wet glaze with the sharpened handle of an old brush.

3. To create the silver grain, comb the glaze twice (first with a large-tooth comb, then a small-tooth one), then either paint the "links" of the pattern or wipe them off with a ribbon of billiard cloth.

4. The completed finishes: bleached oak (central panel) and pickled oak (stiles and rails).

4

Mahogany

TECHNICAL NOTES

Difficulty Rating

3

Systems

Water and oil

Basecoat

Reddish brown (**red ochre + burnt umber + yellow ochre**) OR red-orange (**red ochre + yellow ochre + chrome orange**) alkyd, eggshell finish

Glazes

Glaze #1: Gouache + water OR beer + pigment

Glaze #2: Oil (3 turpentine + 1 oil + drier)

Palettes

Gouaches

Alizarin crimson

Burnt umber

Cassel earth

Black

Artists' Oils

Burnt sienna

Alizarin crimson

Burnt umber

Cassel earth

Brushes and Tools

Glazing brushes (for oil and water)

#100 spalters (for oil and water)

Badger brush

Flogger

#40 teeth spalter

Cat's tongue brush

Burlap

Billiard cloth

Assorted small flat brushes

Square two-header

#40 spalter

Exercises

See pages 157–165 and 166 (top)

See also the recipe for "Diaspro di Bohemia" (page 123)

Reference Drawings

See Drawings 28 and 29

Most varieties of mahogany are found in tropical areas, including the West Indies, Cuba, the Dominican Republic, Central America, Mexico, and Brazil. All types of mahogany—including "female mahogany" (actually a member of the cedar family, prized by woodworkers for its beautiful figure) as well as various cuts such as feather, moiré, and knotted—have very tight grain patterns and exhibit a range of colors, from light orange-blond, to red, to dark reddish brown. This exotic hardwood is strong and durable but easy to saw and carve. It was first used in Europe during the 18th century for furniture-making as a support for fine-art painting, and in the United States during the same period to make Chippendale-style furniture. Its popularity increased significantly in the 19th century, especially during the French Empire and English Victorian periods, when its use was expanded to include interior paneling, making small objects, and construction, primarily for finishing the interiors of ships. Mahogany has always been an imported commodity for European and North American woodworkers, and its price varies, depending on the quality. Central American mahogany, which is fairly inexpensive but poorly figured, is widely used nowadays, while the beautiful and far more expensive Cuban and Dominican mahoganies are rare. Shown in this demonstration is an example of Santo Domingo mahogany, whose grain patterns are highly varied. If you're attempting to match a lesser grade of mahogany, its characteristics can be altered as needed.

1. Lightly sand and dust off the cured basecoated the surface, then degrease it as shown on page 32. Draw the boards on the surface using a straight edge and a 5H pencil. Glaze up the surface with a glazing brush and glaze #1 (see Technical Notes) + **Cassel earth** or **burnt umber + black** as shown in the exercise on page 157. Flog the surface as shown on page 157 to a medium grain. Let dry.

2. Apply a thin layer of glaze #2 (see Technical Notes) + **burnt umber + alizarin crimson + burnt sienna,** then stretch it out with a spalter as shown in the exercise on page 157.

3. While the surface is wet, load a #40 teeth spalter with glaze #2 and various colors from the palette. Begin outlining the basic shape of the figure grain as shown in the exercise on page 159. Add the side graining with a cat's tongue brush, creating mahogany's characteristic dark streaks. Soften with a clean spalter.

4. While still wet, use a piece of folded burlap to refine the figure and side graining by dragging it over the surface as shown in the exercise on page 159.

5. With a ribbon of used billiard cloth, wipe off the main grain lines of the figure so that they are very distinct. Use a small flat brush loaded with glaze #2 + **burnt umber** to add a dark shadow above the highlighted grain lines, then smooth out the figure with a #40 spalter, working from the outside toward the heart. Refine the side graining with the square two-header, exerting pressure while dragging it down the surface so that it makes two light tracks on each pass. Add tiny knots wherever you had planned them, then smooth them out with a #40 spalter. Let dry for one full day before overglazing (see step 7).

6. The straight graining on the stiles and rails is done with the same glaze and palette. To create the grain lines, paint dark streaks with the cat's tongue brush, giving them some movement. Repeat using the two-header loaded only with untinted glaze, to create the mahogany's characteristic vertical streaks. Following the direction of the streaks, smooth out with a #40 spalter. Let dry for one full day.

7. Overglazing: Dust the surface with whiting by dipping a folded rag into a can of whiting, then gently tapping it over the surface. (This procedure should *not* be confused with degreasing, which would destroy the surface if done at this point.) This absorbs any of the oil glaze's remaining greasiness, thus preventing the water-based overglaze from beading up. Dust off the excess whiting, then glaze the surface with glaze #1 (see Technical Notes) + **alizarin crimson + Cassel earth** as shown on page 157. Use a badger and a

skunk brush to manipulate the glaze with butterflies and cat's eyes (see page 166), then use a spalter to add moiré effects (page 164) throughout. Add crosspores (page 165) and small moirés (page 165) in the light areas. Let dry.

8. Varnish with two coats of satin-finish or semigloss oil-based varnish. (Do *not* use an acrylic or other water-based varnish, which would reactivate the reversible overglaze.)

USING OTHER MEDIA

The overglaze (step 7) can also be done in an oil-based glaze, which provides more time to create the final effects.

1. Glaze and flog one panel at a time; let dry. Apply a thin coat of oil-based glaze, then sketch out the figure with a teeth spalter.

2. Add the side graining with the cat's tongue brush.

3. Soften with a clean spalter, working from the outside toward the heart.

4. Refine the figure graining with a piece of folded burlap. Repeat for the side graining.

5. Use a ribbon of billiard cloth to wipe off the main lines of the figure.

6. Use a small flat brush to add a dark shadow above the highlighted grain lines, then smooth out with a #40 spalter, working from the outside toward the heart.

7. Drag the square two-header over the side graining, exerting pressure so that it leaves two light tracks. Let dry.

8. Use the cat's tongue brush to create the straight graining on the stiles and rails.

9. Refine the straight graining with the square two-header. Smooth out with a #40 spalter. Let dry.

1

2

3

4

5

6

7

8

9

10. Gently dust the oil-glazed surface with whiting to prepare it for the water-based overglaze. Dust off excess whiting, then apply the glaze to one panel at a time.

11. Use a badger brush to manipulate the wet overglaze with butterflies and cat's eyes.

12. Use a spalter to add moiré effects, crosspores, and small moirés. Soften with a badger brush. Let dry.

13. The completed finish.

10   11   12

13

Cuban Feather Mahogany

As is noted on page 152, feather or crotch mahogany is a grain pattern rather than a variety of mahogany. The best feather mahogany is obtained from Cuban mahogany. Because it is rare (and, therefore, very expensive), feather mahogany is always cut and used as veneer. Its splendid decorative effect is used mostly in furniture and panels, where it is usually shown with straight or figured mahogany on the stiles and rails.

There are actually a few types of the "spray" or "flame" that is characteristic of this cut; some are relatively straight, while others are narrow. Before you begin painting, it is important to study several examples, either by visiting a museum of decorative arts or by researching them in magazines and books.

In this recipe, the finish is created using a combination of systems: water first, then oil. This alternative to the oil-then-water recipe used for figure- and straight-grain mahogany (see page 188) will allow you to complete the finish in one day.

1. Lightly sand and dust off the cured basecoated surface, then degrease it as shown on page 32. Use a water-dedicated glazing brush to apply glaze #1 (see Technical Notes) + **alizarin crimson + burnt umber + black** as shown in the exercise on page 157.

2. While the surface is wet, use a glazing brush loaded with glaze #1 + **burnt umber + black** to design a spray or feather shape using a slight S movement. Smooth out with a badger brush using a figure-eight motion.

3. While wet, use a fringed sea sponge (see "Elm, Amboina, and Thuja Burl," page 175) that has been moistened with water and wrung out to wipe off glaze from either side of the spray. You'll need to work quickly or the glaze may dry before you're done. Start at the bottom, staggering the lengths of the strokes. Begin each stroke in the heart of the spray, applying very little pressure to the sponge so that it creates a set of fringed streaks. Following the S shape of the spray, gradually increase pressure as you drag the sponge away from the spray and down toward the bottom of the panel. The side graining on either side of the top of the spray is done in the same way, but an even amount of pressure is applied to the sponge throughout. Smooth out the spray from the heart outward to build up dark areas under the lighter, sponged-off marks. Let dry.

4. Dip the veinette in water, then ruffle its hairs by combing them with a pet comb. Use the veinette to connect the fringes that extend into the heart of the spray with a wavy stroke. Emphasize these by softening them with a badger brush as you work, working from the heart outward. Let dry. If necessary, accentuate certain fringe shapes with the tip of the wet sea sponge.

5. Glaze the stiles and rails as shown in the exercise on page 157 using the tinted glaze from step 1. Add some dark streaks with the glazing brush, then wipe off the surface with a dampened sea sponge, giving the grain a slight movement. Soften with a badger brush. Let dry. I recommend that a coat of shellac be applied at this point to protect the surface from the remaining brush work.

6. Overglazing: Use a glazing brush to apply glaze #2 (see Technical Notes) + **Cassel earth + alizarin crimson** to the surface, then smooth it out with a spalter. Using a teeth spalter held nearly flat against the surface, add some dark streaks of **black + alizarin crimson** within the spray; smooth it out with the spalter once more.

7. While the surface is wet, use a skunk brush to manipulate the surface with small moirés (see page 165), and a spalter for the moiré effects (page 164) and crosspores (page 165). Smooth out the surface with a spalter. Repeat for the straight graining. Let dry for at least one day.

8. Optional: To heighten the effect, apply a second overglaze, this time using a reversible water medium (gouache or beer glaze) instead of oil. Gently dust the surface with whiting to prevent the water-based glaze from beading up. (This procedure should *not* be confused with degreasing, which would destroy the surface if done

1. Apply the glaze to the entire surface, then add the softly curving "spray" or "flame."

2. Smooth out with a badger brush, working it in a figure-eight motion.

3. Use a damp, frayed sea sponge to wipe off glaze from either side of the spray. Gradually increase pressure on the sponge as you drag it away from the spray and toward the bottom of the panel.

4. Apply an even amount of pressure to the sponge to make the side graining.

5. Working from the heart outward, smooth out the spray with a badger brush. Let dry.

6. Use the veinette to connect the fringes that extend into the heart of the spray with a wavy stroke.

7. Soften with a badger, again working from the heart of the spray outward. Let dry.

8. Apply glaze to the stiles and rails, then add dark streaks.

9. Wipe off with a damp sea sponge, giving the grain a slight movement. Let dry.

10. Apply the overglaze to the central panel and smooth it out with a spalter. Add some dark streaks within the spray with a teeth spalter.

11. Smooth out the dark streaks with a spalter.

12. Manipulate the rest of the surface with moiré effects, small moirés, butterflies and cat's eyes, and crosspores. Apply overglaze to the stiles and rails and repeat.

13. The completed finish.

at this point.) Dust off the excess whiting, then glaze the surface with glaze #1 (see Technical Notes) + **Cassel earth** as shown on page 157. Manipulate the glaze with a few moiré effects, then flog the surface as shown in the exercise on page 157 while following the contours of the graining on either side of the spray.

This step could also have been done at the end of step 7 by flogging the wet overglaze after it has been manipulated with moiré effects, or by spattering the manipulated, dried overglaze with a dark tone (**black + Cassel earth**), then immediately softening the spatters with a #40 spalter to create the pores. Let dry.

9. Give the finish more depth by varnishing it with two or three coats of semigloss- or gloss-finish varnish. If the optional reversible overglaze was added (see step 8), do *not* use a water-based varnish, as it will reactivate the overglaze.

USING OTHER MEDIA

For a longer working time, steps 1 through 5 can be done with an oil-based glaze (see the Technical Notes for glaze #2). Work with the same colors, but use a piece of eraser or corkboard instead of the sea sponge to make the spray, and a folded rag instead of the sponge for the side graining.

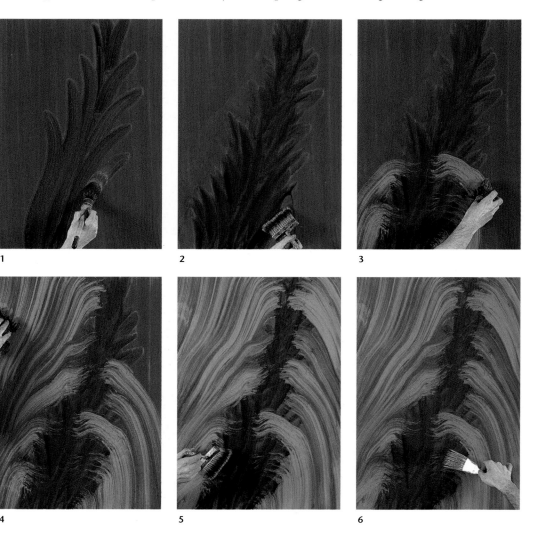

7

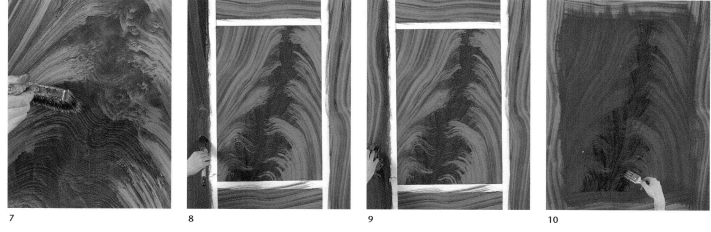

8

9

10

11

12

13

Bamboo

TECHNICAL NOTES

Difficulty Rating

2.5

System

Water (acrylics)

Basecoat

Straw yellow (**white + chrome yellow + a touch of yellow ochre**) OR pale green (**green + white + a touch of burnt sienna**) alkyd, eggshell finish

Acrylic Glaze

1 matte medium + 2 water

Palette

Artists' Acrylics

Chrome yellow

Raw sienna

Yellow ochre

Raw umber

Burnt umber

Chrome green oxide

Brushes and Tools

Glazing brush

Spalter or disposable brush

Badger brush

Water-dedicated rondin

Striping brush

Striping edge

Assorted small flat and pointed brushes

Exercises

Strié (page 206)

Outlining Bamboo (page 166)

Striping (page 303)

Bamboo is native to tropical regions in Asia, Africa, and South and Central America. There are hundreds of different species, which range in color from light yellow, to deep ochre, to brown or green, and can be spotted, streaked, or solid. These woody grasses have long, straight shafts with rings at regular intervals. Shown in this demonstration is Asian yellow bamboo, which is used for a variety of purposes. Bamboo became popular in Europe in the 18th century, when halved bamboo stalks were used to create ornate oriental decor. Later, real bamboo was replaced with plaster or wood and painted with faux bamboo.

Before trying to paint bamboo, read Chapter 11, "Trompe l'Oeil: Faux Moldings and Grisaille," for information on shading, highlighting, and perspective.

1. Lightly sand and dust off the cured basecoated surface. Use a straight edge and a 5H pencil to draw bamboo shoots of slightly varied widths. There is no need to measure these precisely. Simply mark the intervals indicating the width of the shoots on a piece of tape placed along the top of the panel, then move the tape to the bottom of the panel and mark the intervals on the surface as they appear on the tape. Draw the vertical lines between the corresponding marks at top and bottom.

2. Glaze the panel with acrylic glaze (see Technical Notes) + **raw sienna + raw umber + chrome oxide deep** varied with other colors from the palette. Apply the glaze using up-and-down strokes only, then strié the surface with a clean, dry spalter or disposable brush as shown in the exercise on page 206. Smooth it out with a badger brush. Let dry. Repeat if the surface needs more texture or color. Let dry.

3. Using a wide flat brush, vary the colors of the shoots by applying acrylic glaze tinted with any of the following transparent mixtures: **yellow ochre + raw umber,** or **burnt sienna + raw umber,** or **chrome oxide deep + burnt sienna.** Let dry. Use a 3H pencil to draw the "rings" between the sections of each shoot. They should curve slightly to create the illusion of form. So that they conform to the rules of perspective, keep in mind that the rings above eye level should curve upward, those below eye level should curve downward, and those more or less at eye level should curve less.

4. Create a dark brown by mixing **burnt umber + raw umber + raw sienna** (no glaze is added). As shown in the exercise on page 166, outline the shoots by painting the gap and the darkest shadow between the shoots as well as the rings. Let dry.

5. Load a large water-dedicated rondin or striping brush with glaze + **raw umber.** Use the rondin and the striping edge to paint the first shadow as shown in the exercises in Chapter 11. (Refer also to the drawing on the opposite page for an analysis of the elements of light and shadow.) Let dry.

6. Use the rondin and the same glaze mixture to emphasize the part of the shadow that's closest to the edge of each shoot. It should be about two-thirds the width of the first shadow. Let dry, then add the ring shadows by painting a thin line of the glaze directly over or immediately above each ring, and a fat, broad stroke about 1/8 inch below. Let dry.

7. Repeat step 6 to add the final and darkest part of each shadow, which should be about one-third the width of the first shadow. Use the striping brush and the same glaze mixture to add "splits" (which are caused by growing branches) to the segments of some selected shoots. There should be a tiny knot at either the top or bottom point of each split.

8. Use a small pointed brush loaded with **white + yellow ochre** thinned with a little water to add highlights to the shoots. Use the reference drawing on page 195 to see where the highlights should be placed. Repeat for the rings and the splits. Let dry.

9. Varnish with two coats of satin-finish acrylic varnish.

USING OTHER MEDIA

Although bamboo can be painted using oil media, they have no clear advantages over acrylics.

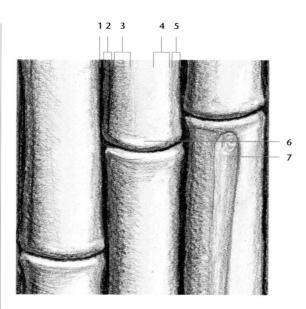

Light source is above and to the right.

1. Outline of stalk

2. Shadow accent

3. Shadow halftone

4. Highlight halftone

5. Cast shadow (from adjacent stalk)

6. Highlight accent

7. "Split" caused by growing branches

1. Draw the basic outlines of the bamboo shoots on the basecoated surface.

2. Apply glaze using only vertical strokes, then strié. Smooth out with a badger brush. Let dry.

3. Vary the colors of the shoots by applying a range of transparent glazes with a wide flat brush. Let dry.

4. Draw the "rings" between the sections of each shoot.

5. Outline the shoots and rings with dark brown paint. Let dry.

6. Paint the shadows, shown here on the left side of each shoot. Let dry.

7. Emphasize the part of each shadow that's closest to the edge of the shoot, which should be about two-thirds the width of the initial shadow. Let dry.

1

2

3

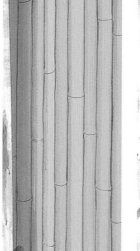

4

5

6

7

8. Add the ring shadows by painting a thin line of the glaze directly over or immediately above each ring, and a fat, broad stroke about $^1/_8$ inch below.

9. Paint the final and darkest part of each shadow, which should be about one-third the width of the initial shadow. Add "splits" to some of the segments.

10. Add highlights to the shoots, rings, and splits.

11. The completed finish.

8

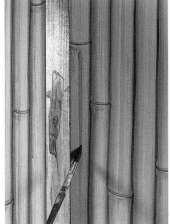

9

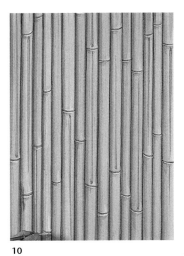

10

11

Marquetry

Like pietre dure (see page 132), marquetry produces elaborate ornamental designs by fitting together small pieces of wood and other materials (such as marble, metal, or ivory) like a jigsaw puzzle into a wood veneer. The background is often a book-match striped or streaked wood such as satinwood (page 171), Brazilian rosewood (used in this demonstration), or amaranth. In a book-match layout, the design of each segment is a mirror image of its opposite, but there should be a dark-and-light contrast between them.

This recipe demonstrates an alternative masking technique to the one used for pietre dure. Instead of a frisket mask, I used an isolating coat of shellac to seal off and protect each part of the design as I completed it. Another technique used to create faux marquetry involves painting faux woods on pieces of a commercial oil-primed paper or an architect-grade vellum with one glossy and one matte side, then cutting them up to fit the puzzle pieces of the design, pasting them on a surface with glue, and varnishing well.

1. Lightly sand and dust off the cured basecoated surface, then degrease it as shown on page 32. Draw the design on the surface with a 5H pencil. If you worked out your design on a sheet of paper, you can transfer it to the surface using either the tracing-paper or the pounce technique (see Chapter 11).

2. To paint the rosewood, apply glaze + **alizarin crimson** + **burnt sienna** to one of the four central panels as shown in the exercise on page 157. In this example, the glaze was applied at a 45-degree to the central axis of the surface to create book-match panels. Add some dark streaks of **alizarin crimson** and **burnt umber.** Smooth out with a #100 spalter, then strié it with a dry flogger, exerting very little pressure on the brush. Soften with a badger brush; let dry. Repeat on the panel that lies diagonally opposite. Let dry.

3. With a lettering brush, apply shellac to the areas of the rosewood panel you want to seal off and protect from subsequent applications of glaze. (I use thinned-down shellac [1 shellac + 1/3 denatured alcohol]

because it dries in just 5 minutes.) You can make sure you haven't missed any spots by illuminating your work closely and viewing it at an angle. Since the shellac is shiny and the gouache glaze is flat, you'll be able to tell immediately which parts have been varnished. Let dry.

4. Wet a sea sponge, then wring it out so that it's just damp. Use it to remove the dried glaze from wherever it shouldn't be, including the central design and the other two panels. Because the gouache glaze is reversible, any areas that haven't been sealed with shellac will wipe off easily. Regardless, you should proceed with caution.

5. Repeat steps 2, 3, and 4 on the other two panels. After the dried glaze has been removed, touch up any little mistakes or accidents with some water-thinned acrylic and a small pointed round brush.

6. The rest of the design was done in the same manner using several wood-graining techniques, but in just one step and with a reversible water glaze. As each area was completed, it was protected with a coat of shellac, and the excess glaze was wiped away with a damp sponge. Use a variety of colors, opposing warm to cold and dark to light for maximum effect. This technique can be time-consuming, and there will always be little "accidents" that need touching up, but these can be corrected with acrylics after the entire surface has been glazed and shellacked.

7. If the design requires it, shadows can be added with a translucent acrylic glaze (1 matte medium + 1 water + **Payne's gray** + **alizarin crimson**). Use a fine, long pointed brush or a quill pen and black waterproof ink to outline each "puzzle piece" of the ornamental design.

8. The frame was painted in Amboina burl (see page 178), and the thin border stripe was painted in rosewood with a fan brush.

9. Varnish with three coats of gloss-finish oil-based varnish. Sanding between the second and third coats will create a look similar to that achieved with the French polish technique, in which shellac is rubbed on with a pad.

1. Draw the design on (or transfer it to) the basecoated surface.

2. To paint the rosewood panels, apply glaze to two diagonal panels at a 45-degree angle to the central axis of the surface, then add some dark streaks. Smooth out with a spalter, then strié with a dry flogger. Let dry.

3. Seal off the areas of the panels that should be protected from subsequent applications of glaze with a coat of shellac.

4. Use a damp sea sponge to wipe away the areas of dried glaze that were not shellacked.

5. Repeat steps 2, 3, and 4 on the two remaining panels.

6. Using reversible water-based glazes, render one element of the design at a time, using a different faux wood (A). Let dry, apply an isolating coat of shellac, then wipe away excess glaze with a damp sponge. Repeat (B) until the design is completed.

7. If desired, add shadows with a translucent acrylic glaze.

8. Outline each element of the design with black waterproof ink. Let dry.

9. The completed finish.

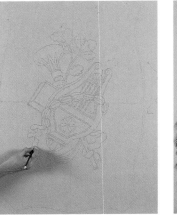

1

2

3

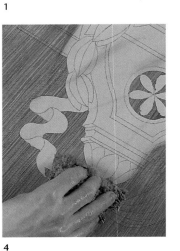

4

5

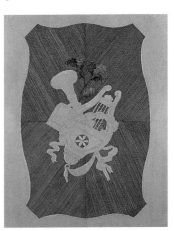

6A

6B

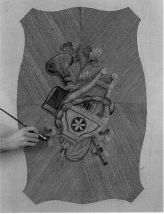

7

8

Patinas and Textures

Patina was originally the name given to the thin green film (verdigris) that forms on bronze or copper as a result of oxidation due to exposure to the elements over time. In decorative painting, patina refers to the modification of a surface to look as though it has been altered by the effects of weather, physical stress, dust, or time.

Before the early 20th century, decorative painters used patinas only to match preexisting, older work, or to imitate bronze oxidation; patinas were not used over basecoats or gilded surfaces for purely decorative effects. Over the years a patina would develop naturally without the intervention of the decorative painter. In a 19th-century cafe, for example, the smoke of gas lamps, cigars and pipes, and cooking stoves, as well as the effects of day-to-day use, weather, and time, all took their toll on painted surfaces. At the start of this century, decorative painters began to devise techniques to provide an immediate simulation of the long-term effects of aging. These techniques were used to soften the brightness of new paint or gilding, to lend finer tonalities, and to accentuate relief areas and architectural details. Ever since then, patinas have been utilized not for budget reasons but for decorative purposes and because of time constraints. Later, new techniques such as ragging and sponging were invented not just to imitate a particular patina but to achieve decorative effects.

In this dining room, a subtle green rendition of tricolor glazing (see page 213) featuring a stenciled and painted frieze and vertical border is accented with painted boiserie cabinets and crown moldings with a gilded and aged stripe molding (page 223).

Creating a Patina

The term *glazing* should not be confused with *patina*. Glazing is the action of applying a glaze—the transparent film of color used over a basecoat—for various treatments, including wood graining, marbling, and patina effects. When a painter refers to glazing a wall, this might be the first step of wood graining, not necessarily a final glaze effect such as ragging. On the other hand, reference to a patina or a glazing finish concerns a recipe, not the action of glazing. In short, while glazing refers to the action of applying a glaze, patina refers to a technique.

TYPES OF PATINAS

A patina can take on a variety of different looks, depending on the material over which it is applied, so there are many different patina techniques. Some patinas incorporate methods that create a raised surface, giving them a textured look. Two basic methods are used for the various patina techniques: positive and negative. In the *positive method*, glaze is applied to a surface with different types of tools. Sponging on, spattering, and veining are positive methods. In the *negative method*, glaze is removed or displaced with different tools. Strié, stippling, ragging, sponging off, and wiping off are all examples of negative methods.

- *Aged patinas* are often the result of dust, smoke, or humidity stains. Frequently seen on paneling and furniture, the method is used not so much to fool people into thinking that something new is old, but usually to give the project a more harmonious aspect, to lessen the intensity of colors, or to accentuate an architectural relief. The basic technique consists of applying a thin glaze over a surface, smoothing it out by stippling it, and wiping off the raised portions, leaving the relief areas clean and the crevices darkened with glaze. The whole piece is then stippled to soften the transitions.
  Crackling is another type of aged patina, simulating the effect of crazed varnish or old paint. Crackling can be either transparent or opaque. An example of a transparent crackle applied to a surface can be seen in the recipe for "Handmade Tile with Crackle Finish," page 249.

- *Distressed patinas* are often the next step after the aged patina, since the distressed appearance would generally not be visible before the effects of age. Distressed patinas imitate the physical wear and tear on such items as a piece of furniture or a painted panel, caused by normal usage over the years. The areas that show greatest wear are those subject to the most contact: around a door knob, the lower portion of a baseboard or chair leg, the edges of a tabletop. Distress is also evident when paint begins to crackle due to weather conditions. This patina is often done with a dry brushing technique or colored wax sticks, before which the surface sometimes is actually hit with dull knives or other blunt objects to give the effect of handling over the years.

- *Decorative patinas or glazing finishes* refer to all decorative effects such as ragging, sponging, stippling, spattering. These techniques do not aim to imitate any existing natural finishes but are used to change a basecoat's appearance, to make it more interesting, to give depth, or to modify a color. Stippling a burnt sienna + burnt umber glaze over a green-ochre base, for instance, will yield a Tabasco tone that would be impossible to achieve with only a straight basecoat. Creating successful decorative patinas requires an understanding of colors and how they interact with one another. (See pages 33–35.)

- *Textured or raised patinas* are those with a raised effect that is actually three-dimensional, such as old plaster walls. Such patinas are often accomplished by adding to the basecoat a textural ingredient—such as sand, sawdust, whiting, compound, or modeling paste—which thickens the paint, allowing it to be "shaped" on the surface with a stippling brush, roller, or glazing brush. Once dry, the surface is then glazed with a patina.

SUITABLE APPLICATIONS

Patinas are the most versatile decorative painting technique because they can be done on virtually any surface given the right preparation. Thousands of patina variations can be created on paneling, floors, walls, furniture, even hardware and other small objects. Patinas are suitable for any decor as long as they are done with the appropriate technique and colors. In classical decor, a patina effect works wonderfully to give the sort of worn feeling that is the hallmark of old decor. Patinas can also be used to create certain decorative effects in modern settings.

CHOOSING THE RIGHT TECHNIQUE

Before reading this section, review "Influential Movements in Decorative Painting," page 15. Patinas used to simulate the effects of age—traditionally thought of as French techniques—aim for great accuracy in tonalities, areas of wear and tear, and subtlety of relief. A decorative patina that utilizes the greater freedom (and spontaneous immediacy) of water-based glazes is classified as an Italian technique, but again may be considered French if it employs oil-based glazes. In creating any patina, however, the considerations of decor are more important than the technique you use to create it.

PREPARING THE SURFACE

Surface preparation for patinas and textures varies, depending on the technique used and the look desired. The same recipe can be done on a flat or satin basecoat, with water- or oil-based glazes. The following suggestions are meant only as general guidelines; through experimentation and practice you can develop your own variations.

- *Aged patina, oil-based:* Very smooth basecoat in satin or eggshell sheen; patina in oil-based glaze
- *Aged patina, water-based:* Flat basecoat with visible brushstrokes; patina in water-based glaze

- *Distressed patina:* Flat alkyd basecoat with visible brushstrokes; patina in oil-based glaze
- *Textured patina:* Heavy-bodied oil- or water-based flat basecoat; patina in oil- or water-based glaze, as appropriate

Lighter glazes require basecoats that are only slightly absorbent (satin or eggshell sheen). Heavier glazes need more absorbent basecoats (matte or eggshell). The final effect will direct the type of preparation:

- *For a light and delicate patina,* use an alkyd basecoat, either satin or eggshell finish, over a smooth surface.
- *For a medium-effect patina,* use an eggshell or flat alkyd basecoat over a medium prepared surface.
- *For a more textured and distressed patina,* use an alkyd or latex basecoat with visible brushstrokes or a heavy-bodied flat alkyd or latex over a medium prepared surface.

Unlike the basecoats for wood and marble (which can only vary up to a point since they are meant to imitate natural materials), all the basecoats and glaze colors given in the following recipes can be completely changed or new ones invented, depending on the color you wish to obtain.

PREPARING THE GLAZE

As with surface preparation, glaze preparation will vary depending on the final effect desired. Mixing a glaze for a patina can be tricky, but an understanding of color theory (see pages 33–35) will help you to become more efficient at mixing by enabling you to anticipate the effect of different glazes over various basecoats. Transparency is the most important characteristic to keep in mind when preparing glaze for patina effects. Using pigments that are less opaque (such as raw sienna, burnt sienna, burnt umber, raw umber, Cassel earth, alizarin crimson, and emerald green) will result in glazes that are more transparent. Ready-made oil- and water-based glazing liquids can be purchased, or you can mix your own (see page 29).

Following are some general suggestions; check the technical notes for each recipe and experiment with your own combinations to complete this list:

Oil-Based Glazes. Oil-based glazes are recommended for finer or smoother effects.

Basic oil glaze = 2 to 3 turpentine + 1 linseed oil + drier + colorant + whiting (if necessary for body)

Basic modified commercial oil glaze = 1 glazing liquid + $^3/_4$ kerosene + $^1/_4$ linseed oil + colorant

Water-Based Glazes. Water-based glazes are often used for more distressed looks, though you can achieve similar results with oil glazes.

Basic acrylic glaze = 1 matte medium + 1 to 3 water + whiting (if necessary for body) + gel retarder (10% maximum, if necessary) + colorant

Basic gouache glaze = 1 tube of gouache + $^1/_2$ pint of water (or less)

Basic beer glaze = 1 beer + pigment

A commercial water-based glaze can be used either straight out of the can or diluted slightly with water.

Tips on Preparing Glazes for Patinas
- The color of the basecoat should be close in tonality and intensity to the intended final glaze.
- Whiting is useful for imparting body to very liquid glazes so they don't run. Both whiting and talc are good matting agents (particularly for oil glazes) to dull down glazes that are too shiny.
- When using a reversible water-based glaze over an oil basecoat, the basecoat first needs to be degreased to keep the glaze from repelling (see page 32).
- Because all of the patina techniques (with the exception of crassé or drybrush) remove the most volatile part of the glaze—the solvent—the more you work

the surface, the thinner the application of glaze will be, and thus the faster it will set and start drying.
- Always work from the top to the bottom (ceiling to crown to wall to baseboard) to avoid drips over a finished area.
- To achieve a smoother finish, improve color control, avoid heaviness and dark accumulations in corners, it's better to glaze a surface two or three times with a light, transparent glaze than once with a darker glaze.
- For large surfaces (anything larger than a door), mix your glaze in a bucket, using a round glazing brush to stir in the color and to blend the glaze.
- When glazing a large wall, the most efficient method is to work with two or three painters. One painter applies the glaze, the second manipulates it to create the decorative effect, and the third finishes up and helps the other two with tasks like moving ladders, touching up corners, base moldings, and joints, and retaping surfaces.

VARNISHING

There is some controversy among decorative painters about whether patinas should be varnished. Some think that a patina should never be varnished because the varnish may affect the glazing, by ruining the uneven effect of the sheen—the hallmark of a handmade finish—by sealing a surface that is supposed to look aged and distressed, or by turning it yellow. (An oil-based glaze varnished with an acrylic varnish will turn yellow within two days; an oil-based varnish itself will turn yellow over time, although slowly and less noticeably.) Other painters believe that varnish will protect the patina, permit maintenance (cleaning), equalize the shine, and make the surface more durable. I support both views—sometimes it's better to varnish when protection is required; in other instances, varnishing should be avoided because it will ruin the effect of the patina. If you are doing a job for a client, advise the client on the pros and cons of varnishing and talk it over with him or her.

Patina Exercises

The exercises below and on the following pages illustrate the most fundamental of decorative painting techniques. In fact, many of the recipes in this book employ variations of these techniques, so in at least one sense they provide a good place for a beginner to start. To allow for maximum working time, an oil-based glaze is used in each demonstration.

Note that after the initial layer of glaze is applied and before it is ragged, stippled, or striéd, it must be *crisscrossed*, that is, worked with the glazing brush from top to bottom, then side to side, then from top to bottom once more. Crisscrossing evens out the glaze and eliminates brush marks, yielding a smooth, consistent working surface.

RAGGING

Ragging is a negative method of manipulating paint (see page 202). Using a glazing brush, glaze the surface with an oil-based glaze (a water-based glaze should be used only on small surfaces), "greasing up" the surface well and making sure there are no dark spots. Crisscross the glaze with the glazing brush, then stipple it with the same brush to break the brushstrokes (photo 1). To create the ragging effect, use a cotton rag, ribbed T-shirt, or cheesecloth held loosely between all fingers in the baseball hold (see page 37) so that the cloth forms a rosebud (photo 2). While the surface is still wet, hit it with the cloth in a repetitive manner similar to the motion used when sponging on or dabbing with the chiqueteur brush (see pages 79 and 87). The movement is all in the wrist: When you raise the cloth, turn your wrist from left to right to vary the pattern, working from left to right and from top to bottom, overlapping the hits so no area is missed (photo 3). Change the configuration of the cloth often to expose clean areas; this will ensure that it picks up the glaze evenly. Work methodically rather than randomly, hitting the surface with the cloth consistently, as if you were carefully reading a page in a book: Don't skip words or skim paragraphs; instead, hit the surface one "word" at a time (photo 4).

1

2

3

4

STIPPLING

Stippling is another negative method of paint manipulation. For this technique, it's preferable to work with an oil-based glaze, but a water-based glaze can be used on small surfaces.

Glaze up and stipple the surface as noted in "Ragging" (see page 205) using a glazing brush (photo 1). Hold a stippling or patina brush in the baseball hold (see page 37) as if you were prepared to throw thousands of balls. It is important to keep the movement in your wrist rather than your elbow, or you will tire quickly and the strokes will be heavier and less controlled. If you use the right

motion, the stippling brush should literally bounce off the surface. When you first begin with a clean stippling brush, run a little glaze on it with the glazing brush and work it in a cloth so it won't pick up too much glaze and leave a lighter spot where you started. Work across the surface, from left to right and top to bottom, using a rapid, jerking wrist motion, turning the brush left and right to break any identifiable repeat patterns (photo 2). Wipe off the brush very often with a clean cloth so that you pick up and move the glaze but avoid adding to it (photos 3 and 4).

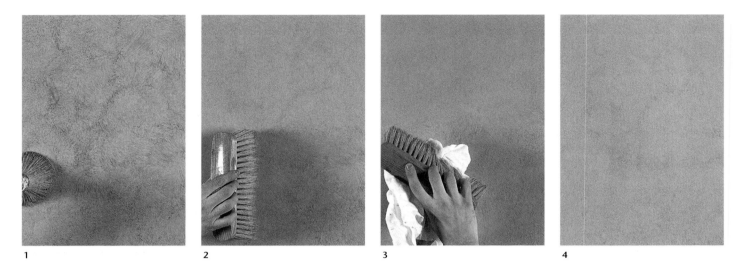

1   2   3   4

STRIÉ

Strié, or striping, is another negative method. It is generally done in oil glaze, but can be done in a water-based system on small surfaces. Glaze up the surface with a glazing brush, crisscrossing to even out the glaze and finishing with the last strokes in the direction of the strié (photo 1). Then, using a spalter, tooth spalter, or disposable brush held in a drummer's or pen grip (depending on the amount of pressure you wish to use—the more pressure, the deeper the strié), drag the brush over the wet surface from top to bottom (not side

to side), overlapping the previous stroke by one-quarter on each pass (photo 2). Keep your lines straight by locking your wrist and moving only your arm and elbow. Focus on the previous stroke, not on the brush. The more parallel you hold your brush to the surface, the coarser the strié will be; the more perpendicular to the surface, the finer the strié will be (photo 3). In order to manipulate the glaze consistently, wipe off the brush after almost every pass in a clean rag held like a claw in your other hand.

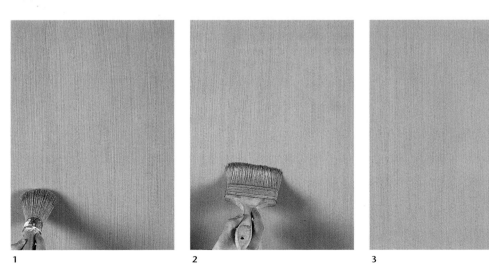

1   2   3

AGED STRIÉ

Aged strié, a variation of "Strié," opposite, is also a negative glazing method. Glaze up your surface with an oil-based glaze or a thick water-based glaze (1 matte medium + 1 water) and some color (choose a light tone in keeping with the basecoat), using a big glazing brush with a lot of glaze. While still wet, use a clean glazing brush to add color from the palette (raw umber, burnt umber, yellow ochre, or another shade depending on the basecoat),

placing it randomly in somewhat vertical strokes (photo 1). Break up this application by sponging off the entire surface (see page 80), using a sea sponge with a water-based glaze and cheesecloth with an oil-based glaze (photo 2). While wet, strié in the direction of the grain as described above with a used disposable brush or a spalter (photo 3). The more you strié, the lighter and more even the texture will become.

1 2 3

CRASSÉ OR DRYBRUSH

Crassé (pronounced crah-SAY), which means "dirt marks" in French, imitates the scuffs and dirt marks seen on old painted *boiserie* or woodwork (see page 223). It is a positive method of paint manipulation done with an old, worn spalter or teeth spalter and some dark gouache colors on the palette (raw umber, burnt umber, burnt sienna, raw sienna, Cassel earth, chrome green oxide).

Often the painter spits on the palette, touches the saliva with the tips of the teeth spalter, and mixes it very slightly with some of the colors (photo 1). Since this method requires a dry brush to create a fine strié, the object is to barely wet the hairs, just enough to mix them with a little color while remaining almost dry. Using

the conductor or drummer's hold (see page 37), position the teeth spalter vertically over panels (photo 2) and sideways over relief areas (photo 3), then slide it on the surface to leave darkened areas and ridges. This makes the surface look as if the wood were coming through the paint, or as if the ridges were darkened by dirt. If spitting on your palette seems repulsive, you can wet an industrial sponge instead and clip it onto the palette. Each time you need to moisten the brush, run its tip over the wet sponge, then mix it with the gouache. You can also use acrylics for crassé, but because they dry so quickly they tend to clot the brush hairs, whereas gouaches are reactivated by the moisture in the brush, so that clotting is prevented.

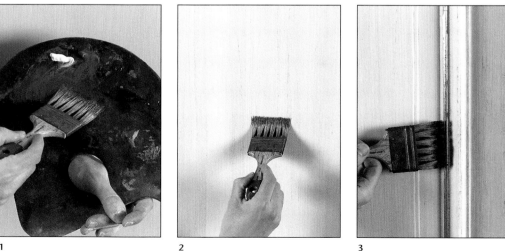

1 2 3

WIPING OFF

The negative method of wiping off is used on areas with three-dimensional architectural details such as moldings, flutings, bas-reliefs, or ornaments to emphasize their detail by simulating the dust and dirt that accumulates over time within their fine crevices.

Glaze the surface with an oil-based glaze (photo 1), then stipple it with the glazing brush or a stippling brush to achieve a fine, even "grain." Wipe off the carved and flat surfaces, using a white lint-free fine cotton rag that has either been folded into a hard pad or wrapped over a small wood block or dowel (a piece of wooden handrail is best) or over your thumb, depending on the element you're working on (photo 2). (The rag must be hard so that it doesn't wipe the glaze out of the fine crevices.) Whichever configuration you choose, keep turning the rag to expose a clean side so the wipeoffs are really clean. While the glaze is still wet, smooth out the wipeoffs with a little stippling, then wipe off the surface again. Let dry, then apply a second glaze to reinforce the relief areas; wipe off the surface using the same technique while concentrating only on the reliefs. This can also be done on a small surface using a reversible water-based glaze and a wet chamois skin instead of a rag.

1

2

"ROPEY" AND HEAVY-BODIED BASECOATS

A "ropey" basecoat is basepaint that has been thickened so that it has the consistency of yogurt. It is used for such aged patinas as old painted *boiserie* (see page 223), or whenever visible brushmarks are desirable (see photo at right). For a water-based paint, mix acrylic gesso or flat latex paint with whiting; for an oil-based paint, mix flat alkyd paint, whiting or zinc white, and turpentine. (Refer to the technical notes for each recipe to determine the correct proportions for these ingredients.) Brush on a ropey basecoat with a glazing brush or a flat brush, applying pressure in order to leave a distinct strié or rope effect. Let dry, then apply a second coat in the same manner.

The formula for a heavy-bodied basecoat, which is even thicker than a ropey one, contains joint compound or modeling paste. A heavy-bodied basecoat can be so thick that its ingredients are most thoroughly mixed with a power drill fitted with a mixing tip. This type of basecoat is used to create highly textured surfaces such as distressed Italian walls (page 216), as well as three-dimensional finishes like Provençal walls and jigouille (pages 217 and 218).

STRIPING A MOLDING WITH A RONDIN BRUSH

A rondin is a fat skunk-hair brush with a short wooden handle (see page 45). Its round, thick hairs hold a generous load of paint or glaze, and are perfect for painting relief surfaces, both flat and curved, such as stripe moldings and other narrow details on paneling. For this task, you must use a rondin whose width matches that of the molding you're intending to paint. Also, the rondin is held in a specific way; this is the only situation in which the brush hold described below is used.

Load the rondin with a fluid paint or glaze. Hold the brush by pinching the hairs between your thumb and index finger just above the ferrule; the handle rests in the palm of your hand (see drawing). As you run the brush hairs over the face of the molding, guide their path by running your middle finger along its side. By pinching the hairs, you ensure that they will flex to fit the contour of the molding (see photo). When the brush is out of paint, reload it, then overlap part of the previous stroke to ensure seamless coverage.

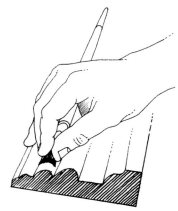

Watermark Patina

TECHNICAL NOTES

Difficulty Rating

1

System

Oil

Basecoat

Gray-green **(white + burnt umber + chrome green oxide + a touch of burnt sienna)** alkyd, satin or eggshell finish

Oil Glazes

Glaze #1: 2 turpentine + 1 oil + whiting + drier

Glaze #2: 1 turpentine + 1 oil + drier

Palette

Artists' Oils

White

Yellow ochre

Cadmium red

Raw umber

Burnt umber

Chrome oxide deep

Brushes and Tools

Glazing brush

Cheesecloth

Old stiff spattering (small glazing) brush

Palette knife (for spattering)

Square stippling brush

Exercises

Ragging (page 205)

Stippling (page 206)

Spattering (page 86)

This decorative patina is an interpretation of the marks that water could make on old wallpapers. The technique can be done in any color, but the color of the glaze should be close to that of the basecoat so that the finished look is very subtle. An effective and rapid technique, watermark patina works well on walls and other large surfaces as well as on small objects or furniture. It looks best in contemporary settings.

Before you begin working on your surface, create a small sample to ensure that the glaze will "open" to your satisfaction in step 4.

1. Lightly sand and dust off the cured basecoated surface. Use the glazing brush to apply a medium layer of glaze #1 (see Technical Notes) + **white + chrome oxide deep + raw umber + burnt umber + cadmium red** + a touch of **yellow ochre,** which is a gray tone slightly darker than the basecoat. Crisscross the glaze as noted on page 205.

2. While the surface is still wet, stipple it with the same glazing brush as shown in the exercise on page 206. This will break up the brush marks and prepare the surface for the next step.

3. While still wet, rag the surface with cheesecloth formed into a rosebud shape as shown on page 205 to produce a medium-fine texture, then very lightly stipple it as shown on page 206.

4. While the surface is still wet, barely dip the spattering brush in mineral spirits, then use it to spatter the entire surface to "open up" the fresh glaze (see page 86). Before you start, test the spatter in an inconspicuous area to see how quickly and to what extent the glaze opens. If the glaze doesn't open, it either means that it's begun to set because you waited too long before spattering, or that it isn't oily enough. If the glaze opens too much

and starts running, it either means that you loaded the brush too heavily with mineral spirits, or that the glaze is too oily, in which case you should add some turpentine to the mineral spirits. Once you've worked out any glitches, spatter the whole surface, working methodically from left to right and from top to bottom.

5. Optional: To add more depth and detail, spatter the still-wet surface with wet glaze #2 (see Technical Notes) + **chrome oxide deep + burnt umber** + a touch of **white** here and there.

6. While still wet, lightly stipple the surface with the square stippling brush as shown in the exercise on page 206 to smooth out any unevenness that may be evident. Let dry.

7. Finish with eggshell- or satin-finish oil-based varnish if needed.

ALTERNATE TECHNIQUES

You can also spatter the surface with a chiqueteur brush instead of a spattering brush, which will produce more open marks than are shown in the demonstration. Follow steps 1–3, then dip the chiqueteur in mineral spirits and spin it between your fingers in a bucket to remove excess thinner and to tassel the hairs. Proceed with the fine dabbing of the chiqueteur as shown in the exercise on page 87, wait until the glaze opens (usually 10 to 15 seconds), then stipple the surface finely to smooth it out.

USING OTHER MEDIA

If you're working on a small area (no larger than 2 feet square), this technique can also be done in fluid acrylics, which is spattered with denatured alcohol instead of mineral spirits, but the result won't be as delicate.

1. Before you start, it's advisable to make a small sample of the finish covering steps 1–4 to ensure that the glaze "opens" properly when it's spattered with mineral spirits.

2. Apply the glaze, then crisscross it.

3. Stipple the wet glaze with the glazing brush.

4. Immediately rag the surface with cheesecloth.

5. Spatter the still-wet glaze with mineral spirits.

6. If desired, spatter the surface with glaze to add depth. Stipple lightly to smooth out any unevenness. Let dry.

7. The completed finish.

1

2

3

4

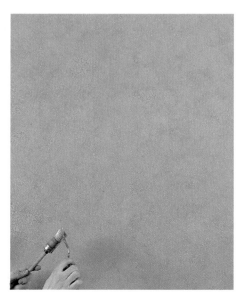

5

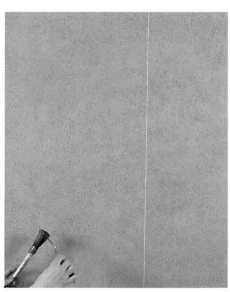

6

Tricolor Glazing

TECHNICAL NOTES

Difficulty Rating

1.5

System

Oil

Basecoat

Pale yellow ochre (**yellow ochre + white + burnt umber**) alkyd, eggshell or satin finish

Oil Glaze

3 turpentine + 1 oil + drier + whiting OR 1 glazing liquid + ³/₄ kerosene + ¹/₄ linseed oil

Palette

Artists' Oils

White

Yellow ochre

Raw umber

Burnt umber

Violet

Brushes and Tools

Large and small glazing brushes

Cheesecloth

Spattering (small glazing) brush

Palette knife (for spattering)

Exercises

Stippling (page 206)

Ragging (page 205)

Spattering (page 86)

This decorative patina, which simulates the effect of old walls or leather, is wonderful for walls and other large surfaces since it lends depth and texture to otherwise flat areas. It works well on surfaces that are not very smooth because the texture helps to obscure the imperfections. It works well in both traditional and modern settings.

1. Lightly sand and dust off the cured basecoated surface. Use a large glazing brush to glaze the surface heavily with the glaze + **violet** + **white** + **raw umber** + **burnt umber** as described on page 205. Stipple the surface with the same glazing brush as shown on page 206.
2. While the surface is still wet, load a small glazing brush with glaze, then touch it to the **burnt umber** and **raw umber** on the palette. Create some variations on the surface by making some marks or marbling effects (not spots or dots). Don't cover the whole surface, but let a lot of the background show through.

3. While wet, stipple the surface with the large glazing brush.
4. Bunch the cheesecloth into a rosebud shape, then immediately rag the still-wet surface as shown in the exercise on page 205, until it looks nicely textured. This step breaks up the variations left by the glazing brush in step 2.
5. Optional: If you wish to add to the effect, either while the surface is still wet or after it dries, spatter it with glaze + **raw umber** + **burnt umber.** Let dry.
6. Finish with flat- or eggshell-finish varnish if needed.

USING OTHER MEDIA

If you're working on a small to medium-sized surface—and don't mind having to work *very* quickly—this technique can also be done with an acrylic glaze (1 matte medium + 1 water). Instead of ragging the surface with cheesecloth, sponge it off with a damp sponge (see page 80), then stipple it with a stippling brush.

1

2

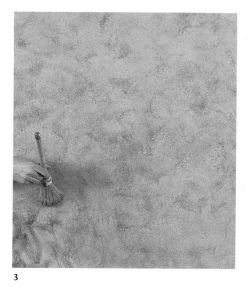

3

4

1. Apply and crisscross the glaze, then stipple it with the glazing brush.

2. Add some variations with a small glazing brush. Create marks and marbling effects rather than spots or dots, and leave a lot of background visible.

3. Stipple the surface with the large glazing brush.

4. Break up the marks added in step 2 by immediately ragging the surface with cheesecloth.

5. The completed finish. This example was spattered with glaze after the surface had dried.

5

Distressed Italian Walls

This technique imitates the old lime walls that can be found in many towns throughout Italy. Similar to aged lime stucco but with a slightly dimensional texture, this finish is fairly smooth to the touch, not rough like a heavy sand texture. The coloration is generally uneven because lime-washed walls often are not brushed evenly and the action of sun and weather discolors certain areas. The technique is very appropriate for walls that are not perfectly prepared, as well as for a more rustic look.

Because the acrylic paint dries quickly, it's recommended that steps 2–6 be done by two to three people working a section at a time: One to apply each of the three colors, one to stipple the surface before it dries, and one to assist the other two people.

1. Prepare three values of the same color in three different pails using the heavy-bodied paint with univeral tints or acrylics and mix with an electric power drill. For the lightest value, tint the heavy-bodied paint with **white + yellow ochre + chrome yellow.** Prepare the medium value the same way, but make it darker by adding more yellow ochre. Repeat for the darkest value, but add even more **yellow ochre** as well as **raw sienna + raw umber.** Test the three colors to see how they look when dried. Though they should all be the same hue, each should have a distinct value.

2. Lightly sand and dust off the primed surface. Choose three different disposable brushes or large glazing brushes. (I recommend disposable because they are very cheap and this technique is especially hard on brushes. Number the brushes and their respective pails so you don't put the brush in the wrong pail.) Using the medium-value paint and its brush, cover 60 to 70 percent of the surface with large, heavy marks.

3. While the paint is still wet, cover the remaining 20 percent of the surface that is still untouched with the darkest value, overlapping the medium value here and there.

4. Cover the remaining surface with the lightest value, again overlapping the other colors here and there.

5. While the surface is still wet, touch the damp sea sponge to a little **raw umber** and **burnt umber,** working it on the palette in a circular motion. Touch the sponge to surface as shown in the exercise on page 79, but use a much more open technique to add distressing and depth here and there.

6. While wet, stipple the surface heavily (see page 206) to "melt" the underwork. The more you stipple, the more the variations will fade, so if you want a more textured look, stipple just a little. Let dry.

7. Optional: At this point you can leave the surface as is, or you can lightly glaze it with two or three colors as shown in the recipe for "Tricolor Glazing" (see page 213). Use an acrylic glaze (see Technical Notes) + **raw sienna + yellow ochre + raw umber** varied with other colors from the palette. Sponge off the surface with a damp sea sponge as shown on page 80. Let dry.

8. Smooth out and age the surface with a medium sanding, using either 150-grit sandpaper or a sanding block. Dust it off thoroughly.

USING OTHER MEDIA

Although the water-based heavy-bodied paint is easier to handle, this recipe can also be done with an oil-based paint (a flat-finish alkyd) mixed with whiting ($1/2$ flat alkyd + $1/2$ whiting).

1. Prepare three values of the same color of heavy-bodied paint in three different pails.

2. Cover 60 to 70 percent of the primed surface with large, heavy marks of the medium-value paint.

3. While the paint is still wet, cover most of the remaining untouched surface with the darkest value.

4. Cover the remaining surface with the lightest value.

5. Using an open technique, sponge on darker colors to distress the surface and add depth.

6. While wet, stipple the surface heavily to "melt" the underwork. Let dry.

7. The finish can be considered complete at this point, but can be glazed if greater depth is desired (see step 8).

8. Optional: Lightly glaze the dried surface with two or three values of the same color, then sponge off with a damp sea sponge. (See "Tricolor Glazing," page 212, for more information.)

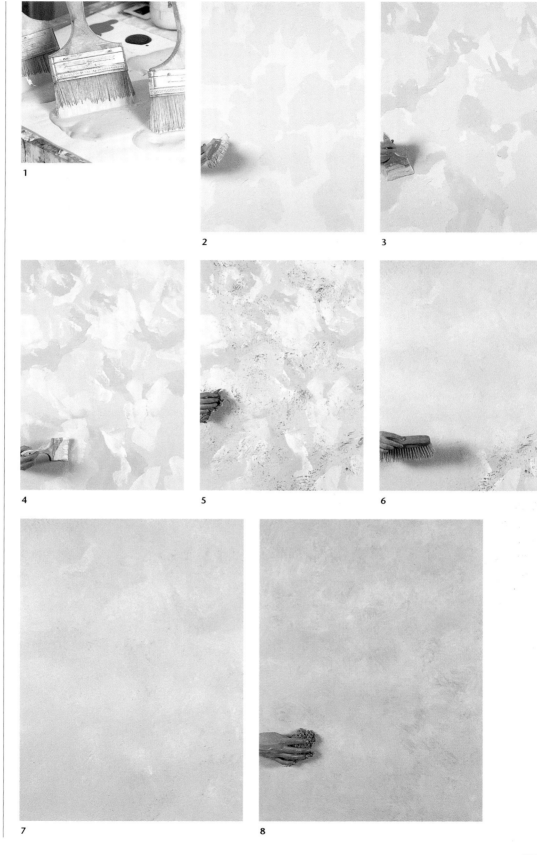

1

2

3

4

5

6

7

8

9. The completed finish.

9

Raised Textures: Provençal Walls and Jigouille

TECHNICAL NOTES

Difficulty Rating

2

System

Water (acrylics OR gouaches)

Basecoat

White oil-based primer

For Jigouille, Step 5

Straw yellow (**white +
yellow ochre + raw umber**)
latex, satin finish

Heavy-Bodied Paint

1/2 joint compound + 1/4 flat
white latex paint + whiting

Glaze

Acrylic (1 matte medium + 2
water) OR gouache (gouache
+ water)

Palette

Artists' Acrylics OR Gouaches

White

Raw sienna

Yellow ochre

Burnt sienna

Raw umber

Brushes and Tools

Glazing brush

Sea sponge

Stippling brush

Compound knife

Exercises

Sponging Off (page 80)

Stippling (page 206)

Sponging On (page 79)

Wiping Off (page 205)

*See also the recipe for "Tricolor
Glazing" (page 212)*

More three-dimensional than distressed Italian walls, these raised textures have a brushed or troweled look that seeks to imitate old walls found in the Provence region of France that were sometimes brushed with lime paint and the brushstrokes left visible. These techniques, which work particularly well on rough, uneven walls, can be done in any colors and glazed with complementary or contrasting tones.

PROVENÇAL WALLS

1. Prepare the heavy-bodied paint by combining joint compound and white latex in the bucket and mixing with an electric power drill. Add whiting a little at a time while stirring. Do a sample to test that the paste can hold its shape; it should not flatten out when you stipple it with a glazing brush. If it does, add more joint compound and whiting.
2. With the glazing brush, brush the paint heavily over the primed surface, leaving obvious crisscrossed brushstrokes in all directions. Let dry well (at least 2 hours). Sand with a sanding block to smooth out the surface slightly.
3. Overglaze: Glaze the surface with a water-based glaze (see Technical Notes) tinted with various colors from the palette, as shown in the recipe for "Tricolor Glazing" (see page 212). Sponge off the surface as shown in the exercise on page 80, then stipple it to smooth it out. Let dry.
5. Sand well with a block, then dust off. Sponge on some off-white (**white + yellow ochre**) to achieve a chalky look. Let dry. Sand lightly.

JIGOUILLE

1. Prepare the heavy-bodied paint as for Provençal walls (see step 1 above).
2. Lightly sand and dust off the primed surface. Using a large glazing brush or a disposable brush, cover your surface heavily with the heavy paint mixture, stippling it with your glazing brush as you apply it.
3. While wet, stipple the surface with a dry stippling brush (see the exercise on page 206) to create a network of tiny "mountains" that hold their shape. Let the surface set for about 20 minutes. (Timing will depend on the temperature and the thickness of the paint.)
4. When almost dry to the touch but not cured, flatten the ridges with a clean compound knife, wiping it off frequently in a rag as you work. Work almost parallel to the surface in all directions and with very little pressure; the object is to flatten the surface, not to scratch it. Let dry thoroughly.
5. Lightly sand and dust off the surface. Basecoat it with the tinted latex paint (see Technical Notes). Let dry.
6. Overglaze: Using the glazing brush and a water-based glaze (see Technical Notes) + **raw sienna + raw umber + yellow ochre**, glaze the surface, varying the tonality with colors from the palette (**burnt sienna, burnt umber,** and **raw sienna**) as shown in the recipe for "Tricolor Glazing" (see page 212), then stipple it with the stippling brush.
7. While the surface is still wet, wipe it off with a clean rag folded into a pad (see page 205), turning it often to expose a clean area. Remove glaze from the tops of the "mountains" and leave it in the tiny crevices. Let dry. (A gouache overglaze is wiped off with a damp, folded chamois.)
8. Repeat step 7 with another tone if you want to accentuate the crevices. Let dry. To achieve a chalkier, aged effect, dust the surface with powdered pigment in white, raw umber, or another shade.

USING OTHER MEDIA

The heavy-bodied paint can also be prepared with oil-based paint and compounds or oil-based zinc white in cans and whiting. Apply the mixture with a compound knife, then stipple it with a stippling brush. When it is almost set, flatten it with the compound knife, then let dry. Overglaze the surface with either a water-based glaze (see Technical Notes) or an oil-based one (2 turpentine + 1 oil + drier), then wipe off. (Oils give you more time to wipe off.)

Raised Textures: Provençal Walls and Jigouille

1. Provençal walls: Brush the heavy-bodied paint over the primed surface, leaving crisscrossed brushstrokes in all directions. Let dry.

2. Sand with a sanding block to smooth out the surface slightly.

3. Glaze the surface with various colors as shown in the recipe for "Tricolor Glazing" (see page 212).

4. Sponge off the surface.

5. Stipple the surface to smooth it out, then let dry.

6. Sand well, then dust off. For a chalky look, sponge on some off-white glaze. Let dry, then sand lightly.

7. The completed finish.

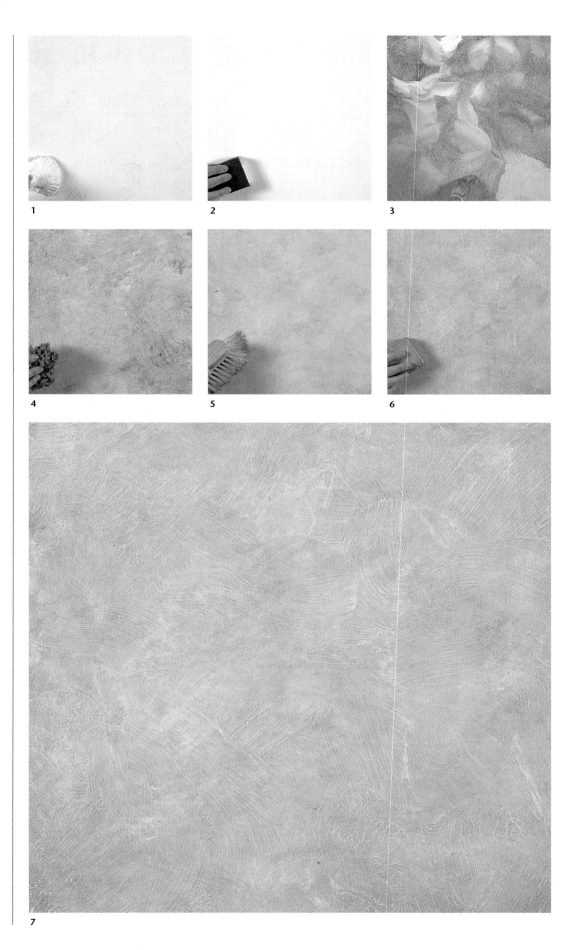

1

2

3

4

5

6

7

1. Jigouille: Cover the surface heavily with the heavy-bodied paint, stippling it with the glazing brush as you apply it.

2. Stipple the wet paint with a dry stippling brush to create a network of tiny "mountains." Let set for about 20 minutes.

3. Using very little pressure and working almost parallel to the surface, flatten the ridges with a clean compound knife. Let dry thoroughly, lightly sand and dust off the surface, then basecoat it with latex paint. Let dry.

4. Glaze the surface with various colors from the palette. While wet, wipe off the glaze from the tops of the "mountains" and leave it in the tiny crevices. Let dry.

5. The completed finish.

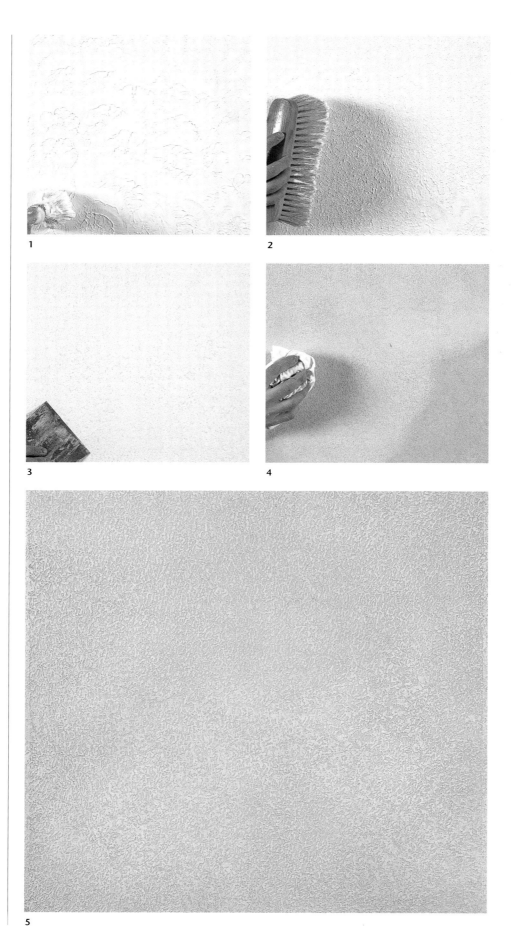

1

2

3

4

5

Old Painted Boiserie with Aged Gilding

Paneled walls in 17th- and 18th-century Europe were made of handcarved oak painted with a mixture of rabbitskin glue, whiting, and pigment. Because this water-based paint dried very quickly, visible brushstrokes, which ran with the grain of the wood, often remained. The painted room was sometimes ornamented with gilded strip moldings or other adornments, and used various colors for the stiles and rail, moldings, stripe, and sometimes also featured marbleized baseboards and grisaille painting over the doors. (For a better understanding of the period style and choice of colors, consult books on 18th-century interior decor.) The porous paints easily absorbed dirt and humidity, which eventually discolored it, giving it a beautiful aged look.

Often called French patina, this technique aims to duplicate the patina these painted *boiseries* took on after many decades. Be aware that at the time all the gilding had a saturated tone and was left unglazed; its subtle glow is produced only by wear over time. Reproducing this look requires a few tricks to add 100 years to newly painted millwork. (See Chapter 7, "Metal Patinas and Gilding," for more information on gilding.) This technique is particularly appropriate for various classical settings. It is also used to age and distress new millwork for a more rustic decor. Hundreds of tonalities can be made to work with this technique, so research the particular style and period to get the right hue.

1. Prepare a ropey basepaint (see Technical Notes), then tint it with a light, cold greenish gray (**raw umber** + **burnt umber** + **ultramarine blue** + **yellow ochre**). Stipple the paint on the ornaments first, using the glazing brush to cover all areas. Brush the paint on the flat areas and the molding following the direction of the grain. To leave visible brushstrokes, apply pressure to the glazing brush, or use a spalter to strié the flat areas. Let dry.

2. Make the thick paint a shade darker by adding **ultramarine blue** + **raw umber** + **Payne's gray,** then use it to paint the stiles, rails, and the inset molding. Let dry.

3. Mix a beige-gray glaze (glaze #1 + **raw umber** + **white** + **raw sienna** + **yellow ochre** + **burnt umber**), then apply it to the surface with a glazing brush, crisscrossing as noted on page 205. Make deep striés over the wet glaze with a spalter or disposable brush as shown in the exercise on page 206.

4. Spray the ornament with water to keep wet longer. Apply glaze to it, then stipple it with the glazing brush to reach all the nooks and crannies. Wipe off the buildup with a damp rag or elephant ear or sea sponge. Complete the rest of the flat surface by glazing it heavily and dragging the spalter strongly to create a nice strié as shown on page 206. Let dry.

5. Overglaze: With glaze #1 + **raw umber** + **burnt umber** + **burnt sienna,** glaze the stiles and rail once more to produce more variations within the surface, then strié. Let dry.

6. Prepare glaze #2 (see Technical Notes), then tint it with **raw umber** + **burnt umber** + **yellow ochre** + a touch of **ultramarine blue.** Using the glazing brush, apply it heavily to the entire surface.

7. While it is still wet, touch the tip of the glazing brush to the **black, raw umber,** and **yellow ochre** on the palette, then add some variations to the surface as shown in the recipe for "Tricolor Glazing" (see page 212). Smooth out the variations with a disposable brush, then sponge off as on page 80 to even them out further. While still wet, wipe off the ornaments with a damp rag as shown in the exercise on page 208, then strié the surface with a spalter as shown in the exercise on page 206. Let dry.

8. Paint the ornaments and molding with yellow ochre as shown on page 239. You can also drybrush some **red ochre** on the tip of the ornaments for the look of water gilding (see page 207). Apply 3-hour gold size; when the size is at the right tack, leaf the moldings and tip-gild the ornaments as shown on pages 239 and 240. Let dry.

9. To age the gilding, tint glaze #1 with **burnt umber** + **raw umber,** then apply it

with a pointed glazing brush or rondin brush. Wipe off the glaze with a wet sponge and smooth it out with a badger brush. Let dry.

10. Switch to the gouache palette. Spit on the palette or barely wet the tip of the used teeth spalter. Very lightly load the tips of the brush with **burnt umber + raw umber** or **yellow ochre + black,** working them on the palette in circular motion. Use the teeth spalter to drybrush the surface as shown in the exercise on page 207, following the grain of the wood. This will simulate the wood showing through the paint in the areas of most wear (on the edges) and the accumulation of dirt. The more you drybrush the surface, the more distressed it will look.

11. To age the ornaments, very lightly load the teeth spalter with **burnt umber + red ochre** gouache, then touch the brush to high-relief areas. This technique approximates the red bole that shows through the gold on worn water-glazed gilding. (See "Using Other Media," below, for an alternative aging technique.) For

extra authenticity, dip a folded rag into a container of raw umber pigment, dust the surface with it, then brush off the excess.

USING OTHER MEDIA

This technique can also be done using an oil system, following the same steps. Prepare the heavy-bodied paint by adding whiting to a flat alkyd basepaint. For the overglaze, use a mixture of 3 turpentine + 1 oil + drier + artists' oils.

The ornaments can also be aged with a wax bar, which is a tinted wax used by furniture finishers for touchups. Wax bars are available in a few earth colors, or you can make your own by melting beeswax in a double burner, adding pigment, and pouring it into a plastic lid or other shape. (Note that making your own wax bars requires caution, as well as protective gear—an apron, gloves, and a face mask—and immediate access to a fire extinguisher.) Drag the wax bar across the surface, hitting only the high-relief areas to leave a trace of color. Let dry.

1. Stipple the ropey basepaint over the entire surface. While the paint is wet, strié the flat areas with a spalter. Let dry.

2. Paint the stiles, rails, and inset molding with a darker value of the ropey basepaint.

3. Spray the ornaments with water so they'll stay wet longer, then apply a lighter glaze to the entire surface.

4. While wet, strié the flat areas with a spalter. Stipple the ornaments with a glazing brush, then wipe off the buildup with a sea sponge. Let dry.

1

2

3

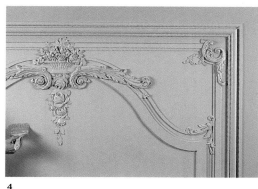

4

5. Glaze the stiles and rails again, then strié. Let dry.

6. Apply glaze heavily to the entire surface.

7. While wet, add some variations, then smooth them out.

8. Sponge off the surface to even out the variations further.

9. Wipe off the ornaments with a damp rag.

10. Strié the flat areas with a spalter. Let dry.

11. Paint the ornaments and stripe moldings with yellow ochre; let dry. Apply 3-hour gold size, let set to the right tack, then gild the ornaments and moldings (see pages 234–241 for more information).

12. To age the gilding, apply a dark glaze.

13. Wipe off the glaze with a wet sponge, then smooth it out with a badger brush. Let dry.

14. Use the teeth spalter to drybrush the surface and the ornaments.

15. The completed finish.

5

6

7

8

9

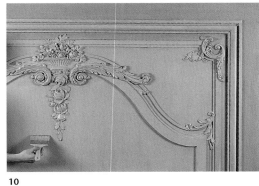

10

11

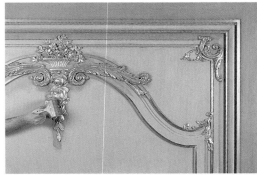

12

13

14

15

Crackle Effects

TRANSPARENT CRACKLING

This elegant effect simulates the fine crackling seen in the varnish of old paintings or on old basecoats. The look is often a result of age and of stress caused by humidity, unstable substrates, or incompatible mediums. There are many ways to obtain the crackling, but the basic rule is that you are putting a fast-drying paint or varnish over slow-drying paint or varnish that has not yet cured. In this case, the crackle effect occurs because the gum arabic or shellac dries and cures very fast, but the oil size dries more slowly; hence the upper layer is stretched and will crack as the lower layer continues to dry.

Ready-made crackling products are sold at art supply and home decorating stores. Different products will produce different types and degrees of crackling, as will the thickness of application and the temperature. Experiment to find the effect you want.

1. Lightly sand and dust off the basecoat or dried glazed finish. Apply a thin, even coat of crackle varnish #1 with the varnishing brush, stretching it out with the spalter. Allow the size to tack up, then test it by pressing your knuckle lightly to the size. (Do *not* use your fingertip; that will ruin the size.) It is ready when you barely feel your knuckle stick, or when you hear a slight squeak when you gently drag your knuckle across the surface.

2. When the size is ready, use the spalter to apply crackle varnish #2 (see Technical Notes). If the size is at the right tack, the gum arabic or shellac should not bead too much (if it only beads slightly, see if stretching it out with the spalter fixes the problem).

3. Let dry. Cracks should appear within 2 to 4 hours. To hasten the process and produce larger, almost instantaneous cracks, use a hair dryer. Let dry for 24 hours.

4. Tint glaze #1 (see Technical Notes) with **raw umber + any color similar to the background** to achieve a very dark tone. Apply the glaze with the glazing brush, crisscrossing it as noted on page 205. Stretch the glaze with the spalter, then stipple it as shown in the exercise on page 206. Let set for 15 to 30 minutes, then wipe off with a clean, soft white cotton rag folded in a pad as shown on page 208. The wiping off will leave the dark glaze only in the fine cracks, making the network of veining more evident. Let dry.

OPAQUE CRACKLING

Opaque crackling differs from transparent crackling in that you are actually crackling a coat of paint rather than a transparent varnish. This requires a satin-finish alkyd or latex basecoat over which an organic glue is applied, then allowed to dry for 15 to 20 minutes. A latex basepaint in a contrasting color is then painted over the glue in one pass, so that the glue is disturbed as little as possible. The principle remains the same: A fast-drying paint applied over a slow-drying glue will crackle and let the base show through. Applying a thin coat of paint over a thick application of glue will result in large cracks; a thick coat of paint over a thin application of glue will produce small cracks. In both cases, the crackle effect is immediate.

ALTERNATIVE TECHNIQUES: OPAQUE CRACKLING

Apply a satin-finish alkyd basecoat to the surface. Allow it to set but not cure. Once dry to the touch, paint over it with an eggshell-finish latex paint of a different color. Let dry. It will take about 10 hours to see results. Use the hair dryer if you want faster crackling.

You can also basecoat the surface with an eggshell-finish latex paint, let it dry fully, then paint over it with gum arabic solution or organic glue. Let dry for 15 to 20 minutes, then apply latex paint over the glue in a single application; don't rework it with the brush. The crackle effect will be immediate.

1. Transparent crackling:
Apply a thin, even coat of 3-hour gold size, then stretch it out with the spalter. Allow the size to tack up.

2. Apply diluted gum arabic or clear shellac, then let dry. Cracks will appear within 2 to 4 hours.

3. To hasten the process and produce larger cracks, use a hair dryer. Let set for 12 hours.

4. Apply a dark glaze, let set for 15 to 30 minutes, then wipe off. The glaze will remain only in the cracks.

Opaque crackling: A thick coat of paint over a thin application of glue will produce small cracks (photo 1), while a thin coat of paint over a thick application of glue will yield large cracks (photo 2).

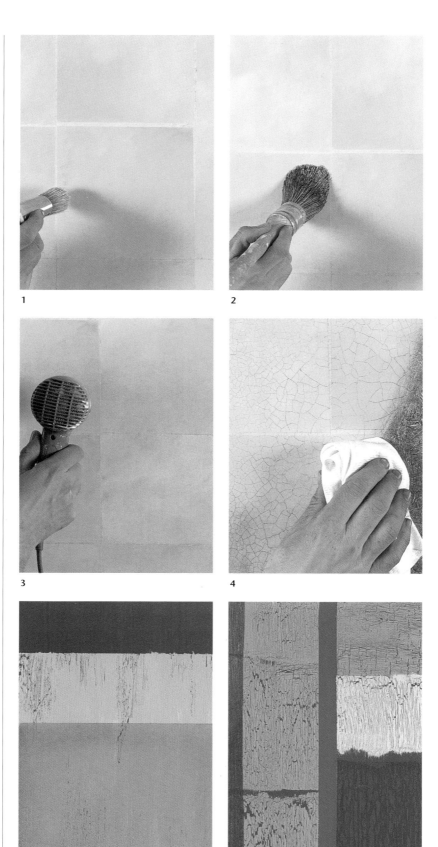

Metal Patinas and Gilding

Metal patina effects are used to give any kind of plaster, composite, or wood ornaments or statuary the look of a heavy bronze or other semiprecious metal. Real bronze is expensive, but the patina it acquires over many years outdoors can be simulated with a simple recipe. Metal patinas are a timeless finish—bronze was discovered in prehistoric times—and works in classical as well as modern settings.

The technique of gilding entails applying extremely thin leaves of gold, copper, or aluminum one at a time over a special type of adhesive, generally a product called gold size. Gilding is a specialized craft in itself and is often handled by professional gilders. This book presents an overview of gilding as it applies to decorative painting; for more complete information, consult a book on gilding.

This living room features trompe l'oeil ornamental friezes set off by gilded stripe moldings.

Creating a Metal Patina

Metal surfaces develop patinas due to oxidation, which results from the application of chemicals or the natural effects of weather that alter the aspect of the metal. The best-known patina is rust, which turns iron orange-brown and makes its surface rough. Copper turns green, bronze turns green or tarnishes, silver tarnishes, and aluminum becomes white. Decorative styles of the 19th century often imitated such patinations, painting bronze verdigris effects on plaster bas-reliefs or plaster or composite ornaments that were affixed to wood or paneling.

TYPES OF METAL PATINAS

Patinations can be done in several different ways:

- The most often used technique employs glazes over a metallic basecoat of bronze or aluminum powders mixed in a medium. This is an easy method that produces very efficient patination.
- Another very good technique—but more time-consuming—uses glaze over a surface that has been gilded with gold leaf or with Dutch, copper, or aluminum leaf. (An example of this is shown in the recipe for "Old Painted *Boiserie* with Aged Gilding," page 220.)
- A third technique uses glazes over a regular basecoat to achieve effects such as rust or verdigris. An older method of imitating bronze metal or antique bronze used a basecoat of yellow ochre.
- A fourth technique entails applying chemical solutions or pastes to real metals to produce actual oxidation. This method, which requires manipulation of toxic products, is not used in decorative painting.

SUITABLE APPLICATIONS

For the greatest impact, metal patinas are used on three-dimensional objects or surfaces in relief. The raised portions are wiped off, leaving the patina mostly in the recessed areas (as it would be in real metal patination) and accentuating the details.

BASIC PROCEDURE

For all techniques, surface preparation must be as smooth as possible. Oil is generally used for the basecoat and is brushed on; for bronze effects, bronze powders are mixed with special varnishes or acrylic medium and either brushed or sprayed on.

The glazing medium can either be oil- or water-based. These recipes use water systems because they dry fast and allow the following steps to be done soon after. On large surfaces the overglazing should be done in oil. Both oil- and water-based varnishes work equally well for the finish coat.

Refer to the general patina procedures in Chapter 6 (see pages 203–204). Bronze powders are toxic, so be sure to wear a mask and gloves when handling and mixing them. Bronze powders can be mixed with any of several specialized oil-, water-, or lacquer-based mediums; ask your supplier for advice. If you can't locate or don't wish to use these commercial preparations, you can make your own. For a water-based medium, use an acrylic varnish with the powders (some excellent metallic colors are available already mixed from certain acrylic manufacturers). For an oil-based medium, use satin-finish oil-based varnish and bronze powder. You can also use 3-hour gold size, covering it with the powder when still slightly tacky and then brushing out the excess; seal it with shellac or an oil-based varnish.

Natural Bronze

TECHNICAL NOTES
Difficulty Rating
2
System
Water (acrylics)
Base or Basecoat
Dutch metal leaf OR metallic gold paint (see step 1)
Glazes
For Natural Bronze
Acrylic (1 matte medium + 1 water)
For Green Bronze
Oil (3 turpentine + 1 oil + drier)
Palettes
Artists' Acrylics
Raw umber
Burnt umber
Chrome oxide deep
Black
Artists' Oils
Raw umber
Burnt umber
Chrome oxide deep
Black
Brushes and Tools
Glazing brush
Disposable brush OR patina brush
Veinette OR badger brush
Rag OR chamois
Exercises
Stippling (page 206)
Wiping Off (page 208)

Bronze is composed mainly of copper mixed with some tin and sometimes zinc. Its coloration depends on the amount of each element present, as well as on whether the patina has been produced chemically. There are hundreds of bronze variations, including brown, green (shown on page 231), red, and silvery blue. The following recipe can be used for any of those shades, according to the colors on your palette. This technique is best used on three-dimensional details or objects to highlight the relief areas.

NATURAL BRONZE

1. Apply a layer of Dutch metal leaf (see page 236 for detailed instructions) or apply a coat of metallic gold basepaint to the prepared surface. The gold metallic paint can be purchased ready-made, or can be mixed from scratch by combining bronze powder with 1 turpentine + 1 linseed oil + 10% drier, acrylic medium, or lacquer. Let dry. Coat the surface with oil-based eggshell-finish varnish, water-based satin-finish varnish, or shellac. Let dry.
2. Glaze the surface heavily with glaze (see Technical Notes) + **burnt umber + raw umber,** then stipple it with a disposable brush or a stippling brush.
3. While still wet, wipe off the ridges of the reliefs as shown on page 208. Smooth out with a veinette or badger brush. Let dry.
4. Repeat steps 2 and 3 with a darker tone (**burnt umber + black**). Keep in mind

that the darker the glaze as compared to the basecoat, the more careful you must be because every detail will show. Let dry.
5. Wax with a clear, natural beeswax (either paste or liquid) or finish with an eggshell-finish oil-based varnish.

USING OTHER MEDIA

If you're working on a large surface, step 4 should be done in an oil-based glaze (2 or 3 turpentine + 1 oil + drier + same palette in artists' oils).

GREEN BRONZE

To create green bronze, use the same base and technique as for natural bronze, but with an oil-based glaze and a slightly different palette (see Technical Notes).
1. Apply the first oil glaze in a deep green tone (**chrome oxide deep + raw umber**) in the same manner as in step # 2 for "Natural Bronze." Using a disposable brush, stipple it as shown in the exercise on page 206, then stipple it again with a clean stipple brush. Wipe off (see page 208) and stipple again. Let dry.
2. Apply a darker glaze (**chrome oxide deep + black + raw umber**). Wipe off, then stipple. Repeat. Let dry.
3. Wax with a clear, natural beeswax (either paste or liquid) or finish with an eggshell-finish oil-based varnish.

1. Natural bronze: Over gold leaf or metallic basepaint that's been sealed with varnish or shellac, apply a heavy coat of glaze, then stipple it.

2. Wipe off the ridges of the reliefs, then smooth out with a veinette or badger brush. Let dry.

3. Repeat step 1 with a darker tone.

4. Wipe off the ridges as in step 2. Let dry.

5. Stipple the entire surface, then let dry.

6. The completed finish.

1

2

3

4

5

6

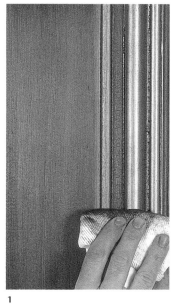

1

1. Green bronze: Over gold leaf or metallic basepaint that's been sealed with varnish or shellac, apply a heavy coat of oil glaze, then stipple it. Wipe off the ridges of the reliefs, stipple again, then let dry. Repeat with a darker glaze.

2. The completed finish.

2

Verdigris

The verdigris technique imitates the oxidation seen on bronze and copper statues and ornaments that have been exposed to the elements. Areas of low relief take on a light green tone and other parts appear medium green. Because they are most often polished, the ridges of the relief retain a little of the bronze's original goldish color. This technique is wonderful on three-dimensional objects such as small statues, ornaments, and moldings. It is also a good method to use for imitating oxidized copper and zinc.

1. Lightly sand and dust off the cured basecoated surface. With a glazing brush, apply the **metallic gold** acrylic paint with a drybrushing action (see page 207). As you work, soften certain spots by stippling them with a disposable brush (see page 206). Let dry.
2. Using a clean, dry glazing brush or a small spalter, drybrush the entire surface with a dark verdigris tone (glaze + **white + Veronese green + raw sienna** varied with colors from the palette). Wipe off the ridges as shown on page 208 so they are left clean. Soften as you work by stippling. Let dry.
3. Repeat step 2 with a lighter verdigris (add more white to the glaze used in step 2) and drybrush it in spots. Wipe off the ridges, softening with the disposable brush as you work. Let dry. Repeat one more time if necessary.
4. Load a small fat pointed brush with a very light verdigris tone (add even more white to the glaze used in step 2) and glaze the insides of the low reliefs. Stipple them with the disposable brush, then wipe off the ridges as on page 208. Let dry.
5. Here and there, drybrush some spots with acid green (glaze + **chrome green oxide + yellow ochre** + a touch of **white**) to add more warm tonalities. Let dry.
6. With a flat brush held in the drummer's grip (page 37) and on the side, hit the ridges and high reliefs by drybrushing on some gold metallic acrylic paint to make the reliefs pop out. (This simulates the areas of real bronze that have been polished back to their original shade.) Let dry.
7. Wax with a clear, natural beeswax (either paste or liquid) or finish with an eggshell-finish oil-based varnish.

USING OTHER MEDIA

If you want more working time for a large surface, you can use an oil glaze for the final overglazing that gets wiped off (see step 4).

1

2

3

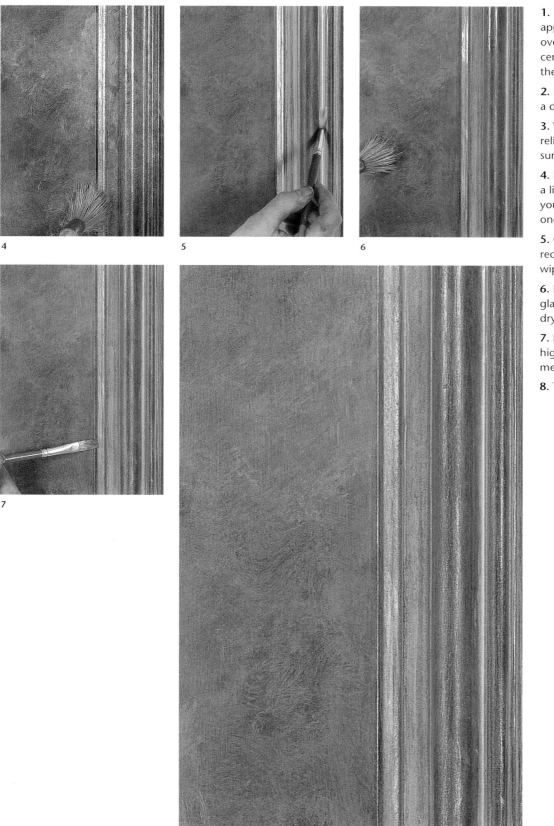

4

5

6

7

8

1. Using a drybrush action, apply gold metallic paint over the basecoat. Soften certain spots by stippling them. Let dry.

2. Drybrush the surface with a dark verdigris glaze.

3. Wipe off the ridges of the reliefs. Stipple the entire surface. Let dry.

4. Repeat steps 2 and 3 with a lighter verdigris. Soften as you work. Let dry. Repeat once more if necessary.

5. Glaze and stipple the recesses of the relief, then wipe of the ridges. Let dry.

6. Drybrush an acid green glaze here and there. Let dry.

7. Drybrush the ridges and high reliefs with gold metallic paint. Let dry.

8. The completed finish.

Gilding

Gilding is the act of applying an extremely thin metal leaf (0.4 to 0.8 micron) over any type of surface (including furniture, walls, plaster, wood, metal, and leather) using a type of glue called size to adhere the leaves. Since the earliest civilizations, gold has been a symbol of wealth and rank. Through the ages, gold has been used to ornament walls and furniture, and some of the most remarkable gilding work can still be found throughout Europe in many 18th-century palaces. Rather than making solid gold furniture, items were made of wood that was then covered with real hand-beaten gold leaves. Gold leaf is quite expensive, but its spectacular effect really cannot be duplicated by any paint. The much cheaper Dutch metal leaf does come close to the look of actual gold, but it must be varnished to prevent oxidization.

TYPES OF METAL LEAF

True gold leaf is made of real hand-beaten gold, or gold mixed with a small percentage of other alloys to give it a different color or tonality. Leaf made of other metals, such as copper and aluminum, is also available. Gold leaf is sold in different packages: in books about 3 1/8 inches square, with 25 pages to a book and 20 books to a pack; and in 67-foot-long rolls measuring 1/8 inch, 1/4 inch, 1/2 inch, and 1 inch wide, and ranging up to 4 inches wide with most sizes in between. Copper and Dutch metal leaf are sold in 6-inch-square leaves. Leaf may either be loose-surface (not attached to the book) or patent (held on the page by a thin red powder, which allows for easier manipulation but makes the gold appear duller).

Various types of metal leaf are available for use in gilding techniques:

- *Gold leaf* comes in different colors and different karats, or weights. The color or tone of the gold is obtained by adding a small amount of an alloy, such as copper, silver, or palladium. The higher the weight, the purer the gold: 24k, 23k, 22k (most often used), 18k, 16k (lemon gold), 14k, 12k (white gold), as well as moon gold (pinkish gold) and palladium (silvery gold tone). Be aware that 12k gold has a high silver content and therefore will oxidize; the others won't.
- *Copper leaf,* which contains 100 percent copper, generally has a pinkish hue, and is also available as a variegated leaf (multicolored). *Dutch metal leaf,* an alloy of copper and zinc, is the kind of copper-alloy leaf most often used because its color is closest to that of real gold. All leaf containing copper oxidizes and must be sealed.
- *Aluminum leaf,* made of aluminum, will not oxidize but has a rather cold look.
- *Silver leaf,* made of silver, has a slightly warmer tone, but will oxidize rapidly and must be sealed.

TYPES OF GILDING

There are two types of gilding: *oil gilding* and *water gilding.* If the size is oil-based, the process is known as oil gilding; if it is water-based it is called water gilding. Because it is less time-consuming and easier to work with (and thus more economical), gilding is often done with oil size, a kind of slow-drying varnish that stays open for a certain amount of time. The size is applied over a satin-finish basecoat and left to dry for a certain amount of time (anywhere from 3 to 12 hours, depending on the type of size). When the size is at the right tack, the leaf is applied either with a gilding tip (see page 52) or directly from a book of leaves. This a fairly easy technique, especially with Dutch metal leaf, and can be done over very large surfaces.

In gilding processes using water size, the "glue" is water combined with melted gelatin, which is then brushed over a tedious preparation of a minimum of twelve coats of gesso and bole. Then, while the size is still wet, the leaves are applied with a gilding tip. The water size stays open for 3 to 5 minutes, so only a small area can be gilded at a time. Primarily used for gilding over wood, water gilding produces the most beautiful results of any gilding method. Since this is the most time-consuming and difficult technique and is best left to the specialists, it is not covered here.

BASIC PROCEDURE FOR OIL GILDING

Oil gilding can be done on any flat surface or a surface with relief areas, as long as it is prepared correctly. Surface preparation must be absolutely smooth, without any imperfections, because gold leaf is so thin (0.4 to 0.8 microns) it won't hide anything; in fact, its reflective quality will magnify imperfections. The work area must be as dust-free as possible because the size must be allowed to set up for a time and it will tend to attract particles of dust to its sticky surface.

Oil sizes come in several varieties, depending on open time. Quick size (also called 3-hour size) is ready in 3 hours and stays open for 3 to 6 hours. Slow size will be ready to be gilded on in 12 hours and stays open 12 to 24 hours. These times are only averages; they may vary widely, depending on the humidity and temperature of the worksite. The thinner the leaf, the less tacky the size should be. There is also a synthetic size, which is a water-based acrylic size (not to be confused with water gilding) that is ready to be gilded in 15 minutes and stays open for 48 hours.

With an oil size you can use any type of leaf: gold of different karats, copper leaves of different shades, aluminum, silver, or palladium. Since real gold leaf does not oxidize, it does not need to be varnished; this is fortunate because varnish kills the natural shine. Leaf that does oxidize (copper, Dutch metal, and silver) must be sealed with shellac or an acrylic or oil varnish. Since real gold leaf loses its natural shine under heavy glaze, use Dutch metal leaf for the gilding process if you plan to glaze it. (For more information on aging a gilded surface, see page 220.)

GILDING TIPS

When gilding, keep the following points in mind:

- Contrary to glazing methods, a surface should be gilded from the bottom up so that if loose leaves fall or flake the pieces won't stick to a sized area that has not yet been gilded.
- Work in a draft-free area, since metal leaf is astonishingly thin and will catch the slightest movement of air, making it impossible to lay the leaf properly. Even your own breath can disrupt the proper application of the leaf.
- Many factors affect the gilding process. The gold size may be too tacky or not tacky enough; the leaf may stick to the paper on which it's mounted; "holidays" or "bald spots" in the leafed surface indicate that the size may have been applied unevenly, or may not have been allowed to set to the right tack; the burnishing process may scratch the surface; humidity will also have an effect on the process. Unfortunately, no amount of written information can replace the actual experience of gilding, so experiment and practice.

Gilding Exercise

The basic principle is the same whether you use real gold or Dutch metal leaf; what varies is the tack of the size and the way the leaf is handled. Dutch metal leaf can be picked up with your fingers, but real gold leaf must be manipulated with a gilding tip (see "Tip-Gilding," page 240).

Basecoat your surface with oil-based paint in satin or semigloss finish. Use yellow ochre if you don't want any cracks to show, red ochre if you want it to look like aged water gilding, white if you're using silver or aluminum leaf. Note that acrylics can be used on small areas.

GILDING STEP-BY-STEP

Once the basecoat has cured, sand it lightly, then dust if off. Using a varnishing brush, apply 3-hour size to small areas and 12-hour size to larger surfaces (photo 1). (If you want to wait a day before gilding, use a 12-hour size.) Cover the surface well and evenly; stretch out the size by crisscrossing it with a #100 spalter (see page 205). A spot of size that's thicker than the rest will be tackier and will show when the process is complete. It's always a good idea to tint your size with artists' oils or universal tints (in either yellow ochre or red ochre) so you can see what areas you have covered and how evenly you have applied it. The size has reached the proper tack when it is almost dried; when you touch your knuckle to it you should barely be able to feel it. You can also run your finger over the size with a slight pressure; if you hear a little squealing noise, it's ready (professional decorative painters say the size is "singing").

If you're using Dutch metal leaf, you can apply it directly out of the book. If you're working with real gold, or gilding only the highest reliefs of an ornament, apply the leaf with a gilding tip. (See page 240 for instructions on working with a gilding tip.) You can cut the book in half or thirds to accommodate the size of the area to be gilded (photo 2). If you're using real gold leaf, score it by folding the orange paper it's mounted on, then running your fingernail over the fold. I prefer using loose leaves to patent leaf, but patent leaf is easier to use if you're a beginner.

Gently place the book over the surface, then press the leaf onto the surface with your finger or a soft bristle or stencil brush (photo 3). Remove the orange paper and continue pressing on the leaf with a soft, very clean and dry squirrel-hair brush such as a chiqueteur brush (photo 4). Do *not* touch any exposed size. For Dutch metal leaf, use a soft-bristle brush to push the leaf into any crevices. Repeat the process until the sized surface is completely covered.

Burnish lightly by gently brushing the gilded surface to see if there are any "holidays," or areas that were missed (photo 5). Patch up any cracks with more leaf and give the surface a good burnishing with the same brush used previously or a large pad of soft sterilized cotton (photo 6). If you used real gold the surface can be left as is or given a slight patina (see page 220). If you used an oxidizing leaf (Dutch metal, copper, or silver), you must seal the surface with a varnish. The varnished surface can be left as is or glazed.

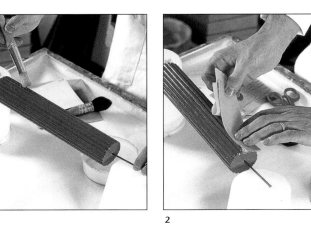

1

2

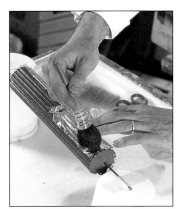

3

4

5

6

Basic Gold Leaf Applications

The following recipes explain how to leaf a flat surface such as a wall or ceiling, how to leaf a stripe molding, and how to tip-gild an ornament. These recipes use the oil-gilding technique (see page 234) because it is much easier and less time-consuming than water gilding. The processes are similar for all types of leaves. Unless you are creating an aged effect, try to find a basecoat as close as possible to the leaf color so the small cracks won't show.

GILDING A FLAT SURFACE

This application employs the same technique as shown in the exercise on page 236. It requires a book of loose leaves rather than patent. (A large roll of leaf—measuring 4 inches × 3 inches × 67 feet—is faster, but requires 2 to 3 people to apply it.) The demonstration shows aluminum leaf applied over a base of yellow ochre instead of white so that it could be seen more clearly in the photographs.

1. Basecoat the surface with the appropriate color; let dry. If you're gilding a large area, before applying the size it's a good idea to mark the surface with a 5H pencil in a grid of 6-inch squares so you have guidelines to keep your leaves straight.

2. Tint 3-hour or 12-hour size with a color similar to the basecoat, then apply it with a varnishing brush. (Use 12-hour size if your surface is over 30 square feet.) Wait until the size reaches the proper tack (heavy leaves will require more tack).

3. When the size is ready, hold the book of loose leaves between your thumb and index finger as if you were making the "okay" sign. Pull the top page back toward you until only one-quarter of the protective paper holds the leaf. Beginning at the lower left, touch the bottom of the leaf to the surface and gently roll the leaf up onto the surface in one smooth motion. Put the next leaf to the right of the first, overlapping by ⅛ inch and roll it on as before. Proceed in the same manner until the row is complete.

4. Repeat step 3 to apply the second and subsequent rows, always moving from left to right and overlapping all edges as described above. It is very important to be consistent in the way you lay the leaves; they should overlap like roof tiles, with the top one overlapping the one below, so when you burnish the surface in one direction you won't tear the leaf (see step 5). To minimize scratching (and thus dulling the finish), wait 12 hours before burnishing the leaves.

5. After all the leaves are laid, burnish them with a large, soft, clean, dry squirrel-hair brush such as a chiqueteur brush. Holding the brush like a pen (see page 37) and perpendicular to the surface, burnish the leaves at a 45-degree angle, working from upper right to bottom left. The object is to flatten the overlaps, not pull them. To keep from scratching the leaves, wipe off the brush as it picks up *skewings,* which are loose flakes or scraps. Then repeat the burnishing with a dry cotton pad, again moving in the same direction. Continue refolding the pad to avoid scratching the surface with skewings. Once the wrinkles are flattened, get rid of the overlaps by burnishing the outside edges of each leaf. Add more leaf to touch up the biggest cracks. In the photographs, small cracks are visible because the background color is not matched to the leaf color; if it had been, these tiny cracks wouldn't show. If you're working with aluminum leaf, as here, there is no need to varnish unless you want to glaze over the leaf (see page 220).

1. Gilding a flat surface:
When the size is ready, hold
the book of loose leaves
between your thumb and
index finger.

2. Beginning at the lower
left, touch the bottom of the
leaf to the surface.

3. Gently roll the leaf up onto
the surface in one smooth
motion.

4. Repeat steps 2 and 3 to
complete the first row,
overlapping the leaves by
1/8 inch.

5. Repeat steps 2–4 to apply
the second and subsequent
rows of leaf.

6. After all the leaves have
been laid, burnish them with
a chiqueteur brush. Repeat
with a dry cotton pad.

7. Eliminate the overlaps by
burnishing the contour of
each leaf.

8. The completed finish.

1

2

3

4

5

6

7

8

GILDING A STRIPE MOLDING

Gilding a stripe molding employs the same principle as gilding a flat surface, except that you use a rondin brush to apply both the basecoat and the size. For this technique, it is helpful to tint the size so you can clearly see the areas that have been covered as it is applied. A roll of leaf is used instead of a book. Although most gilders prefer to use leaves cut into small bands and apply them with a gilding tip, the roll is much faster and easier for beginners.

1. Apply the basecoat with a rondin brush. (If you're just working on the stripe molding, you can use artists' acrylics; use an alkyd basecoat instead if you're painting a large area and plan to glaze it before gilding. If the stripes are extremely narrow, you can skip the basecoating step and apply a well-tinted size directly to the prepared surface.) Let dry.

2. Once the basecoat has dried, tint some 3-hour size with **yellow ochre** or **red ochre** artists' oils or universal tints, depending on the effect you want (see page 236) and apply the size to the surface.

3. When the size reaches the right tack, hold the roll of leaf at its axle between your thumb and index finger and pull out 10 to 12 inches of leaf with the other hand. Touch the leaf to the stripe and gently rub it on the surface with your index finger. An alternate method is to hold the roll between your thumb and middle finger and push the roll down on the stripe with the index finger of the other hand. Two people working together can make the process easier: As one unrolls and stretches the leaf over the molding, the other can rub it on the surface.

4. Once the leafing is complete, burnish the surface with a squirrel-hair brush and then a small pad of cotton (see page 236).

1. Gilding a stripe molding: Apply tinted size to the surface.

2. When the size reaches the right tack, apply the leaf to the stripe. Either hold the roll of leaf at its axle between your thumb and index finger and gently rub it on the surface with the index finger of the same hand while pulling the strip of leaf with the other, or . . .

3. . . . hold the roll between the thumb and middle finger of one hand and push the leaf down on the stripe with the index finger of the other.

4. Burnish the leafed surface with a chiqueteur brush. (For a gilded stripe molding that's been "aged" with glaze, see page 223.)

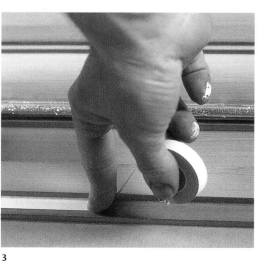

1

2

3

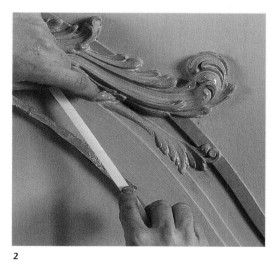

4

TIP-GILDING

In contrast to solid gilding, which covers an entire area, tip-gilding entails applying leaf only to certain parts of an ornament, particularly the higher reliefs. In spite of its name, tip-gilding doesn't have anything to do with the fact a gilding tip is used to apply the leaf; a gilding tip can be used for other gold-leaf applications, and is always used to apply real gold leaf, which was used in this demonstration. Tip-gilding is a good method to use when you don't want the gilding to be too imposing, or if you want to give the reliefs of an ornament great emphasis, especially when aged. The principal is the same as shown in the exercise on page 236, except that only the areas of high relief are gilded, using tinted size, a gilding tip, and an assortment of pointed brushes. The instructions explain the process using a book of leaves, but this technique can also be done with patent leaf, which is easier to handle but will require more touchups since it won't cling to the deeper crevices the way loose-leaf gold will.

1. Basecoat the areas to be gilded; let cure. Once the basecoat has dried, tint some size and apply it to the surface by drybrushing it on only the highest reliefs.

2. When the size reaches the right tack, prepare the gilding tip by running it twice over your hair, nose, or cheek to put a slight film of grease on it (not to add an electrostatic charge, as is often mistakenly thought). Or, before you begin, rub a little Vaseline on the back of your left hand (or your right hand if you're left-handed) and run the tip over it each time you need to grease it.

3. Use a piece of double-sided tape to attach the book of leaves to small piece of rigid cardboard twice as long as the book, fold the page back, and hold the setup between your thumb and index finger as if you were making the "okay" sign. Using the slightly "greased" gilding tip, pick up and apply the leaf by flicking the gilding tip on the edge of the leaf in a swift but gentle motion. If the leaf is not perfectly flat on the book, blow on it gently to flatten it. Because the leaves are so thin and are easily ruffled by the slightest movement, be sure not to pick up the leaf until you are standing close to the surface to which it will be applied (no more than 2 feet away). Gently lay the leaf over the sized surface, then push it softly with the gilding tip, but avoid getting size on the tip.

4. Continue the leafing process in the same way until all sized areas are gilded. If you need smaller pieces for tiny areas and touchups, cut the leaves by running your fingernail over the leaf.

5. Gently burnish the leaves with the chiqueteur brush while holding a small tray beneath your hand to catch the skewings for use in touching up. Load the chiqueteur with skewings by dipping it into the tray, then run it over small cracks and hard-to-reach places.

6. If you want to glaze the leaf, apply a clear coat of very watered-down acrylic; otherwise, the water-based glaze will bead up on the real gold leaf. (You can also use a mixture of 1 cup of hot water + 2 or 3 gelatin capsules. Stir until the gelatin has melted, let cool, then apply the mixture to the leaf with a sponge. If you are using Dutch metal leaf, you can apply an oil-based glaze directly to the surface.) If desired, proceed with the aging process using water-based glazes described on page 220.

1. Tip-Gilding: Once the size is at the right tack, lightly grease the gilding tip.

2. Using a swift but gentle motion, pick up the leaf by flicking the greased gilding tip on its edge.

3. Gently lay the leaf over the size surface.

4. Burnish the leaves with a chiqueteur brush while holding a small tray beneath your hand to catch any skewings, for use in touching up.

5. Load the chiqueteur with skewings, then run it over any small cracks or hard-to-reach places. (For an ornament that's been "aged" with glaze, see page 223).

1

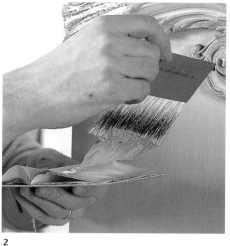

2

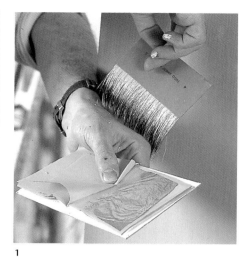

3

4

5

Tile

Tile comes in many forms, but it is tile made of baked clay or similar material, popularly known as ceramic or earthenware tile, that concerns us here. Such tiles are sometimes glazed with a glasslike paste that is tinted or painted and then fired in a kiln at a high temperature, which varies according to the type of material being fired. When mass-produced, tiles are quite even in shape and color and are available in numerous styles. A trip to a tile store will reveal an enormous diversity of pattern, shape, color, and thickness. Handmade tiles, less widely available, vary somewhat in coloration, and even differ a bit in size and shape within a given type or pattern.

The floor of this music room, which is adorned with a variety of faux finishes, is graced with a central motif and border of faux mosaic tile as well as faux travertine.

Painting Faux Tile

Since mass-produced tile is widely available and relatively inexpensive to install, tile is simulated purely for decorative reasons; for example, in order to create a certain motif or color combination that can't be found in a real tile, or to match existing old tiles. It's also practical to paint tile in places where the installation of real tile would be difficult, such as over a curved wall.

SUITABLE APPLICATIONS

Earthenware can be traced to prehistoric times, but the development and use of tile is attributed to the Greeks and the Romans, who also innovated mosaic art—tiles made in small, square pieces that fit together to form intricate pictures and designs. Magnificent mosaic floors with detailed depictions of life in those ancient societies remain intact, now installed for our viewing pleasure in major museums. But during the Middle Ages, handpainted tiles became more popular for floors. Mosaics were also less favored during the Renaissance, when new materials and techniques made floor and wall tile more accessible and widely used in many kinds of rooms. In the 17th and 18th centuries, handpainted decorative tiles became very prized by the nobility. Then, in the 19th century, tile finally became available to millions through the mass production of a tile industry that provided its product for kitchens and bathrooms in homes all over the world. There are still a few manufacturers that make handpainted tiles, but 90 percent of tile manufacturing is now mechanized. As for mosaic tile, nowadays it is installed by only a few skilled artisans.

Simulation of this timeless material works well in both traditional and modern settings, wherever you would find real tile: on floors, walls, wainscoting, tabletops, and countertops. Faux mosaic has even wider application—from all kinds of small objects to entire floors. The style, coloration, and pattern of the tile determines its suitability for a particular setting. For example, a handpainted tile with a provincial motif might not be appropriate in a bathroom fitted with art deco fixtures and accessories.

Also note that floors and other surfaces that normally get wet—such as countertops, backsplashes, and areas behind stovetops—need special surface preparation and finishing (see "Special Considerations," below).

CHOOSING THE RIGHT TECHNIQUE

Before reading this section, review "Influential Movements in Decorative Painting," page 15. Since you'll be imitating something that is handpainted (most probably in a loose manner), the Italian style is often the preferred method. However, if the pattern incorporates trompe l'oeil, the French style will achieve the best results. Where it's hard to make a clear distinction, the general rule is: More spontaneous and loose painting calls for Italian technique; more detailed and precise work calls for French.

LAYOUT

Draft your layout and design completely before you start drawing it on the surface to be painted. Consult magazines, books, and other documents to find references for your pattern. Study designs characteristic of a chosen period to avoid making an error in style.

BASIC PROCEDURE

As most tiles are very smooth, the intended surface must be prepared well. To begin, I recommend an oil-based primer followed by two coats of eggshell-finish alkyd basepaint. After lightly sanding the cured surface, draw your layout with a 3H or 5H pencil, ruling straight edges into grid lines that are very thin and light so that you can barely see them once they are painted over.

Because it dries quickly, allowing for almost immediate overglazings and the efficient use of tape to organize the surface, most faux tile is painted in acrylics, using a glaze of 1 gloss medium + 1 or 2 water + artists' acrylics. When simulating handpainted tiles, remember to keep the technique simple and spontaneous. Because real ceramic tiles, though decorated by hand, are generally lined up and painted in a row at a quick pace, the brushwork technique is usually kept to a minimum of strokes. To add a transparent crackle effect, an oil-based size is applied to the completed surface, then a layer of gum arabic solution (see the recipe for "Transparent Crackling," page 224).

To impart a glasslike sheen to your faux tile, use an oil- or water-based satin-finish or semigloss varnish (see "The Finish Coat," page 59). For some types of tile and most mosaic tiles, a low-sheen varnish, either flat or eggshell, is used.

Special Considerations
Surface preparation for faux tile in kitchens and bathrooms must be meticulous. Allow it to dry fully before proceeding. After painting your tile, seal it with two or three coats of acrylic varnish. Surfaces that are exposed to constant and/or direct contact with running water (such as shower walls) or that require vigorous cleaning are not appropriate for faux tile. The finish can take some moisture, but there's a danger that the substrate (whether wood or plaster) will also pick up moisture and cause peeling or cracking. (This is true for any type of faux finish, whether wood, marble, or an aged patina.)

The surface preparation for a floor mosaic must also be very thorough and fully cured before proceeding. A wood floor must be sanded down to the raw wood to remove any stain, wax, or varnish, then repaired as needed, fixing all cracks with wood filler. Apply two coats of oil-based primer, then two coats of an eggshell-finish alkyd basepaint, waiting 24 hours between coats. After painting your mosaic and letting it dry thoroughly, apply at least three coats of eggshell-finish acrylic floor polyurethane. The cured second coat should be *screened*— lightly burnished with a buffer fitted with a wire mesh screen to eliminate roughness— before the last coat is applied. The number of coats and the type of varnish may vary, depending on the type of floor and the medium used to paint the faux finish. Floors should be maintained by adding a coat of varnish every year.

TILE EXERCISES
The technical notes of each of the recipes in this chapter lists exercises that will help prepare you for painting faux tile. In addition to those, it would be beneficial to review Chapter 11 in order to practice the exercises for "Striping" and "Fading" and to study the recipe for "Polychrome Ornaments."

When designing a grid for faux tiles, avoid drawing rigid layouts with tiles that are all the same size (left). The dimensions of faux handmade tiles (center) and mosaics (right) should vary slightly, and their layouts should be slightly uneven.

Faux Handmade Tile with Crackle Finish

When tiles are crafted by hand, they are not uniform either in thickness or in size. In addition, the uneven temperature of a wood-burning kiln causes crackling and uneven coloration, giving each tile a beautiful, individual look, compared with the sterile uniformity of cheaper, mass-produced tiles. This type of faux finish looks great in any room where tiles would be used: bathrooms, kitchens, foyers, hallways, and living areas that have Mediterranean or other rustic decor. This recipe is a bit time-consuming, so if you consider your investment of time plus materials, it isn't necessarily cheaper to create faux tile than it is to install actual handmade tile. But, as noted earlier, simulation allows you to work on curved surfaces and other places where tile is hard to install, though mostly to create particular color combinations and other customized decorative effects.

The tiles painted for the demonstration are squares, which usually measure 3 × 3 or 4 × 4 inches, and rectangles, which are generally 3 × 5 inches. Handmade tiles are also available in many other shapes, including hexagons and octagons. Before you begin, visit a tile store to survey a range of shapes and dimensions.

1. Lightly sand and dust off the cured basecoated surface. Draw your grid on the surface with a 5H pencil. Using a glazing brush, glaze the surface for the yellow tiles heavily with glaze #1 (see Technical Notes) + **white** + **chrome yellow** + a touch of **yellow ochre**. Stipple the surface with a stippling brush as shown in the exercise on page 206, then smooth out with a codtail or badger brush. Let dry.

2. Your grid should still be visible (though just barely); if not, redraw it very lightly. Tape off every other tile with low-tack white tape, then glaze the exposed tiles individually with glaze #2 (see Technical Notes) + **white** + **chrome yellow** + **yellow ochre**, varying the tonality as shown in the recipe for "Tricolor Glazing" (see page 212) by adding **raw sienna, chrome yellow,** and **white**. Stipple the surface, then smooth it out with a codtail or

badger brush, wiping the brush as often as possible. Let dry.

3. Gently remove the tape; if necessary, use a hair dryer to soften the adhesive. Repeat step 2, first by taping off the remaining tiles, then by applying glaze. Although immediately adjacent tiles should be glazed to create a contrast of value (dark to light) between them, this should not be done in a systematic way. Let dry.

4. Using glaze #2 + **chrome oxide deep** + **chrome green oxide** + **raw sienna** + **yellow ochre** + a touch of **burnt sienna** (to tone down the greens), paint the Amazon green tiles as described in step 2. Note that the row of darker green rectangular tiles along the bottom of the composition are a darker value of the square tiles. Let dry.

5. Lightly sand and dust off the surface, then glaze the yellow tiles with the transparent crackle effect as described in the recipe for "Transparent Crackling" on page 224. Apply crackle varnish #1 (see Technical Notes), let it set to the proper tack, then apply a well-stretched, generous coat of crackle varnish #2 (see Technical Notes). If simply allowed to dry, cracks will appear in 2 to 4 hours. To speed up the process and produce larger, almost instantaneous cracks, let set for 15 to 30 minutes, then dry with a hair dryer.

To vary the crackle patterns, I waited a day before applying a crackle effect to the Amazon green tiles. The effect (shown on page 248) was done with a commercial transparent crackle varnish product by Lefranc & Bourgeois that is applied and can be manipulated in the same way as my crackle varnish recipe. Let dry for 24 hours.

6. Using the glazing brush, coat the yellow tiles with glaze #3 (see Technical Notes) + **raw umber.** Stipple the glaze, allow it to set for 15 minutes, then wipe it off as shown in the exercise on page 208. Fold a cotton rag several times to make a hard pad, or wrap it around a small block of wood. Keep unfolding the rag to expose clean areas so that it wipes off the surface effectively, leaving dark tones only in the cracks to make them more visible. Repeat

1. Glaze the surface heavily, stipple, then smooth out with a codtail or badger brush. Let dry.

2. Redraw the grid if necessary, tape off every other tile, then glaze, stipple, and smooth out each individual tile.

3. Vary the tonality within each tile by adding lights (A) and darks (B) to the surface. Let dry.

4. Remove the tape, then repeat steps 2 and 3 for the remaining tiles. Let dry.

for the green tiles, but this time tinting glaze #3 with **chrome oxide deep.** Let dry.

7. Varnish all the tiles with a gloss- or semigloss-finish oil-based varnish. This step has a dual purpose: While imparting a nice sheen to the tiles before adding the trompe l'oeil grout lines (see step 8), which will have a matte finish, it also seals the gum arabic portion of the crackling varnish, which is reversible. Let dry.

8. Using a striping edge and flat brush as shown in the exercise on page 303, paint the grout lines in medium-gray acrylic (**white + raw umber + burnt umber**)

thinned with water. Lines are painted one tile at a time to impart an effect of unevenness. Let dry.

9. With an off-white acrylic mixture (**white + yellow ochre + raw umber**), paint the highlight beneath the grout lines and at the edges of each tile, using the technique noted in step 8. Let dry.

USING OTHER MEDIA

This recipe can also be painted in oils using a gloss-finish varnish tinted with artists' oils and working over a white basecoat.

1

2

3A

3B

4

5. Glaze, stipple, and smooth out the surrounding tiles as described in steps 2 and 3. Let dry.

6. To create the crackle effect, apply 3-hour size, let set to the proper tack, then apply a coat of gum arabic. Let cure for 24 hours before applying the oil glaze.

7. Apply the oil glaze, let set for 15 minutes, then wipe off.

8. Varnish the tiles, then let dry. Use a striping brush and edge to paint the grout lines and the highlights.

9. The completed finish.

5

6

7

8

Faux Handpainted Blue Delft Tile

Delft tile dates from the mid-17th century and takes its name from the city of its origin in Holland. It is one of many forms of tin-glazed earthenware known collectively as delftware. The white tiles, handpainted with cobalt blue designs, are produced to this day. This recipe can be also be used to simulate many other handpainted tiles, including the famous Spanish and Portuguese *azulejos,* Swedish stove tiles, and tiles such as faience and majolica crafted in French and Italian Mediterranean locales. The only things that change are the design and coloration, but all the tiles are very decorative, and their patterns are limitless. These handpainted tiles were often used as borders to frame fields of solid-colored tiles, and were sometimes featured as center panels framed by unadorned tiles. You have very broad choices in using this recipe, which can be applied to all sorts of traditional, as well as contemporary, settings.

In this recipe, the crackles are handpainted on selected tiles instead of using the size-and-gum-arabic crackle varnish shown in the previous recipe (see page 246). Although that finish would also work well here, I wanted to show yet another crackling technique.

1. Lightly sand and dust off the cured basecoated surface. Transfer your tile grid as well as the design motif to your working surface as discussed on page 306. (The design shown in this demonstration, an essence burner with a decorative garland, adorned an early 18th-century Swedish stove pictured in a book. Note that Delft craftsmen painted their designs directly on the surface of the tiles, using only a very roughly drawn light sketch as a guide.)

2. Use the glazing brush to cover your drawing heavily with a mixture of glaze (see Technical Notes) + **white** + a touch of **Payne's gray.** Sponge off the surface as shown in the exercise on page 80, then smooth it out with a badger or veinette brush. This step fixes the drawing and makes its outline barely perceptible, creating a nice background that looks slightly aged and uneven, as though the surface were baked in a wood-burning kiln. Let dry.

3. Load a fat pointed brush with glaze + **ultramarine blue + cobalt blue + a touch of black.** (This mixture will be used in subsequent steps, so place it in a small jar—a baby-food jar or film container—into which you'll dip your brushes.) With the fat brush, paint a transparent shadow. Let dry. Load a medium brush with the same mixture, then go back over the shadow, using the same tone but placing it a third of the way inside the shadow to create a fading effect. (Refer to the exercise on page 304 and the recipes for "Circular Medallion" and "Grisaille Ornament" for a more detailed discussion of this technique.) Let dry, then repeat to darken selected areas. Let dry.

4. With a long, pointed synthetic brush dipped into the glaze mixture that was used in the previous step, paint a complete outline of the tiles over your barely perceptible pencil sketch. Let dry.

5. Use the same glaze mixture and the striping brush to paint the trompe l'oeil effects shown on page 303. But note that in this example the effect is created solely with shadows; no highlights are used. Note also that the faux molding appears deliberately handpainted, which is consistent with the character of these tiles. Refer to pages 300–304 for more information on trompe l'oeil striping and fading.

6. For the border tiles, load the synthetic spalter with the blue glaze and paint each tile individually. Allow the brushstrokes to be obvious, as they often are on real handpainted tiles. Let dry.

7. Load a fine, long, pointed synthetic brush with the blue glaze used in previous steps. Paint the crackles based on your own very close observation of crackle patterns found on real tiles, plates, bowls, and other ceramic items. The pattern should look similar to a chaotic cobweb. Simulate it on only a few tiles, and here and there, then let dry.

To simulate chips in the tile surface (where dirt is most likely to accumulate quickly), overglaze a few of the small areas formed by the intersection of the crackle lines. Let dry.

8. Varnish with gloss- or satin-finish acrylic varnish. Let dry.

9. Paint the joint lines with a striping brush loaded with the blue glaze darkened with **burnt umber.** Vary the width of the lines so that the dimensions of the tiles also vary slightly, and to mimic the appearance of handlaid tiles. Add highlights using pure acrylic **white.**

USING OTHER MEDIA

This recipe can be painted in oils, using a glaze of a gloss-finish oil-based varnish tinted with artists' oils.

1. Apply a heavy coat of glaze over the grid and design.

2. Sponge off, then smooth out with a badger brush or veinette. Let dry.

3. Begin delineating the design with transparent shading. Let dry.

4. Apply the same glaze to the dried shadows, but place it a third of the way inside the shadows to create a fading effect. Let dry.

5. Outline the contours of the design with an even darker value. Let dry.

6. Use a striping edge to complete the design and outline the edges of the tiles. Let dry.

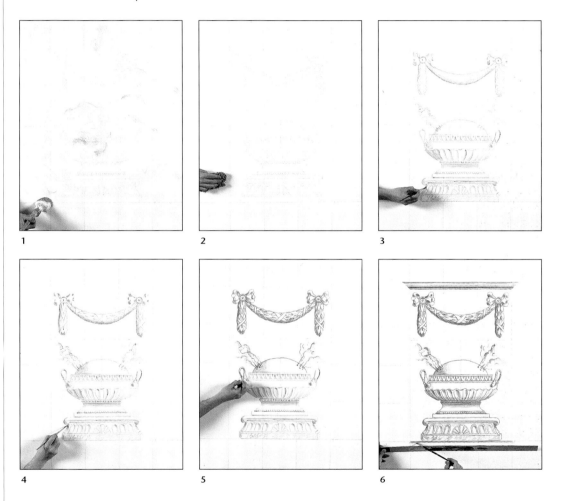

1

2

3

4

5

6

7. Glaze each border tile individually, leaving visible brushstrokes. Let dry.

8. Add fine crackles to a few tiles. Let dry.

9. Simulate chips in the tile; let dry. Varnish, let dry, then paint the joint lines and highlights. Let dry.

10. The completed finish.

7

8

9

10

Mosaic

Mosaic is one of the oldest decorative art forms. Created by the ancient Greeks and used extensively by the Romans, mosaic art was raised to an unsurpassed level during the Byzantine empire. The principle is simple: Colored squares (called *tesserae*) 1 × 1 inch or smaller, made of glass, marble, or clay, are formed into designs or pictorial patterns and embedded in cement in walls, floors, or ceilings, and sometimes are used to decorate columns and objects of various kinds. Mosaic tiles of different colors may be cut to fit a particular design and are mixed so that when viewed at a distance, the assembled colors are merged by the eye into particular shades, much like the Pointillist painting technique of Georges Seurat.

Broken pieces of chinaware are also sometimes used to form mosaics, the finest examples being those created by Spanish architect Antonio Gaudí, who used the technique as embellishment on building facades and in a park in Barcelona. There is also a form called *micro mosaic* that uses tiny glass strings or sticks glued to a base to form a very small design or picture, sized to fit a tabletop, other furniture inset, or framed as a small picture.

Faux mosaic can be placed almost anywhere; add friezes and borders to the areas named above. Since virtually any subject matter can be used—landscape, figural, portrait, animal, trompe l'oeil, lettering, floral, geometric, or abstract patterns—reference sources for design inspiration are unlimited. Consult books, magazines, and other printed sources for ideas, and, during museum visits, observe actual mosaic patterns and how the tiles are cut and pieced together.

1. Lightly sand and dust off the cured basecoated surface. Trace your design over the surface, using either the tracing-paper technique or the pounce technique (see page 306), or draw it directly on the surface with a 5H pencil. Use the glazing brush to glaze the surface with glaze (see Technical Notes) + **white** + **yellow ochre** + **raw umber**, adding some touches of **raw umber** + **ultramarine blue.**

2. While the surface is wet, sponge it off (see page 80) then smooth it out with a badger brush. Let dry. This procedure varies the tonality of the tiles, while sealing and muting the penciled design.

3. Use a flat synthetic brush loaded with glaze + **chrome yellow** + **yellow ochre** modified with **white** or **raw sienna.** Paint one tile at a time, going back to vary some here and there if there isn't enough contrast among them. Let dry.

4. Glaze the light blue tiles with glaze + **ultramarine blue** + **white** + **raw umber** applied in the same manner as described in step 3. Let dry.

5. Glaze the red tiles with glaze + **cadmium red** + **red ochre** + **white** modified with other palette colors. Let dry.

6. If the colors seem too intense at this point, tone them down with a thin layer of off-white glaze (see step 1). Apply the glaze to each set of *motifs,* rather than to the entire surface.

7. Using a long, fine-pointed synthetic brush, paint the fine grout lines with a water-thinned mixture of **white** + **raw umber** + **ultramarine blue** + a touch of **black** modified with other colors of the palette to darken some parts and lighten others. Study the layout well. Note that rather than a sharply ruled square grid, the grid should be uneven, following the contours of the design. Let dry.

8. If you want to give your mosaic an aged look, apply a layer of glaze tinted with **raw umber** + **white** + **yellow ochre,** varied here and there with **white** and **raw umber.** Sponge off with a sea sponge, then soften with the badger brush. Let dry. For added distressing, sponge on an off-white glaze (glaze + **white** + **yellow ochre**). Let dry.

9. If the mosaic has been painted in an area that is out of reach, there is no need to varnish it. Otherwise, proceed as follows: Lightly sand and dust off the surface. Varnish with a flat-finish varnish. (Choose the medium based on the location of the mosaic.)

Mosaic

1. Draw or transfer the design to the surface. Glaze the surface, sponge it off, then smooth it out. Let dry.

2. Working within one color family, glaze one tile at a time, making sure there is sufficient contrast among adjacent tiles. Let dry.

3. Repeat step 2 for the remaining color families.

4. If at any point the colors seem too intense, apply an off-white glaze to each set of motifs rather than to the entire surface.

5. Add any remaining motifs. (Here, a vertical red border has been added.) Let dry.

6. Paint the grout lines, working darker in some areas and lighter than others.

7. As you work, be sure to preserve the uneven character of the grid. Let dry.

8. To "age" the surface, apply a light raw umber glaze. Sponge off, then smooth out. Let dry.

9. For added distressing, sponge on an off-white glaze. Let dry.

10. The completed finish.

ALTERNATE TECHNIQUES

This recipe can be applied over a medium-gray base, with each tile individually painted with a flat brush and leaving a space between tiles to let the base serve as the grout line. It can also be rendered by "printing" each individual tile, using a potato or a dense foam or dish sponge that's been carved or cut into a 1 × 1 inch square. Load your printing tool with opaque paint instead of glaze, and use a different color for each element of the mosaic.

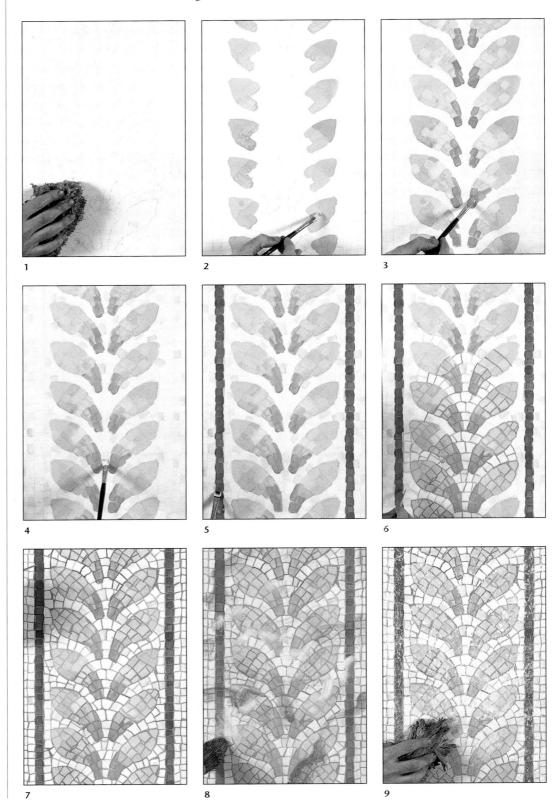

254

Organic Materials

Materials of animal origin have been used decoratively since ancient times. Some of these materials, like skin and bone, were once parts of living animals that, by various processes, were preserved and used to embellish objects and surfaces.

Organic textures are classified into four basic categories: skin, which includes a variety of leathers and hides; bone, such as ivory and horn; scales, like tortoiseshell and shagreen (a type of sharkskin); and shells, such as mother-of-pearl. Except for leathers, most of these materials are available only in limited quantities and in small sizes; some, like ivory, shagreen, and tortoiseshell, are rare (and thus extremely expensive) or protected by environmental laws.

In addition to faux palisander, gilding, and trompe l'oeil, this entryway is painted with striking tortoiseshell insets.

Rendering Organic Materials

In most cases, the primary reason for imitating organic materials is cost. In addition to the high price of the materials themselves, their installation often requires many steps and thus considerable expense, while painting them only requires a thorough surface preparation (see "Basic Procedure," below). Naturally, their beautiful colors—and, in some cases, surface design and translucency—make organic materials very decorative.

SUITABLE APPLICATIONS

Organic materials have been used throughout the ages to ornament both objects and surfaces. Some materials, such as ivory and mother-of-pearl, were carved to make small objects. Others had practical uses as well; for example, parchment was the surface on which the first manuscripts were written and illustrated.

During the Renaissance, many organic materials were first used as inlays in furniture, frames, cabinets, and the like. In the early 18th century, the famous French cabinetmaker Andre-Charles Boulle (1642–1732) began incorporating intricate inlay patterns of tortoiseshell, ivory, ebony, and mother-of-pearl, combined with brass and tin, into his furniture designs. This type of inlay became very fashionable in France and England, and was widely imitated through the 19th century. During the 1930s, the art deco style made great use of these materials, especially shagreen, leather, and ivory, by incorporating them into marquetry and using them to cover small objects and furniture.

Customarily used even today in marquetry or as veneers for furniture and cabinetry, organic materials can work well in both traditional and modern decors, as long as they are suitably integrated as an element of a given style. Their natural dimensions should be observed closely to avoid undermining the credibility of the finish. As for faux marble, stone, wood, and metal, finishes that simulate organic materials should only be applied to surfaces or objects on which their real forms would be used. For more information on appropriate sizes and applications, refer to the recipe and technical notes for each organic texture.

CHOOSING THE RIGHT TECHNIQUE

Before reading this section, review "Influential Movements in Decorative Painting," page 15. Unlike marble, the French and Italian styles of decorative painting for organic textures are distinct, with either one or the other perceived as preferable for each specific finish. In general, a looser, more theatrical technique, such as that used for tortoiseshell, can be considered Italian, whereas a more precise rendering can be attributed to the French approach.

In general, organic textures exhibit great variations in color. This is especially true of leather, which can be dyed to virtually any hue. Consequently, the recipes in this chapter offer color suggestions rather than strict rules, so that efforts can be focused primarily on technique.

LAYOUT

Because they are usually confined to small, precisely defined areas, a design or grid must be drawn directly on the prepared surface. Use a 3H or 5H pencil to make dark, sharply drawn lines. Keep in mind that while leather and parchment can be used in any size up to a square yard, the other organic materials demonstrated in this chapter range from tiny (just a few inches square) to a maximum of 8 × 10 inches. Plan your design well before painting, and avoid making the units of the design too large, using too few units per surface area, and painting the scale of the finish out of proportion to the size of the unit.

Before attempting to incorporate organic materials into a marquetry design, refer to the techniques shown in "Pietre Dure" (page 132) and "Marquetry" (page 197).

BASIC PROCEDURE

With the exception of most skins and some scales (see page 257), the surfaces on which organic materials are painted must be very smooth in order to best simulate the ways in which the real materials are used. The basic surface preparation consists of skimcoating and basecoating with an oil-based primer, each followed with a sanding, then two coats of eggshell-finish alkyd basepaint. See "Surface Preparation," pages 53–55, for detailed information on preparing specific types of surfaces.

Depending on the finish, acrylic glazes (1 matte medium + 1 water + artists' acrylics), oil-based glazes (2 or 3 turpentine + 1 oil + drier + artists' oils), or reversible water-based glazes (either gouache or beer) can be used. The proportions of the glaze ingredients will vary for each recipe.

The varnish can also be either water- or oil-based, depending on the recipe's requirements: Use an oil-based varnish over reversible water-based or oil-based glazes, and a water-based (acrylic) varnish over acrylic glazes only. Wax can be applied over any glaze medium. The sheen of the finish coat depends on the texture of the finish; for example, parchment should have a flat finish, which can be achieved by applying wax or matte varnish, while tortoiseshell should have a semigloss sheen.

ORGANIC MATERIALS EXERCISES

All the exercises required to master the techniques used to render organic materials are covered in other chapters. In addition to the exercises and recipes listed below, see also "Making a 'Cut' with Sandpaper," page 56.

- From Chapter 2, "Marble": See "Sponging On" (page 79), "Sponging Off" (page 80), "Spattering" (page 86), and "Dabbing with a Chiqueteur Brush" (page 87).
- From Chapter 4, "Sandstone and Limestone": See "Taping a Block Layout" (page 140).
- From Chapter 6, "Patinas and Textures": See the note on crisscrossing the initial application of glaze (page 205), as well as "Stippling" (page 206) and "Strié" (page 206). See also the recipes for "Tricolor Glazing" (page 212) and "Raised Textures: Provençal Walls and Jigouille" (page 217).
- From Chapter 10, "Stenciling": See "Cutting a Stencil" (page 285).

Ivory

Ivory is very hard, compact, homogeneous bone matter that can be polished to a satin finish. Elephant tusk is the principal source for ivory, with smaller quantities taken from hippopotamus, walrus, and narwhal tusks. Ivory has been worn as jewelry and carved to make boxes, statuettes, and other small decorative objects since ancient times. During the 18th century, it was widely used as inlays for furniture as well as decorative objects. Its popularity as a decorative medium, which peaked in the 19th century, encouraged the hunting of elephants on a massive scale, a practice that continued unabated until the elephant population reached a dangerously low ebb in the 1970s. In the 1930s, followers of the art deco style revived the use of ivory as inlay for furniture. Because environmental protection laws have made the ivory trade illegal in many countries—yet another reason to paint faux ivory—other types of bone are used as substitutes.

The fact that real ivory has a tendency to yellow as it ages doesn't make faux ivory a good candidate for using an oil-based glaze or varnish, both of which also yellow with time. If an aged ivory is desired, the glazes should have a slightly stronger yellow tone. Regardless of color or medium, ivory should never be painted in units larger than 3 × 6 inches.

1. Lightly sand and dust off the cured basecoated surface. Draw the grid or motif on the surface with a sharp 3H or 5H pencil. (In the demonstration, a staggered 2 × 4 inch tile design—similar to what might be found on a decorative box—is shown.) Use a small spalter or disposable brush to apply a mixture of glaze (see Technical Notes) + yellow ochre to the surface.
2. While the glaze it still wet, use the same brush to add streaks of chrome orange (raw sienna + yellow ochre + raw umber).
3. With a dry used spalter, strié the still-wet surface to a fine strié as shown in the exercise on page 206. Let dry.
4. Tape off every other tile with low-tack tape. Using glaze + various colors from the palette, strié the exposed tiles with a small spalter, creating contrasts by making some tiles warm and others cool. (The higher the contrast, the better the tiles will read.) Let dry. Remove the tape, then repeat this step on the remaining tiles. Let dry.
5. With a spattering brush or small stencil brush, spatter some glaze + raw umber as shown in the exercise on page 86. Following the direction of the strié, soften as you work with a dry spalter to create pores as shown in the recipe for "Pickled Oak" (see page 186). Let dry.
6. To unify the surface and mute the stronger contrasts, use a spalter to glaze the entire surface with a mixture of 1 matte medium + 1 water + white + a touch of chrome yellow. Strié immediately with a dry spalter. Let dry.
7. With a long pointed synthetic brush and a mixture of raw umber + a touch of white + raw sienna thinned with a little water, paint some very thin cracks or splits of the sort that often occur in old ivory boards. Hold the brush like a pen (see page 37) and use your pinkie finger as a maulstick. (See also "Alternate Technique," below.) Let dry.
8. Retrace the grid with a very sharp 5H pencil. Wax the surface with clear beeswax (see page 61), then polish it once the wax has set.

USING OTHER MEDIA

This recipe can also be done using an oil-based glaze (3 turpentine + 1 oil).

ALTERNATE TECHNIQUE

A finer and more accurate method for making the cracks (see step 7) can be used with either water or oil media. After step 6, score the surface with a pin in the same way that you would paint them with a brush. Then glaze the entire surface with oil-based glaze (see "Using Other Media," above) + raw umber, smooth it out with a spalter, let set for 15 minutes, and then wipe off the surface with a folded pad as shown in the exercise on page 208. The glaze remains only in the fine cracks so that they are clear and distinct. Let dry, then proceed to step 8.

1. Glaze the surface, then add streaks of chrome orange.

2. Strié the wet glaze with a dry used spalter. Let dry.

3. Tape off every other tile, then apply and strié another coat of glaze to create contrast among the tiles. Let dry.

4. Spatter the surface with some dark glaze.

5. Following the direction of the surface, soften the spatters to create pores. Let dry.

6. To unify the surface, glaze the surface, then strié with a dry spalter. Let dry.

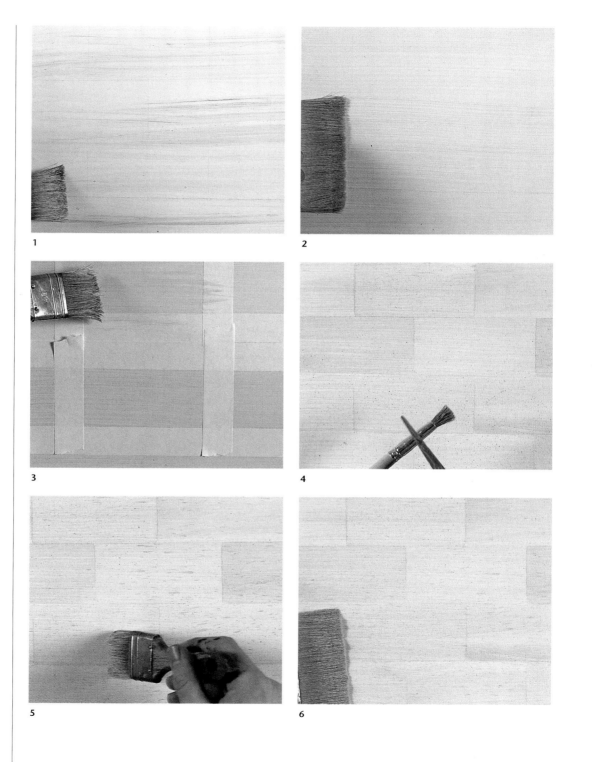

1

2

3

4

5

6

7. Paint some very fine cracks. Let dry.

8. Retrace the grid with a sharp pencil.

9. The completed finish.

7

8

9

Leather

TECHNICAL NOTES

Difficulty Rating

1.5

System

Oil

Basecoat

Color will vary, depending on the intended color of the finish

Medium brown (**raw sienna + burnt sienna + raw umber** + a touch of **white**) alkyd, eggshell finish

Oil Glaze

3 turpentine + 1 oil + drier

Palette

Artists' Oils

Raw sienna

Burnt sienna

Burnt umber

Ultramarine blue

Brushes and Tools

Glazing brushes

Square OR patina stippling brush

Codtail brush

Ribbed T-shirt cloth OR cheesecloth

Spattering (small glazing) brush

Palette knife (for spattering)

Exercises

Ragging (page 205)

Stippling (page 206)

Spattering (page 86)

See also "Applying a Wax Finish" (page 61) and the recipe for "Tricolor Glazing" (page 212)

Leather is converted from animal skin or hide by means of a process known as *tanning*, in which the hide is treated and preserved with a specially prepared solution. Leather has served several functional purposes since prehistoric times, but has been used decoratively only since the Middle Ages, when it was used to cover books and small objects. During the Renaissance, embossed leathers such as Cordova leather (see page 292) were prized as wall coverings. In the 1930s, leather squares were used to cover walls in art deco decor, and leather again saw a resurgence in the 1970s as a covering for furniture as well as walls. Leather is currently used somewhat sparingly as a decorative element.

A leather's thickness and texture depend on the animal from which it is taken, its age, and the way its skins are tanned. Some types, like cowhide, are thick, while others, such as lambskin, are thin. Some are rough-textured like goat; others—calfskin, for example—are very smooth. Some have a napped finish, while others are smooth. Color can vary greatly, as most skins can be dyed to virtually any color.

This basic recipe can be varied by changing color or adding texture (as shown in the recipe for "Parchment" on page 265). The basecoat should be about two value steps lighter than the final effect you want to achieve. The size of a leather wall covering unit should generally not exceed 1 square yard.

1. Lightly sand and dust off the cured basecoated surface. Draw the panels on the surface with a 3H pencil, leaving dark lines. (At this point, you can either tape off every other unit or proceed with the recipe and make your "cuts" with a piece of sandpaper as noted in step 3.) Apply a thin layer of oil glaze (see Technical Notes) + **burnt umber + raw umber,** then crisscross and stretch it out as described on page 205.

2. While the glaze is still wet, very lightly touch the glazing brush (it should remain almost dry) to some of the palette colors (**raw sienna, burnt sienna, raw umber, burnt umber, ultramarine blue**), then use it to create some variations within the surface as shown in the recipe for "Tricolor Glazing" (page 212). Once the paint has been completely discharged from the brush, use it to stipple the surface. Smooth out some of the cloud-shaped forms as you work.

3. If you did not tape off every other square in step 1, place a piece of 100-grade sandpaper face down on the wet surface and use its edge to leave a distinct line of demarcation between two panels as you stipple the surface with the glazing brush. Create contrast between the two panels by opposing light to dark and warm to cool colors. (See "Making a 'Cut' with Sandpaper," page 56, for more information.)

4. Stipple the still-wet glaze once more, this time with either a patina or square stippling brush (the square one produces a finer and more even stippling). As shown in the exercise on page 206, work methodically to obtain a fine stippling while leaving slight variations.

5. Use a ribbed T-shirt rag or cheesecloth gathered into a rosebud shape to rag the wet glaze as shown in the exercise on page 205. Working from left to right and from top to bottom, hit the surface methodically, rotating your wrist and overlapping the previous hit so no area is missed. Smooth out the surface very lightly, working the codtail brush in a figure-eight motion.

6. While the glaze is wet (or after it has dried), spatter it with glaze + **raw umber** as shown in the exercise on page 86. Use a fine spattering so that it can be smoothed out if it looks too contrived. Let dry.

7. Faux leather can be varnished with a satin-finish oil-based varnish, but it looks most authentic when it's been finished with clear beeswax or carnauba wax (see "Applying a Wax Finish," page 61), which gives the surface an uneven and slightly oily appearance.

USING OTHER MEDIA

Because it requires that the surface remain wet for the entire process, this technique makes it difficult to work with water media unless you are painting small, discrete units. For more information, see the recipe for "Parchment," page 265.

1. Apply a thin layer of glaze. Use a lightly loaded glazing brush to create some variations, then use it to stipple the surface.

2. Stipple the wet glaze again with a patina stippling brush.

3. Rag the wet glaze, then smooth out lightly.

4. While the glaze is still wet (or after it has dried), finely spatter the surface.

5. The completed finish.

1

2

3

4

5

Parchment

The word "parchment" is a corruption of the name of the ancient city of Pergamum, where parchment was invented in the 2nd century B.C. Parchment is goat, sheep, or calfskin (which is referred to as *vellum*) that has been treated with lime and other substances to make it durable and rot-resistant. Originally developed as a writing surface, parchment was often used during the Middle Ages for illuminated manuscripts and paintings. Throughout the 19th century, then more routinely during the art deco period of the 1920s and 30s, parchment was used as a sort of veneer for certain types of furniture. Like leather, it can also be used to cover walls, and should be painted in units no larger than 1 square yard.

The following recipe specifies acrylics as an alternative to oils (as shown in the recipe for "Leather," page 263), though it is easier for beginning decorative painters to work in oils, which have a much longer working time.

1. Lightly sand and dust off the cured basecoated surface. Prepare the heavy-bodied paint (see Technical Notes) in a pail, then mix it either by hand or with an electric power drill fitted with a mixing tip. Use a glazing brush to apply as well as stipple it. (See "Raised Textures: Provençal Walls and Jigouille," page 217.)

2. While the paint is wet, use a patina stippling brush to stipple the surface as shown in the exercise on page 206, but to a finer texture. Let cure fully.

3. Use a sanding block covered with 150-grit sandpaper to sand down the surface as described on page 56, then dust it off. Using thin lines, draw the units of parchment with a sharp 3H pencil.

4. Tape off every other unit with blue tape. Use the glazing brush to apply glaze (see Technical Notes) + **white** + **yellow ochre** + **raw umber**, twisting and turning the brush as shown in the recipe for "Tricolor Glazing" (see page 212).

5. While the surface is wet, touch the same glazing brush to some of the palette colors—**raw sienna, burnt sienna**, and **raw umber** OR **burnt sienna, raw umber, and ultramarine blue**—changing the combination for each panel in order to create contrast—light and dark, cool and warm—between units.

6. To soften the contrast within a unit, sponge off the still-wet surface with an old fringed sea sponge as shown in the exercise on page 80, then stipple it with the stippling brush as shown in the exercise on page 206. Smooth out with a codtail or badger brush. Remove the tape while the surface is still wet, then use a wet elephant ear sponge or folded rag to clean off any bleeding, which is likely to occur when working on a textured surface. Let dry.

7. Repeat steps 4–6 for the remaining units. Always create contrast between adjacent units so that they read individually. Once the remaining units have dried completely, you can overglaze any that seem too light or lack sufficient contrast by using the same technique but a more transparent glaze.

8. Spatter some cool tones of glaze + **raw umber** + **ultramarine blue** as shown in the exercise on page 86. Dab off any excess with a rag. Let dry.

9. Use a fine, long, pointed synthetic brush loaded with glaze + **raw sienna** + **raw umber** to vein the surface with a barely perceptible trembled veining, making lightning-shaped forms here and there. Proceed as shown in the exercise on page 80, but make the veining finer and more sparse. Let dry.

10. Parchment can be varnished with a satin-finish oil-based varnish, but it looks most authentic when it's been finished with clear beeswax or carnauba wax (see "Applying a Wax Finish," page 61), which gives the surface an uneven and slightly oily appearance.

USING OTHER MEDIA

This recipe can be done in oils using the technique described in the recipe for "Leather" (see page 263). The formula for an oil-based heavy-bodied paint, which can be used with oil or water glazes, is $3/4$ zinc white + $1/4$ turpentine + sieved fine oak sawdust.

1. Apply and stipple heavy-bodied paint; let cure. Sand and dust off the surface, then draw the units in pencil.

2. Apply the glaze, twisting and turning the brush to create variety, then add touches of some of the palette colors to create contrast.

3. Sponge off the wet surface with a fringed sea sponge.

4. Stipple with a stippling brush, then smooth out with a badger brush. Let dry.

5. If necessary, overglaze and sponge off units that are lacking in contrast. Let dry.

6. Spatter some cool tones; dab off excess with a rag. Let dry, then paint fine, thin veins. Let dry.

7. The completed finish.

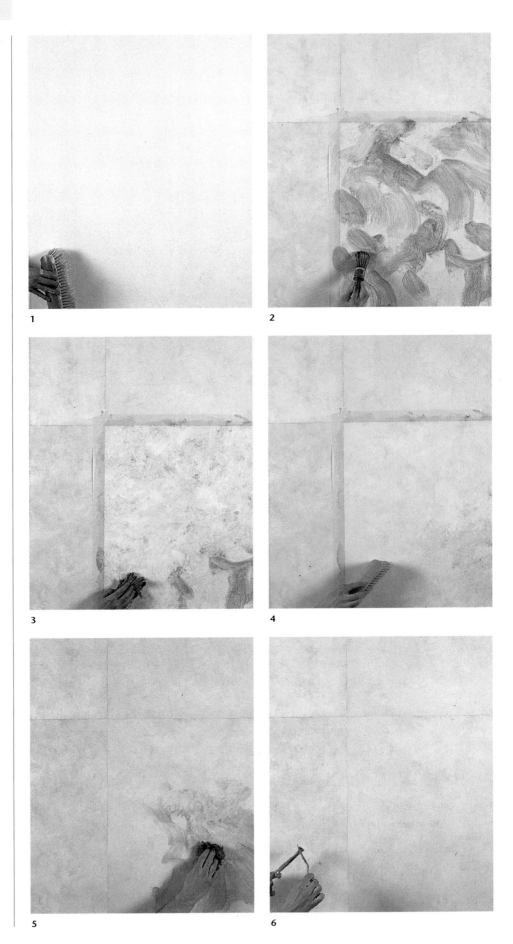

1

2

3

4

5

6

Mother-of-Pearl

Mother-of-pearl is a shiny, pearlescent substance that lines the shells of certain mollusks. It has been used decoratively since prehistory, mostly as jewelry and as inlay for small objects and furniture. Its highly reflective surface, which changes appearance as the light source shifts, can only be imitated with special pearlescent, iridescent, or interference acrylic paints or mica powders. These are made in many different hues and are very transparent. Since color choice is dictated by the desired final effect, no colors are specified for these materials in the technical notes. (The colors cited specifically in the recipe were used to create the finish shown in the demonstration photographs.) Available only in small concentrations, mother-of-pearl should be painted in units no larger than 5 × 6 inches.

1. Lightly sand and dust off the cured basecoated surface. Using a 5H pencil, draw the units of the finish directly on the surface with thin lines, then tape off every other unit. Apply glaze + **pearlescent color** or **mica powder** to the surface with a synthetic spalter. Smooth out with a badger brush. Let dry.
2. With a chiqueteur brush or synthetic spalter, apply a medium gray mixture of glaze + **black** + **ultramarine blue** + **pearlescent** or **mica blue**. Vary this tone by adding streaks of **alizarin crimson** and **ultramarine blue**; strié slightly as shown in the exercise on page 206. Smooth out

the wet surface with the badger brush, working it in a figure-eight motion.
3. Manipulate the wet glaze with moiré effects as shown in the exercise on page 164, then smooth it out well with the badger brush. Let dry.
4. In a pail, mix some **silver mica powder** or **silver pearlescent paint** with gloss-finish acrylic varnish ($^1/_5$ to $^1/_4$ mica powder or pearlescent paint + $^4/_5$ to $^3/_4$ acrylic varnish), stirring until thoroughly homogenized. Apply the mixture with a synthetic spalter; while the paint is wet, use the same brush to manipulate the surface here and there with moiré effects. Let dry.
5. For added depth, apply a coat of untinted gloss-finish acrylic varnish.

USING OTHER MEDIA/ALTERNATE TECHNIQUE

Another, more traditional recipe involves metallic leaf. Apply aluminum leaf or silver leaf to your surface, let dry for two days, then seal it with a coat of shellac or diluted oil-based satin varnish (1 varnish + $^1/_5$ thinner) and let dry. Apply an acrylic glaze (1 gloss medium + 1 water) + **alizarin crimson** + **ultramarine blue** + **black** with a spalter, and then manipulate the wet glaze with moiré effects (see page 164). Smooth out with a badger brush. Let dry, then varnish with a semigloss oil-based varnish.

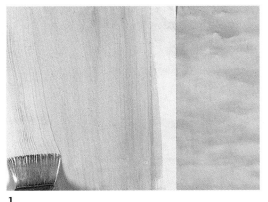

1

2

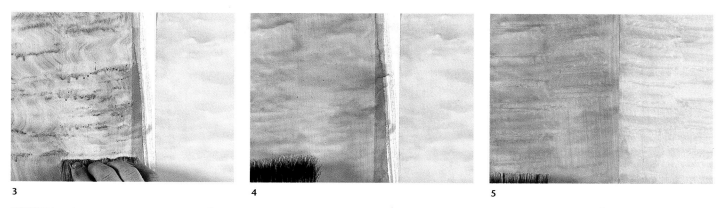

3   **4**   **5**

6

1. Apply a pearlescent glaze with a synthetic spalter, then smooth out with a badger brush. Let dry.

2. Apply another coat of glaze, then add streaks. Strié slightly, then smooth out.

3. Manipulate the wet glaze with moiré effects.

4. Smooth out with a badger. Let dry.

5. Apply a mixture of mica powder or pearlescent paint and acrylic varnish, then manipulate with a few moiré effects. Let dry.

6. The completed finish.

Tortoiseshell

Tortoiseshell is the hard, translucent substance that covers the bony plates of all turtles' shells (in particular, the hawksbill turtle). It is mottled with dark dots laid in different patterns. The size of the shieldlike scales varies, depending on the size of the turtle and the part of the shell they are taken from, but they never exceed 8 × 6 inches. The scales on the upper part, or *carapace,* are bigger and thicker, while those on the underside, or *plastron,* are smaller, finer, and more delicate in design, which makes them more prized. The pattern of the dots also varies: The central scales are arranged in a "spinal pattern," or a pronounced ridge, while the side scales have a more blotchy design. Colors also vary: Some shells are greenish, others yellow or brown; the red is dyed.

Most tortoiseshell used to come from Vietnam and now comes from Madagascar, the Philippines, Cuba, and California. Genuine tortoiseshell is fairly expensive. Imitating it is more economical as well as environmentally friendly. As have the other organic textures, tortoiseshell has been used throughout the centuries to ornament small objects, jewelry, boxes, chests, and picture frames. The decorative use of tortoiseshell reached glorious heights during the 18th century, when the famous French cabinetmaker Andre-Charles Boulle used it as inlays on furniture in conjunction with pewter, brass, ivory, ebony, and other materials to create remarkable decorative work known as Boulle marquetry.

RED TORTOISESHELL

1. Lightly sand and dust off the cured basecoated surface. Use a 3H pencil to draw the units (scales) on the surface, then tape off every other unit with low-tack tape.
2. Apply glaze #1 (see Technical Notes) + **black** with a synthetic spalter, adding some variations here and there. While the glaze is still wet, sponge off the surface as shown in the exercise on page 80, but by lightly rolling and dragging the sponge. Smooth out with a badger brush. Let dry.
3. Use the glazing brush to apply a heavy mixture of glaze #2 (see Technical Notes) + **black** + **cadmium red** to the surface, smooth it out with the badger brush, then create a spotted pattern by rolling and dragging an old fringed sea sponge over the surface. (For an example of this technique, see the recipe for "Elm, Amboina, and Thuja Burl," page 175.) Smooth out the surface, then let dry.
4. Following the direction of the pattern, spatter the surface with **black,** then smooth out with the badger brush. Let dry. For added depth, apply a transparent mixture of glaze #2 + **cadmium red** + **chrome orange.** Carefully remove the tape before the glaze has dried fully, then clean off any seepage that may have occurred. Let dry.
5. Tape off the remaining units, then repeat steps 2–4.
6. Varnish with a gloss- or satin-finish acrylic or oil-based varnish.

1

2

3

4

5

6

1. Red tortoiseshell: Apply glaze, adding variations here and there.

2. Sponge off the wet surface by lightly rolling a fringed sea sponge. Smooth out with a badger brush. Let dry.

3. Following the established direction of the surface, apply a darker glaze.

4. Smooth out with a badger brush.

5. Roll and drag the sea sponge to create a spotted pattern. Smooth out, then let dry.

6. Spatter with a dark glaze, then smooth out. Let dry. (If desired, apply a transparent orange overglaze, then let dry.)

7. The completed finish.

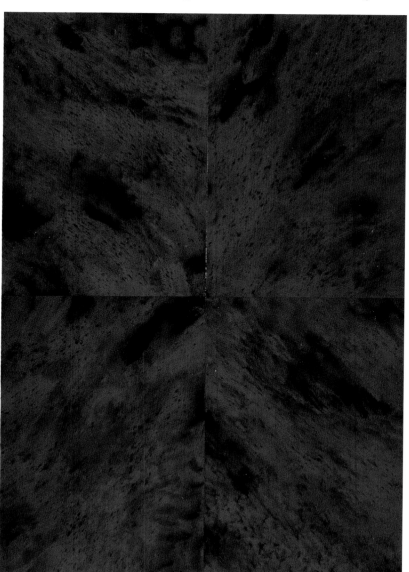

7

YELLOW TORTOISESHELL

1. Lightly sand and dust off the cured basecoated surface. Use a 3H pencil to draw the units (scales) on the surface, then tape off every other unit with low-tack tape.

2. Apply glaze #1 (see Technical Notes) + **yellow ochre** + **raw umber** with a synthetic spalter. While the surface is wet, use a glazing brush to add streaks of glaze #1 + **burnt umber** + **black** in a directional pattern, then smooth out with a veinette or badger brush. Sponge off as shown in the recipe for "Elm, Amboina, and Thuja Burl" (see page 175) to break the pattern, then smooth out in the direction of the surface. Let dry.

3. Overglaze: Apply glaze #1 + **chrome yellow** + **raw sienna** + **yellow ochre** with a synthetic spalter. While the surface is wet, use a fat pointed synthetic brush loaded with various palette colors (**raw sienna** + **raw umber** + **burnt umber** + **black**) to paint a dotted pattern following the established direction of the surface. Soften as you work with the badger brush or veinette. Let dry.

4. For added depth and detail, apply a transparent mixture of glaze #2 + **chrome yellow**. Carefully remove the tape before the glaze has dried fully, then clean off any seepage that may have occurred. Let dry.

5. Tape off the remaining units, then repeat steps 2–4.

6. Varnish with two coats of semigloss acrylic or oil-based varnish.

1. Yellow tortoiseshell: Apply the first glaze, then add dark streaks. Smooth out with a badger or veinette.

2. Sponge off the wet surface to break up the pattern.

3. Smooth out with a badger following the established direction of the surface. Let dry.

4. Apply the overglaze, then use a fat pointed brush to paint a dotted pattern.

5. Soften as you work with a badger or veinette. Let dry. (If desired, apply a transparent yellow overglaze, then let dry.)

6. The completed finish.

1

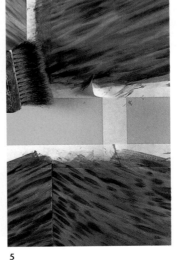

2

3

4

5

Snakeskin

TECHNICAL NOTES

Difficulty Rating

2

Systems

Water (gouache) and oil

Basecoat

Color will vary, depending on the intended color of the completed finish

Off-white **(white + raw sienna + raw umber)** alkyd, eggshell finish

Glazes

Glaze #1: Gouache (gouache + water)

Glaze #2: Oil (2 turpentine + 1 oil + drier)

Palettes

Gouaches

White

Yellow ochre

Raw umber

Burnt umber

Chrome oxide deep

Artists' Oils

White

Raw sienna

Burnt sienna

Chrome oxide deep

Brushes and Tools

For Gouaches

Glazing brush OR synthetic spalter

Disposable brush OR small stippling brush

Elephant ear sponge

For Oils

Glazing brush

Small stippling brush

Chiqueteur brush (for applying the mineral spirits)

Exercises

Stippling (page 206)

Dabbing with a Chiqueteur Brush (page 87)

Snakeskin is leather prepared from the tanned skin of a snake; it is composed of scales (as is lizard, crocodile, and alligator skin) whose pattern and size will vary depending on the animal. The color will also vary, since most of these skins can be dyed. The sizes of the pieces will vary, though they should not exceed the maximum unit size in which the real material is actually used, usually no larger than 5 × 16 inches.

Snakeskin is expensive, as snakes aren't generally bred for their skins. It has been used in decoration mostly for covering small objects such as boxes and chests. The art deco style of the 1930s used snakeskin as inlay for certain furniture and objects.

1. Lightly sand and dust off the cured basecoated surface, then degrease it as shown on page 32. Draw the units on the surface with a 3H pencil, then tape off every other unit with low-tack blue tape.
2. With a water-dedicated glazing brush or synthetic spalter, apply glaze #1 (see Technical Notes) + **yellow ochre + raw umber + chrome oxide deep** varied with other palette colors.
3. While the surface is wet, use the same brush to add glaze #1 tinted with **burnt umber + chrome oxide deep** to create a dark line down the center of each unit.
4. Use a disposable brush or a clean small stippling brush to stipple the still-wet surface as shown in the exercise on page 206. For each unit, begin by stippling half the surface, working from top to bottom. Before stippling the other half of the unit, flip the brush so that each side of its bristles will manipulate the colors it has already been soiled with. The stippling should be heavy; avoid overworking the surface or the stipple will become too fine. On the final pass, run the brush down the center of the surface to emphasize the spinal ridge. Let dry.
5. Remove the tape and clean off the remaining units with a damp elephant ear sponge. Tape off the remaining units, then repeat steps 2–4. Seal the surface with a layer of diluted shellac (1 shellac + 1 alcohol) to ensure that the gouache will remain unaffected when the oil glaze (see step 6) is dabbed with mineral spirits (step 7). (Although the dried gouache won't be reactivated by either the oil glaze or the mineral spirits, it could be abraded by the action of the brush, as the glaze is applied and then dabbed with mineral spirits.) Let dry.
6. Use an oil-dedicated glazing brush to apply glaze #2 (see Technical Notes) + **white + raw sienna + burnt sienna + chrome oxide deep** to the surface. Working from top to bottom, smooth out with a spalter, then stipple finely with a small stippling brush, working on the sides of each unit before the center.
7. As shown in the exercise on page 87, dab the wet surface with a chiqueteur brush very lightly loaded with mineral spirits, but work from top to bottom in a straight line down the center of each unit; the brush will make larger, coarser "scales," further emphasizing the central spinal ridge. Once the brush is nearly empty, dab it on either side of the ridge; the scales will be much smaller. Let dry.
8. For the finish, apply turpentine-diluted wax with a brush (see "Applying a Wax Finish," page 61). Let dry for 1 hour, then buff with a clean rag. (An example of snakeskin with this finish can be seen on page 279.)

USING OTHER MEDIA

The second part of this finish is usually done with an oil-based glaze, but if you don't mind working very quickly you can use acrylic airbrush inks thinned with water. Use denatured alcohol and a sea sponge to "open up" this type of glaze.

1. Apply glaze to each unit, then add a dark line down the center.

2. Working from top to bottom, stipple one half of the surface, then flip the brush and repeat on the other half.

3. On the final pass, stipple the central spinal ridge. Let dry. Seal the surface with thinned shellac, then let dry.

4. Apply an oil glaze.

5. Working from top to bottom, smooth out with a spalter, then stipple finely, working on the sides of each unit before the center.

6. Dab the surface with a chiqueteur brush loaded with mineral spirits. Work from top to bottom down the center of each unit, then dab each side. Let dry.

7. The completed finish.

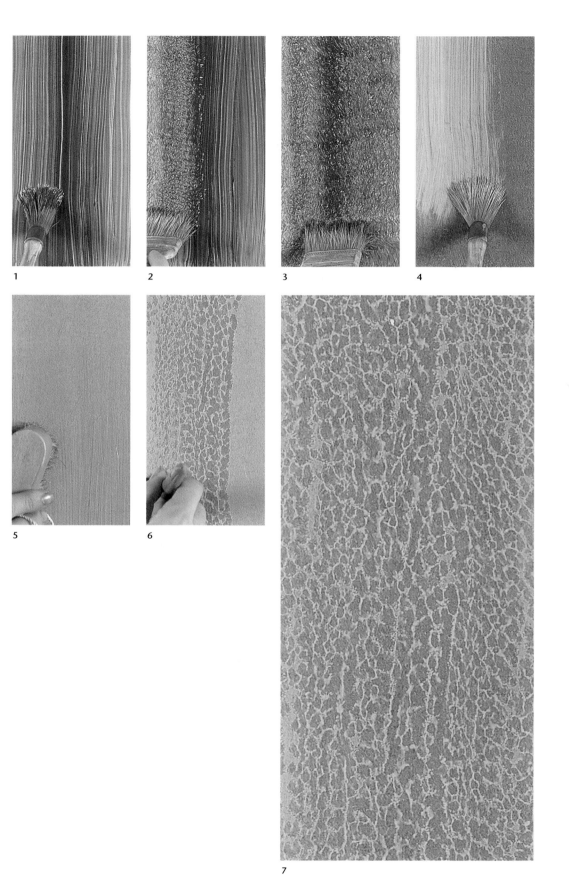

1

2

3

4

5

6

7

Shagreen

Shagreen is a skin taken from certain types of sharks and stingrays. These substances are also referred to as *galuchat,* which is derived from the name of the late 18th-century French sheather who was the first to use it decoratively. Shagreen features tiny round scales that radiate from a central ridge, where they are wider and unidirectional; the scales are smaller and more random toward the outer edges of the skins, which are no larger than 12 × 7 inches in size. It has a milky color but can be stained, most typically with off-green, bluish green, or beige tones. Shagreen skins are tanned, ground flat, stained, then usually applied to wooden surfaces such as furniture or small boxes. The height of shagreen's popularity came in the 1930s with the art deco style, when it was widely used in furniture and objects by cabinetmakers such as Jacques-Emile Ruhlmann (1879–1933).

In the demonstration for this recipe, an art deco–style layout was used, incorporating shagreen with snakeskin, palisander (a type of Brazilian rosewood), ivory, and mother-of-pearl. Refer to books about art deco to research designs typical of this style.

SHAGREEN

1. Lightly sand and dust off the cured basecoated surface, then degrease it as shown on page 32. Use a sharp 3H pencil to draw the units of your design directly on the surface, then tape off every other unit.

2. With a small glazing brush, apply a medium-value grayish green mixture of glaze #1 (see Technical Notes) + **white + chrome oxide deep + raw sienna + burnt sienna.** While the glaze is wet, use the same brush to add a dark streak of glaze #1 + **burnt sienna + burnt umber + a touch of chrome oxide deep** down the center of each unit.

3. While the surface is still wet, use a disposable brush or a clean small stippling brush to stipple each unit as shown in the exercise on page 206, as well as in the recipe for "Snakeskin" (see page 274). For each unit, begin by stippling half the surface, working from top to bottom.

Before stippling the other half of the unit, flip the brush so that each side of its bristles will manipulate the colors it has already been soiled with. As for snakeskin, the stippling should be heavy; if the surface is overworked, the stipple will become too fine. Let dry.

4. Cut the stencil for the scales using one of the techniques described on page 285. This kind of stencil design, which features many small, pebble-shaped windows, is easier to cut from a sheet of Mylar with an electric stencil cutter than using an X-Acto knife to cut stencil paper. Draw the design directly on the Mylar with a fine-tip felt marker. To emphasize the skin's central spinal ridge, make the windows for the scales in the center of the stencil slightly larger than the rest. It's best to cut two or three different stencils so that the pattern of the skin will vary.

5. Place one of the stencils over one of the units so that the large scales of the spinal ridge are positioned over the dark central streak, then tape it down so it won't move. Cut a small (6 × 6 inch) square from a fine, clean rag, fold it in half once, wrap it over your index finger or roll it into a point, then moisten its tip on a damp sponge. Wipe the tip of the rag over the stencil in a gentle circular motion. The slight moisture in the rag reactivates the gouache and removes it from the windows to expose the basecoat beneath. (This is an example of the "negative" method of stenciling; instead of applying paint or glaze, is it being removed from the surface.) Take note: If the rag is too wet, the moisture might seep under the stencil and reactivate areas that shouldn't be. This makes a mess that can only be remedied by wiping the surface clean and starting over from step 2. Let dry.

6. Repeat step 5 for the remaining taped-off units. So that the patterns of the skins are as diverse as possible, change the orientation of the stencils by flipping and turning them. Let dry.

7. Before shellacking (see step 8), vary the configuration of some of the spinal ridges

to create the impression that all the units are different skins. Using a well-worn flat brush lightly dampened on a moist sponge, change the shapes of some of the larger scales by reworking their edges. Let dry. Use a small brush loaded with acrylic **white + burnt umber + ultramarine blue** to lighten the scales of the spinal ridges. Add a slightly more bluish shadow at the edge of each of these scales. Let dry.

8. Seal the stenciled units with a coat of thinned shellac (1 shellac + 1 alcohol) to ensure that the gouache will remain unaffected when the oil glaze (see step 9) is applied. (Although the dried gouache won't be reactivated by the oil glaze, it could be abraded by the action of applying it with the brush.) Let dry.

9. Remove the tape, clean and tape off the remaining units, then repeat steps 2–8.

10. Overglazing: Use an oil-dedicated glazing brush to apply a thin layer of glaze #2 (see Technical Notes) + **white + burnt sienna + ultramarine blue** to all of the shagreen units. Crisscross the glaze as described on page 205, then stipple it as shown in the exercise on page 206 to a fine texture. Dip a spattering brush in mineral spirits, then gently spatter the surface as shown in the recipe for "Watermark Patina" (see page 209). This adds depth by opening up the glaze, especially along the sides of the units. Let dry.

11. Using a striping brush and striping edge, paint joint lines (which will conceal any evidence of overlap between units) by mixing fluid acrylics to create a greenish blue that blends with the color of the shagreen (**white + chrome oxide deep + burnt sienna + ultramarine blue + raw umber**). Let dry.

PALISANDER

The technique used to create this finish is similar to that used for rosewood (see page 197) and Italian-style walnut using a water-based glaze (page 181).

1. Apply glaze #1 + **Cassel earth**, then flog it as shown in the exercise on page 157.

2. Using a square two-header loaded with glaze #1 + **burnt umber + black**, grain the surface as shown on page 162. Soften with a badger brush, working perpendicular to the grain lines to create a ridge. Let dry.

3. Overglazing: Apply glaze #2 + **burnt umber + Cassel earth + alizarin crimson**, then use a spalter to manipulate it with some moiré effects (see page 164). Let dry, then finish with wax (see below).

SNAKESKIN, IVORY, AND MOTHER-OF-PEARL

To create the snakeskin panels on the stiles and rails, see the recipe for "Snakeskin," page 274.

For the ivory border (see "Ivory," page 260) and the mother-of-pearl inlays (see "Mother-of-Pearl," page 268), be sure to create contrasts of color and value among units.

VARNISHING

Apply turpentine-diluted wax with a brush (see "Applying a Wax Finish," page 61). Let dry for 1 hour, then buff with a clean rag.

ALTERNATE TECHNIQUES

The following shagreen technique, which is similar to the one used in "Watermark Patina" (see page 209), is less complex and produces a less detailed surface than the one described above: Over an off-white alkyd basecoat (see Technical Notes), apply a medium-dark greenish gray oil glaze (glaze #2 + **raw umber + burnt umber + chrome oxide deep**). Stipple it to a fine stipple, then, while still wet, spatter the entire surface very gently with mineral spirits. Use a small pointed brush lightly loaded with mineral spirits to create the scales of the spinal ridge. Let dry.

Using either acrylics or oils, another technique involves stenciling white scales over the stippled effect (see step 1). In this case, the stenciling technique, which is positive (in which paint is applied) rather than negative, is a little easier, although the effect is not as realistic. Let dry, then overglaze as described in step 10, above.

1. Apply glaze to each unit, then add a dark streak down the center.

2. Working from top to bottom, stipple one half of the surface . . .

3. . . . then flip the brush and repeat on the other half. Let dry.

4. Position and affix the stencil, then use the tip of a slightly damp rag to reactivate and remove the dried gouache glaze from within the stencil windows.

5. Let dry, then remove the stencil. Change the shapes of some of the larger scales by reworking their edges with a moistened flat brush. Let dry.

6. Lighten and add subtle shadows to the scales of the central ridge. Let dry.

7. Seal the surface with thinned shellac, then let dry. Apply and stipple the overglaze, then spatter with mineral spirits. Let dry.

8. Here, the snakeskin panels have been added.

9. The completed finish, with joint lines, snakeskin stiles and rails, palisander corners, and mother-of-pearl and ivory inlay.

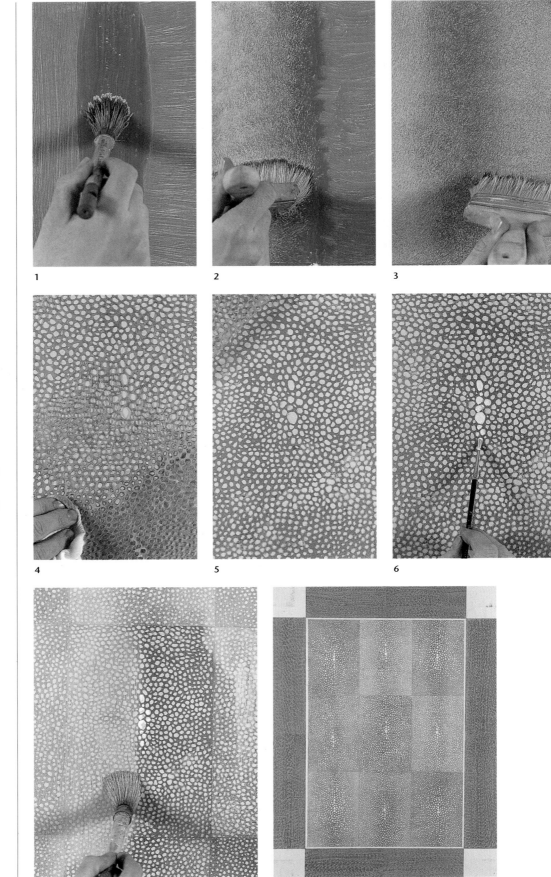

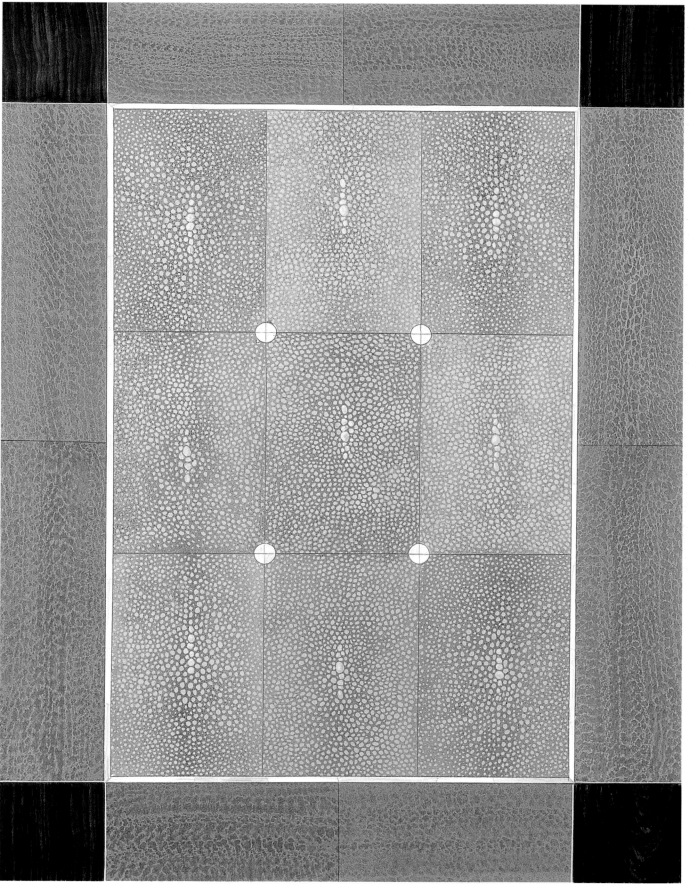

9

Stenciling

When you wish to repeat a single motif many times, stenciling—applying paint to a surface through the open areas of a stencil—is the perfect decorative painting technique. By designing and cutting your own stencils, you can create any motif, in any style, custom-fit to any size or proportion; several *overlays,* or multipart stencils, can be cut to produce multicolor and complex patterns. The time spent cutting the stencil is more than justified by the time saved and the accuracy guaranteed when a motif is repeated by stenciling, rather than rendering it freehand each time.

This stenciled living room uses a monchrome palette, for a subtle tone-on-tone look. The circular medallions (faux) between the triglyphs on the crown molding (real) were painted using trompe l'oeil techniques (see Chapter 11).

Stenciling Basics

The openings in a stencil through which paint is applied to a surface are called *windows*. The material from which the stencil is cut—the "positive" part of the stencil—defines the shapes of and relationships among the windows. Narrow strips of paper or pieces of copper wire known as *bridges* are used to connect the areas surrounding a window to a loose piece of stencil material in its center. For example, a bridge would be required to hold the center of the letter "O" in place, or the midrib and veins within a leaf.

A stencil can be cut from any material that can effectively mask off a surrounding surface. Once cut from parchment or leather, stencils are now most commonly cut from sheets of paper or plastic.

- *Stencil paper or stencil board* is a thin, opaque, poster board–like paper that is either coated with a protective layer of wax or waterproofed with linseed oil. It is inexpensive, durable, and easy to cut with an X-Acto or craft knife. Stencil paper can be used as purchased with oil-based paints; if used with water-based paints, it must be sealed after it's been cut on both sides with three coats of thinned shellac (1 shellac + $^1/_2$ alcohol; this mixture penetrates the paper well).

  A paper stencil can also be cut from a sheet of heavy, gloss-finish paper (similar to the kind used to make drawdown board or bristol board), which is then sealed on both sides with two to three coats of thinned shellac. I find these homemade stencils are quite durable and can be used with either oils or acrylics.
- *Mylar* (which is generically referred to as polyester film) is a thin, flexible transparent plastic that comes in a range of thicknesses; 5 mil is a good choice for stencils. It can be easily cut with an X-Acto knife or an electric stencil cutter (see page 285). Mylar works well with both oil- and water-based paints, and although it doesn't need to be sealed after cutting with thinned shellac, it tends to curl after several applications of water-based paint. Its transparency makes it easier to align motifs accurately.

LAYOUT

To find pattern ideas for your stencil, review books, magazines, and photographs of fabrics, carpeting, architectural ornaments, and historical designs. Upholstery fabrics, both woven and printed, are a great source of inspiration for me, especially Italian and French textiles, which have some spectacular designs.

Only very rarely will you be able to use a motif taken from reference materials as is; even stencils taken from copyright-free stenciling books require adjustments in size in order to establish good proportions relative to the surface to be stenciled. You might also have to simplify elements of a motif that are too detailed, or add bridges to effect a workable, solid stencil. With the wide availability of photocopiers, it's easy to reduce or enlarge a pattern. Once you have the correct size, then any necessary design adjustments can be made.

To copy a pattern from a fabric, place the fabric on a flat surface and secure it with tape, making sure the design remains straight. Lay gridded tracing paper or vellum over a section that will cover a full repeat. (A full repeat takes in all elements of a textile design, which are then printed over and over in a continuous flow without apparent interruption.) Trace one full repeat pattern with a pencil. Remove the tracing paper from the fabric, place it on a white surface, then go over the pattern with a felt-tip pen, making sure to outline the design elements carefully. If necessary, add more space between design elements to avoid ending up with hair-thin areas of stencil that will surely break after using it just once or twice.

STENCILING TECHNIQUES

Stenciling can be done in one of two ways: The paint can either be *applied to* or *removed from* the surface.

- As its name suggests, with the *positive method,* the stencil is placed on the surface and the paint is applied through the stencil windows. The most widely used stenciling technique, the positive method can be used with any medium, whether oil- or water-based, transparent or opaque, or even heavy or three-dimensional in texture.

- With the *negative method,* a reversible water-based paint is applied to the surface and allowed to dry, then the stencil is placed on the surface and the paint is removed through the stencil windows with a slightly damp cloth. This is a far less popular way of stenciling, but it produces great effects. An example of this technique is used to create the shagreen finish shown on page 279.

For motifs that require prints with sharp, clean edges—for instance, a multicolor Victorian-style stencil—it's recommended that the stenciling surface be smooth and flat. If you want to stencil even a slightly textured surface, it's likely that the paint will bleed or smudge unless you work with a very dry medium and that the edges of the prints won't be sharp. However, there are instances where softer prints are desirable, such as on an aged, textured patina, whose stenciled prints should look old and somewhat worn.

SUITABLE APPLICATIONS

Because of its versatility and ease of application, stenciling has long been a very popular decorative painting technique. It is quite cost effective in allowing the simulation of beautiful but expensive fabrics or wallcoverings, and can be longer lasting than both. Stenciling is also a good technique for creating friezes and other repetitive ornamentation on wood paneling and furniture.

Since the Middle Ages, when it was first used in the West as a decorative painting technique, stenciling has usually been thought of as most appropriate for rustic or provincial interiors, and after the 17th century was rarely used in castles or other grand residences. During the 19th century, a resurgence of interest in stenciling gave rise to some of the most spectacular and intricate

examples of this craft, many of which are still used to exemplify the great artisanship of the Victorian era. Today, stenciling is most commonly used to recreate period designs, to simulate expensive fabrics such as damask, and to decorate the walls, floors, and fabrics of virtually any room in a home.

CHOOSING THE RIGHT TECHNIQUE

Before reading this section, review "Influential Movements in Decorative Painting," page 15. The Italian approach usually applies strong, translucent color (usually water-based paint) over textured surfaces using an uneven method of application, so that it that looks as though the print has worn away in places. In contrast, the French (also the English) technique is more rigid and elaborate and often employs several overlays to compose one motif, and several colors for each pattern.

BASIC PROCEDURE

In general, your intended surface should be smooth, but slightly textured surfaces, such as distressed Italian or Provençal walls (see Chapter 6), can also be stenciled.

Before you begin stenciling, you will need to place removable registration lines on the surface; these will provide important aids for positioning the stencil correctly. Use a snap line (see page 48) to apply vertical chalk lines at even intervals. The size of the interval is usually the exact width of the stencil motif. When working with opaque stencil materials, cut little triangular registration windows into the stencil at points corresponding to the position of the chalk lines (but make sure they don't interfere with the stencil motif), then use them to line up the stencil with the chalk lines.

Since it's likely that you'll be working with several copies of the same stencil, you must number your stencils and prepare a map of your walls so that you have a record of exactly which stencil was used where. This is extremely important, since the cutting from stencil to stencil is never exactly the same, even when all the copies are cut using the original as the template (see page 285). When it is necessary to return the stencil to surface, whether for touchups, for additional applications of color (such as in "Multicolor Stenciling," page 286), or for dimensional effects (as shown in "Embossed Leather," page 292), you must reposition each stencil on its original spot.

In calculating how many stencils will be needed to complete a job, you can figure on getting 10 to 18 prints from each stencil before it will have to be repaired or thrown away. You might also need to cut an additional three or four stencils that are specially adapted to fit motif into corners, returns, ceilings, and baseboards.

Some decorative painters spray a low-tack adhesive on the backs of their stencils to keep them in place. It's efficient, but it has a tendency to leave a gluey residue on the working surface, and stencils may stick to each other when they're put away between painting sessions. I prefer to use low-tack tape (see page 48), which I apply in many places around the perimeter of the stencil, especially securing the top edge. The tape becomes a hinge, so when I want to check on the progress of the stencil, I simply lift the bottom only. When dropped back into place, the stencil repositions itself exactly where it was, the tape hinges having kept it from shifting.

Oil-based paints are the most frequently used with the positive technique, but water-based paints (acrylics) also produce excellent results, especially when a transparent and uneven look is desired. (In general, gouaches and beer glazes are too fluid for the positive technique, though they can be used to great effect with the negative technique.)

Stenciling is quite different from most of the other decorative painting techniques covered in this book, as it requires a medium with a dry, pastelike consistency (cut with very little thinner), which also keeps it from running. For transparent prints, load the brush with very little paint; for opaque prints, load the brush more heavily, but make sure the paint is not fluid.

Oil paints for stenciling = artists' oils + a touch of turpentine + drier

Acrylic paints for stenciling = 1 matte medium (optional, depending on degree of opacity) + 2 artists' acrylics (in tubes) + a touch of water

There are a few methods for applying the paint to the surface; each produces a slightly different effect. One technique, which produces opaque prints, uses a short-handled stencil brush (see page 45) held in a pen grip (page 37) to tap the surface repeatedly, using a stipplelike motion, working from the center of the motif to the edges. Another method, in which the stencil brush is held like a pen and worked in a circular motion, is more likely to yield translucent prints.

Both brush and stencil should be cleaned off frequently to prevent paint from building up in the heel of the brush or around the edges of the windows, which could cause smudging or bleeding. It's best to have a separate brush for each color you're working with, and to work with two sets of brushes, so that you don't have to wait for one to dry if you need to clean it in the middle of the process. This is especially important if you're working with acrylics, which in addition to drying quickly in this case are dry in consistency, which in turn cause brush hairs to stiffen, so that brushes require more frequent cleanings.

The final procedure of varnishing is generally omitted in stenciling, mainly to preserve the difference in sheen between the stencil and the background. Because most stenciling is done in irreversible paint, the additional protection of a varnish is usually not required. But if you elect to varnish your stencils—for extra protection in high-traffic areas, or when an even shine is desired—refer to "The Finish Coat," page 59.

Stenciling paints should have a dry, a pastelike consistency, so very little binder and thinner are added when colors are mixed. Load the stencil brush evenly by picking up a little paint, then working it on the palette with a circular motion.

Stenciling Exercises

Before you can begin cutting a stencil (see below), you must make some important decisions. In addition to working out the motif's design at a scale that is appropriate for your surface, you must decide how many colors will be used to make the prints. Although a single stencil can be used to make multicolor prints (see page 286), you might want to consider cutting several overlays, one for each color. Cutting overlays can be something of a challenge, especially for a beginner, since each part of the stencil must align perfectly with the others to produce a complete motif.

Since stippling is one of the primary application methods used for stenciling, it's recommended that you prepare for a stenciling recipe by practicing that exercise (see page 206) but use a stenciling brush instead of a stippling brush.

CUTTING A STENCIL

After you've copied or created a new stencil motif on a sheet of gridded tracing paper or vellum (photo 1), made any necessary corrections or adjustments, then made a photocopy, enlarging or reducing the motif so its size is in correct proportion to your working surface, you're ready to cut the motif from the stencil material.

Cutting Stencil Paper or Heavy Gloss-Finish Paper with an X-Acto Knife. Mark both the stencil paper and the final photocopy of the stencil motif with registration lines. Apply spray adhesive to the back of the photocopy, then lay it on the stencil paper. Align the registration marks carefully, then smooth out the photocopy (photo 2). Use an X-Acto knife to cut through both the photocopy and the stencil paper to remove the windows of each design element (photo 3). When all the windows have been cut, peel the photocopy off the stencil (photo 4). If you cut the stencil from gloss-finish paper, or if you're planning to stencil with acrylics, apply three coats of thinned shellac (see page 282) to each side of the stencil.

Cutting Mylar with an Electric Stencil Cutter. If you prefer to work with a transparent plastic stencil material such as Mylar, you can cut your stencils with an electric stencil cutter, which has a heated cutting tip. When working with Mylar, an electric cutter is easier to use than an X-Acto knife, especially when cutting small windows.

Place a sheet of 5-mil Mylar over the final photocopy of the stencil motif, then trace the design with a permanent fine-tip felt marker for transparent film. Lay the Mylar over a smooth piece of glass, which will enable the tip of the cutter to glide over the Mylar and protects the underlying surface from its heat. After the windows have been cut, remove any ridges left around the perimeter of the windows by sanding down both sides of the stencil with a sanding block. Because it is plastic, Mylar doesn't require a protective coat of shellac.

Cutting Additional Copies. To make additional copies of a stencil, *always* use the original as your template so that the copies are as consistent as possible. Place the original over another sheet of stencil paper or Mylar, stencil the motifs with a dark, opaque color (such as black, blue, or red), let dry, then cut out the windows. Seal paper stencils with thinned shellac.

Repairing Stencils. Paper stencils can be repaired by gluing on a piece of stencil paper cut to the shape of the damaged area, or taping both sides of a loose or broken area with a small piece of masking tape and cutting off the excess with an X-Acto knife.

Because it is resistant to glue, Mylar can be difficult to repair, though a broken piece can usually be fixed with masking tape.

1

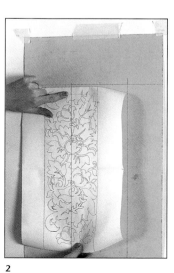

2

3

4

Multicolor Stenciling

The process for stenciling single-color or multicolor prints is essentially the same, except for the number of applications of color that are required; for example, a three-color stencil requires that a stencil be placed on the intended surface three different times, to permit the application of three different colors. This technique can be accomplished in one of two ways: by using several overlays—one stencil for each color—or by using a single stencil and masking off those parts of the motif through which color should *not* be applied. I recommend using the "taping-off" technique whenever possible, not only to avoid the extra work of cutting a separate stencil for each color, but as a precaution against potential registration and alignment problems when overlaying the stencils. For example, with the motif I used for the demonstration, it was easier to mask off windows for each pass than to cut three different stencils. However, if you elect to cut a separate stencil for each color, make sure they all fit together perfectly, and pay particular attention to the accuracy and alignment of registration marks.

This recipe demonstrates the basic stenciling technique; the only variables are pattern, color, and medium. The optional "aging" step works beautifully on stenciled textured surfaces, such as distressed Italian and Provençal walls (see Chapter 6).

1. Lightly sand and dust off the cured basecoated surface. Use the glazing brush to cover the surface with acrylic glaze (see Technical Notes) + **yellow ochre** + **raw sienna** varied with other colors from the palette. Strié the wet glaze as shown in the exercise on page 206. Let dry.
2. Cut several copies of the same stencil motif as described in the exercise on page 285. Using low-tack tape, mask off the windows where you want to avoid applying color to the surface; leave exposed only those windows through which you want to apply your first color. Set aside.
3. With the aid of a chalk snap line, place your vertical registration lines. Align the triangular registration windows of the stencil with the chalk lines and tape the stencil to the surface.
4. Prepare a good amount (about 8 to 16 fluid ounces) of acrylic paint for stenciling (see Technical Notes), mixing **white + raw sienna + burnt umber + burnt sienna** well with a palette knife. The mixture should have a pastelike consistency. Very lightly load a 1-inch stencil brush, then apply the paint through the stencil windows (either by stippling or with a circular stroke), varying the tonality with other colors from the palette (in the demonstration, **white, raw sienna, burnt sienna,** and a touch of **chrome green oxide** were used). The paint mixture and application method yield translucent prints with a variegated tonality that suggests depth and age. For more opaque prints, use artists' acrylics straight from the tube thinned with just a little water and use a more heavily loaded brush.

   You must finish the entire room (or other working surface) with this taped-off version of the stencil and the first color before going on to the next. Keep any remaining paint in an airtight container in case you need to do touchups or you decide to use the same stencil on another surface. Let dry.
5. Remove the masks from the stencil, then tape off all the windows except those through which the second stencil paint mixture will be applied. In the example used for the demonstration, I stenciled the foliage with an off-green color (**white + chrome green oxide + raw sienna + a touch of burnt sienna**), following the same procedure outlined in step 4 and again using selected palette colors to vary the color and intensity of the elements. Complete the entire surface with the second color, modifying it with **white** here and there to give these elements a faded effect. Let dry.
6. Remove the masks from the stencil, then tape off all the windows except

those through which the third color will be applied. For these elements of the motif, I used a redder mixture (**burnt sienna** + **raw sienna** + **white** + a touch of **chrome green oxide**). Stencil the last elements with the third color, again varying tonality with both the palette colors and with white alone. Let dry.

7. Optional: For a more distressed, aged effect, lightly sand and dust off the surface, then run a scrub pad here and there over the stenciled areas. To heighten the aged effect, sponge on an off-white glaze (acrylic glaze + **white** + **yellow ochre**) over the entire surface. Let dry.

USING OTHER MEDIA

Oils might be easier for beginners to use than acrylics because they offer a longer working time, but this also means a long wait for each color to dry before the next can be applied. If the stencil is placed over a wet print, the print will smear.

1. To prepare the background for the stenciling, apply and strié a translucent glaze. Let dry.

2. Cut the stencil, then mask off windows where you don't want to apply color to the surface. Affix the stencil to the surface and align it with the chalk registration lines. Using just the first color and stencil configuration, stencil the entire surface. Let dry.

3. The first part of the stencil is complete.

4. Remove the tape from the stencil, then tape off all the windows except those through which the second color will be applied. Complete the entire surface with the second color, modifying its value here and there to produce a faded effect. Let dry. Repeat this step for the third color; let dry.

5. The completed stencil prints.

6. For an aged effect, sponge on an off-white glaze over the entire surface. Let dry.

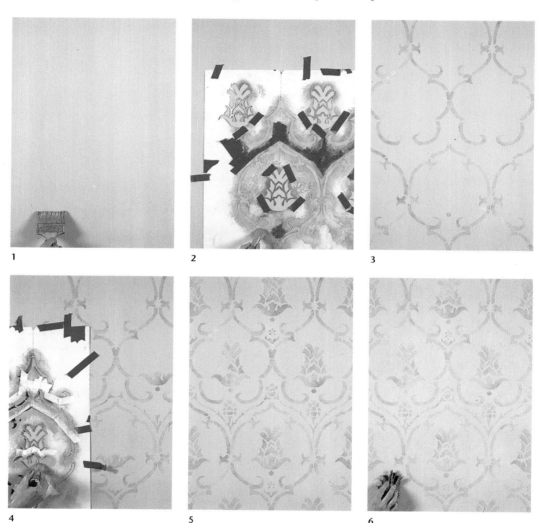

1

2

3

4

5

6

7. The completed finish.

7

Damask

TECHNICAL NOTES

Difficulty Rating

3

System

Oil

Basecoat

*Any color may be used,
depending on the final effect*

Light aqua green (**white +
ultramarine blue + chrome
oxide deep** + a touch of
burnt umber) alkyd,
eggshell finish

Oil Glaze

2 turpentine + 1 oil + drier

Oil Paints for Stenciling

Artists' oils + a touch of
turpentine + drier

Palette

Artists' Oils

White

Raw umber

Burnt sienna

Burnt umber

Ultramarine blue

Chrome green oxide

Chrome oxide deep

Brushes and Tools

Glazing brushes

#60 spalter

Stippling brushes

Stencil brushes

Assorted pointed brushes

Exercises

Cutting a Stencil (page 285)

Stippling (page 206)

Fading (page 304)

*See also the recipe for
"Distressed Italian Walls"
(page 214)*

Damask is a monochrome textile having a woven pattern—positive on one side, negative on the other—that is revealed only by differences in texture or surface sheen, which can be glowing and quite spectacular. The slightly raised pattern has a velvety texture as contrasted with its flatter silky background—or the other way around on the reverse side. Damask is imitated with stencils for decorative purposes, and because painting is more economical and often more durable than covering a wall with the textile itself. The stencil motif created for this recipe was adapted from a book on Italian Renaissance fabrics.

It is important that the sheen of the background differ from that of the stenciled motifs, particularly when working tone on tone as in this demonstration. While the gradated stippling of the background (steps 1–4) is optional, it adds tremendous dimensionality and movement of light to the stenciled surface.

1. Lightly sand and dust off the cured basecoated surface. Using a snap line loaded with white chalk, lay out four horizontal lines; this divides the surface into fifths, which will be painted with three values of the same color to represent the variations in color created by the play of light within the fabric's raised pattern. (These lines are usually spaced so that the lightest color falls in the center of the stencil, but that isn't an absolute rule.)

2. Mix three separate batches of green glaze, using an oil glaze (see Technical Notes) + **white + chrome oxide deep + raw umber + ultramarine blue** + a touch of **burnt sienna.** Reserve one batch as is, then add more **white** to the second batch, and still more **white** to the third batch, creating two lighter values of the original mixture. Set aside.

3. Optional: To make it easier to create fluid transitions among the three values, you can apply an untinted layer of oil glaze over the surface with a rag. This slick, saturated surface will allow the values to "slide" more smoothly when they are faded into one another.

4. As shown in the recipe on page 214, use a separate glazing brush to apply each of the three values to the surface (see also "Tips on Color Mixing," page 35). The darkest value goes at the top and bottom of the surface, the lightest value in the center, and the middle value immediately above and below the lightest value. Working from left to right, use each of the glazing brushes to lightly soften the edges of the sections so that three distinct values remain but appear to merge gradually into one another.

5. Work a #60 spalter in a zigzag, vertical motion to create a wide, jagged edge between each of the values. Start by working the light values into the medium value, then work the medium value into the darker values.

6. Stipple the surface with a stippling brush, working from light (the center) to dark (either the top or the bottom of the surface). To avoid spoiling the gradated effect, do not stop in the middle of a pass, change brushes, or wipe the brush off as you work. Once you've reached either the top or the bottom of the surface, work the stippling brush back toward the center in one continuous motion. Repeat two or three times until you've achieved an effective gradation of the three values. Use a smaller and coarser stippling brush when the transitions seem to be at a midway point, then use a softer, wider stippling or patina brush for the final pass. Let dry. The oil glaze gives the surface a satin sheen.

7. Cut and prepare the stencils using one of the methods discussed in the exercise on page 285. Use a snap line to chalk vertical registration lines, then affix the stencil to the surface. On your palette, prepare the oil paints for stenciling by mixing **chrome oxide deep + burnt umber + ultramarine blue + white** + a touch of **burnt sienna,** then add a little turpentine and drier to give the mixture a pastelike consistency. Put some untinted oil glaze in a palette cup. (To emphasize the matte finish of the stencil prints, you can replace the oil glaze with a mixture of 2 matte-finish oil-based

1. Apply a layer of untinted glaze, then apply three values of glaze: the darkest at the top and bottom, the lightest in the center, and the middle value immediately above and below the lightest. Soften the edges of each section so that the values merge softly there.

2. Work a spalter in a zigzag, vertical motion to create a wide jagged edge between each of the values.

3. Stipple the surface, working from light (the center) to dark (either the top or bottom of the surface). Begin with a stippling brush; when the transitions are at a midway point, use a smaller, coarser stippling brush. For the final pass, use a soft, wide stippling or patina brush. Let dry.

4. The oil glaze gives the background a satin sheen that will contrast with the matte finish of the stencil prints.

5. Cut the stencil, then affix it to the surface. Using a semi-opaque application of paint, begin stenciling at the top and bottom of the motif. When the paint is exhausted from the brush, work it toward the center of the stencil.

6. Stipple the center of the stencil with a stippling brush, working from the center up to the top and down to the bottom of the motif.

7. If necessary, lighten the value of the center of the motif by dabbing it with a clean rag. Let dry.

8. To heighten the three-dimensional look of the finish, add shadows and highlights with a small pointed brush.

9. The completed finish.

varnish + 1 turpentine.) Dab the stencil brush into a little of the oil glaze, then work it into the palette mixture with a circular motion so that the brush is loaded evenly. Using a semi-opaque application of paint, begin stenciling at the top and bottom of the motif. When the paint has been exhausted from the brush, work the brush toward the center of the stencil, to create a more transparent, gradated effect in that area.

8. Use a clean, small stippling brush to stipple the center of the stencil, smoothing it out and making it more transparent. Then work up to the top and down to the bottom; if necessary, dab a large clean rag through the stencil windows to lighten the value of the central portion of the motif further. Let dry. Because the stencil paint

contains little or no linseed oil and only a few drops of turpentine, the print will have a matte finish. This important contrast of matte stenciling over a satin background is what establishes the contrasting light effects, reinforcing the raised-pattern look of damask fabric. Let dry.

9. Optional: To heighten the dimensional effect even further, use a small pointed brush loaded with a darker value of the green paint mixed for step 7 to add thin shadows here and there under selected design elements. Then use a lighter value of the green paint + **white** to add highlights to the tops of some selected elements. Note that this is a very time-consuming process that is usually used only for specially commissioned works. Let dry.

290

7

8

9

Embossed Leather

Embossed leather is also called Cordova leather, named for the Spanish town of Cordova, where the process evolved during the Renaissance. The leather was first heat-embossed with various designs, then after staining was often painted and gilded.

The basic procedure used to simulate the dimensional effect of the embossing is as follows: Stencil a light translucent print, reposition the same stencil on the surface, moving it down approximately 1/8 inch, then stencil a dark translucent print. The areas where the dark print overlaps the light one creates a middle value, which becomes the color of the embossed design, while the lighter and darker areas become its highlights and shadows. This technique can be used to create any type of patterned dimensional finish, such as damask (see page 289; the highlights and shadows in that recipe were painted on instead of stenciled).

1. Following steps 1–6 of the recipe on page 263, paint the surface with faux leather. Let dry. Omit step 7 (finishing the surface with wax) until after the stenciling is completed.

2. Cut and prepare the stencils using one of the methods discussed in the exercise on page 285. (Number the stencils so you can document exactly where each one was used.) Use a snap line to chalk vertical registration lines, then affix the stencils to the surface.

3. Mix the light-value paint, blending **raw sienna** + **yellow ochre** + **burnt umber** + a touch of **white** into a pastelike consistency (see Technical Notes). (A total of 8 to 16 fluid ounces is usually enough for an average-size room.) Place a walnut-size glob of the mixture on your palette and store the rest in an airtight plastic container. Load a stencil brush and begin stenciling in a circular motion. The application should be semi-transparent. To ensure that both the value and color are right, try out the paint in a corner before you do a full stencil. Unfortunately, there are no hard-and-fast rules for evaluating color; in this case, though, it should be no more than one or two value steps lighter than the background.

4. Carefully remove the stencils. With a roll of paper towels, hit the surface here and there, each time exposing a clean area of the roll to blot areas where the intensity of the paint is too strong. Repeat steps 3 and 4 over your entire surface, then let dry fully (at least 24 hours).

5. Mix a darker, warm-brown tone by blending **burnt umber** + **raw umber** + **raw sienna.** into a pastelike consistency for stenciling. Place some of the mixture on your palette. Place some untinted oil glaze (see Technical Notes) in a palette cup.

6. Using the same stencils you used before (refer to your map and stencil numbers for accuracy), reposition each on its previous spot, but move it down 1/8 inch. To ensure that the downward shift is even for all parts of the stencil, you might need to enlist an assistant for this step. Touch the stencil brush to the cup glaze, pick up a little of the dark-value paint from the palette, then work the bristles in a circular motion so that the brush is loaded evenly. Stencil the surface uniformly with a semi-transparent application. Use a small stippling brush to even out certain parts as needed.

7. To simulate leather texture, hit the surface through the stencil windows with a clean, dry cotton rag formed into a "rosebud," as shown in the exercise on page 205. Lift up the stencil to check for imperfections, replace it, then make any necessary corrections. Repeat steps 6 and 7 for the remaining prints until the entire room is completed. Let dry.

8. Optional: For heightened textural effect, add highlights and shadows here and there with a pointed brush. Let dry.

9. Once the surface has cured fully, wax it according to step 7 on page 263.

USING OTHER MEDIA

This recipe can also be painted in acrylics, as long as color and translucency can be managed properly. Although it's easier to correct mistakes when working in oils than it is when working in acrylics, there's a much longer wait between applications of color.

1. Paint the surface with faux leather (see page 263); let dry. Cut the stencils, then number each one. Affix the stencils to the surface, align them with the chalk registration lines. (Keep a careful record of where each stencil was used.) Prepare the paint, then proceed with the stenciling.

2. While the paint is still wet, carefully remove the stencils. Blot areas where the intensity of the paint is too strong by hitting the surface here and there with a roll of paper towels, each time exposing a clean area of the roll. Let dry completely.

3. Reposition each of the stencils on its previous spot, but lower it 1/8 inch. Stencil the surface evenly with a darker tone using a semi-transparent application.

4. Use a small stippling brush to even out the tonality.

5. To simulate the leather texture, hit the surface through the stencil with a clean rag. Let dry.

6. To heighten texture and dimension, add highlights and shadows here and there with a small pointed brush. Let dry.

7. The completed finish.

Trompe l'Oeil

FAUX MOLDINGS AND GRISAILLE

Trompe l'oeil is a French phrase that literally means "fool the eye." In decorative painting, trompe l'oeil techniques use the interplay between light and shadow to create an illusion of dimension and depth. In this book, examples of trompe l'oeil are limited strictly to the painting of three-dimensional architectural details such as moldings, and the ornamental elements of grisaille and polychrome. Though today the term "trompe l'oeil" is broadly used to refer to all manner of painted illusions, including those that seek to imitate marble, wood, and other organic materials, as well as photographically realistic depictions of both animate and inanimate objects, the restricted use of the term in this chapter is actually more faithful to its original definition.

This room juxtaposes real moldings with grisaille ornaments and faux moldings.

Trompe l'Oeil Basics

Within the time-honored traditions of decorative painting, trompe l'oeil techniques are only used to depict inanimate or stationary objects, such as architectural details and still lifes; if well executed, it would be difficult for the viewer to discern the real from the painted. Animate and plant life—animals, portraits, and landscapes—are generally considered inappropriate for trompe l'oeil, simply because the viewer would expect the subject to move, thus sabotaging the painted deception. (These trompe l'oeil compositions are referred to as murals; see list below.)

TYPES OF TROMPE L'OEIL

There are six basic categories of trompe l'oeil painting. The first three listed below—all architectural or surface ornamentation—are covered in this chapter. The last three, which fall primarily within the realms of the fine artist or artisan, are discussed here only briefly; a few books have been written on these topics, which deserve further study.

Regardless of type, trompe l'oeil can be either *monochromatic* (also called *tone-on-tone*), in which several values of one principle color are used; or *polychromatic*, in which subjects are rendered in several different colors.

- *Faux moldings,* which are the most common type of trompe l'oeil, include all manner of decorative architectural detail, such as moldings, columns, niches, and bosses.
- *Grisaille,* a French word that means "shades of gray," is a technique in which several values of one color are used to model form. As the term suggests, grays were traditionally used for this technique, usually a blend of white, a primary color, and its complement, rather than a mixture of black and white. (See "Tips on Color Mixing," page 35.) Faux bas-relief carvings and ornaments are often painted in grisaille.
- *Polychrome ornaments* employ the same three-dimensional painting techniques as traditional grisaille, but uses several colors to render what are usually more complex ornamental forms (such as floral motifs) and styles (like Chinoiserie).
- *Murals* are large-scale trompe l'oeil compositions painted on facades, ceilings, or interior walls that combine three-dimensional architectural elements with landscapes and/or figures.
- *Trompe l'oeil paintings* are fine-art still lifes that incorporate trompe l'oeil techniques. This style of painting, which first emerged in 16th-century Holland and Flanders, is still practiced today.
- *Trompe l'oeil marquetry,* both in stone (*pietre dure*) and wood, were created by Italian artisans during the Renaissance. For more information on how to recreate these incredible masterpieces in paint, see pages 132 and 197.

SUITABLE APPLICATIONS

While trompe l'oeil's primary value is ostensibly decorative, it's likely that its heightened degree of realism was devised to provoke a strong response from the viewer: the amusing realization that he or she has momentarily been tricked into thinking that a two-dimensional image is a three-dimensional form. It is also possible that trompe l'oeil techniques were used for financial reasons; prior to the Renaissance, it was less costly to paint elaborate architectural detail than to actually install it.

The earliest examples of trompe l'oeil can be found in the ruins of Pompeii, where villa walls were painted with faux moldings, columns, and other ornamentation. Trompe l'oeil technique reached its height in Italy during the Renaissance, when such works by masters as Titian, Tiepolo, Raphael, and Michelangelo were framed with a dazzling array of faux architectural details, including moldings, crowns, balustrades, columns, and carvings. Throughout Europe during the 18th and 19th centuries, when grand interiors were lavishly decorated with grisaille and polychrome ornaments, it was common for decorative painters to paint faux moldings alongside real ones, so that it was difficult to distinguish one from the other. (For an example of this technique, see the photograph on pages 280–281.) Whether this was done strictly because it was easier to paint the details than to add new ones, or because those who oversaw such renovations wanted to have fun with viewers remains a mystery.

Because of its long history and somewhat strict decorative traditions, trompe l'oeil is frequently thought of as appropriate only for classic or traditional decor. As long as the intended form is appropriate for a modern setting, and the decorative principles of the space are respected, trompe l'oeil techniques could be used. Trompe l'oeil forms can be painted on walls, millwork, cabinetry, faux wood or marble panels—anywhere real moldings or ornaments would normally be found.

CHOOSING THE RIGHT TECHNIQUE

Before reading this section, review "Influential Movements in Decorative Painting," page 15. The differences between the French and Italian approaches to trompe l'oeil are clearly defined. Both techniques are effective, but each is appropriate for different applications and settings.

Somewhat predictably, the Italian style is loose, bold, and theatrical; from a distance the technique is persuasive, but upon close examination it's obvious that the form has been painted. Also, the fact that most of Italian-style trompe l'oeil painted from the 16th through the 18th centuries was done on large surfaces in *buon fresco*—applying water-based paints over damp lime plaster, so that as the plaster dries the image becomes integrated with the surface—means that artists did not have time to painstakingly blend shadows and highlights, which is feasible only when working on small surfaces or in oils. As a result, highlights and shadows were opaque rather than transparent, so that light and dark areas within forms were modeled with carefully chosen colors rather than a transparent gradation of values.

In contrast, the French technique, which was perfected during the 19th century, uses oil-based media; in addition to being precisely painted, shadows and highlights were transparent and based on a subtle gradation of value. Although it's difficult for viewers to discern, French-style trompe l'oeil has a certain rigidity that could be displeasing; as it has few painterly qualities, it looks almost "too perfect."

BASIC PROCEDURE

Essentially, you must work with whatever surface preparation has been done for the faux finish on which the trompe l'oeil detail is being painted. When painted over faux marble or wood, the surface has been meticulously prepared; over faux block-style stone and certain types of patinas, the surface preparation could be less precise. In general, it's best (and easiest) to paint trompe l'oeil over a smooth, well-prepared surface. If you're planning to paint faux moldings or other trompe l'oeil forms over a faux finish, you must wait until the finish is completely dry before you begin; the entire surface is varnished only *after* the trompe l'oeil has been completed.

To ensure a high degree of accuracy, the profile or image must be carefully drawn on (for moldings) or transferred to (for grisaille and polychrome ornaments) the surface; for more information, see the exercises on pages 305 and 306.

Faux moldings are usually painted in oil; a basic glaze formula is 1.5 turpentine + 1 oil + drier + artists' oils. A generous working time makes an oil glaze easier for beginners to work with, but their drying and curing times require a long wait between painting shadows (which are always painted first) and highlights. I prefer to work with acrylics, especially when the amount of molding to be painted is minimal; since acrylics dry so quickly (in as little as 5 minutes with a hair dryer), shadows can be quickly built up in translucent layers, and highlights can be added almost immediately. The standard acrylic glaze is 1 acrylic medium (use either matte or gloss, to match the sheen of the finish you're painting) + 1 water + fluid artists' acrylics; add gel retarder for hot days or large surfaces. Whether oil or water, the glaze should be neither too thick nor too thin; it should be easy to apply without being runny. To achieve the proper consistency, thicken an acrylic glaze with matte medium and thin it down with water; for an oil glaze, thicken with linseed oil or whiting and thin with turpentine. Note that reversible water-based media—gouache and beer glazes—are not suitable for trompe l'oeil. Because shadows and highlights are rendered by means of layered shifts in value and color, each application of glaze would reactivate the previous ones.

As for any other faux finish, varnishing is always done after the painting is fully dry. This gives the entire surface a consistent, unified sheen and texture.

NOTES ON TROMPE L'OEIL BRUSHES AND TOOLS

Listed below is the equipment used to paint trompe l'oeil compositions. Because these tools are supposed to promote precision and accuracy, they should be used exclusively for trompe l'oeil painting and kept separate from the other tools in your kit so they won't be damaged or accidentally used for other purposes.

Striping Brushes. Striping brushes (see page 43) are used for *striping,* or painting the subtle yet precise gradations of light and shadow that are used to render trompe l'oeil forms. Designed to paint very sharply defined areas, striping brushes are filled

with a lot of bristles or hairs so they can hold plenty of glaze. There are several types of striping brushes; the shape of their hairs determines their use. In addition to striping brushes, a variety of other brushes can be used for this task, including lettering and rondin brushes. Never exert pressure on a striping brush in order to make a thicker line; simply use a larger brush.

Purchase only good-quality striping brushes, and use them only for striping. (It's recommended that you store them in a special box so you won't use them for something else.) Maintain a separate set of striping brushes for each system: one for water (with synthetic hairs) and one for oil (with natural hairs like sable or mongoose). To paint a very thin stripe, use a thin nylon (for water systems) or flat sable (for oil systems) brush (both have razor-sharp edges); for a medium-width stripe, use a flat or angled nylon (water) or natural-bristle (oil) brush; for a wide stripe, use a large nylon (water) or rondin (water or oil) brush. Experiment with a few brushes to find the ones you're most comfortable with, and for those that are most suitable for the molding you're painting and the medium you're using. It takes a little while to "make" a striping brush; use it regularly so it maintains a consistent edge.

Striping brushes have some special cleaning requirements. Rinse striping brushes used with oil media two or three times in clean mineral spirits. Gently massage the hairs between your thumb and index finger, always working from the heel of the brush

If you have a local carpenter make a striping edge for you, make sure that its dimensions are correct.

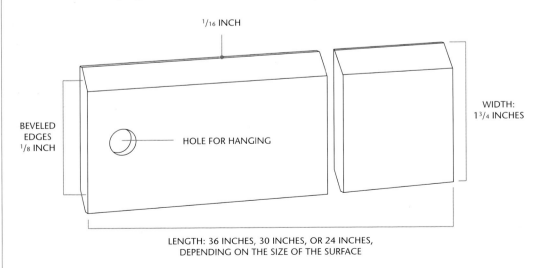

to the ends of the hairs, then wipe them off with a clean rag. Once clean, "grease up" the hairs with lard, shape them to a sharp edge, and store the brush in a box. Before using the brush again, remove the lard by rinsing the hairs in mineral spirits, then wipe them off well.

To clean striping brushes used with water media, begin by rinsing them in water; if the hairs are caked with paint, rinse them again in alcohol. Wash gently with soap and water, letting the soap foam up in the hairs, then rinse well in water. Shape the hairs to a point, dip them in a solution of 1 water + 1 gum arabic, then shape the hairs again. The gum arabic hardens as it dries, forming a protective coating (similar to what is found on a new brush). Before using the brush again, remove the gum arabic by rinsing the hairs in water, then wipe them off well.

Striping Edge. A striping edge (see page 49) is used to guide the path of a striping brush when painting shadows and highlights. Made out of wood that is smooth, light, and flexible yet strong (such as pine, cedar, walnut, or beech), a striping edge is beveled on both edges to keep paint or glaze from bleeding beneath it as the loaded brush is run against it. If you can't find a striping edge at a hardware or paint retailer, check the list of suppliers or have a local carpenter make one for you. Most are about 1³/₄ inches wide, 3 feet long, and ¹/₈ inch thick; if you plan to paint a lot of trompe l'oeil moldings, you should have a few other versions, both longer and shorter, to fit a variety of surfaces. To keep your striping edge from getting damaged, use it only for striping and keep it in a safe place when you're not using it.

Prior to using it, a new striping edge must be sealed with several applications of linseed oil. While in use, it should be wiped off frequently to prevent paint from building up on its edge. At the end of a working session, it should be wiped down with either mineral spirits (if used with oil media) or alcohol (if used with water media).

Striper Cup. A striper cup is a small, long, narrow tin cup furnished with a clip or hook that threads through a shirt buttonhole. Having a cup of glaze so close at hand makes it possible to reload a brush without changing position, which is particularly important when you're in the middle of striping a long line. This traditional decorative painting tool is no longer commercially manufactured, so you can make one by filling a clean, empty 35mm film canister about a quarter of the way with glaze and taping it to the front of your shirt.

For Correcting Mistakes. Always have a clean, small (6-inch-square) rag and a little thinner (either water or turpentine) ready for making corrections (removing an imperfect stripe) or adjustments (defining the end of a stripe) and for keeping the striping edge clean as you work. Make sure you're prepared for such situations, so you don't have to waste time and energy in the middle of a working session looking for a clean rag.

Make your own striper cup by taping an empty film canister to your chest.

Elements of Light and Shadow

As mentioned above, trompe l'oeil forms are modeled by means of a precisely painted gradation of values, which expresses the effects of the direction and quality of the light on the object.

- The *form shadow* is the area of the object itself that is darkened by shadow; little or no light is present because it is on the side of the object opposite the light.
- The *cast shadow* is the shadow that is projected by the object onto an adjacent surface.
- The *highlight* is the area of the object that is directly illuminated because it is closest to the light source.

A gradual shift between the darkest dark (the lowest value) and the lightest light (the highest value) is used to express the three-dimensional volume of a trompe l'oeil form. This shift is achieved by dividing shadows (both form and cast) and highlights into the following components:

- The *halftone* is the transparent portion of shadows and highlights. It is used to represent the transition from the color and value of the surface toward either dark or light. Of course, a different color and value are used to express each type of halftone, one for the shadow halftone, and one for the highlight halftone.
- The *accent* is the most concentrated, most opaque portion of shadows and highlights. It is used to represent the darkest (within the shadow) and the brightest (within the highlight) areas of an object.

In addition to a halftone and an accent, within almost every form shadow lies *reflected light*. Reflected light is the light that is reflected back onto an object from the adjacent surface. This area of a shadow is generally expressed as the same color or value as the halftone shadow; it is usually not as light as any portion of the highlight.

LIGHT SOURCE

It is absolutely essential that the light source be carefully considered when painting a trompe l'oeil form; if shadows and highlights are placed contrary to the predominant direction of the light, or if the degree of contrast used does not reflect the quality of the light, the final result will be jarring and confusing.

Scrupulously painting every kind and source of light in a space can also create visual confusion. When a space is illuminated by more than one source of light, or when it is illuminated primarily by sunlight (whose direction will not only change over the course of a day, but whose quality can also vary, from day to day as well as within a single day), simplify the task by imposing the predominant source and quality of light on all of the trompe l'oeil forms. This strategy will give you more consistent results.

SHADOW AND HIGHLIGHT: COLOR AND CONTRAST

Once you've resolved the issue of light, you must determine the correct colors and values for your shadows and highlights. Instead of always painting shadows in black and highlights in white—a mistake commonly made by beginners—the colors of shadows and highlights must always reflect the local color; that is, color of the surface on which they are painted. For example, a faux molding painted on a mahogany panel that is predominantly dark maroon in color will most likely use burnt umber for its shadow and chrome orange for its highlight. In general, it's best to use cool colors for shadows and warm colors for highlights, because cool colors tend to recede within a composition, and warm colors tend to advance, thus enhancing the modeling of form. These elements of the composition should be subtle and transparent, so try to use transparent colors: zinc white, raw sienna, burnt sienna, alizarin crimson, raw umber, burnt umber, Cassel earth, and lamp black. See "The Faux Palette," pages 34–35, for more information, and test the colors you have on hand before purchasing others.

There are a couple of methods for choosing the correct color for a shadow. One way is to paint a small listel or flat molding (see page 307) or a little piece of wood mounted on a small board with the same color or faux finish as the surface on which you're planning to paint the faux molding. Observe this sample in several locations, noting how various sources and qualities of light affect the color and value of shadows, then use the sample to match the color and value of the shadow that best express the direction and quality of the predominant light source where you're working. (The color of a highlight can be determined using the same technique.) Another way to test a color you've mixed for a shadow is by casting a shadow on the surface by holding your striping edge above it, then comparing the color and value of the actual shadow to the one you mixed.

The colors you mix for your halftones—both shadow and highlight—will serve as the bases for the colors of your accents. When mixing your accents, don't simply use whatever is leftover from painting your halftones. Before you begin painting, mix the colors for *all* the elements of shadow and highlight—halftone and highlight—then test them out on a separate surface. Once you're satisfied, store each of the mixed in a small container and label it, noting its formula and the element of shadow or highlight for which it will be used.

The contrast between shadows and highlights should be strong enough so that they can be seen from a normal viewing distance: As the distance of the viewer from the surface increases, the degree of contrast between shadows and highlights should also increase. For example, the contrast between shadows and highlights used to paint a molding on a ceiling will be greater than those used to paint an ornament on a door. In addition, the contrast between shadow and highlight increases as the height of a molding's or ornament's projections increase. Note how light and shadow are used to render the circular medallion on page 314, as compared to the grisaille ornament on page 317; the latter is much closer to the surface, and thus requires a much subtler transition from dark to light.

Decorative painters must maintain a delicate balance between meticulously rendering the subtle gradations of light and shadow, and overwhelming a form with unnecessary and cumbersome detail. The shadow is the most important part of the form, as it creates most of its volume. In fact, there are times when trompe l'oeil forms are comprised of shadows only; for instance, when painting a molding on a white ground. Always paint the shadows first, then add the highlights.

These drawings illustrate how the elements of light and shadow can be arranged to express form and the direction of a light source. For the sphere and the molding top right, the light source is above and to the left; for the molding bottom right, the light source is below and to the left.

1. Highlight accent
2. Highlight halftone
3. Shadow halftone
4. Shadow accent
5. Reflected light

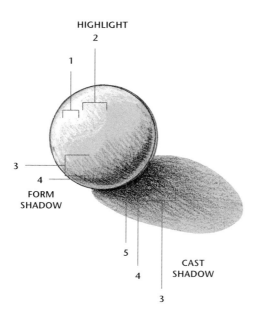

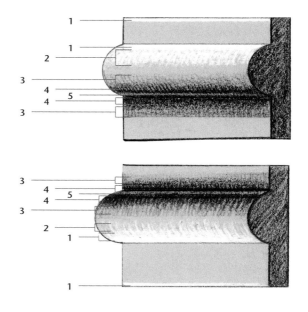

Trompe l'Oeil Exercises

The following is a series of exercises that will guide you in the fundamentals of trompe l'oeil: how to hold a striping edge, the techniques of striping and fading, how to draw a faux molding directly on the surface, and how to transfer a grisaille or polychrome image to the surface.

In addition to these exercises, review "Color Basics" and "The Faux Palette" (pages 33–35), familiarize yourself with "Striping a Molding with a Rondin Brush" (page 208), and use all the completed finishes in this book that feature trompe l'oeil moldings as visual aids.

HOLDING A STRIPING EDGE

A striping edge is used to guide the path of a brush when painting a straight line (see drawing 1). With the beveled side of the striping edge facing toward the surface, hold the end of the edge between your thumb and index finger while resting the other fingers of the same hand on the surface to keep that end of the edge tipped slightly away from the surface. So that the other end of the striping edge remains firmly pressed against the surface, apply enough pressure to your thumb to give the edge a slight curve (see drawing 2). The striping edge must remain perfectly straight and motionless during the striping process. To keep the end of the striping edge from slipping off the surface, use the professional's trick of wrapping it with a couple of rubber bands. Position yourself so that your pencil line is exactly at eye level (you may need to stretch or stoop to do this), then align the edge parallel to and either immediately above or below the pencil line. Once the striping edge is properly aligned, resume your normal stance and begin striping (see "Striping," below).

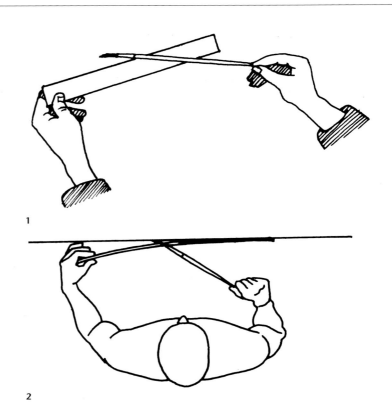

1

2

STRIPING

Although striping a line with a brush and striping edge is not a particularly challenging technique—no more difficult than tracing a straight line with felt-tip pen or marker—it requires some practice and a relaxed frame of mind.

Load your striping brush with the paint or glaze in your striper cup (see page 299). Use the striping edge to shape the hairs and to remove any excess paint or glaze, then use the excess to reload the brush (see photo 1), but be sure to keep the part of edge that touches the surface clean and free from paint. Lightly grasp the end of the handle in the conductor's hold (see page 37) and rest the ferrule on the top edge of the striping edge. Position the handle so that it creates a 45- to 60-degree angle in relation to the surface, but the brush itself should remain perpendicular to the surface. Slide the brush across the edge, always starting at the end of the edge

that's tipped *away* from the surface and moving in one direction (see photo 2). Exert as little pressure on the brush as possible (if you want to paint a wider stripe, use a wider brush). Work at a steady pace (the more slowly you work, the more likely your hand will tremble) and use long strokes instead of small movements. Without moving the edge, go over the stripe once or twice more to even out the application. When the paint has been exhausted from the brush, reload it, then overlap part of the previous stroke to ensure seamless coverage. Keep the edge clean by wiping it off frequently with a rag.

A striping edge can also be used to paint precise vertical stripes (see photo 3): Following the instructions outlined in "Holding a Striping Edge" (see opposite), orient the striping edge on the surface vertically, then slide the ferrule of a loaded striping brush along one side of the edge, always working from top to bottom.

1

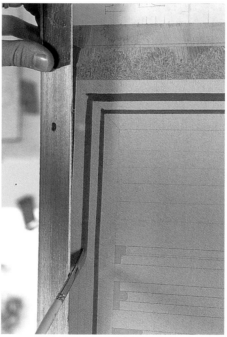

2

3

FADING

Fading is a technique used to create the subtle, gradual shifts in value from light into shadow that express three-dimensional form. For the proper way to hold the brush and striping edge, see "Striping," page 303; for fading, the edge is positioned slightly farther below the pencil line. The painting procedure varies slightly, depending on whether you use oil or water media; with the latter, you have less time to blend the gradations. Note that the instructions below can be used to paint both shadows and highlights, regardless of the direction of the light source and the shape of the molding. Since all of the faux moldings in this book were painted with acrylics, the photos below illustrate the fading technique using that medium.

Fading with Oil-Based Glazes. Prepare a translucent glaze for the halftone and a more opaque mixture for the accent. Load either a soft halftone brush or a short square sable brush with the halftone glaze; using a pencil line drawn on the surface and a striping edge as guides, paint a wide, straight stripe. Rework the stripe with the brush three or four times, so that the side farthest from the pencil line is slightly faded. Run a dry flat bristle or sable brush back and forth over the faded side of the stripe until the glaze is nearly transparent. Load a long, flat striping brush with the accent glaze, then stripe it directly under the pencil line over the still-wet halftone. Rework and fade the accent into the halftone as described above. Let dry. An alternative method is to stripe an untinted glaze before striping the halftone glaze, which makes the fading process a little easier.

Fading with Water-Based Glazes. If you're painting small, short moldings, you can follow the instructions given for oil-based glazes; for moldings that are more than a foot in length, the technique is slightly different because there isn't enough time to fade the glazes by reworking them with a brush. Note that all of the faux moldings in this book were painted with water-based (acrylic) glazes using a wet-on-dry technique.

   While applying a wide stripe of halftone glaze, create a faded edge by lifting one side of the brush slightly (see photo 1). Let dry. Use a narrower brush to apply a second stripe of the same glaze that is two-thirds the width of the first, again fading the edge by lifting one side of the brush (see photo 2). Let dry, then repeat, this time painting a stripe that is one-third the width of the first (see photo 3). Let dry, then add a narrow accent of a more opaque glaze immediately under the pencil line, slightly fading the edge on the same side as the halftone.

1

2

3

DRAWINGS

The drawing on which your trompe l'oeil form is based is crucial to the success of your painting. If the lines of the image are too thick, unevenly drawn, or not perfectly parallel, it will be difficult (if not impossible) to accurately stripe and fade shadows and highlights.

Drawing a Faux Molding. When drawing a molding directly on the surface, use a well-sharpened 3H or 5H pencil to make thin, light lines that won't be visible through the glaze and won't come off when the glaze is applied. Use a notched cardboard template marked with the exact profile of the molding and the arrangement of shadows and highlights to indicate the molding's elements on the surface with a series of simple dashes (see photo 1). Place the striping edge flat against the surface with its beveled side facing toward you, align it with a dash, and run the pencil against its edge (see photo 2). For circular forms, extend the dashes of the template with a compass (see photos 3 and 4).

If you have someone to assist you, you can use a snap line (see page 48) to create long, straight painting guidelines for a molding. The red or blue chalk that comes in the snap line is so intense in color that it is difficult to erase, so replace it with a 1:1 mixture of talcum powder and powdered charcoal or raw umber pigment. Carefully measure the position of the molding, then use a template to mark its line with dashes at both ends of the surface. Unreel the snap line so that you and your assistant are standing at opposite ends of the surface, then give the line a gentle snap by pulling it away from the surface and letting it go. If the snapped lines are too strong, soften them by dusting them lightly with a badger brush and retracing them with a straight or striping edge and a 5H pencil before removing them from the surface completely.

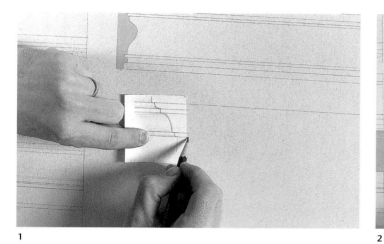

1

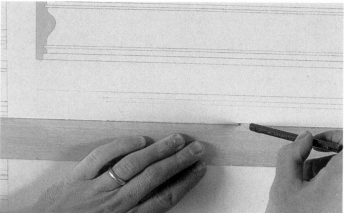

2

3

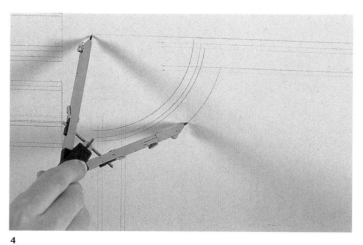

4

TRANSFERS

The following techniques apply to those situations in which you must work out and finalize a more detailed drawing on a separate sheet of paper, as for a grisaille or polychrome ornament. Once the drawing is complete, it can be transferred to the surface using one of the following methods (both can be used to make multiple transfers):

- *Transfer paper.* Sandwich a sheet of artists' transfer paper between the drawing and the surface, then trace over the design with an empty ballpoint pen or 5H pencil. One side of each of sheet transfer paper is treated with a water-soluble graphite-based material. (Do *not* use carbon paper for this purpose.) If you can't find artists' transfer paper, trace the original drawing on a piece of tracing paper, rub graphite over the back of the tracing, then position the tracing on the surface and trace over the design with an empty ballpoint pen. Graphite-based transfer paper is easy to use, but the lines of the transferred image will come off when layered with water media.

    If you're planning to paint with water media, you can make your own transfer paper by coating a sheet of vellum with a mixture of turpentine and red ochre (artists' oils in tubes), then use it as you would artists' transfer paper. (This type of homemade transfer paper can also be used with oil media.) Trace over the design as described above, then allow the transferred image to cure for 2 to 6 hours before proceeding with your painting.

- *The pounce technique.* This method, which has been in use since the Renaissance, is preferred by professionals because it is easy and fast, but the transferred image can require redrawing in pencil. Trace the final drawing on white drafting paper, lay the tracing over a piece of corrugated cardboard, then use a long pushpin or upholsterer's needle to pierce the lines of the design at $^1/_8$-inch intervals. (You can substitute the pin or needle with a pounce wheel, which is made specifically for this purpose.) Always be sure to pierce intersecting lines so that no details are lost. Position the perforated tracing on the surface by taping it along the top, then lightly dab the pattern lines with a pounce bag or pouncing doll (a small rag filled with a mixture of talcum powder and powdered charcoal or pigment, packed with a cotton ball, and closed with a tie, as if you were making the head of a rag doll). (See photo 1.) Remove the tracing to reveal a dotted outline of the design. Evaluate the position and details of the outline, then make adjustments. (If necessary, the outline can be easily wiped off.) Experienced decorative painters can use the outline as a foundation drawing if they are painting within its contours. However, since the dots can be accidentally removed from the surface, or when a layer of glaze will be applied directly over the outline, it's recommended that you connect the dots with a 5H pencil (see photo 2), dust off the excess powder, and refine the drawing as needed.

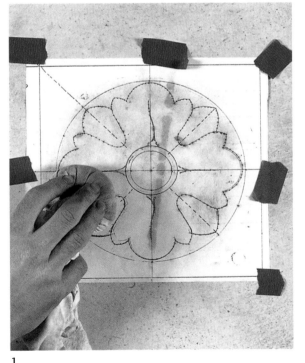

1

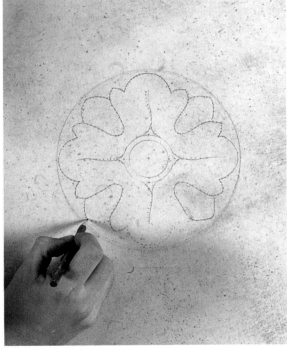

2

Molding Profiles

Striping (page 303) and fading (page 304) provide the technical basis for painting faux moldings, which are essentially comprised of a series of stripes. The drawings below and on pages 308 and 309 are of the nine standard molding profiles; each shows how shadows and highlights are arranged to express form, depending on the direction of the light. These profiles can be combined to produce virtually any configuration.

The drawings were rendered in colored and charcoal pencil so that the elements of shadow and highlight could be clearly discerned; because of this, the transitions between elements are not as subtle and smooth as they would be in a liquid medium. As a general rule, an accent should be approximately one-third the width of the halftone; only when the surface is curved does each fade gently into the other. The light source in each example is assumed to be above and to the left of the molding.

For instructions on how to paint moldings using trompe l'oeil techniques, see page 310.

1. Highlight accent (generally one-quarter to one-third the width of the highlight halftone)

2. Highlight halftone

3. Shadow halftone

4. Shadow accent (generally one-third the width of the shadow halftone)

5. Reflected light

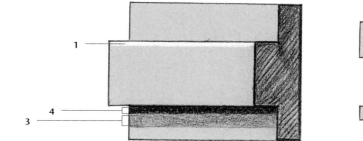
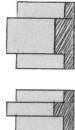

LISTEL OR FLAT

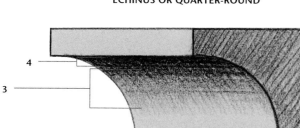

ECHINUS OR QUARTER-ROUND

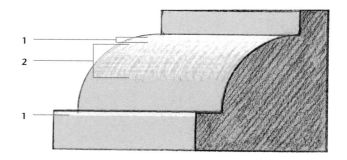

REVERSED QUARTER-ROUND

CAVETTO

The congé is similar in shape to the cavetto, but smaller.

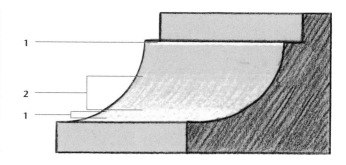

REVERSED CAVETTO

1. Highlight accent (generally one-quarter to one-third the width of the highlight halftone)

2. Highlight halftone

3. Shadow halftone

4. Shadow accent (generally one-third the width of the shadow halftone)

5. Reflected light

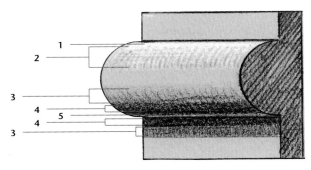
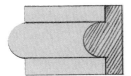
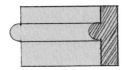
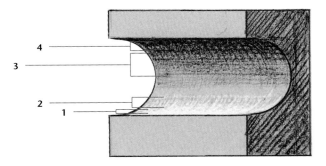

TORUS OR HALF-ROUND

The baguette is similar in shape to the torus, but smaller.

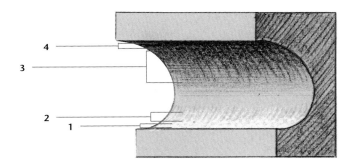

GORGE

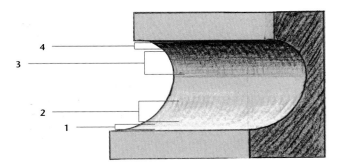

SCOTIA

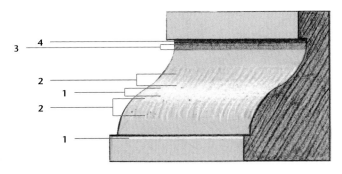

REVERSED SCOTIA

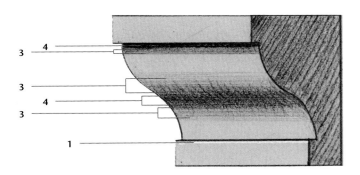

HEEL OR CYMA REVERSA

REVERSED HEEL

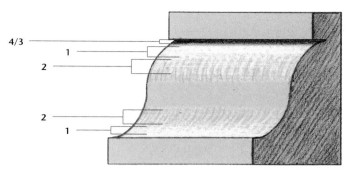

DOUCINE OR CYMA RECTA

REVERSED DOUCINE

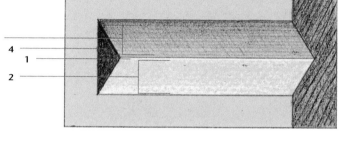

GOUGE, CHANNEL, OR V-GROOVE

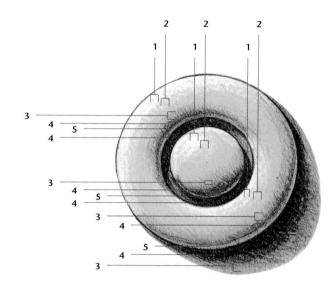

CIRCULAR MOLDING

Shadows and highlights on curved surfaces are rendered the same as on straight ones; only the transitions between gradations are smoother.

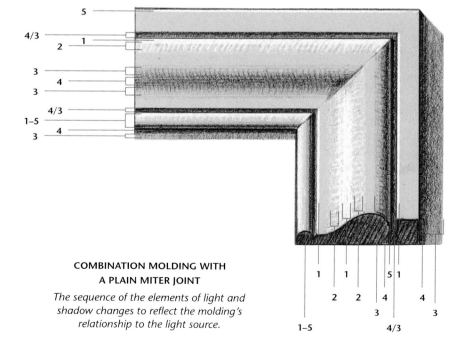

COMBINATION MOLDING WITH A PLAIN MITER JOINT

The sequence of the elements of light and shadow changes to reflect the molding's relationship to the light source.

309

Moldings

As shown on pages 307–309, there are nine basic molding profiles; these can be combined to create virtually any configuration. This recipe demonstrates how these basic moldings, in addition to a few combinations, are painted using trompe l'oeil techniques.

By committing to memory the basic molding profiles and how gradations of highlight and shadow are arranged to define their shapes, an experienced decorative painter can render the effects of light for any type of molding without having to study a drawing or observe a real molding. In the demonstration shown in the photographs add directional, at the left end of each molding I painted its profile in gray, and at the right end I masked off each step in the process, so that in the final photograph the development of the form can be seen. As in the drawings on pages 307–309, the light source painted here is above and to the left of the moldings.

Many of the completed finishes in this book feature faux moldings; in these instances, the moldings were painted directly over the faux finish before the varnishing was done. Before you begin striping a molding on your faux finish, see "Basic Procedure" and "Elements of Light and Shadow," earlier in this chapter.

Note that when painting faux moldings, taping (see page 57) should be kept to a minimum, and should be used only to sharply define the ends of shadows and highlights painted in acrylics; when working in oil, the ends are carefully wiped off with a rag.

1. Use a 3H or 5H pencil to draw the molding profile(s) on the surface as described in the exercise on page 305. Make sure the drawn lines are very thin.
2. Mix a glaze for the shadow halftone using acrylic glaze (see Technical Notes) + **raw umber** + a touch of **Payne's gray.** (The color you mix for your shadows will depend on the local color of the surface you're painting; see "Shadow and Highlight: Color and Contrast," page 300, for more information.) Transfer the shadow halftone glaze to a striper cup, then attach the cup to your chest. Dip

a synthetic flat brush in the cup, then even out the load and "sharpen" the edge of the brush on the face of the striping edge. (You can then use the excess glaze on the striping edge to reload the brush.) Hold and position the striping edge on the surface as shown in the exercise on page 302. Begin striping as shown in the exercise on page 303; working from top to bottom, fade the shadow halftone as shown on page 304. If necessary, use the drawings on pages 307–309 as a guide. Let dry.

3. Use the shadow halftone glaze and a narrower brush to create two more gradations of shadow. Fade the glaze gently; let dry. Add as many layers as necessary to achieve the desired effect. (You may need as many as four or five, depending on the size of the molding.) Let dry.
4. To make a glaze for the shadow accent, add **raw umber + Payne's gray** to a small amount of the shadow halftone glaze. So that the glaze is more fluid for painting the fine line of the accent, thin it down by adding another 1/4 part of water. Stripe and fade the shadow accent with a sharp flat or slanted brush as shown in the exercise on page 304. Let dry.
5. Only once the shadow (both halftone and accent) is completed can the highlight be painted. (The reflected light is painted later.) Mix a glaze for the highlight halftone (acrylic glaze + **white** + a touch of **yellow ochre**). Like the shadow halftone, the highlight halftone must be built up in several layers (although it should remain translucent) because a translucent white glaze covers poorly. (If necessary, use fluid acrylics for this step, as they have better coverage.) Paint broader, faded highlights with the tip of a flat striping brush; for thin highlights, use a long pointed brush, but use the whole length of its hairs instead of just its tip. Let dry.
6. Using the glaze mixed in step 5, stripe the remaining gradations of the highlight halftone. Let dry.

7. Use a warm gray glaze (acrylic glaze + **white** + **raw umber** + **burnt sienna** + **ultramarine blue**) to paint the reflected light. Let dry.
8. To make the glaze for the highlight accent, add **white** to the highlight halftone glaze (the glaze should be more opaque here); if desired, thin it down with a little water. Paint the highlight accent as shown in the exercise on page 304; let dry.
9. If necessary, refine or adjust the shadow highlights with some of the glaze mixed in step 3. Let dry.

USING OTHER MEDIA

When striping and fading, fluid acrylics are somewhat easier to use than tube acrylics.

If you use fluid acrylics, use a glaze formula of 1 artists' acrylics + $1/2$ matte medium + $1/4$ water.

As is noted under "Basic Procedure" (page 297) and the exercise for "Fading" (page 304), fading can also be done with an oil-based glaze (1 turpentine + 1 oil + drier), which is easier for beginners because the longer working time provides an opportunity to develop shadows and highlights slowly and to correct mistakes, but care must be taken to avoid touching stripes that haven't yet dried, and the shadows must be dry before the highlights are painted. Once you've gained confidence in your striping and fading skills you can switch to acrylics, which dry so quickly that the entire process can be completed in one day.

1. Draw the molding profile(s) on the surface with very thin pencil lines.

2. Stripe the first shadow halftones, fading their edges. Let dry.

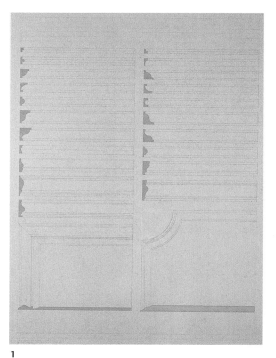

1

2

311

3. Add at least two more gradations for the shadow halftones, fading each gently. Let each dry before adding the next.

4. Stripe and fade the shadow accents. Let dry.

5. Stripe and fade the first highlight halftones. Let dry, then add subsequent layers, fading each as it is added. Let each layer dry before adding the next.

6. Stripe and fade the highlight accents. Let dry.

7. Add the reflected lights. Let dry.

8. The completed molding profiles. *First column, from top:* Listel or flat; baguette; echinus or quarter-round; cavetto; torus or half-round; doucine or cyma recta; heel or cyma reversa; gouge, channel, or V-groove; three combination profiles; combination molding with panel and plain miter joint. *Second column, from top:* Listel or flat; small cavetto; reversed heel; three combination profiles; combination molding with curved corner.

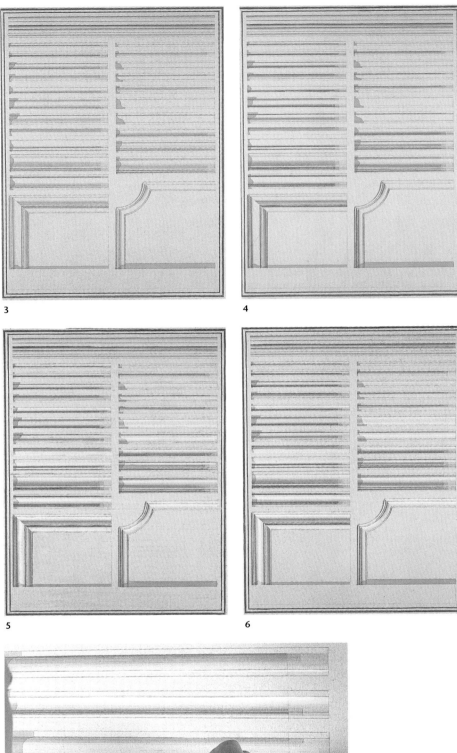

3

4

5

6

7

8

Circular Medallion

While the circular medallion or *boss* shown in this demonstration was painted in the same manner as the grisaille ornament on page 319, because it is symmetrical and simpler in form it is somewhat easier to paint. Use the drawings of the molding profiles on pages 307–309 to identify the shapes used to create the ornament, or to create an ornament of your own design. Refer to "Elements of Light and Shadow," page 300, to determine how the predominant light source affects where highlights and shadows fall on the ornament's complex surface.

The medallion in this demonstration was painted with a grisaille technique (in which several values of one color are used to render form) over a gray stone finish similar to "Interior Limestone of Paris" (see page 141). The palette can be adapted for painting over any faux finish, including marble and wood.

1. Make a pounce pattern by tracing the final drawing and piercing the outline of the tracing. Transfer the image to the surface by dabbing the perforated lines with a pounce bag or pouncing doll as shown in the exercise on page 306. Connect the dots of the outline with a 5H pencil and a compass, then refine the drawing by adding perspective lines to its contours. (The medallion in this demonstration was drawn to be viewed from below and illuminated from directly above.)

2. Mix a glaze for the shadow halftone using an acrylic glaze (see Technical Notes) + **Payne's gray + raw umber.** Load a short pointed synthetic brush with the glaze, then use it to paint the lightest-value shadow halftones. Let dry.

3. Add second, third, and fourth applications of glaze for the shadow halftone, each slightly darker in value, using flat and pointed brushes of various sizes to obtain

a translucent faded effect, as shown in the exercise on page 304. Since acrylics are used, each layer of glaze will dry very quickly; drying time can be reduced further by drying each layer with a hair dryer. When using acrylics, it's easier to paint five translucent layers for the shadow halftone than to try to subtly fade them in just two layers.

4. Mix the glaze for the shadow accent by adding **raw umber** + a touch of **burnt sienna** + **ultramarine blue** and a little water to the shadow halftone glaze. Use short synthetic brush to add the shadow accents. Let dry; where necessary, add a second layer to heighten detail. Let dry.

5. Mix a glaze for the highlight halftone using acrylic glaze + **white** + **raw sienna** + a touch of **burnt sienna**. As for the shadow halftone (see step 3), paint several translucent layers to obtain a subtle increase in value. Let dry.

6. Paint the highlight accent with a more opaque, more fluid off-white glaze (acrylic glaze + **white** + **raw sienna** + a touch of **burnt sienna** in fluid acrylics + a little water). Let dry.

7. Mix a light gray-pink glaze (acrylic glaze + **white** + **raw sienna** + a touch of **burnt sienna**), then use it to paint the reflected lights. Let dry.

8. Use the shadow halftone glaze to conceal any highlight accents that overlap their contours. Let dry.

9. This type of ornament can be varnished with acrylic varnish.

USING OTHER MEDIA

This recipe can also be painted in oils, whose longer working and drying times would only be of benefit to beginners.

1. After transferring the image to the surface (see the exercise on page 306), refine the drawing by adding perspective lines to its contours.

2. Begin by painting the lightest portion of the shadow halftone. Let dry.

3. Continue to build up the shadow halftone by adding progressively darker values (A–C). Let each layer dry before adding the next.

4. Add the shadow accent. Let dry.

5. Begin the highlight halftones, painting several translucent layers to obtain a subtle, gradual increase in value. Let each layer dry before adding the next.

6. Paint the highlight accents using a more opaque glaze.

7. Add the reflected lights. Let dry.

1

2

3A

3B

3C

4

5

6

7

8. The completed medallion.

8

Grisaille Ornament

TECHNICAL NOTES

Difficulty Rating

3.5

System

Water (acrylics)

Basecoat

Grayish off-white **(white + raw umber + ultramarine blue)** alkyd, eggshell finish

Acrylic Glazes

Glaze #1: 1 matte medium + 1.5 water

Glaze #2: 1 matte medium + 1 water

Palette

Artists' Acrylics

White

Yellow ochre

Raw umber

Burnt umber

Payne's gray

Black

Brushes and Tools

Glazing brush

Assorted pointed and flat brushes

Exercises

Transfers (page 306)

Striping (page 303)

Fading (page 304)

See also the recipes for "Faux Handpainted Blue Delft Tile" (page 246), "Moldings" (page 310), and "Circular Medallion" (page 314).

The French word *grisaille* translates roughly into English as "shades of gray." It refers to all trompe l'oeil forms painted with a series of gray values, as well as to any trompe l'oeil painting where a monochrome palette is used (also known as *camaïeu* or tone-on-tone painting). Even grisaille that is based on a strictly gray palette can include more than one color or temperature of gray, from yellow to pink to brown. The technique of heightening the illusion of depth and dimension in grisaille painting with a range of warm and cool grays has been used for centuries, frequently to paint bas-reliefs such as the ornament in this recipe. (See also the recipe for "Circular Medallion," page 314.)

In the following demonstration, a grisaille palette is used to paint an architectural ornament featuring an incense burner surrounded by swirling vines and underlined at its base with acanthus leaves. I drew the design of this ornament, which combines elements from a range of classical examples, from several sources, including books, magazines, and photographs taken in museums and châteaus.

1. Lightly sand and dust off the cured basecoated surface. Transfer the design to the surface using one of the techniques discussed in the exercise on page 306.
2. Optional: Seal the drawing and create a little surface texture (as shown in the recipe for "Faux Handpainted Blue Delft Tile," page 246) by applying a translucent mixture of glaze #1 (see Technical Notes) + **white**, with a glazing brush. This step is recommended primarily for beginners, so that mistakes can be wiped off without affecting the transferred design. Also, this layer of glaze softens the lines of the drawing, making them less visible, especially close up. Let dry.
3. Mix the glaze for the shadow halftone using glaze #2 (see Technical Notes) + **Payne's gray + raw umber +** a touch of **burnt umber.** Use an assortment of pointed brushes to paint the first value of the shadow halftone as shown in the exercise on page 304, fading its edge slightly. Let dry.
4. Using the same glaze, add the next two layers of the shadow halftone, again gently fading their edges as shown in the exercise on page 304. Let each layer dry before adding the next.
5. Mix a glaze for the shadow accent by adding **black** or **raw umber** to the shadow halftone glaze. Use it to define the darkest values (the deepest reliefs) of the ornament. Let dry.
6. Mix a glaze for the highlight halftone using glaze #1 + **white** + a touch of **yellow ochre.** Use an assortment of pointed brushes to lay in the lowest value of the highlight halftone. Let dry.
7. Use the same glaze to add progressively higher values of the highlight halftone, fading their edges as needed. Let each layer dry before adding the next.
8. Mix an off-white glaze for the highlight accent (1 water + **white** fluid acrylic + a touch of **yellow ochre**). Use the glaze to add the brightest highlights to the highest reliefs.
9. Paint the reflected lights. Let dry.

USING OTHER MEDIA

This recipe could also be done in oils, but only to give a beginner a more generous working time. The main drawbacks of working with oils in this case are the long wait between painting shadows and highlights (the shadows must be dry before the highlights can be painted) and their tendency to yellow over time, which would seriously affect the appearance of the grisaille painted with a white-gray palette.

1. Using one of the methods described on page 306, transfer the drawing to the surface.

2. Paint the first value of the shadow halftone, fading its edge gently. Let dry.

3. Develop the shadow halftone by adding progressively darker layers, fading edges and letting each layer dry before painting the next.

4. Use the shadow accents to define the deepest reliefs of the ornament. Let dry.

5. The faux ornament with completed shadows. Depending on the surface, the ornament could be considered finished as this point.

6. Develop the highlight halftones by adding progressively lighter layers, fading edges and letting each dry before adding the next (A). For this type of ornament, the highlight halftones must be very subtly rendered (B).

7. Add the highlight accents to the highest reliefs. Let dry.

8. The completed ornament.

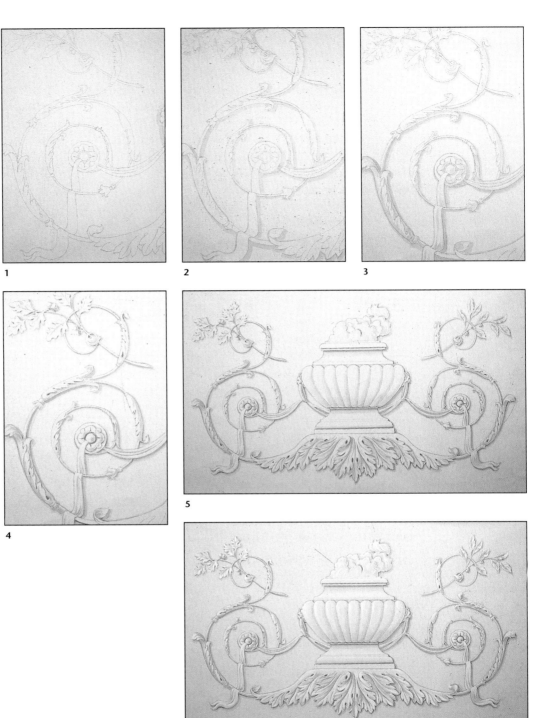

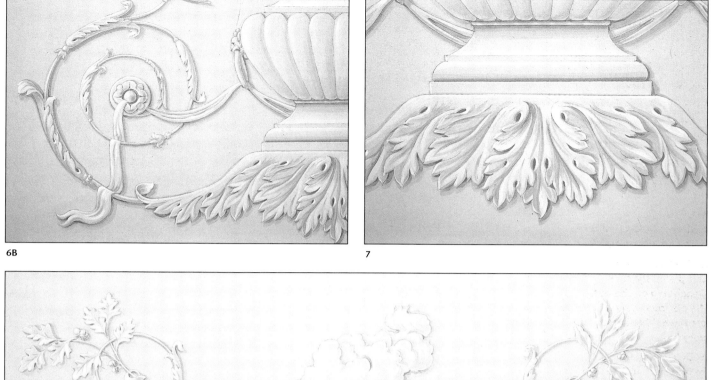

6B

7

8

Polychrome Ornament

A variation on grisaille, the polychrome technique—in which individual elements of a composition are painted in several different colors using trompe l'oeil techniques—was most widely used during the 17th, 18th, and 19th centuries to decorate wall panels or boiserie, doors, and furniture. Typically, these ornaments featured flowers, leaves, vines, draped fabrics, geometric friezes, caryatids, and other decorative elements. Examples of polychrome ornamentation can be found in a variety of different sources—books, magazines, and auction catalogs—and seen in museums and grand residences. When creating a polychrome composition, the designs and colors must be carefully selected to reflect a specific style or period—for example, medieval, 16th century, or 18th-century rococo or Chinoiserie—and arranged to convey balance and symmetry. In the demonstration for this recipe, an armoire is painted with an adaptation of an 18th-century design; the emphasis here is on painting technique rather than accuracy of period or style.

1. Lightly sand and dust off the cured basecoated surface. Patina the surface by following steps 1–3 from the recipe for "Old Painted Boiserie" (see page 220). Over a light greenish gray ropey basecoat (**raw umber + burnt umber + ultramarine blue + yellow ochre**), strié a light gray-green glaze (**raw umber + burnt umber + chrome oxide deep + white + yellow ochre**). Let dry.

2. Transfer the design to the surface using one of the techniques discussed in the exercise on page 306.

3. Each element is painted with several values of one opaque color; subtle gradations from light to dark are used to render three-dimensional form. Begin by mixing the middle value of each of the various colors that will be used, then lighten and darken them as needed as you proceed. Paint all the elements in the same color at one time, rather than one element at a time, so that it won't be necessary to remix any colors.

If you're working in oil, you'll be working wet-on-wet: Apply the middle tone for your base; in a single application of opaque color, rather than a series of translucent layers, add the shadow halftone first, then the shadow accent. Let dry; using the same method, paint the highlight halftone and accent. The same technique and opacity of medium are used when working in acrylics, except that you'll be working wet-on-dry. Paint the shadows first, and wait until the shadows are dry before painting the highlights.

Repeat until all of the elements have been painted. If necessary, use a striping edge to align your stroke for the linear elements.

4. Complex motifs, like the ribbon that winds around the branch on each of the drawers, were broken down into distinct elements. The reverse side of the ribbon was painted first using **yellow ochre,** working from dark to light to create the illusion of a curve. To give the ribbon width, a highlight accent was added along one side and a shadow accent was added along the other. Then the branch and its foliage were painted, using a few values of one green (**chrome green oxide + burnt umber + burnt sienna + yellow ochre + white**). After the branch had dried, the front of the ribbon was painted in an off-white, with shadows in gray and highlights in white, with accents added along each side to suggest width. The front of the ribbon was completed with a double red stripe.

5. After the ornaments are completely dry, distress and age the surface by following steps 5–11 from the recipe for "Old Painted Boiserie" (see page 220). Let dry.

USING OTHER MEDIA

This technique demonstrated here is only one of the hundreds of ways of painting polychrome ornaments. Acrylics are easy to use and recommended in most cases, but oils have an old-world quality that is perfect for imitating 18th-century ornaments.

1. Paint all the elements in the same color at one time. Begin by painting the middle value of each color.

2. Complete the elements of the shadow first; let dry, then paint the elements of the highlight. Let dry.

3. The completed polychrome ornament for the door of the armoire.

4. Complex and overlapping motifs were broken down into discreet elements. On each of the drawers, the reverse side of the ribbon was painted first, then allowed to dry.

5. The branch and its foliage were then added and allowed to dry.

6. The front of the ribbon was painted: first its form (by shading from dark to light), then its design (a double red stripe).

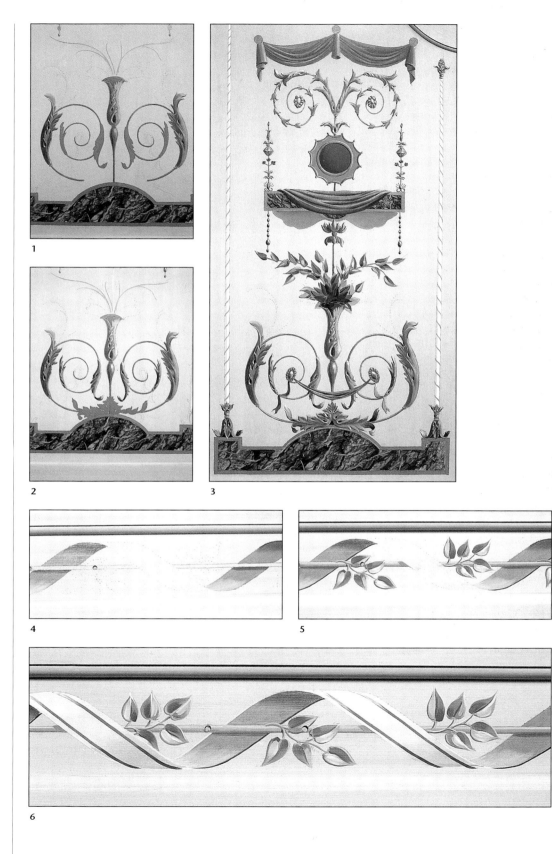

1

2

3

4

5

6

7. The completed armoire, distressed and aged according to the recipe for "Old Painted Boiserie" (see page 220).

7

Reference Drawings

Drawings 1 and 2:
White Veined Carrara
See pages 88–90

Drawings 3 and 4:
Yellow Flower
See pages 91–93

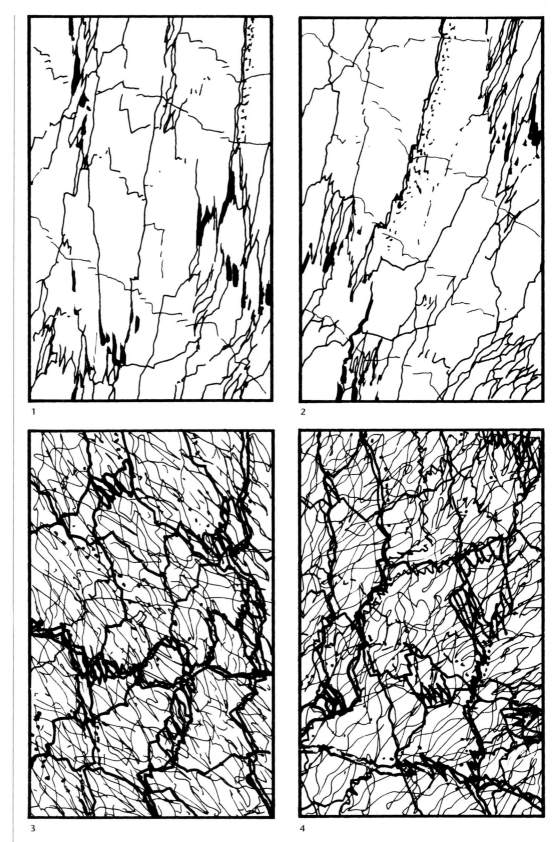

1

2

3

4

Reference Drawings

Drawings 5 and 6:
Rouge Royal
See pages 94–96

Drawings 7 and 8:
Sea Green
See pages 97–99

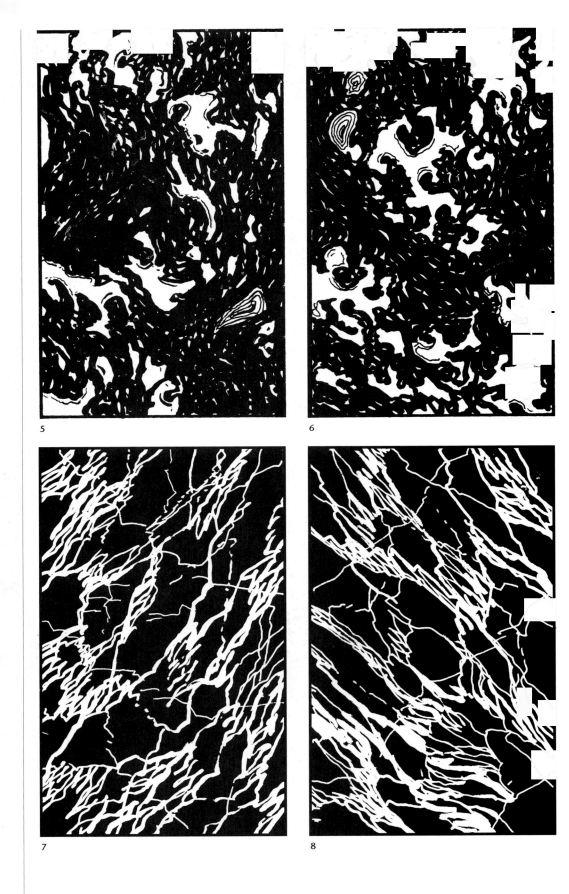

5

6

7

8

Drawing 9:
Imperador
See pages 100–102

Drawings 10 and 11:
Portor
See pages 103–105

Drawing 12:
White Brèche
See pages 106–108

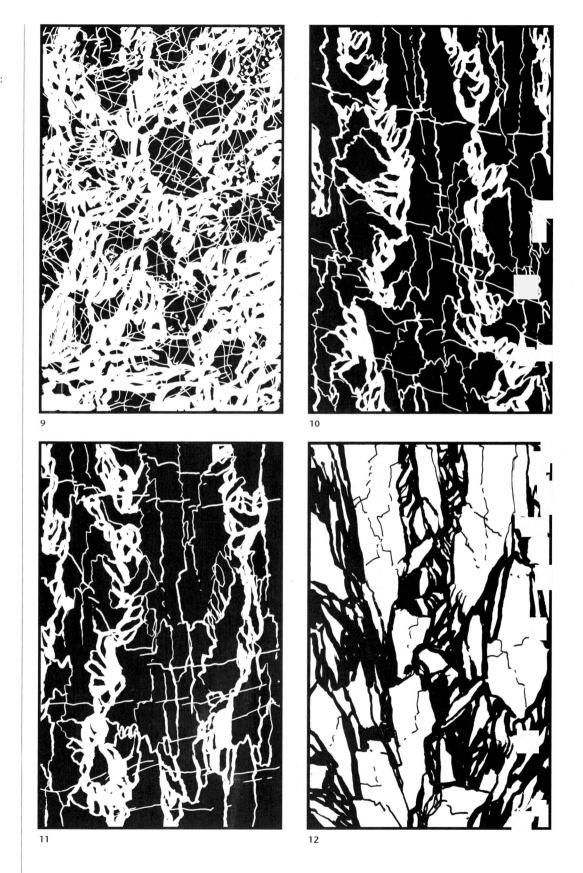

9

10

11

12

Drawing 13:
White Brèche
See pages 106–108

Drawings 14 and 15:
Violet Brèche
See pages 109–111

Drawing 16:
Algerian Onyx
See pages 129–131

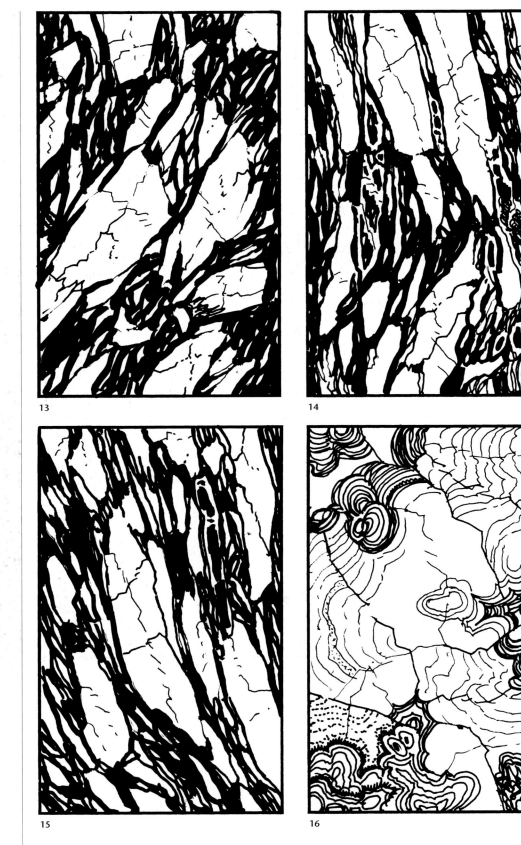

13

14

15

16

Drawing 17:
Bird's-eye maple
See pages 172–174

Drawing 18:
Elm burl
See pages 175–178

Drawing 19:
Thuja burl
See pages 175–178

Drawing 20:
Walnut
See pages 179–181

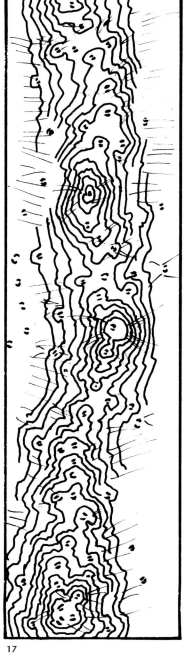

17

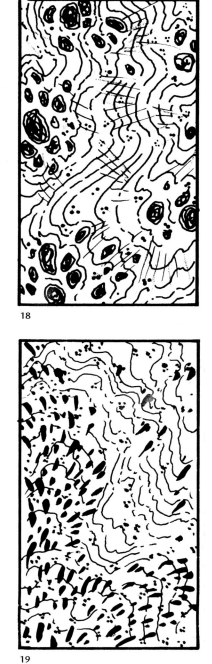

18

19

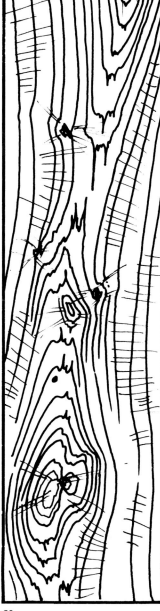

20

Drawings 21–22:
Walnut
See pages 179–181

Drawing 23:
Figure grain oak
See pages 182–187

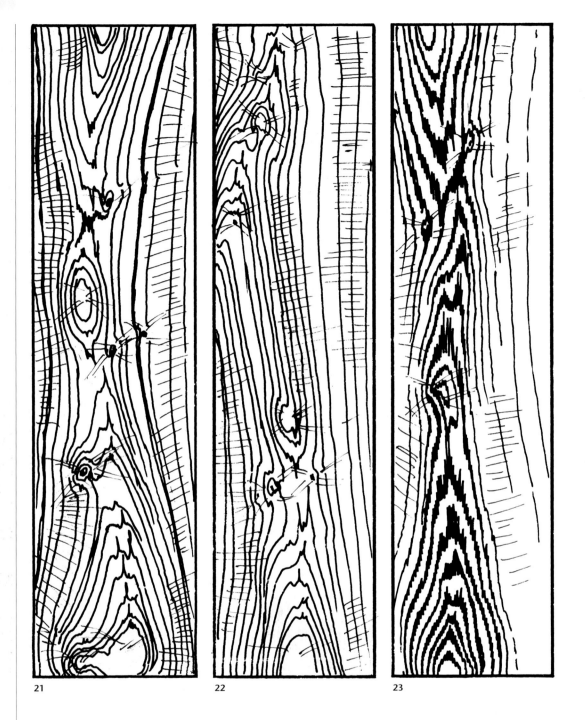

21 22 23

Drawings 24 and 25:
Figure grain oak
See pages 182–187

Drawing 26:
Silver grain oak
See pages 182–187

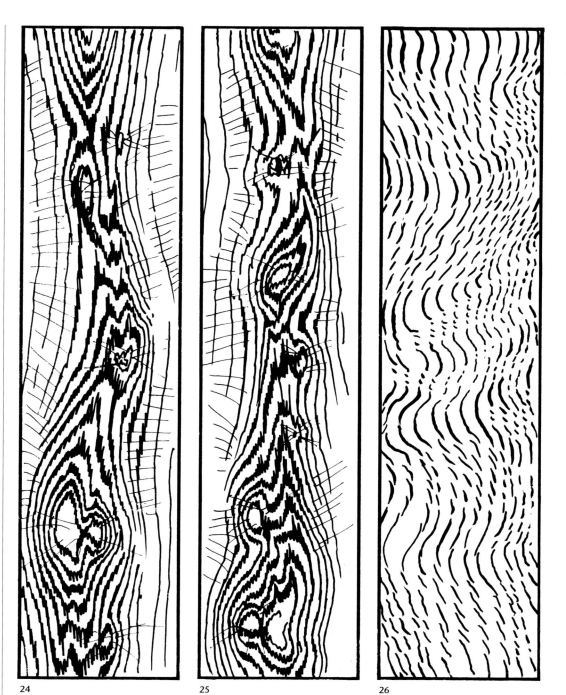

24

25

26

329

Drawing 27:
Silver grain oak
See pages 182–187

Drawings 28 and 29:
Figure grain mahogany
See pages 188–190

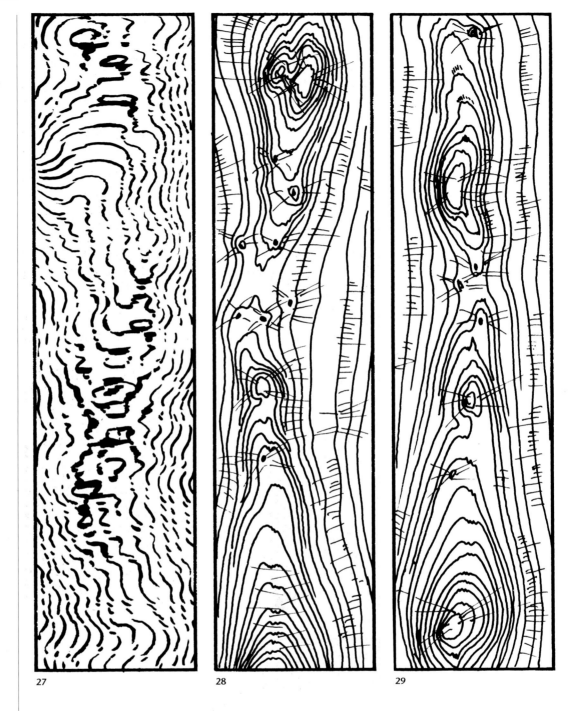

27   28   29

Drawings 30 and 31:
Feather mahogany
See pages 191–193

Drawings 32 and 33:
Tortoiseshell
See pages 270–273

Drawing 34:
Shagreen
See pages 276–279

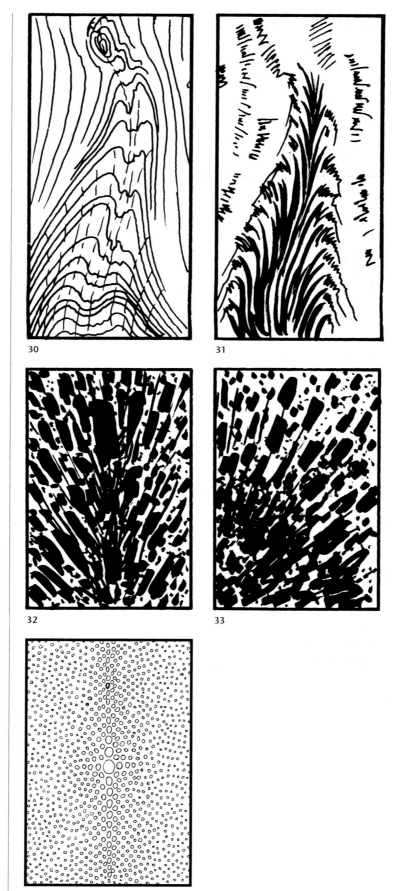

30

31

32

33

34

Source Directory

Listed below are the manufacturers, importers, and retailers for many of the materials used in this book. Because space limitations prohibit a comprehensive listing, readers should not restrict their choice of products and retailers to those listed in this directory, and should investigate local sources, including paint, hardware, art supply, hobby, and craft stores, as well as regionally manufactured and distributed products.

The manufacturers and importers in this listing generally sell their products exclusively through retail outlets, which are a consumer's most dependable source for decorative painting materials and supplies. Your local retailer's knowledgeable personnel can advise you on your purchases, and if you need something that they don't have in stock they will usually order it for you. If you can't find a store in your area that carries a particular item or will accept a request for an order, or if you need special technical assistance, a manufacturer will gladly direct you to the retailer nearest you that carries their products, and will try to answer any other questions you might have.

MANUFACTURERS: PAINTS AND RELATED PRODUCTS

AccuSpray, Inc.
23350 Mercantile Road
Cleveland, Ohio 44122
(216) 595-6860
(800) 618-6860
Manufacturers of high-volume, low-pressure (HVLP) spray guns and related equipment.

Allpro Corporation
3014 U.S. Highway 301 North – #200
Tampa, Florida 33619
(813) 620-4188
Paint supplies and related materials such as brushes, rollers, and glues.

The Flecto Company, Inc.
1000 45th Street
Oakland, California 94608
Varathane varnishes and shellacs.

Golden Artist Colors, Inc.
188 Bell Road
New Berlin, New York 13411
(607) 847-6154
http://www.goldenpaints.com/
Artists' acrylics and acrylic mediums.

The Leneta Company
15 Whitney Road
Mahwah, New Jersey 07430
(201) 847-9300
Draw down cards and chart paper.

Purdy Corporation
P.O. Box 83097
Portland, Oregon 97283
(800) 547-0780
Professional-quality brushes for basecoating, varnishing, and staining.

Sepp Leaf Products, Inc.
381 Park Avenue South
New York, New York 10016
(212) 683-2840
Metal leaf, leafing brushes, and related products; distributor of Mixol Universal Tints.

3M Company
3M Center
St. Paul, Minnesota 55144-1000
(800) 328-5949
Specialty low-tack masking tape and adhesives.

Winsor & Newton
11 Constitution Avenue
Piscataway, New Jersey 08855-1396
(908) 562-0770
Artist-quality tube paints, brushes, and related materials.

Woodworker's Supply, Inc.
1108 North Glenn Road
Casper, Wyoming 82601
(800) 645-9292
Stains, dry pigments, waxes, and other finishing products.

IMPORTERS/DISTRIBUTORS

Pierre Finkelstein Institute of Decorative Painting, Inc.
175 Fifth Avenue – Suite 2162
New York, New York 10010
(888) 8BRUSH8
http://www.pfinkelstein.com/
A complete selection of handcrafted specialty brushes, tools, and other related products made especially for the decorative painter.

Savoire-Faire
P.O. Box 2021
Sausalito, California 94966
(415) 332-4660
FAX (415) 332-3113
Fine-art products made in France, including Sennelier oil paints, Lascaux acrylics, and Isabey brushes. Call or write for a list of local retailers.

MANUFACTURERS/RETAILERS

The following manufacturers also distribute their products—basepaints, varnishes, glazing liquids, and basecoat brushes and rollers—through their own retail outlets. Call or write for the location nearest you.

Benjamin Moore & Co.
51 Chestnut Ridge Road
Montvale, New Jersey 07645
(800) 334-0400
http://www.benjaminmoore.com/

The Sherwin Williams Company
101 Prospect Avenue N.W.
Cleveland, Ohio 44115
(216) 566-2000

RETAILERS

Art Supplies
The following retailers offer complete selections of artist- and professional-quality decorative painting products and supplies. Call or write for the location nearest you.

Kremer Pigments, Inc.
228 Elizabeth Street
New York, New York 10012
(212) 219-2394
Dry pigments and specialty products such as dry shellac, mediums, varnishes, and resins.

Mann Brothers
757 North LaBrea Avenue
Hollywood, California 90038
(213) 936-5168
(800) 245-MANN

New York Central Art Supply
62 Third Avenue
New York, New York 10003
(212) 477-0400
(800) 950-6111

Pearl Paint Co., Inc.
308 Canal Street
New York, New York 10013-2572
(212) 431-7932
(800) 221-6845

Professional Paint and Home Remodeling/Building Supplies
The Home Depot
2455 Paces Ferry Road
Atlanta, Georgia 30339
(770) 433-8211

Janovic/Plaza
30-35 Thomson Avenue
Long Island City, New York 11101
(718) 392-3999

ASSOCIATIONS AND ORGANIZATIONS

International Faux Finishers Association (IFFA)
P.O. Box 2747
Norcross, Georgia 30093-2747
(770) 381-7373
FAX (770) 381-6424

Painting and Decorating Contractors of America (PDCA)
3913 Old Lee Highway – Suite 33B
Fairfax, Virginia 22030
(703) 359-0826

Society of Decorative Painters (SDP)
393 North McLean Boulevard
Wichita, Kansas 67203-5968
(316) 269-9300
FAX (316) 269-9191

Stencil Artisans League, Inc. (SALI)
P.O. Box 920190
Norcross, Georgia 30092
(770) 455-7258
FAX (770) 455-6097

TRAINING AND INSTRUCTION

Pierre Finkelstein Institute of Decorative Painting, Inc.
175 Fifth Avenue – Suite 2162
New York, New York 10010
(888) FAUXART
http://www.pfinkelstein.com/
Workshops, seminars, and lectures on decorative painting. Call or write for more information.

Index